DATE DUE

GAYLORD			PRINTED IN U.S.A.

From
Prison
to
Power

Lengyel

BOOKS BY THE SAME AUTHOR

HITLER
THE DANUBE
TURKEY
DAKAR: OUTPOST OF TWO HEMISPHERES
SIBERIA
THEY CALLED HIM ATATÜRK
KRISHNA MENON

From Prison to Power

by Emil Lengyel

Follett Publishing Company · Chicago
1964

First Printing

MANUFACTURED IN THE UNITED STATES OF AMERICA
Designed by Bedno Associates

FOLLETT PUBLISHING COMPANY
1000 West Washington Boulevard
Chicago, Illinois   60607

To
RUTH AND MICHEL FRANCK
my friends

Contents

List of Illustrations

ACKNOWLEDGMENTS

THANKS to Louis Zara, whose perspicacity and patience helped to fill many a gap in this book; to Arnold G. Leo, Jr., whose keen eyes helped to detect more scope for improvement; to the editors of *The New York Times Magazine* for permission to reprint portions of my article about the national anthems of new countries; to the editors of the *Reporter* for permission to reprint excerpts from my article about Israeli technical aid to Ghana; to Sir Robert Jackson, for his readiness to be of help in the face of an overwhelming schedule; to Assibi Abudu, who brought Ghana closer to me; to his wife Margaret J. G. Abudu, for her permission to profit from her enlightening study *Ghana—One-Party State;* to Edwin P. Booth, Professor Emeritus of Historical Theology of the School of Theology of Boston University, for his recollections of the academic career of Archbishop Makarios; to administrative officials of Boston University for information about the scholastic record of Makarios; to the officials of Lincoln University, Pennsylvania, for a similar record of Kwame Nkrumah; to Raouf Boudjakdje, Cultural Attaché of Algeria, for much useful information; to many officials of the former Délégation Generale of Algeria, for insights into a disturbing problem; to Kasimir Piechoviak, Cultural Attaché of Poland, for placing the public addresses of Wladyslaw Gomulka at my disposal; to Dr. Fazil Kutchuk, Vice-President of the Republic of Cyprus, for many revealing statements about his country's communal problems; to Jomo Kenyatta for his willingness to answer questions even though the pressure of events prevented the consummation of this plan; to the information officers and cultural attachés of Cyprus, Ghana, Hungary, and Indonesia for material about the careers of biographees in this book, and to many others in some of these countries who probably prefer not to have their names mentioned; to Anne Jurkowski, who relieved me of much of my burden as chairman of the Social Science Department of Fairleigh Dickinson University, Rutherford, N.J., during the parturition of the manuscript of this book; to my friends Flory and Miklós László for the days of leisure they provided to overcome my "battle fatigue" while struggling to meet the deadline of my manuscript.

My deep gratitude to Livia, always cheerful and understanding, in spite of her "manuscript widowhood" and to Peter for his encouraging words and perceptive comments.

From
Prison
to
Power

Introduction

The genesis of a book may be of interest to the reader, especially if the subject is unconventional. Unconventional is the word for the backgrounds of the men whose biographies are presented here: from the lowest degradation to the highest pinnacle of fame—from prison to power.

The idea occurred to the author when he was meditating—not on one day but over many years—on the prison experience he had shared with other young people in a faraway land. He tried to recall their lives in prison and then attempted to correlate those details with the information he had gathered about them after they were all liberated. Although not one of this group reached any "pinnacle," the author had some direct insight into the influence of detention, specifically upon such young people.

The place of detention was Siberia, and I was a prisoner there for nearly two years. This all happened so long ago that my readers may think of it as another age. I was very young then, just out of my teens. I recall the bitterness with which I envisaged my future in that prison. I was a studious young man, and I feared that I would be weaned drastically from my working habits. Would any of us be able to make up for the time we would lose there?

We had been members of the Austro-Hungarian army, now we were prisoners of war in Siberia. We had been taken prisoner by the Russians in the midst of the First World War and shipped off to Siberia. Our status? We were of the lowest rank of Austrian officers.

In our detention camp we observed one another closely, living in a tight little community. How did the detention affect us, our character traits, and our modes of living? Above all, how did we feel about the violent interruption of the accepted norms

3

of young people? We were on our own, without the guidance of tutorial and paternal authority, left utterly to our own devices. The Russian government provided for our room and board. The pocket money we received—paid by the International Red Cross—took care of our trifling extra expenses. We did not have to perform work of any kind for the authorities who had put us into prison. Our time was our own, and we could use it as we pleased.

No sooner were we settled in our Siberian prison camps than some of us resumed the studies that had engaged us before we had entered the army. Our day began with the break of dawn. We rose with the sun, and in Siberia the sun rose sometimes at two in the morning. Foreign languages were the most important subjects of our studies. We worked away at them all day, until we nearly dropped from fatigue. And let me repeat it, we were driven by nobody except by ourselves. All over the camp were similar study circles: here, for instance, to learn shorthand, there to study anatomy, the favorite subject of the ex-students of medicine.

There were also the others, who, not driven by our ambitions, formed quite another group. Until late into the day they lounged in their bunks. Eventually, they, too, settled down to a daily occupation: playing cards. They did that hour after hour, staking vast amounts on the cards, the accounts to be settled after the war.

Both groups were convinced—this we had in common—that we never would be freed. Month followed month, and interminably, the war dragged on. The antagonists, the great powers, did not appear to be able to come to grips with one another in the nauseating trench warfare of those years. It was a boxing match of giants, and they were deadlocked in a mortal clinch.

Days can be terribly long when there is no variety and the scene is always the same, offering only the endless Siberian *taiga*. This is especially true when one has limited experience of the extent and meaning of time—when one is very young—and when one's home seems to be faraway, at the end of the most distant galaxy. How would we ever reach the end of that galaxy once the war was over? Of course, it would never be over. Could one walk to the end of the galaxy, since one could not count on the inefficient Trans-Siberian Railway?

Meanwhile, there were the daily problems, eternal problems, and also the bleak prospects of each new day. We bought books, we built up a small library, we acquired musical instruments, and we even got an orchestra started. But one could not always read those books, nor always listen to Bach and Handel. Then there were the faces, day after day, the same sad and hopeless faces. They were the faces of males, males everywhere. We yearned so for different companionship that we came to hate those faces because they were not the faces of girls. Also, because they looked so sad. Yet there were ample reasons for sadness.

Hatreds degenerated into quarrels, useless, synthetic quarrels, and then came the fights. There was that incident, for example, when I became involved in a duel. The Russian dentist appeared on his periodical visit; the prisoners formed a line. Who was first? I was first, said I. I was first, said another, and we began to spit venom—because, I suspect, he was a male, not a girl, and I, too, was a male, and not really because anyone cared about who was first in line. I hated him, he hated me. A point was reached where the flow of blood alone could cleanse the wounds we had inflicted on each other's dignity.

Solemn-faced young men—teen-agers—met to arrange the duel. Sabers? What kind? Pistols? What kind? The words of hatred had been serious. Heavy sabers were decided upon. First blood? Or should we duel to utter incapacity? Not merely first blood because our deeply injured honor could not be cauterized by mere scratches. To utter incapacity then! The protocols were drawn up and the seconds read and signed them. Then the principals deliberately signed them. And now the duel.

Prisoners of war could have no access to sabers, obviously. The protocol, however, provided that the duel should be fought after we had been liberated—and were back home! Everybody knew that there would be no liberation and that our homes lay at the outermost limits of the farthest galaxy. So all this dueling was sheer nonsense. Yet it made sense because it provided us with some excitement. This was part of the prisoner's *fata morgana*. We had to pretend that we could wield heavy sabers. We had to pretend that we were free men.

There were countless such incidents. At first, we thought that only our camp produced such nonsense. Then we learned that the other camps, too, suffered from similar ailments. We also learned the term for this affliction: the barbed wire disease.

Eventually, we did get home. Did we fight the duel? Of course not. One fought imaginary duels only behind the barbed wires, when one's mind was afflicted.

This is how the idea for this book *From Prison to Power* was slowly conceived. What was the influence of jail not on people like us but on those who later reached the highest pinnacles of power—on political prisoners who became the leaders of their states? In the case of my fellow prisoners, the detention did have some effect. A few prisoners, not many, became mentally deranged. These were among the "oldsters," that is, people in their thirties. On the other hand, many prisoners became afflicted with melancholy. Did they rid themselves of it after their liberation? Probably they did. We found that prison life was not responsible for any new character traits. Rather it emphasized and accelerated the dominant old traits. People endowed with strong working habits labored harder in detention than they would have done at home. People who were apathetic worked even less in the prison camp than they would have done in their normal lives.

While there are certain similarities in the reactions of political and war prisoners—possibly other prisoners, too—there is a basic difference in the conditions that led to the imprisonment of these two groups. The soldier who becomes a prisoner of war is forced by his nation, in the nature of his career as a soldier, to run the risk of being captured. The political prisoner, on the other hand, undertakes risks which his government scorns. The subjects of the biographies in this book were confined to jail because of infractions of prevailing laws. Most of them were confined by governments that ruled their homelands as colonial powers. The Communists were imprisoned by their own national governments. Tito, a Communist, was imprisoned by an anti-Communist regime. Kádár and Gomulka were the victims of ideological disputes within the Communist party.

The ex-prisoners in this book ultimately became leaders in their countries. Who can guarantee that all of them will still be at the helm by the time this manuscript is set into type? Such is the turnover in contemporary history. However, whatever their ultimate fates, the biographees in this volume have played historic roles. While they were molded by their countries, they were also the molders of the histories of their nations. The former prisoners in this book who ascended to power were all born in the twentieth century, with the possible exception of Kenyatta, whose year of birth is uncertain. Each is at the head of the country which he helped to build and whose destiny is linked with his. His own life history thus overlaps that of his nation's. These men all acted in the manner of charismatic leaders—men destined by forces inherent in themselves to influence and dominate whole masses of people; so they believed and so they conducted themselves until they came to guide their countries. The biography, the man, and the history of his country thus became intertwined.

Two of the best-known prisoners who reached power are Marshal Tito of Yugoslavia and Prime Minister Nehru of India. In the course of time, Tito became "Mr. Yugoslavia" and Nehru "Mr. India."

India is not merely one of the largest countries in the world. It has the largest population in the entire non-Communist world, and geographically, is a subcontinent. Indeed, it is a world with so infinite a variety of peoples and conditions that i' is hard to describe. Nehru will be treated in the Epilogue of this book in connection with his prison experience. It would be impossible to place him solely within the framework of his country, and entirely within the framework of this work. Besides, he has been already the subject of many biographies and of a vast literature. The full history of Nehru within the context of India cannot be condensed into a single chapter.

Yugoslavia's history for almost a quarter of a century has been intertwined with the biography of Tito. His wartime role as head of the Partisans' struggle against the German and Italian occupying forces will eventually furnish the substance of many epics. After the war he started a process within the Communist party that marked the beginning of a new historic sequence which may be described most aptly as a revolution within a revolution, for it was certainly not a counter-revolution. Again it would be impossible to condense such a vast history within a chapter. Only Tito's life in prison and its possible impact upon him will be discussed in the Epilogue.

ABOUT PRISONERS AND MEN

There is a paradox at the heart of the study of ex-prisoners who reach power. They were rebels, and then, later, they became the staunchest supporters of authority. They were rebels against a system they considered odious. As rebels they were opposed to any kind of restraint and took the risks that brought them to jail.

"Jail"—"gaol"—means "cage," in its Latin origin. "Prisoner" is derived from the term "to be seized." The prisoner is seized and confined in a cage. Normally, cages are for animals. A caged man ceases to be a man, temporarily at least, and becomes an un-man. Can a greater indignity be inflicted on *homo sapiens?* Even within the prison walls the caged un-man's movements are restricted. Silence is the rule in many jails, and because the prisoner is deprived of his speech the un-man becomes even more animal-like. The paradox is that while fighting for freedom the political prisoner experiences the ultimate in un-freedom. The common criminal may not be able to restrain his savage impulses. But the fighter for freedom is espousing the cause of his fellow nationals, his fellow men. Unnatural is his lot while he strives for the highest aspirations of humanity.

Unnatural also is his attitude toward the social framework within which he has to live. Today that framework is the nation. Once it was the religion. At other times it has been the arbitrary rule of the emperor, or the *polis*—the city-state of the Greeks. Nations are sustained on ideas and ideals. One of the major ideas is that of legitimacy. Power is derived from a fountainhead, as, for example, from the people in the democracies; their will is expressed by democratically elected governments. In autocracies power is derived by divine right, or from a closed Establishment. In colonial possessions power is derived from the ruling elite. Whatever the origin of power, the hold upon the people is constantly tightened by the rulers. The rulers are not to be dislodged from power—the spirit of legitimacy they represent demands unyielding resistance to change, the maintenance of the status quo. The rebel who becomes a political prisoner has scant respect for a legitimacy the validity of which he questions. The legitimacy to which the state is committed seems, to him, arbitrary and tyrannical. It is illegitimate legitimacy. The rebel opposes an ideology which is sanctified by tradition and the power of the authorities. It is because of his own integrity that the rebel violates the rules and, in essence, declares, "Better be honest and be free in jail than be craven and un-free at large." When confined to jail he is free in his wide-ranging thoughts. In the interest of his human dignity the prisoner is willing to give up the appurtenances of his personal dignity, including his freedom.

These are some of the reasons why political rebels risk confinement in the cage. There are other reasons, too, some not quite so altruistic. Compared to the slaves at large, the caged man appears still to be free. He has demonstrated the high value of the freedom he claims for himself by running the risk of the jail. He has demonstrated the fact that his freely ranging thoughts represent danger to the official establishment. He has become a "witness" to his political creed—a martyr. As a martyr he is suffering for the cause of his people. Those people will look at his daring act as the incarnation of the ideas they lack the courage to express themselves. They will owe thanks to him and will strive to loosen his fetters. The courage he displays in resisting the autocratic powers demonstrates his worth and his ability to represent his people. His fame spreads through the length and breadth of the land. And his martyrdom often leads to his resurrection. Has any hill been more dazzling than the hill of final indignity, Calvary, upon which the crosses were erected? The suffering endured in martyrdom may inaugurate exaltation and, ultimately, even deification.

To turn to more recent times, has the stentorian voice of any potentate been listened to with as much respectful attention as the weak voice of a frail little man in the jails of India? Gandhi, with the aid of those countless prison terms he served, became the "Great Soul"—Mahatma. The words he spoke from within the prison walls echoed with greater resonance than the loudest trumpets of the autocrats. He needed no mechanical amplifiers to carry his voice to all of India, indeed, to the four corners of the globe.

In the same way, Kwame Nkrumah, when he was released from a British jail, faced the most ecstatic crowds of his career. Poland's Wladyslaw Gomulka also had a far larger number of followers *after* his release from prison. "Where there is sorrow there is holy ground," said Oscar Wilde. He uttered these words from within prison walls, and his voice issued from the depths of his innermost being—*De Profundis*. Thus the political prisoner offers himself as a sacrifice for the freedom of his people. His is the vicarious atonement for the greater glory of the common cause. His prison cell may be crawling with noisome creatures, and yet it is also the dwelling place of his glory. In the eyes of his followers he occupies a majestic pedestal in the center of his shrine of detention, which may yet become a place of pilgrimage.

Nehru spoke about his years in prison in a triumphant tone. His pride in his once-caged condition was reflected in the prominence he accorded to it in his autobiography. A few of the chapter titles tell the story: "Lucknow's District Gaol," "In Bareilly and Dehra Gun Gaols," "Alipore Gaol " "Back to Prison," and many more.

The same was true of Tito when he talked to his biographers of his life in jail. He expected and received homage for the martyrdom he had suffered.

Give unto men, made lowly wise,
The Spirit of self-sacrifice . . .

And so we trace the road that brings the rebel to the jail. An explorer of the depths of the human psyche, Dr. Theodor Reik, believed that there might be a streak of masochism—no doubt, subconscious and well-disguised—in people of high ideals who start on their careers while suffering from psychic ill-treatment, from non-appreciation, and from a total lack of understanding. "We know," he wrote in his *Masochism in Sex and Society,* "that the best of men have drawn sweetness from their sufferings by anticipating their future appreciation in their imagination."

The most painful experiences of their lives, their keenest disappointments, and the contempt they have elicited may serve to become the turning points to happiness and self-esteem.

Reik quotes Beethoven's apt phrase, *Aus Leiden Freuden,* suffering leads to joy. According to Reik, the question whether it is happiness or unhappiness that urges on creativity—statesmanlike acts in the case of the political prisoner—becomes unimportant. It is unessential compared to the prospect of being praised and esteemed.

Goethe knew the deep significance of the ecstasy of suffering:

Arrows, transpierce ye me,
Lances, coerce ye me,
Bludgeons, so batter me,
Lightnings, so shatter me,
That all of mortality's
Vain unrealities
Die and the stars above
Beam but eternal love!

These are some of the motivations that lead the rebel toward his self-inflicted martyrdom. In the course of this work, we shall ask and examine what the jails have done to these self-appointed, self-anointed martyrs who have ascended from prison to power.

1

A Jailbird Near Nowhere: Kwame Nkrumah

Geographers describe one point on our globe as "Nowhere." This is the place where the two zeros meet—the intersection of zero latitude and zero longitude—where the Equator is intersected by the Meridian of Greenwich—Nowhere. This point is located in the Gulf of Guinea, the tropical sea that washes West Africa's underbelly. Closest to Nowhere is the city of Accra, capital today of the Republic of Ghana. Jails so close to Nowhere are the closest approximations to hell. Kwame Nkrumah was once one of the jailbirds incarcerated in Accra.

It is a very bad hole, indeed, that prison of Nkrumah's. One can judge that by looking at the "homes" of the common people of Accra. Most of these homes are swish huts, so named because of the way mortar is laid on in West Africa—swish-swash. When the bottom of the black sky drops off in a tropical storm, releasing the contents of an aerial water reservoir, many of the huts collapse. Then the work of reconstruction begins—swish-swash.

The roofs of these huts are made of thatched straw, which reeks with the sweetish smell of decomposition; huts of the more affluent residents are covered with sheets of corrugated iron. In all cases, the square windows of the huts are never more than gaping holes. Pallets are rolls of rotting straw, chewed up by insects the large variety of which would delight zoologists. The naked floor serves as the cupboard. One can take in at a glance what "comforts" a prison cell would offer here nearest to Nowhere. Jail cells serve the purpose of making their inmates yearn for

11

the amenities of their homes. What Inferno could have made Nkrumah long for the pleasures of the swish hut?

HAPPY DAYS IN JAIL

Nkrumah spent two terms in jail, the second term near Nowhere. The first period was spent up-country in what was then the British colony of the Gold Coast. "It was a very lonely existence," Nkrumah was to reminisce years later, "but surprisingly enough, I enjoyed it. It was the first time in thirteen years that I had been able to remain quiet and undisturbed in one place for any length of time. . . . At least I could be left with my private thoughts and whatever plans evolved could not be immediately squashed by the majority. I was allowed to read books, but these as well as letters that came had first to be censored by the District Commissioner. Newspapers were forbidden."

The second term was served at James Fort in Accra. The time was 1950, and Nkrumah had been imprisoned on a charge of sedition and of fomenting an illegal general strike. Life in that prison was less bucolic, and he was not alone in his cell—he shared it with eleven other "politicals," lodged there by the British masters of the Gold Coast.

A bucket in a corner of the narrow cell was the latrine of the twelve men. "If only we had been permitted the flimsiest of straw mats to partition the thing off," Nkrumah sighed. But they were not permitted to do that. Life in the cell was harsher than in a swish hut. The prisoners' stomachs were constantly upset by the wretched food. What was their food? Corn porridge without sweetening for breakfast; for lunch, boiled cassava, *gari* (farina) with red pepper, or dry cornmeal. On special days the prisoners were given a watery soup which contained a minute scrap of meat, as hard as a bullet. To relieve his stomach distress, Nkrumah adopted the habit of fasting a day or two every week.

Prisoner Nkrumah was the moving spirit of the Convention People's Party of the Gold Coast, and he had to devise means in his cell to keep in contact with his co-workers. How was he to do it? Since he had no permission to get newspapers he could not learn what political events were taking place in the outside world. Not even a stub of pencil could he have, nor a piece of paper. His professional life, his entire political career, he felt, depended on his getting hold of these basic items. It was a day of triumph when one of his followers managed to smuggle a small pencil into the jail. But how was he to get paper? There was toilet paper, but the share doled out to each prisoner was small. Since some of his cellmates had stronger stomachs than he, Nkrumah exchanged his food with them for toilet paper on his days of fast. A bowl of watery soup for so much toilet paper. On those pieces of paper he wrote African history.

He had to hide the extra paper and his treasured pencil from the guards and to bide his time until dark. The prisoners were thought to be asleep; the guards would become drowsy in the unventilated fort. A street lamp shone faintly into Nkrumah's cell, and by its light he did his work. Feverishly, he wrote, covering sheet after sheet of toilet paper, directives to the free members of the Convention People's Party about strategy and tactics.

A revolution was sweeping the colonial world, and the British had the prescience to take account of it. A few years earlier they had freed India, thereby dropping a liability to gain an asset. An enemy before, India had become a friend, and the London government was now prepared to follow the pattern set in that Asian subcontinent.

In few places of Africa was the will for independence more determined than on the Gold Coast, and nowhere else was there a more effective leader than Kwame Nkrumah, albeit he led his campaign for freedom from a stifling cell in a tropical city near Nowhere.

The jail, however, was the best possible setting for this campaign, and Nkrumah knew it. He knew it because he could see himself in the proper perspective of history. In his prison cell he was a martyr; he bore the indignity of being a prisoner and suffered for his convictions so that his people might become free. But martyrdom was not enough—that he knew, too. The forces of the freedom fighters had to be lined up, a platform constructed, and the strategy of the movement devised. His movement had to have a popular appeal which could be expressed in slogans, songs, emblems and pageants that were simple, easily understood, and attuned to people who lacked sophistication. He had to link the people together to form a community of like-minded brethren.

He constructed a platform the main plank of which was to "fight relentlessly by all constitutional means for the achievement of 'Self-government Now' for the chiefs and the people of the Gold Coast."

Then he had to devise a party greeting, something simple and striking. Because of the many languages of the Gold Coast the word must be in English—the *lingua franca* of the colony. The chosen word was "Freedom," with the accent on the second syllable—Free-*dom!*—to distinguish it from the everyday variety of freedom movements. This was to be a different type of freedom.

A salute was also needed, a special salute that set apart the true believers. He found one: the elbow resting on the hip, the palm fronting outward. Outsiders may not have found it a gesture of overwhelming strength but it was distinctive, and that was important. It was also somewhat puzzling, which made it even more distinctive.

Finally, he needed a party song, a rhythmic stream of strains that would sweep people into the torrent of the movement with the invincible force of a tropical storm. And the song was a paean: "There shall be victory for us!"

All these preparations for Gold Coast independence were made in the "think tank" of a prison cell. There was to be a general election in February, 1951, and if the people of the Gold Coast manifested a sufficiently strong will to be free of the colonial bondage, the British would not stand in the way.

As a man's age is reckoned in the tropics, Kwame Nkrumah was not the youngest of men. At forty-two he had to hustle. Even though in jail, he was elected by an overwhelming majority, and thus began a chain of events. The Gold Coast became Ghana, the first African country to gain independence in the twentieth century. Then came the "independence explosion" of the entire continent. The fame of Kwame Nkrumah skyrocketed; he was soon the best known statesman of Africa. Before tracing his career, let us look at the soil from which he grew.

SATURDAY'S CHILD

Nkrumah was born on a Saturday and that is the only certainty regarding the date of his birth. The month is not sure, nor is the year, although he considers September 18, 1909, his birthday. He was born in the village of Nkroful which is in the Axim district of the western portion of what was then the Gold Coast. The boy was a member of the Nzima group of the Akan tribe of western Ghana, neighbors and kinsfolk of the Ashanti and the Fanti. Akan is the main dialect of the Twi language group, spoken by about a million people.

Nkroful is situated on a bluff flanking the Subri river. Even today it has no electricity or regular water supply, in spite of the fact that it has become a place of pilgrimage not only for Ghanaians but also for people from outside Ghana. The inhabitants live in wattle huts, mud huts, swish huts, or bamboo compounds, but spend most of their time in the narrow alleys separating their abodes. Their kitchens are outdoor ovens, and their sitting rooms are the unpaved, dusty alleys which serve admirably as settings for quarrels, friendships, and endless gossip. Only in inclement weather is the hut used during the day. Residents otherwise spend the entire day on the dusty alley floors, surveying the colorful village scene, eavesdropping on the women's quarrels and on their cooing words to children. There is not enough full-time work for all the able-bodied young men. But they manage to live—that is, to eat—since the extended family group is a mutual protective association and who would dare to turn a kinsman away from the family stove?

A short distance from Nkroful, people speak many other dialects, even different languages. In Ghana there are some seventy different languages—and half a dozen are major ones. Thus primitive societies both bind people together and insulate them. The kinship groups are strongly self-centered, with their own creeds, modes of ancestral worship, moods, ways of life. Nkrumah was born into a matrilineal society where his mother's influence was dominant.

Nkroful was very, very beautiful to the Saturday child who was to become one of Africa's leading statesmen. It was beautiful because it was his birth place. Squatting on the high, stony ground that was situated in a steep escarpment, he could survey the stream and the adjacent swamp, and he saw the entire universe—the microscopic globe of his childhood.

That world was pervaded by another one—an invisible world of souls. That is why Saturday's child had many prenoms—Francis Nwia Kofie Kwame Nkrumah—expiatory offerings to dead individuals that could help as well as harm. Ghosts were real people to Nkrumah because he was endowed, or cursed, with a vivid imagination. To die quickly, that is what he wanted. Then he would become a ghost, able to pass through walls and locked doors.

Some fifty miles from Nkroful, in the town of Half Assini in the narrow panhandle projecting into the Ivory Coast which was then part of French West Africa, lived his father, a goldsmith who apparently had several wives. Nkrumah's mother lived away from him most of the time, and Kwame was her only child, although the boy had several half-brothers. Kwame was nearly three years old when his mother escorted him to his father on the coast. The boy wanted to sleep in her bed. "I remember how I used to be angry when my father came to sleep in our bed and I insisted on sleeping between them. Several times he tried to explain to me that he was married to my mother, but I told him that I also was married to her and that it was my job to protect her."

Kwame was rarely denied anything by his mother, but she tried not to display her affection too openly. Thus, whenever it was her turn to serve the family meal, Kwame was the last to get his food.

In the sub-Saharan Africa of those days, Christian missionaries were as prominent as the savanna and the bush. First among them were the Moravian Brethren, pioneers in introducing Western religions to Africa. Then came the Church Missionary Society, followed by Baptists and Methodists. But it was a German Catholic missionary, George Fischer, who detected the potentialities of Saturday's child, and began to take more than passing interest in him. He converted both the boy and his mother to Catholicism, relieving the parents of the responsibility and financial burden of his education. For eight years Kwame Nkrumah attended the missionary school near Half Assini, where he stood out among his fellow pupils.

While still a teen-ager, he became a student-teacher in the town of Half Assini, his father's place of residence. One day the principal of the Government Training College in Accra audited a class conducted by the boy. He prevailed upon Kwame's parents to let the young scholar study at the school which later achieved fame, first as the Prince of Wales College, and then as Achimota College.

At that time the school had an African assistant principal, Dr. Kwegyir Aggrey, and Kwame fell under his spell. "You can play a tune of sorts on the white keys of a piano," Dr. Aggrey used to say, "and you can play a tune of sorts on the black keys. But for harmony, you must use both black and white."

Kwame was also influenced by Dr. Benjamin Nnamdi Azikiwe, or "Zik," who was among the first to call Africans to action against their colonial rulers. As editor of the newspaper *African Morning Post*, "Zik" set forth his views in blistering words, many of which were to sear the mind of Saturday's child. Now Nkrumah began to reflect on an electrifying concept. Was it really possible that black people could rise to the level of the whites? To him, white had always appeared as a superior color.

A STUDENT AND A TEACHER

The Western creed of Catholicism which Nkrumah had embraced, now exerted a strong influence on him. In the rich symbolism of the Church he saw the fulfilment of an aim. "Catholic," after all, meant "universal," and white people were not the only component parts of the universe. God's children were blacks, whites, and of other colors, and he sought to impress this upon his pupils, while clarifying his own thoughts and convincing himself of the correctness of his views. When teaching, he was able to analyze some of his own character traits. He had the capacity to focus the peregrinating attention of the fancy-free youngsters in his classes. With the intensity of his feelings, his earnestness, and his resonantly convincing arguments that the beliefs of his creed were far more than mere Sunday exercises, he found that he could cast a spell over his pupils.

Nkrumah graduated as a teacher in 1930 and was given a teaching job in the Roman Catholic school of the historic town of Elmina, on the coast. The records of the town opened new vistas to him. He learned how the greedy whites had penetrated Africa behind the protective shield of their creed. Don Diego d'Azambuja, a Portuguese adventurer-navigator, had petitioned the tribal chief at Elmina to accord him permission to build a Christian church for the greater glory of God and the benefit of the natives. That permission granted, the church was built and it became the center of slaving operations. Before being transported overseas, the slaves were converted to Christianity.

From Elmina the young man was transferred to Axim, erstwhile center of the white man's greedy gold operations. Inland from Axim, in the Ancobrah river basin, he came across the diggings that gave the coast its name. For two years he taught at the Roman Catholic Seminary, Amissano, a small mission center.

Young Nkrumah came into contact with numerous European educators in his teaching career. Some were helpful and encouraging, while others were condescending. What made the whites have that feeling of superiority? After all, they were intruders in the black people's land. The mere color of the skin did not make people mentally superior. Skin colors were due to successful biological adjustments and did not influence the quality of the brain. Indeed, there were far more colored than white people in the world and surely the white minority could not speak for the non-white majority.

The whites had despoiled his land, Nkrumah decided. Why had Africa not been able to set its will against the white man's greed? He was eager to become acquainted with the source of the white man's strength. The center of authority on the Gold Coast was Britain, and Nkrumah wanted to complete his education there. But first, he had to pass preliminary tests. Would he be able to compete with the Westerners?

He could express himself well and had the gift to stir an audience. Was this a sign of intelligence and of knowledge? Perhaps it was only the projection of a deep-seated will to stand out from the crowd. The entrance tests to the British schools might tell him how much he was worth. Academic tests, however, are not designed to measure the non-academic capabilities of young men. In two crucial tests—in mathematics and Latin—he failed. Here, then, was the answer to his questions. He should be content to be a teacher at home. It was at least better than working on a cocoa plantation, like so many other young men he knew.

THE BLACK MAN'S BURDEN

Increasingly, life in the United States had begun to attract ambitious young West Africans. America had a large Negro population and produced colored leaders of note. The United States was spurting ahead of Europe in many fields, including education. Nkrumah was a Catholic; Catholics were strengthening their positions in America, forming a powerful lobby. For a time he played with the idea of becoming a priest—not in the bush, but a prince of the Church, a bishop. It is true that America was in the midst of a depression then, but it still looked like fabulous affluence to the impecunious young African. An uncle helped him to obtain passage to the United States. The year was 1935. He planned to remain for a short time but stayed fully ten years.

His first contact in the United States was an "African" one. After a probationary period he got a scholarship at the first Negro school of higher learning, founded in 1854, Lincoln University, which is located forty-five miles southwest of Philadelphia. At the time it had a student body of 160 and a faculty of 25. (Some thirty years later it had a student body of 372 and a faculty of 42.) Although several religious faiths were represented at Lincoln, it was affiliated with the Presbyterian Church. This fact gave a new orientation to the young man from the Gold Coast.

In those days the United States was in a state of intellectual ferment, for the values of the nation were being reappraised. Young intellectuals taxed capitalism for failing to fulfill its promise of a more abundant life. It was fashionable among the younger generation to protest against the established order, to be left-wing. Bright young Americans were beguiled by various forms of collectivism, especially socialism and communism. In many parts of the world other young and not-so-young capitalists were attracted to an altogether different form of collectivism: its name was fascism. To these capitalists, fascism seemed to be the wave of the future, the universal remedy that would put recalcitrant labor in its place, elevate the nation and national authority into godheads, extol war as the sign of the supreme sacrifice of man for a cause, and reorganize the world order. For the young people from Africa, fascism appeared to be a satanic force, while the opposite end of the political spectrum seemed to be the universal nostrum.

Instead of theology, Nkrumah selected economics and sociology as his majors at Lincoln. He is not economics-minded now and could not have been in those days. But having turned to socialism he had to study economics, which was its pivot. His *bête noire* was colonialism, the handmaiden of capitalism. Through economics he hoped to ascertain the nature of the forces that propel social classes into power, thereby creating the Establishment. If the Gold Coast became free one day, what economic system should it adopt?

He studied sociology because of his concern with the intrinsic nature of social forces. He observed that in the West, society was being transformed from a status-minded to a performance-centered community. Nkrumah was very much interested in the philosophy and application of Western values which, he felt, might be turned to fruitful use by the emerging social units in Africa. Should that continent become really free, what new social forces were likely to emerge?

He was an African Faust, this young man from the Gold Coast. Economics and sociology alone did not seem to provide the answers he was seeking. So he turned again to theology, to the search for the infinite within the finite, to the longing for the whisper of intuition which may be a sign of communion with supernatural powers.

He gained admission to the Lincoln Theological Seminary in 1939, the same year in which he graduated as a bachelor of arts with a major in sociology and economics. At the same time he arranged to continue his studies in philosophy and education at the University of Pennsylvania in order to get his master's degree.

His funds were always low, and now they were running out. This would have been the time to return to the Gold Coast. Then World War II broke out; temporarily, at least, his road to Africa was blocked. And so he continued his studies of philosophy. Who of the philosophers had the key to the kingdom of knowledge? He was attracted to several philosophers. One of them was that austere Prussian, Immanuel Kant, with his categorical imperative: "So act that you could will the maxim of your action to be a universal law." The search for the correct action, as for truth, was basic to man, Nkrumah believed. But there were always those counter-forces that sought to divert man from the path of truth, those challenging natural forces that dared human resourcefulness to devise the right replies.

Nkrumah was also attracted to the theories of Hegel, especially to his dialectic ideology. He saw in them an explanation of historical evolution as well as of the process of mental resolution: a thesis will always call forth a contradiction—antithesis—and the conflict between the two will produce a synthesis.

The young Gold Coast scholar was impressed by the fact that Hegelian dialectics was employed by Karl Marx in his dialectical materialism, the theory which states that social and economic changes are the result of materialistic forces—that it is economic needs, especially the methods of production, which are mainly responsible for the dialectic oscillations. Nkrumah pondered whether the dialectical techniques might not disclose insights which would help the student of history to peer into the secrets of the future. During his stay in Pennsylvania he certainly could not have foreseen that the time would come when he would link his own name to that of Marx—Marxism-Nkrumahism would become the official creed of an independent country in Africa of which Nkrumah was to be the head.

In still another German philosopher, Schopenhauer, the

young man from the Gold Coast found not merely insights but also scholarly relaxation. Did he agree with Schopenhauer's vitriolic criticism of Hegel: "All the books dealing with Hegel's secrets have managed to keep them." Schopenhauer's adventurous generalizations appealed to Nkrumah because they confirmed his own belief that stronger than the power of abstract thinking in the realm of philosophy was the force of intuitive comprehension. He agreed with this sophisticated German that the primeval seed was the human will. The real substance of the human world was the expression of man's will and the projection of his ideas.

Schopenhauer led Nkrumah to Nietzsche, the categorical philosopher of power and self-assertion. Conflict was an immutable force and the assertion of will was its resolution. The meek represented the foundations upon which the strong constructed their innovations and projections into the future. Yes, when all was said and done, it was the image of the Superior Man, as envisaged by Nietzsche, that made the strongest impression on the student from the Gold Coast. He could not foresee then that the assertion of the will power he learned from the teachings of Nietzsche would one day lodge him in the cell of a jail near Nowhere and that after a period of turmoil and tribulation he would create a nation named Ghana.

At the University of Pennsylvania, Nkrumah also studied methods of education. He abandoned the idea of becoming a priest or preacher. His courses in education, he hoped, would provide him with the skills necessary to convey to students some of the esoteric knowledge he had acquired.

In 1942 he received two academic degrees. (He already had that of the bachelor of arts from Lincoln.) The University of Pennsylvania conferred upon him the degree of Master of Science in Education. Lincoln gave him the degree of Bachelor of Theology. In February, 1943, he received the Master of Arts degree in Philosophy from the University of Pennsylvania.

What impression did Nkrumah make at Lincoln? The 1939 Lincoln Year Book carried the following notice about him: "As a freshman he quite easily and interestingly adjusted himself to Lincoln and the new environment and graduated a fine and polished gentleman intent on the economic resurrection of his beloved native land."

Nkrumah was moonlighting as an assistant in philosophy to a Lincoln faculty member, Dr. George Johnson, who recalls that

Nkrumah marked papers for him and oversaw the assigned read-ing. Nkrumah says that he had become a full instructor in philoso-phy, first year Greek, and Negro history. "Negro history was a most popular subject and the classroom was always packed to capacity," he recalled in *Ghana; The Autobiography of Kwame Nkrumah.* "I think I enjoyed lecturing on this subject as much as my audience appeared to enjoy listening. Another course which I liked was social philosophy; this also attracted a lot of students to my class. However, I never considered myself anything more than a novice and it was consequently a very pleasant surprise to me when in 1945—the year I left America—I was honored by the *Lincolnian* [the magazine of Lincoln University] which voted me 'the most outstanding professor of the year'."

"He has given me great satisfaction," Dr. Johnson wrote in a letter of recommendation for Nkrumah on February 11, 1941. "He is as able intellectually as any assistant I have ever had; he is conscientious, exemplary in conduct, and gives promise of great usefulness. He is a candidate for the ministry under the care of the Chester Presbytery—and expects to pass his ecclesiastic exam-inations and receive licensure April next. . . . One of his papers, 'Primitive Education in Africa,' was considered by his instructors meritorious. enough to be published in the January, 1941, *Educa-tional Outlook,* the magazine published by the School of Educa-tion, University of Pennsylvania."

Another Lincoln professor, Dr. Laurence Foster, wrote about Nkrumah as a student on January 11, 1951: "His anthropo-logical interests prompted several college-born papers and a fruitless doctor's dissertation. Purposeful; an African nationalist."

Another comment on the same day about Nkrumah both as a student and as a teacher from the late Dr. Miller: "Courteous, somewhat aloof. Very religious; led prayer services and tended other religious services conscientiously. Good student. Overdog-matic on certain points of social anthropology. Was Dr. Johnson's 'ace-boy' in history and philosophy. . . . Embittered by some undetermined cause late in his seminary course."

Nkrumah was underpaid, as were most teachers at the time. America had not yet been swept by the "revolt of the professors" for living wages. So inadequate were their salaries that ivy-league college professors were going around in worn-out shoes, and were sometimes unable to eat their fill or to support their families.

Thus it was that Professor Kwame Nkrumah, "outstanding

teacher of the year," had to get moonlighting jobs. The best of these were occasional invitations to preach in Negro churches in Pennsylvania and in New York. During vacations he had a chance at times to go to sea as a steward. He also had a "steady job" as a welder at the Sun Shipbuilding Yard at Chester, Pennsylvania, close to Lincoln University.

On the night shift, from midnight until eight, he worked in all kinds of weather. So intense was the cold on some of those nights that his hands seemed to freeze to the bars of steel he was handling. In the early morning hours he put his welding tools aside and hurried to his classroom to assume another role, that of an esteemed scholar explaining esoteric points of the profound philosophies of Hegel and Kant.

He aspired to the scholar's "labor union card," Doctor of Philosophy diploma, which he felt would provide him a better opportunity to obtain a permanent position at one of America's schools of higher learning. But he was reaching beyond his grasp and had to abandon his project. However, after he had made his name in Africa, Lincoln presented to him the honorary doctorate— an LL.D. As President of Ghana he proudly called himself Dr. Kwame Nkrumah.

In the United States, though, he had not escaped the black man's burden. One of the most memorable incidents of that portion of his life happened to him in a bus depot. It was a hot summer day in Baltimore, and as he waited for his bus in the station he became very thirsty. Looking around he saw no sign of water. He stepped up to the ticket window and asked the clerk for information: where could he get a drink? The white-skinned attendant pointed to a corner of the waiting room: "There." And "there" was a brass spittoon.

But he encountered kindness, too, in his peregrinations and on his jobs in America, especially among his colleagues, both black and white. He was respected for many of his excellent qualities particularly because of his vast capacity for work. His students as well as his associates were impressed by his eagerness to continue learning, his ability to think through problems to conclusions which he verified by consulting established authorities, the economic use he made of his time, wasting neither moments nor motions.

In May, 1945, he left New York for London. "It was not until the boat sailed out from the harbor," he wrote in his autobiography, "and I saw the Statue of Liberty with her arm raised as if in a personal farewell to me that a mist covered my eyes: 'You have opened my eyes to the true meaning of liberty,' I thought. 'I shall never rest until I have carried your message to Africa'."

TO BRITAIN

He had spent ten years in the United States, the formative years of his political thinking and of his working habits. More than ever he realized that the black man could not afford to have white masters. In the intellectual ferment of America's depression and war years, he had developed a strong antipathy to fascism and much sympathy for the left-wing. He would have been out of the swim of the times if he had not become a radical.

For years the right-wing seemed to be riding high in many parts of the world outside the English-speaking countries. During those years the so-called Axis, of Germany-Italy-Japan, appeared to be on its way to victory. It would have been the victory of die-hard nationalism and militarism. For a time the German and the Japanese gave the impression of being invincible. It was a long heartbreaking period before the anti-Fascist alliance brought its opponents' war machines to a halt. V-E Day—Victory in Europe —opened the Atlantic Ocean to travel again. In May, 1945, Nkrumah took passage to London.

The center of his African universe was the British capital. He wanted to get his bearings and to acquaint himself with the governmental system of that land. He wanted to take the measure of the British ruling race and learn the causes of the subordinate position of Africa. In the United States he had learned about will power, and his action-batteries were fully charged. He was still young, and few of his contemporaries possessed his advantages—a thorough education and an indomitable will power. He believed that if a man wanted something intensely—well, there was no reason why he should not get it.

Coming from American academic circles he was attracted to that towering institution of liberalism, the London School of Economics. It appealed to many bright young people from all parts of Britain's global empire. It was the bulwark of the British Labour party, now in power, and above all, it was the sounding board of the erudite Harold Laski, a man of deep sympathy for the underdog.

Through that school he could more easily set up contact with British sympathizers, important members of the party at the helm, and fellow Africans with established positions in London.

"I associated myself with all political movements, and also with all parties," he wrote later, "and I felt that the Communist party in England was fortunate in having among its leaders personalities such as Mr. Emil Burns, Mr. Palme Dutt, and Mr. Harry Pollitt."

Ostentatiously he would unfold his *Daily Worker,* surrounded by businessmen with copies of *The Times, Manchester Guardian,* and *Daily Telegraph.* "I could . . . then watch as pairs of eyes were suddenly focused on me. But the gaze of these bowler-hatted gentlemen was not in any way hostile and the atmosphere was always one of mild amusement."

Was he a member of the Communist party? In Britain it was nobody else's business. There no one would censor his words or deeds. In Britain even the most inflammatory speech was protected by the country's democratic traditions. At home, on the Gold Coast, a British possession, he might have spent his life in jail for a lesser offense.

This dark-skinned Faust, this Kwame Nkrumah, still hungered insatiably for knowledge. He continued to immerse himself in sociology, philosophy, economics, and theology, and now he added practical politics to his studies. In the relaxed atmosphere of Britain, "subversive" African organizations of students and of others were proliferating. The West African Students' Union at London had been founded in 1925 and was now an incubator for native African leadership. Ambitious Mr. Nkrumah worked himself into the vice-presidency of the organization. Here he was closely connected with the bearers of legendary names, including William Edward Burghardt Du Bois, former professor of Greek, of Latin, of history, and of economics, director of publications of the National Association for the Advancement of the Colored People; with George Arthur Padmore, whose honors included the commandership of the "Most Venerable Order of the Knighthood of the Pioneers of the Republic of Liberia" and of the "Great Band of the Humane Order of African Redemption." These two "grand men" of Negro liberation movements, one as old as the mountains and the other younger even than Nkrumah, felt that the independence of colored people could be achieved only by organized mass movements engaged in positive political action.

Zealous Mr. Nkrumah became the general secretary of the

working committee of the Fifth Pan-African Congress in Manchester.

During the war the victorious Allies had made a solemn pledge in the Atlantic Charter to "respect the right of all peoples to choose the form of government under which they will live." Now was the time to fulfill the pledge. Britain had won the war but in so doing she had lost her strength to retain her empire.

Nationalism was the established church of the Western world now, and its creeds spread to the colonies. As nations, the countries of the West had grown powerful and rich. African societies would have to be remodeled in the image of the new godhead. But could those societies achieve their rights without arms? Obviously, they could not set their primitive weapons against the sophisticated arms of the West. Would Britain, France, and the other colonialists be perceptive enough to realize that colonialism was becoming as obsolete as the bow and arrow? They ought to be able to see, Nkrumah and his associates thought, that the friendship and trade of the former colonies would weigh more on the scale than the retention of nominal rule.

The young Africans were heartened when, in 1947, the British government freed the Indian subcontinent, where India and Pakistan had laid the foundations of an independent existence. The Africans were particularly impressed by the pre-independence work of a shriveled little Indian, Mahatma Gandhi. Not force but will power counted in the affairs of people, India's Great Soul declared. Nkrumah, the disciple of Nietzsche, heard the echo of the teachings he had absorbed.

Britain, as he saw it, was motivated also by other forces. The post-war world was now engaged in the battle of the giants. The wartime allies had fallen out among themselves, and the world was split into two parts on ideological grounds. Or were the ideologies mere smoke screens for power rapacity? It was under the banner of freedom that the West was marching into battle. Free-*dom*. The word resounded in Nkrumah's mind. How could the Occident claim to be the defender of liberty as long as it held the Gold Coast in bondage—and the other coasts, too, and vast interiors of continents? But should the West remain attached to its antiquated ways there was the challenger, the Soviet Union. A new game of diplomacy was now open to the champions of colonial liberation, a new balance-of-power policy in which the scales were held by the weak, and not the strong.

Nkrumah established contact with leaders of the colonial people of French West Africa, especially Leopold Senghor, political leader in Senegal and a noted poet, who was to play a historic role in the transformation of the sub-Saharan colonial possessions of France. Also, he became associated with another nimble politician of French West Africa, Félix Houphouet-Boigny, leader in the political movement of the Ivory Coast, adjacent to the Gold Coast.

"Words fade away, but the print remains." Young Africans in London quoted the Latin proverb when they applied for funds in their attempt to establish publications. In 1946 funds became available for a time to start a periodical, the *New African;* however, they were forced to stop publication shortly thereafter. "Towards Colonial Free-dom," a pamphlet Nkrumah wrote, was smuggled into the Gold Coast and had an impressive circulation there. He had become the young agitator whom people were watching.

By now the Gold Coast was astir, too. That meant the articulate portion of the colony, not the primitive tribesmen in the bush. It was intellectuals who began to give shape to the future, hoping that others would fall into line. To achieve political results a political movement had to be established. This was done by a respected author-politician, Dr. Joseph Danquah. He was the founder of the United Gold Coast Convention, UGCC.

Dr. Danquah, author of studies on Akan customs and religion, was more an idea-man than a practical politician. It was he who first suggested that the Gold Coast be named after a long departed mid-Saharan state—Ghana. Centuries before, Ghana had existed in the western Sudan, hundreds of miles to the northwest of the site of the Gold Coast. A family tree was needed for the projected independent state and Ghana was handy.

The awkward designation of the UGCC indicated the difficulties the independence movement had to overcome. Why was it called a Convention? Why not the more easily understandable "Party" or "Movement"? And what was the meaning of the word "United"? The British ruled over a conglomerate of chieftains on the Gold Coast, many of whom were considered godlike creatures and were venerated as divinities. They were invested with magic powers, conferred upon them by such symbols as the golden stools. Some of these chieftains had been headhunters until the British discovered their practices.

The Convention needed a practical politician to run it, and Nkrumah was recommended for the post. From Nietzsche he had learned about the pervasive force of will power; in America he had become acquainted with the methods of public relations, advertising, propaganda, and the importance of methodical organization. It was on November 14, 1947, that Nkrumah left England to return to the Gold Coast. He had been away from home for a dozen years. Meanwhile, his fame had spread in the colony. He was secretary-general of the Convention.

CREATING A NATION

"When I took up my appointment as general secretary," he wrote in his autobiography, "I found, on going through the minute book, that thirteen branches had been formed throughout the country. On looking further into the matter, however, I discovered that this was entirely incorrect. In actual fact just a couple of branches had been established, and these were inactive."

He had to start from scratch, this former teacher, shipyard welder, preacher, philosopher, propagandist, inhibited exhibitionist. It was in a room of a Catholic School in the inland town of Tarkwa that this organization against the authority of the British and, perhaps, also of the chieftains held its first meeting. The avowed objective of the UGCC was to "insure that by all legitimate and constitutional means the control and the direction of the government shall within the shortest time possible pass into the hands of the people and their chiefs."

The wording of this program should be noted: constitutional means . . . shortest possible time . . . people . . . and their chiefs. "Constitutional means" ruled out the application of force—and this betokened the influence of Gandhi and of the new revolution, i.e. without the shedding of blood. The "shortest time possible" indicated the urgency with which the colonial world began to view the timetable of events. Then note the curious juxtaposition of "people" and "chiefs," indicating the chasm between them. Were the chiefs not people, were they superior creatures, gods in human form? Even though the British were the masters of the Gold Coast, they had had to rule through the major chiefs—and that was the substance of British "indirect rule."

Nkrumah has said that his mother told him he was the descendant of two minor chiefs. This seems to be an afterthought, a fairy tale, for no documentation of this statement has ever been produced. Nkrumah knew that it was hard to break into the circle of the Gold Coast native rulers, protected by the magic of their golden stools. He was jockeying to get closer to the center of power.

The secretary-general of the Convention did not like the cautious ways of Dr. Danquah, nor those of the "respectable" people behind the Convention. He began to lay the foundations of a secret organization from which the chiefs—headhunting and otherwise—were to be excluded. He called it "The Circle," the program of which was summarized in service, sacrifice, and suffering. The scope of The Circle went far beyond the Gold Coast. After all, that colony had been shaped as a result of a power struggle between the British and the French (who controlled vast areas in that region) and because of the administrative convenience of those rulers. The Circle was to support the claims of an All West-African National Congress which was to create a Union of African Socialist Republics. "At such time as may be deemed advisable, The Circle will come out openly as a political party embracing the whole of West Africa."

THEN THE CPP

Rioting broke out on the Gold Coast on February 28, 1948. It started because of an attempt on the consumers' part to have the price of imported goods reduced and it was directed against the local European and Syrian traders. The spirit of Gandhi did not prevail at these riots; twenty-nine Africans were killed. The UGCC was blamed for the trouble, and its major leaders were arrested, including Nkrumah. At first he was held in Kumasi, in the heart of the Ashanti country; then he was transferred to Lawra, in the Northern Territories. On that occasion his complicity could not be proved and he was released after a short period of detention. A British investigation of the troubles by the Watson Commission found that he was "imbued with a Communist ideology" and that he had "never abandoned his aims for a Union of West-African Soviet Socialist Republics."

Among his cautious comrades the belief spread that their arrest and suffering was his fault. So he was demoted from the post of secretary-general to that of the treasurer. Undaunted, he decided that only young people had the spirit to stand by their convictions. He founded the Committee on Youth Organization which was to be a section of the national movement. Still convinced that only the printed word could amplify the human voice, he established the *Accra Evening News.*

Backed by the Youth Organization he decided to break with the cautious UGCC and in June, 1949, he formed the Convention People's Party, CPP, to fight relentlessly by all constitutional means for the achievement of "Full Government Now" for the chiefs and the people of the Gold Coast.

Kwame Nkrumah had a new degree now. Proudly he called himself P.G.—Prison Graduate. Suffering was one of his qualifications, also a prerequisite for membership in The Circle. On June 12, 1949, at a public meeting in Accra, he set forth details of the CPP. He faced an audience of some sixty thousand people who lifted their faces to him, black faces encasing gleaming teeth. He spoke English to these thousands, a language most of them did not understand. Yet, as he spoke they seemed to comprehend far more than the political concepts that could be expressed in mere words. They understood that this was the man who would have the power to give them free-*dom* and that, above all, with this man's aid they would now become human beings and not anthropoid vegetables in the tropical soil. As they looked at him they were lifted out of their everyday pettiness and cares. Members of that audience were components of a godlike and majestic unit of a sovereign nation that soon might be able to conduct its own affairs. When that time came, the white supermen would no longer stalk in their midst.

"BARAKA" AND "CHARISMA"

Will power was the force that elevated man above himself. Saturday's child, facing the sea of black faces, saw the teachings of Schopenhauer and Nietzsche corroborated by his own experience. In complete command of his audience, he felt intoxicated with the ferment he caused in the thinking of all these people.

The Moslems, of whom there are many in Ghana, have a word for this state of elation and command. They call it *baraka,* "being blessed." Only persons endowed with those attributes can soar aloft on the wings of the power of their will. The ancients knew about this state of elation. They employed a Greek word to describe it—*charisma,* "gift." It is a divine gift, bestowed upon a privileged individual as evidence that divine grace has fitted him for the office to which he has been called. Nor is that enough. The charismatic leader must be convinced that he can perform the unusual deeds which everyday people will call miracles. It may have been on that June day of 1949 that Kwame Nkrumah, P.G., discovered his charismatic powers. "It was a great day," he said, "and my heart felt very full as I stood up to acknowledge the deafening cheers of welcome from an excited crowd."

But first there were two of the three S's of The Circle to fulfill—sacrifice and suffering. In January, 1950, disturbances broke out on the Gold Coast, and a state of emergency was declared. Nkrumah was arrested on January 21, and charged with "inciting strikes and seditions." He was lodged in James Fort prison, the place near Nowhere, and there he was held for over a year. He had ample opportunity to indulge in sacrifice and suffering.

"In a very short time," he wrote later, "prisoners lose all their individualism and personality; they become a set type in an unhappy world of their own. They lose confidence in themselves and are so unequipped to meet the outside world that it is little wonder they hanker for the misery and boredom of their prison cells, a protective shelter for their lost and shattered souls."

That is true, no doubt, of the rank-and-file prisoners, in detention pens for criminal acts. They are weak creatures, many of them. But it is not true of people endowed with the grace which the ancients called *charisma* and which the Moslems name *baraka*. These unusual people look upon their imprisonment as a challenge to which they must find the proper response by probing their inner resources. In their cells they steel themselves for the additional hardships that will confront them after they are released from prison. That strength will give them great competitive advantages over their rivals who have been spared the sacrifice and suffering of jail. In comparison with the hardships of the jail, the trial of life in freedom will be easy for them.

Thus the soul of Kwame Nkrumah was not shattered. He found himself a charismatic leader. Also, he had learned from his teachers in Pennsylvania, quoting Nietzsche and Schopenhauer, that will power could overcome even prison bars.

A MAN TO POWER BORN

Ghana is situated in the part of West Africa which used to be known as the "white man's grave." Those graves were prepared for the white men because of harmless-looking little creatures, such as mosquitoes, which injected death into men in the form of malaria and yellow fever—especially if the man's skin was white. White men ruled the universe but they succumbed to mosquitoes more easily than the black man who was used to the stings of all sorts of creatures. The rows of graves of the white pioneers kept other Caucasians away.

There were no such graves in many other parts of Africa, of course, especially not in the extreme North, beyond the Sahara, and in the extreme South. Neither were there such graves in the highlands of East Africa—the White Highlands. Because of this the white people proliferated there, and becoming strong and aggressive they said that the land belonged to them, not to the natives.

There were no such vested interests of the whites in West Africa, except for the graves. The Gold Coast was right at the core of the vast graveyard. Now, however, in the middle of the twentieth century, there were all kinds of drugs which immunized men against the stings of the tiny creatures: not even the white people had to die. But since the nationalist movement had begun in the colonies, white men no longer cared to move into this area. For Nkrumah it was easier to oust the colonists from the former grave-yard than it would have been in the salubrious highlands. He was in a strategic position to get a historic process started, and he did. He would probably have been unable to do it if he had not first gone to America and Britain, and if he had not learned about the superior qualities of the man who dared to act. And so he became the pioneer of all African freedom movements.

It was somewhat easier for him to act than if he had been a political leader in a French colonial region, or in any of the areas belonging to the Belgians or the Portuguese. The British people were the most adult in their political thinking, and they had learned not to fight incontestable facts. They had also learned that they would retain many advantages in the colonial areas if they could manage to retreat gracefully. And this they did.

First, however, the British had to test the people of the Gold Coast and their prisoner in his nauseating cell. Were the people of the Coast able to agree on a clear-cut and acceptable program? Did Nkrumah possess statesman-like qualities or only a big mouth? They called a general election in February, 1951. The CPP won 35 of the possible 38 electoral seats. Nkrumah waged his campaign from his cell, and he won the constituency of Accra Central with 22,780 votes out of the 23,122 polled. On February 12, Nkrumah changed his address. From the prison cell he moved into Government House. Officially he became known as the Leader of Government Business and he also held the portfolio of Communications and Public Works. This was a probationary period. The following year he became the prime minister.

There he stood now, in the full blaze of world publicity, a black African who had won against the British Empire. As he faced ecstatic masses in front of Government House he did not look a superman. All the world could see that he looked like any of the tens of millions of colored people—of medium height, sometimes wearing a colored toga-like garment, sometimes a conservative Western-style business suit. It required close observation to notice some special features in his appearance. He had a protruding forehead, very broad. He had sad eyes which could become gay, too—evidently a man of quickly changing moods.

Ghana was still passing through a probationary period. In July, 1953, Prime Minister Nkrumah proposed his motion for the independence of the Gold Coast. Popularly, this became known as the Motion of Destiny. Now the National Assembly—until then partly "white"—became an all-African legislature. In 1956 elections were again held, and again the CPP won the majority. In March, 1957, Ghana became fully independent, though the British queen was regarded as the nominal head of state. The new country joined the United Nations as its eighty-first member.

Ghana's independence was the signal for Africa's "independence explosion." The movement spread to the adjacent regions, including France's vast colonial territories—French West Africa and French Equatorial Africa. Eventually, the most populous of all African countries, Nigeria, reached full independence. From the West the area of "spontaneous combustion" spread to the center of the continent, to the former Belgian Congo, and then irrepressibly on to the White Highlands of the black continent, to the African "Horn" in the extreme East, and across the desert belt into Mediterranean Africa where the die-hard resistance of the Algerian *colons* was overcome. A few years ago Africa was the continent of colonies, an appendix of Europe, now Africa had become a vast reservoir of newly independent nations, introducing a new structure to the United Nations.

Ghana was a member of the Commonwealth of Nations, previously known under other names: the British Empire and the

British Commonwealth. The empire was extinct, and the word "British" had been dropped from the designation of the Commonwealth, which was now comprised of fully independent nations— independent in foreign relations and defense matters, too—linked to the other members, including Britain, the *ci-devant* mother country, by common consent and by the desire to derive benefits from mutual assistance and consultation. Ghana was the first black member to gain admittance to the all-white Commonwealth. It was as a Commonwealth member that Ghana recognized the queen of Britain as the symbol of unity, but no more.

On July 1, 1960, the ultimate step was taken. Ghana became a republic, while retaining her seat in the council of the Commonwealth countries. Thus the queen ceased to be the nominal head of state. By a nearly unanimous vote Kwame Nkrumah became the president of the Republic of Ghana.

Until 1957 Nkrumah had remained unmarried. In that year, when he was nearly fifty, he married an Egyptian, Miss Fathia Halim Ritzk. Their first child, a boy, was named Kweku. Their second child was also a boy.

Was there significance in the fact that he had married so late, and an Egyptian and not a Negress? Whisperers read all sorts of significant explanations into his marriage: Nkrumah had not married sooner because he was wedded to his political work. Now however, his great work was accomplished. And why an Egyptian? During his formative years abroad, in Britain and the United States, his ideas of feminine beauty had been shaped. At the same time, the white woman he married was an African, and thus African suspicions might be put to rest. These explanations may have been right or wrong. There is also another possibility that should not be disregarded. He may have been attracted to his lady irrespective of considerations of race or geography.

A CONTROVERSIAL AFRICAN

"I pledge with all my life my support to the Convention People's Party and my leader Kwame Nkrumah." This was the beginning of an oath which party officials were called upon to swear to Nkrumah. A prominent American Negro writer, Richard Wright, heard it recited and he asked Nkrumah for a copy of it, but his request was ignored. Wright was therefore compelled to paraphrase the oath from memory and the rest of it reads something like this: "I swear to follow my Leader's guidance, to execute faithfully his command, to resist with all my power all imperialist attempts to disrupt our ranks, to strive with all my heart to rebuild our lost nation. So help me God."

This is an instance of the cult of the personality, which has been practiced in some of its most extreme forms in Nkrumah's Ghana. The following is the Declaration of Faith of Ghana's Young Pioneers, a government-sponsored organization:

> Nkrumah does no wrong. Nkrumah is our leader.
> Nkrumah does no wrong. Nkrumah is our Messiah.
> Nkrumah does no wrong. Nkrumah never dies.

At meetings where the President of Ghana is present such religious songs as "Lead, Oh Kindly Light" are intoned.

The likeness of Nkrumah is everywhere: on postage stamps, in countless issues of newspapers, in the names of streets, squares, and boulevards. The most prominent place in all Ghana, the square in front of the legislature, is occupied by his statue. Everywhere people are reminded of his famous sayings: in bronze and marble, over the radio, on the cinema screens, in public buildings. There is a Kwame Nkrumah University in Kumasi, the capital of the Ashanti country; Kwame Nkrumah Steel-Works at Tema. There is Kwame Nkrumah this and Kwame Nkrumah that in every nook and corner of the nation.

His official designation is: Osagyefo Dr. Kwame Nkrumah, President of the Republic of Ghana. *Osagyefo* is an Akan word, which is usually translated as "Deliverer" or "Redeemer." He is also called *Tufuhene,* "Warrior Chief."

We have seen that native chiefs in Ghana derive authority, magic power, and even divine rights from the golden stool. The Ashantis believe it contains the soul of the nation, and that if it were destroyed, they would perish. Nkrumah devised two stools for himself, one of them called the Seat of State, placed in the legislature, and the other designated as the Chair of State, in the Presidential Palace.

The Seat of State consists of a dozen parts. The actual seat is called *Osramfa,* "crescent moon," and it is described officially as the symbol of the influence of "feminine disposition and of nature on the well-being of the society and state." Then there is the egg-shaped backrest which "symbolizes the common sharing of the responsibility for the welfare of the nation;" the bowlegs of the seat symbolize "all that comes under detestable pride," (whatever that may mean). Other parts symbolize feminine beauty, male power, and God's presence in society. *Akosane,* a wheel-like shape, is the "Ghanaian symbol of reincarnation." The same seat contains also symbols of good fortune, old age and dignity, the supremacy of the nation, and many other things.

It is the same with the Chair of State, which contains symbols of wisdom, manliness, "the perfect home, purity, sanctity, and the Ghanaian tradition that the head of State must be the embodiment of wisdom." And the head of state is enthroned on all of this magnificence. The role of these fantastic chairs is unequivocal. Through them Nkrumah must convince the tribal chieftains that his power is superior to theirs, and that he derives it from tribal traditions no less than from divinity. The chairs he devised were meant to be the ultimate in golden stools; they were to place all the tribal chieftains in the deepest shadow. By means of the two chairs the Osagyefo was to establish his claim as the first one in the earthly pantheon of authority.

All of this sounds either infantile or fantastic in the West. But Ghana is not that, say some Ghanaians of penetrating insights, when interpreting these names and symbols. Margaret J. C. Abudu, an American married to a brilliant Ghanaian sociologist, writes in *Ghana—One Party State:* "The African does not take words as literally as does the man in the West. His use of church hymns merely expresses the view that the president of his country occupies a position no less exalted than a tribal chieftain."

Interpreting the word *Osagyefo,* Mrs. Abudu derives it from two Akan words: *Osa,* "war," and *gyefo,* "bearer," meaning leader in war. The most important tribal group in Ghana, that of the Ashantis, was in the habit of addressing its paramount chiefs or kings as *Osagyefos* or *Otomfuos.* When addressed in these terms, President Nkrumah wants no more than to be identified with power that is not lower than that of the traditional regional kings.

"Nkrumah's charisma" says Mrs. Abudu, "appears to be the product more of the overenthusiasm of party zealots than of his own design."

At the opening of the third session of the second parliament of the Republic of Ghana, Nkrumah was offered the presidency for life, but he refused the honor. That refusal appeared to amount to a basic policy declaration:

"It is essential," he said, "that the people shall freely exercise their sacred right and duty of self-expression through voting. Therefore, while I thank the House for the faith and solidarity expressed in the motion to confer the life Presidency on me, I submit most humbly that the most conclusive way to demonstrate this singular support is by securing the return of me and my party, the Convention People's Party, to power at the five-yearly elections of parliament."

Was Nkrumah playing coy?

WHAT HAPPENED TO FREE-DOM?

The most prominent P.G.—prison graduate—of Africa is Osagyefo Kwame Nkrumah. From personal experience he knows what it means to be tucked into a noisome cell in the deepest tropics, in the city of Accra, which is the nearest point on land to what the geographers call "Nowhere," at the intersection of zero latitude and zero longitude. He also knows that a man shut off from the companionship of men at large becomes an unman and a zero.

Yet, he has pushed through several laws, the object of which is to have people reduced to the level of zero through incarceration and deportation. The Deportation Act which he sponsored authorizes the exclusion of any person whose presence in the country is not deemed to be conducive to the public weal. The Preventive Detention Act is even more drastic: it invests the government with the power to detain suspects in political matters for periods of up to five years without trial. A distinguished political scientist and the former leader of the National Liberation Movement, Dr. Kofi Busia, was one of Nkrumah's first victims. Dr. Busia was lecturing in the Netherlands when the National Assembly in Accra passed a National Assembly Disqualification Act excluding any member absent for not fewer than twenty consecutive sessions without the Speaker's permission. This act, sponsored by Nkrumah, was tailor-made for Busia, who had been absent for twenty consecutive sessions.

Without military training of any kind, Nkrumah assumed control over Ghana's armed forces, dismissing a competent British officer—not his yes-man—whom he himself had hired. By him and him alone would thenceforth be made all "necessary appointments" to the armed forces. He declared states of emergency in key areas of Ghana from time to time, prohibiting public meetings, requisitioning vehicles, and imprisoning "saboteurs."

Periodically, Ghanaian newspapers have reported attempts on Nkrumah's life. Confirmation of such attempts has been hard to obtain. Nkrumah blames the political opposition, hinting at "clandestine and dangerous activities of certain individuals deliberately calculated to subvert and endanger the security of the State."

Nkrumah had some of the earlier standard-bearers of the national independence movement detained, including Dr. Danquah, the mentor of his formative years, the very person who had launched him on his political career. The opposition of the CPP was the United Party, members of which he had jailed on the charge that they were plotting to overthrow the government. He had some of his formerly closest associates, as for instance K. A. Gbedemah, minister of health, and Kojo Botsio, minister of agriculture, removed from their government posts.

When asked by a visiting American scholar, Gwendolen M. Carter, about the treatment meted out to the opposition, Nkrumah replied: "I feel the same way as you do about the opposition. If only they would act the way I did when I was in opposition. I always made it clear that I would not resort to violence. . . . But when I ask the opposition to sit around the table with me and give me their criticism, they will not do so. They organize in cells and they plan violence. What can I do if they threaten to assassinate me?"

Does this sound like mania of persecution? To some people it does, while to others it is a statement of incontrovertible facts.

And later, in the same conversation:

"I don't want to make much of myself but, in a way, this nation is my creation. If I should die, there would be chaos. This is a new country. It is not like Egypt which has centuries behind it and where it does not matter so much if a break occurs and a new regime is established. They can stand it but we could not."

On February 1, 1964, following a nationwide referendum, Ghana became an official one-party Socialist state. The government contended that in the week-long voting, 99.9 per cent of those who cast ballots voted "Yes" for proposals giving Kwame Nkrumah dictatorial powers. Actually, in most areas the voters found that the "No" boxes had been removed by government-appointed polling officials. In other areas the slits of "No" boxes were sealed. Ghanaians were warned by the government-controlled press and radio that anyone who failed to vote or who dared to vote "No" would be prosecuted as a "counter-revolutionary." The government proclaimed that it had the machinery to detect the "No" voters.

Under the referendum, the Convention People's Party of Nkrumah was established as the "leading core of all organizations and the vanguard of the people in their struggle to build a Socialist society."

This clause had been taken almost verbatim from Article 126 of the 1936 Soviet Constitution which made the Communist party the "leading core" of private as well as of government institutions. Another clause in the law approved by the referendum eliminated the last existing check against dictatorial rule—that of the free judiciary. The President dismissed Sir Arku Korsah as Chief Justice after the high court acquitted three high officials accused of treason.

The official party organ, *Evening News,* of Accra, commented that the referendum meant that the party had a "mandate to transform all expressions of the state—economic, social, and cultural—into organizations for the interest of the revolutionary classes." Then the paper added: "It follows automatically that it is illegal for non-party elements to conduct propaganda or any form of agitation against the People's Party."

"Ghana is turning into a major disappointment among the newly independent African states," commented the New York *Times.* The *Economist* of London reminded Nkrumah that it was he who had said, when the British were still in control, that the "courts of law should be absolutely independent of the executive."

President Nkrumah had moved from his official residence, Flagstaff House, into the seventeenth-century Christianborg Castle of Accra, an erstwhile slave fortress on the cliffs overlooking the harbor. There he was under the protective shield of his security forces. Was he a slave now of his own policies?

THE BALANCE OF POWER IN REVERSE

"When two elephants fight, it is the grass beneath, which is trampled," an African proverb says. Africa is the grass and the elephants are the superpowers. Foreign affairs are an important business of the state, even in Africa. Nkrumah's place in history will be determined partly by the way he conducts foreign affairs.

"A fellow traveler," his adversaries say, "who makes common cause with the Communists—look at his involvement with the Soviet Union, and China, and the European satellites." The Soviet Union was helping to build a 540-mile railway from Kumasi into the Republic of Upper Volta, on top of Ghana in the north. Also it helped to launch the Ghana State Farms Corporation. A *kolkhoz,* the adversaries lamented. A *sovkhoz,* Nkrumah may have corrected them, "an experimental farm to show our people new methods of cultivation."

Then there was China, too, assisting Ghana in trade and technical matters. "China is an underdeveloped country, like us," Ghanaian officials said, "and the exchange of information may be of aid." An economist from Communist Hungary, Jozsef Bognár, was asked by Nkrumah to participate in the preparation of Ghana's new State plan. The President of Ghana lashed out at the "Western imperialists and colonialists" when visiting the Eastern-bloc countries. In 1961 he was awarded the Lenin Peace Prize.

Yet, in economic matters Nkrumah remained in close contact with the United States and other members of the Western alliance. These countries were called upon to play leading roles in Ghana's Second Development Plan, ending in 1964, which allocated nearly a billion dollars to the development of agriculture and industry. Ghana's most ambitious development project, the Volta River Plan, was undertaken with the assistance of Valco— the Volta Aluminum Company—an American-sponsored concern headed by Edgar Kaiser. Several American loans were made to Ghana, including one for the Akosombo Dam and the adjoining power station and lines. Another American loan took the form of a $54 million investment guarantee to Kaiser and Reynolds which covered their Valco investment. A loan of $110 million was approved by the Washington government for the construction of an aluminum smelter. The World Bank, too, with its headquarters in Washington, announced a $47 million loan to the Volta project. "We are grateful to the United States government for its assistance," Nkrumah said at the opening of the National Assembly on October 2, 1962.

Great Britain signed an agreement with Ghana for a training mission which consisted primarily of naval and air elements to assist in the development of Ghanaian armed forces.

On the basis of his record, Nkrumah may be said to be a "fellow traveler" both of the East and the West. As to his links to the East, this is what Nkrumah had to say:

"The government of Ghana has genuinely followed a policy of independence and non-alignment. I have said again and again that this does not mean a neutral attitude in our relations with the rest of the world. What it means is that we shall maintain the courage of our convictions and shall judge every political problem on its merits and adopt whatever policy or measure we believe will do most to safeguard our own independence and further our national interest."

Then, harking back to his student days in Pennsylvania:

"Thomas Jefferson, a great American, stated what defines clearly my conception of non-alignment in his inaugural address some 170 years ago. He said in connection with American foreign policy: 'Peace, commerce, and honest friendship with all nations, entangling alliances with none'."

Nkrumah does no more than the leaders of many other countries of the "Little League." There is a struggle for positions between the two great world powers. Most countries in the Western hemisphere were counted among the "safe" members of the Western group. What was the result? The United States overlooked them. The Soviets, in turn, ignored the interests of the satellites. Then came Castro in the Americas and the Hungarian Revolution of 1956 in the satellite world. As a consequence, America and Russia no longer took their "safe" areas for granted.

Members of the Little League, of which Nkrumah's Ghana is one, are drawing benefits from the jealousies of the world powers. They know that the United States has sunk billions of dollars into foreign aid to keep ahead of the Ivan Ivanoviches. In turn, the Soviets were forced to expend money to keep up with America's Joneses. Nkrumah has learned to play on the fears and jealousies of the giants. If he were not known as a "fellow traveler" he would be no more than an also-run in the billion dollar sweepstakes. In turn, should he not receive large sums from Washington he would get no more than a sumptuous meal with vodka on his visits to Moscow. His policy of non-alignment has lined up Ghana for the largesse of both Washington and the Kremlin.

AN INTERESTING EXPERIMENT

Because Nkrumah was opposed to being in the tow of the major powers, he decided to take part in an interesting experiment about which more than a word must be said.

On Ghana's Independence Day in 1957, the Minister of

Commerce and Industry of Israel stayed on in Accra after the celebrations were over. He suggested close trade relations. The Ghanaian government was receptive, and a short time later the first shipload of assorted industrial goods was on its way from Haifa to Ghana.

This trade relationship developed into something far more ambitious. Soon thereafter, Israel was invited to play a role in the new country's economic development. Why Israel, of all places, a tiny country? Because she herself is a developing country, faced with problems similar to those of Ghana. The main problem was how to raise two blades of grass where only one grew before, how to create industries for an area's untapped resources, and how to introduce social reforms without recourse to strong-arm methods. Israel's own record in social development and in raising living standards fired Nkrumah's imagination. He knew that technical advisers from rich countries were adjusted to different standards, and their concepts of aid to backward nations tended to be grandiose. The contrast was well described by an African official: "I spent two months in the United States on a study tour. At the end they asked me what I thought of America and I said that it was wonderful. Fabulous! Fantastic! Then they asked me what I had learned and I said: Nothing! You see, America is too big for us. The smallest project I saw cost millions. Israel is closer to the problem we are up against."

That is how Israel's role in the development of Nkrumah's country came to be proclaimed through eye-catching posters, and was featured prominently in the capital, and elsewhere, too. At the intersection of two main streets in Accra, for instance, a new building for the Ghana Trades Union Congress was going up. It was being erected by the Ghana National Construction Company, jointly owned by the Ghana government, which held 60 per cent, and the Solel Boneh Company, a large construction firm belonging to Israel's nationwide labor union, the Histadrut, which held 40 per cent.

Israel's participation in the economic growth of Nkrumah's country included the building of highways, an airport, a fishing harbor, a cooperative bank, and even some assistance in the country's major development project, the Volta River Plan. The first steamship line of black Africa, the Black Star Line, was also jointly owned—the Ghana government holding 60 per cent of the stock, and the Zim Israel Navigation Company holding the rest.

Merchant marine officers were trained by Israeli experts

at the Accra Nautical Academy. Israeli instructors were training armed forces at the air-force base of Giffard Camp, near Accra.

From Ghana, Israel's ambitious technical assistance program spread first to other parts of West Africa and then to other regions of the continent. As a result, one of the world's newest and smallest countries acquired a prestige in many parts of Africa that can be compared only with that of the United States and other major powers that have undertaken aid programs in developing areas. The initiative on the side of Ghana had come from Nkrumah.

THE DISMAL SCIENCE

In the beginning there was economics, according to Karl Marx. Not a dismal science but one that interpreted history and was to serve as a guide to political leaders. Nkrumah studied Marx in America and in Britain. Is he adept in economics? We have the testimony of one of his advisers that he read a report of more than a hundred pages on the guiding principles of one of Ghana's Consolidation Development Plans in not more than forty-eight hours. We also have the testimony of other people that he is bored with economic details.

But Nkrumah knows the elementary rules of economic growth in developing countries. He knows that when the earth was created there was the land—and not industrial plants, as many people seem to believe. He also knows that the first attention of his government should be directed to the development of land; then to the industries that process the fruits of the earth; then to the ways of transporting them to the markets; then to the ways of distributing them; and then—and only then—to the creation of more sophisticated industries. Such industries are essential, too. Without them Ghana would produce raw materials in which there is world-wide competition and would be forced to import industrial products that are controlled by world-wide cartels. "Under conditions of monopoly capitalism," Nkrumah read in one of the reports of an economic adviser from the Communist bloc, "it was not worthwhile for capital to establish highly developed processing industries on a continent where manpower was still unskilled. Opportunities were therefore created only for the production of raw materials and of foodstuffs which were important to the developed countries, while the colony was regarded as a market for the colonizing country's own products."

Does Ghana's economic policy reflect Nkrumah's own convictions? Foreign credits will be employed mainly to establish government enterprises that pay for their costs within a short time. Private initiative on small-scale projects and private enterprise are not discouraged. Nkrumah knows that in primitive economies they are powerful incentives. But since there is not enough capital accumulation for large projects, the nation must come into the picture, not as the enemy of the individual, but as the collective will of millions of citizens. Foreign industries are not encouraged, because as long as a country is dependent on them there is no real free-*dom*. Nkrumah has learned this from that bewhiskered prophet of the doom of capitalism and the dawn of collectivism, Karl Marx. To him a large portion of socialism in a nation's economic diet is not merely a spice but also a life-sustaining vitamin. Nkrumah has his own interpretation of Marx, which he calls "Marxism-Nkrumahism," another sign that he does not think lightly of himself.

THE AFRICAN BOLIVAR

"Africa must unite!" Osagyefo Nkrumah said in the address he delivered at the conference of the African heads of state and governments in Addis Ababa, Ethiopia, on May 24, 1963.

He had become known as "Mr. Ghana." Why not "Mr. West Africa" or "Mr. Africa"—*tout court?* The historic accidents of the colonial period and the administrative conveniences of the *ci-devant* masters need not be perpetuated. Logic requires that the African nations should be integrated. That way they could more easily obtain risk capital for their urgently needed industrial developments. And industrial developments they need very urgently. Free-*dom* is a wonderful thing, but free-*dom* without bread is servitude. One cannot remain the Osagyefo in the midst of millions of disgruntled people. Even the affluent countries have to integrate. The United States did that long ago, and recently we have seen the creation of the European Economic Community, which should lead to the United States of Europe. In Latin America there have been many attempts to get together on economic matters. Within the Communist bloc there are the groping attempts of the Comecon.

It was western Africa that Nkrumah had aimed at in his organizing work as a student in Britain and America. He was the vice-president of the West African Student Union. He served subsequently as the secretary of the West African National Secretariat. He was one of the secretaries of the Fifth Pan-African Conference. His convictions were consistent on that score. As the President of Ghana he launched one movement after another, and supported many others, in the interest of African integration.

His capital, Accra, had served as host to the first All-African People's Conference in 1958. In the same year it became the site of a conference of Africa's independent states. There were eight at that time. It was Nkrumah who had rushed to the aid of Guinea's Secou Touré, also in 1958, after France had broken relations with that country, formerly part of her colonial empire. Following this up, Nkrumah sponsored a Ghana-Guinea union which was expected to be the nucleus of further integration. Two years later, with the failure of the Federation of Mali (the union of Senegal and Soudan, former parts of French West Africa) Nkrumah pursued his aim. After a hurried visit to Bamako and friendly discussions with Modibo Keita, the President, Nkrumah announced that political association would be established between Ghana and the Soudan—which now assumed the name of Mali. The union of Ghana, Guinea, and Mali was proclaimed on July 1, 1961. Enthusiastically, the three heads of states initiated quarterly meetings, but the union remained on paper. Cynics suggested that Ghana was too rich in natural resources, while Mali and Guinea were too poor.

Then came the crisis of the former Belgian Congo where all the furies of international hell broke loose, and the coreland of Africa was falling apart. Again Nkrumah took the initiative by approaching nine African states—Ethiopia, Guinea, Liberia, Mali, Morocco, the Republic of the Sudan (former Anglo-Egyptian Sudan), Tunisia, Libya, and the United Arab Republic—to form a consortium for the aid of African nations that might find themselves in a similar situation. He headed a drive to draw up an African Charter that would condemn neo-colonialism, establish economic, cultural, and political committees for cooperation, and eventually provide for an African Consultative Assembly and a joint African High Command. The charter was approved in January, 1961, by the heads of state of Guinea, Mali, Morocco, by the president of the Algerian Provisional Government, and by the foreign minister of Libya. This was at the Casablanca Conference.

The following year Nkrumah served as a host to several

international conferences, including an All-African Farmers' Conference, the African Freedom Fighters' Conference, and a World Without Bomb Conference.

At the Addis Ababa conference of 1963 Nkrumah addressed the representatives of thirty-two independent African states, instead of eight as he had done five years earlier. He spoke of the teachings of history, of inculcating integration, of the "sacred task" of the heads of government not to hesitate in the attempt to tackle the question of African unity, and of the "popular determination" to let that unity assume definite shape.

He presented his plan to the conference, and it was a bold one: a common market for Africa; and African currency with an "African monetary zone"; an African Central Bank; and a continental communications system. A commission was to draw up details for a common foreign policy, a common system of defense, and a common African citizenship.

How seriously should these recommendations of Nkrumah's be taken? "The mouse that roars," contemptuous Nigerians commented, and advised the Osagyefo to compare the size of his country with that of theirs. While there was integration to be made, would not Nigeria be the natural "integrator," the African country with the largest population?

And what did the observer's common sense tell him about Nkrumah's Great African plans—his attempt to become the Bolivar of the continent? First, history revealed that Bolivar—the Great Liberator—was not so successful in his attempts at integration either. Look at the cluster of countries in America which speak the Spanish tongue and have similar backgrounds. The observer noticed that once frontiers were drawn, no matter how unnatural, they exhibited a tendency to stay put. What would happen to Nkrumah's own job, should there be a United Africa? He would want to become its head. But so would others. And if he could not be in the saddle, would he still want to have a United Africa? Frontiers created a large number of vested interests not only in politics but also in economics.

Frontiers created divergent interests also in loyalties. Look at the case of the Republic of Gabon, which used to be a part of French Equatorial Africa. Before the French came, it had belonged for a time to the Portuguese, who had carved up Africa in any which way and then stood back to admire their handiwork. The shape of one of their territories resembled a chest of drawers, and so one of their high-spirited bureaucrats recommended that it be named "cabinet"—Gabon. And it was.

In due time the French acquired the region; then it became independent. The "chest of drawers" got all the appurtenances of national sovereignty: a government, a constitution, a national anthem, a flag, and a seat in the United Nations. Gabon's anthem is very moving, and brings tears to the eyes of emotional citizens who today are ready to die for their flag—the banner of the "chest of drawers." Gabonians are not likely to transfer their loyalty from their own flag to the banner of an inchoate Africa, filled with alien people with whom they have nothing in common. And that must also be true for the other nations, new or otherwise.

In addition, effective integration requires a cohesive force and a strong belief that unity will bring higher living standards. Western Europe is already almost integrated by its thick network of communication facilities and electric power lines. Because of the colonial rule, Africa's trade in the past was directed outward, not inward. She has no continental transport lines, except the air. The prerequisites for the realization of Nkrumah's grand design of integration are thus absent. A more modest project, such as the Colombo Plan of the Asian nations, may have a better chance of success. This is a mutual stimulation and assistance society, with rich uncles who stand in the background, ready to help out in case of need.

OPINIONS—FRIENDLY AND OTHERWISE

There has been much tongue wagging about Nkrumah in Western chancelleries. And there have been many typewriting exercises in editorial offices. At first he was the "Miracle of Africa," the pioneer who got things started, a man whose career was a landmark in world history. Then, precipitately, he became an "autocrat" and a "tyrant." That wise British daily, the *Guardian* commented: "Nkrumah's precepts in colonial days was 'Seek ye first the political Kingdom.' He has both sought and found it, and having found it has kept it to himself."

The *Economist* of London, probably the most quoted weekly in the English language, remarked on Nkrumah's charge of collusion between his political opposition and foreign powers: "This argument in casuistry is worthy of the most devious neo-colonialist."

There is the other side which presents Nkrumah's role in an entirely different light. According to that version, he cannot be compared with the leaders of well-established countries which have old traditions. He had to create a nation out of a conglomerate of tribal loyalties that had been born in the desert and the bush. Simple backwoodsmen are in no position to grasp the meaning of political opposition in Western terms. Such opposition appears to them as attempts to shatter the authority of the government. Nkrumah had to establish his place as superior to even the most important chieftain. "I believe that Nkrumah would like to rule in a settled society," wrote the astute political observer John Hatch in the August, 1962, cover story of *Africa Today,* "with an acceptance of constitutional methods and observances of the rule of law."

Then continuing: "Nkrumah believes that Ghana is still in peril of potential civil war. The opposition which arose in the traditionally restless Ashanti region in 1954 began in violence and has retained that character ever since. Inside the Convention People's Party discussion and argument abound."

Before charging that the Africans—and Nkrumah—are unable to operate a democracy, certain facts of the past should be noted. The heritage that the British bequeathed to the former Gold Coast was not an unblemished democracy. Part of that legacy left behind by the former rulers was the Preventive Detention Act.

With what twentieth-century historical figure can Nkrumah be compared? Speaking to me in Accra, Sir Robert Jackson, one of the President's advisers, compared him with Turkey's Mustapha Kemal Atatürk. Both men had to create new nations; one of them working with the elements of an Oriental dynastic structure, the other with the odds and ends of a tribal society. Their work had to be on a monumental scale, and the temptation was strong to employ the techniques of a Hitler or a Stalin. Nkrumah did nothing of the kind. There were not many political detainees in Ghana, Sir Robert said, and their treatment was not cruel. In most cases, they were released after short prison terms. Having been a political prisoner himself, Nkrumah knew how martyrs were created.

Impartial observers sought to follow the arguments of both sides. Ghana, of course, was not a country like Britain where civic liberties grew out of national traditions. As the "founding father" of his country, Nkrumah was entitled to recognition of his historic deeds. But he has all the media of persuasion at his disposal to present his views to his country and to the world, and perhaps he can afford to be less touchy about exercises of casuistry and criticism.

"THE LION AND THE FOX"

Kwame Nkrumah is an enigma—and so are all human creatures, particularly statesmen. Statesmen are faced with a conspiracy of unknown factors to which they cannot address themselves with unequivocal solutions. Part of their strength consists of their enigmatic nature. Inscrutability disarms opposition and surrounds a person with an aura of mystery. Statesmen have to be foxes and lions, or else they are doomed to fail. How much of Nkrumah is the lion, how much the fox?

He exhibited leonine strength when he converted a colony in the "white man's graveyard" into an independent nation. He was also a pathfinder and a pioneer. Out of his land and due largely to his efforts came the light that was to illuminate the Dark Continent. And so he told the rest of Africa: "This is what you can do!" And he told the colonial rulers: "And this is what you cannot do!" His work is not finished yet. The Portuguese are still in Africa with their colonial ways, and the Afrikanders have their system of *apartheid*. Nkrumah has proclaimed a crusade against them.

As for the fox—he feeds his people with the promise of national grandeur—the union of West Africa, of all Africa. He represents his attacks on neo-colonialism as the substance of his innovations, in fact, as the very essence of the African New Deal. He releases a torrent of slogans that impress the unsophisticated. Are we in the presence of a man drunk with power?

If consistency is a virtue, then it must be credited to Nkrumah. He became a Marxist Socialist during his time in the United States and in Britain partly because of the pressures of the economic conditions he experienced, but largely because of his personal inclinations. He had seen capitalism in the colonialism of the British: he had seen the polarization of wealth under the old order. To him, real democracy called for a large measure of economic equalization. He did not originate the balance-of-power politics practiced by the developing countries of the world. It resulted from a competition between world powers which all but forced bystanders to extract the benefits of the historic rivalry.

Nkrumah is one of the men in our gallery who was not kept in jail for years. However, even his months in prison did make an impression on him. He had learned to overcome hardships and to look for the rainbow at the end of the horizon. The challenge of the prison hardships had evoked a self-sustaining response in him and had strengthened his determination to combat those forces which had turned his humanitarian and constructive intentions into antisocial aberrations. In his "think tank" cell, he had been able to concentrate on the solutions to problems which he, as a free man, might have to face. Both strength and courage were necessary to surmount the hardships of the jail. He had stood the test and was now conscious of his strength. After such an experience the other trials of life seemed trifling.

Nkrumah's use of the power he has acquired—not the force but the restraint that he may be able to reveal should he feel more secure in his place before the international jury of nations—will be another test of his strength. Throughout history the words of Lord Acton echo: "Power corrupts; absolute power corrupts absolutely." Nkrumah's strength will be manifested by his ability to resist the temptations of absolute power. Does he have this kind of strength?

The story of Ghana's Kwame Nkrumah, like every story, ends with a question mark. Life itself is a question mark, especially in a developing civilization that has not yet found its meaning and is groping toward the shaft of light which pierces the depth of darkness that still envelops the heart of Africa.

2

The Man Who Was Not Late: Algeria's Ben Bella

The *panier à salade,* the "salad basket"—the "Black Maria" of the police—drew up in front of the Santé prison of Paris. The rue de la Santé is the longest in the capital, says a grim Parisian joke. People entering it one day may be seen leaving it only years later. In the precise language of bureaucracy, the Santé is the *maison d'arrêt pour hommes,* as well as the *maison de correction pour les condamnés politiques.* Glamorous Paris, *la ville lumière,* has few more lugubrious quarters than the Santé. Normal life is shut off from the jail by a seemingly endless wall which in popular parlance is called the "wailing wall."

On this particular November day in 1956 the massive gate of the wailing wall clicked open, and from the "salad basket" several young men descended. One was Ahmed Ben Bella, who was to make his name in history. He was with three companions, and all four had been kidnaped—not on the ground but in the air. They had been in an airplane traveling between Morocco and Tunisia, two countries friendly to the cause they represented. They had been forced to land in Algeria, into the arms of the French rulers whom they were fighting. That is how, after having been transported across the Mediterranean, they finally emerged in this Paris jail.

Although he was rumpled and bewhiskered at this moment, Ben Bella had a spring and a bounce to his gait. He was a broad-shouldered young man, with pleasant features. Had he smiled, his lively eyes and flashing teeth would have appealed to many young women. For, under more auspicious circumstances, he would have looked like a *jeune premier,* the Frenchwoman's "matinee idol."

These four young men were not only Algerian freedom fighters—*moudjahidine*—they were also the leaders of the movement of the Algerian Moslems against the French masters of their land. It was in the midst of the Algerian insurrection that the "salad basket" disgorged these young men into the Santé court-yard.

The prisoners were well known to millions. Besides Ben Bella, there were Mohammed Boudiaf, Mohammed Khider, and Hocine Aït-Ahmed. Another Algerian insurrectionary leader, Rabah Bitat, joined them later in jail, and they formed a closed circuit known as The Five—*Les Cinques.*

Once France had been the revolutionary land *par excellence,* the first nation to proclaim the humanistic creed of liberty, equality, and fraternity: mankind was not to consist of slaves and masters but of brothers. Forty years later, the French took Algeria by force of arms. Its soil was rich, the climate superb, and Frenchmen, as well as other Europeans from the Mediterranean regions, came to settle there. The immigrants came to be known as *les colons.* Algeria was treated by the French not as a colony, nor even as a protectorate as were Morocco and Tunisia, the two regions flanking Algeria, but as an integral part of France, even though nine-tenths of the Algerian people were not French. The Five had tried to apply the humanistic revolutionary creed of France to their native land; that was their crime.

The Santé was a wretched place even for a jail. A century old, it was a vestige of the preceding age when jails were more like torture chambers. Expanded in the course of time, "modernized," the Santé still remained grim, desolate and hopeless. However, the life of the Five was not too bad there. A little money and some "pull" from the outside could make even the Santé bearable.

The cells of the prisoners were turned into what might be called a combination of a clubhouse, a research center, and a work-shop. Newspapers they had aplenty; they could follow events in their Algerian homeland as well as abroad. The only newspaper not allowed to them was *L'Humanité,* the Communist daily, which was favorable to the Algerian cause.

They had a small library, too: classics, as well as the *vient de paraître* variety, the "new publications." The murder mysteries which modern statesmen boast of reading were not on the young men's reading list. But they did have volumes on politics, psychology, public opinion, advertising, popular economics, agrarian reform, economic development, socialism, and—strangely—also on communism. It may have been the view of the censors here that the

KWAME NKRUMAH

AHMED BEN BELLA

JOMO KENYATTA

HABIB BOURGUIBA

Indonesian Information Service, New York

SUKARNO

ARCHBISHOP MAKARIOS III

JÁNOS KÁDÁR

WLADYSLAW GOMULKA

heavy treatises on communism instead of being a stimulant would be a depressant. Ben Bella and his companion spent their five and a half years in prison making a "great books" study. "We filled notebooks and notebooks," Ben Bella said after he had reached power. "Prison is a good place in which to reflect. It was a permanent polishing of my ideas. Still, I'd rather not have been behind the bars."

Although the young people were Moslem Arabs, the books they read were in French. Since they were more fluent in it than in Arabic—as were many educated Algerians—French was the language they spoke among themselves; also, they were better acquainted with the political vocabulary of the French. At the same time, their bookshelves held an Arabic grammar and an Arabic dictionary. If their cause was to triumph, they should become equally fluent in Arabic, which was to be the language of their nation.

Ahmed Ben Bella was the No. 1 person among The Five. The prison guards themselves noticed this although their jobs called for no psychological insights into their prisoners' minds. Ben Bella, they observed, had that "something" which even more sophisticated people found hard to describe. How did one become a leader, when one was a prisoner, a slave? Certainly one must possess unusual qualities, even if the guards were not shrewd enough to perceive them. Nor did the guards observe that there had been a competition for the leadership in the prison cell, and that Ben Bella had won it. Three of his fellow prisoners submitted to his authority; the fourth, Mohammed Boudiaf, rebelled, and eventually secured his "liberation" to another house of detention.

THE BOY FROM MARNIA

What was the background of this Ben Bella and the root causes that had landed him in jail?

There was no star over the *medina*, the Algerian "town," in which Ben Bella was born on Christmas Day, 1916. His name, Ahmed, is that of Mohammed the Prophet, and also of Al-Mansur, the Victorious, erstwhile Sultan of Morocco.

The *casbah* of the town of Marnia, close to the Moroccan border, was the place of Ahmed's nativity. The town crouches on a ledge of flinty rocks, as if not to trespass on the fertile land of the Algerian coastal plain, that fabled "tell," every square inch of which is worth gold. The *casbah* of Marnia was little different from similar "native quarters" in the rest of Algeria, or anywhere in the Maghreb (Northwest Moslem Africa, with its mixed Arab-Berber population), or, for that matter, from anywhere in the Middle East. It consisted of a maze of warrens, pierced by dark and dank apertures which led into dwellings that swarmed with people living only Allah knew how. Yet, for Ahmed, as for others, the warrens were thrilling places as they resounded with the noise of arguments and quarrels, with the tinkling of the hammers of the silver-, copper-, iron-, and bronzesmiths of the bazaar.

Ahmed was the youngest of six children. His father was a fairly well-to-do *fellah*, "peasant," who operated a seventy-five-acre wheat farm. The father, who had a good Koranic education, made sure that his sons got the same.

Life in such families followed a settled routine, closely regulated by the march of the sun across the sky. Daily, the peasants of the town and of the nearby villages sallied forth from the ledges of their hills, walking long distances in the searing heat. Some owned a piece of land, many did not. Nearly all the good land belonged to the *colons*. Those peasants who could find no work on European land were thrown upon the charity of their kin and fellow Moslems, for the latter were under obligation to provide alms, *zakat*, for the poor. For these people it was mainly a problem of food and sanitation. The few lived twice as long as the many; wealth belonged to the few, poverty to the many. Most of Ahmed's kinsmen were part of the grey mass of the faceless whom the West came to know as the host of common folk afflicted with disease, ignorance, and poverty—D.I.P.

THE EDUCATION OF A BOY

Schools were not for the "native" children, the Moslem boys. In school they would have learned the history of the Great French Revolution and—remember?—Algeria was France—France in Africa, and not a colony or a protectorate. In this part of France the ideas of the French Revolution were subversive.

Perhaps it was better for people to spend their lives in the numbing bliss of ignorance, letting the radiance of that wonderful Mediterranean sun anesthetize their senses. Those who worked little, needed little to keep them alive. And, Allah the Compassionate saw to it that His children somehow lived out their short spans of life.

A few boys, sons of ambitious parents, did attend a school, but of the sort where they learned that their future was in the hands of Allah, although they might have learned just as easily about liberty and equality. Some of these ambitious parents considered letting their sons become leaders in their communities—leaders, that is, at the prayers in the mosques. The town of Marnia had such a school, a dark hole scooped out of the ledge of the hill and separated from a bazaar alley by a creaking door. The school had no window; its light came through an aperture from the alley, which, however, was covered by a tarpaulin against the inclemencies of weather. In various postures the children sprawled on the dirt floor, which was covered with frayed straw mats. At the end of the hole, nearest to the light, an emaciated looking teacher sat on a rickety wicker chair. In one hand he held a grimy copy of the Glorious Koran, in the other a cane. Allah, who had given the Koran to Mohammed the Prophet, was compassionate, but not so the teacher whose duty it was to impart knowledge of the Word to the young disciples. The method of teaching was simple: the teacher croaked a sentence of the Holy Book, the pupils bellowed it back at him. When any of the half-famished children dozed off or failed to reply with enough lung-power the pedagogue's cane flicked at them.

THE "BLACK FEET" AND THE "FIGS"

The "Europeans" of the childhood days of Ahmed Ben Bella formed only 10 per cent of the total population. Who were they? The aristocrats among them were Frenchmen whose ancestors had settled in Algeria during the last century. They had to work their way out of the primitive milieu of this backward Moslem world into the modern age. It was their pride that their unshod feet got dirty in their labors, and so they called themselves *les pieds-noirs,* "the black feet." Other Frenchmen came from the mainland later and also people from Spain, Corsica, Malta, Sicily, and from as far away as Rhodes. The earlier arrivals had got the best land and had prospered. The later arrivals could also prosper, but more work and stronger will power were required. The earliest arrivals, of course, were the "natives," the Moslems. But they had been forced on to the poorest land, and their fate was a sad one except in the case of a small group who made common cause with the master race. These few Moslems served as the "front people" who could be counted on to approve the policies of the Europeans.

"Very well," they would say of everything the French administrators did. The French worked with them, but without respecting them. *Beni, beni, oui, oui,* was the contemptuous description of these yes-men.

Les pieds-noirs, the *colons,* owned most of the land along the Mediterranean, the radiant coastal plain with its rich alluvial soil. To dominate old Algeria, they built a "little France," with attractive modern towns that reminded them of the ancestral homes overseas, to which they were tied by ideology as well as by nostalgia. They were members of the master race, these *colons;* mired in extreme conservatism, they wanted to have the sun halt on its march across the sky.

Contemptuous they were of the native people whom they despoiled. "Little rats" they called them, *ratons.* Also they called them *figuiers,* because, they alleged, the Moslems loitered in the shade of the fig trees.

The government these European settlers established took no notice of the majority. The street signs were in French, perpetuating the memory of army leaders who had defeated the ancestors of the natives. In the public offices there were no inscriptions in the language of the majority of the people. "They cannot read anyway," the European shrugged. Why could they not read? Had the French not been in Algeria for more than a century?

Most of the native boys of Algeria remained *figuiers,* but there were exceptions, and young Ahmed Ben Bella was one of these. A keen-eyed lad, he was not content to let the radiance of the sun benumb his senses. He observed the differences between the lives which his own people led and those which the Europeans enjoyed. The latter owned the beautiful houses, the radios, and the cars, and it was they who in their colorful uniforms, impressed the pretty girls. They were the ones who held the important posts in government and in business. The boy saw all of this but he had not yet reached the stage where it might occur to him to ask the all-important question: Why? He was too young as yet to compare closely the values in his universe—a poor life for the common people—with the values of the *colons'* universe—a good life for the French. The French considered themselves the rulers, and the "little rats" an inferior breed. For the time being, Ahmed wanted only to be of the retinue of the rulers. The road to higher status would come by way of the European school. There people learned how to swagger and also how to work in an organized way. There was a small government school in Marnia, the language of instruction of which was French. From there Ahmed went to the higher grades in Tlemcen, a large town nearby.

Tlemcen boasted not only a European school but also vestiges of his people's history. Those evidences showed that they were not truly inferior people. Far from that, they had a superior culture. Tlemcen contained some sixty Moslem places of worship—mosques—many of them remarkable edifices. The city expressed eloquently the greatness of his own people, the glory that had burst upon the world (in the seventh century of the Christian Era) when the Arabs broke out of their deep desert confinement and, with an irresistible force that dumbfounded Christendom, began their global march both east and west. It had not been long before their desert legions overwhelmed Tlemcen and swept on across the Maghreb, eventually reaching the end of the world, beyond which there was nothing but water, the Atlantic. But the conquerors did not consider even this the end of their mission. They continued their march, wheeling northward, and under their mighty commander, Tarik, they vaulted across the narrows between the Continents. On the European side of the narrows stood a huge rock, and the conquerors named it Jebal Tarik, after their great leader. The European infidels—who could not be expected to speak pure Arabic—mispronounced this name, and the rock came to be called Gibraltar.

Young Ahmed Ben Bella thus found himself in the midst of two cultures of vast contrasts. On the one hand was the glory of the Moslems, reaching back into a brilliant past. On the other was the amazing advance of the modern West toward insights, innovations, and improvements that created conditions for the development of what seemed to be a superior breed of man. Even though he became proudly familiar with the astonishing history of his own spiritual forebears, he was still activated by the West, the winning side today.

He was totally the opposite of the "fig tree" type of native, because competition seemed to be in his blood. He and an acquaintance were walking one day at the foot of the *meshuar*, the citadel, of the city of Tlemcen. Absently, the other youngster picked up a pebble and threw it into the distance. Ahmed stopped in his tracks, picked up another pebble and, rotating his arm strenuously, flung it far, far ahead of the other's stone. Then triumphantly he gazed at his companion. He had turned a careless bit of play into a competitive enterprise.

Having mentally chosen the West, young Ahmed determined to go the whole way. Athletics of every kind appealed to him because they represented the excess energy of the West. Football was the French national sport—the American soccer. So he started "socking" the ball with all his might, and he was skillful at it. He demonstrated that he, too, was a European in his aspirations, in his studies, even in his prowess in sport.

THE SOUND OF DISTANT THUNDER

Drôle de guerre it was at first—the funny war—with a wraithlike front in the west where all was quiet except the conviction that this non-shooting war could not last. The main front coiled around the heartland of France. But the heart of France was not in the fight. The nation was tired—of wars, of excitement, and above all, of its own governments, especially if the Socialists played any part in them. The Industrial Establishment of France had no use for politicians who thought in terms of social values. The motto of the Establishment was "Better Hitler than Blum"—referring to Léon Blum, the Socialist leader who had recently served as Premier. " 'Itler" was different. He was the voice of the future, the man who called himself a National Socialist and came to drive the Socialists out of the Temples of Industry.

Then one day the *drôle de guerre* was over; the war, that is, was no longer droll. It became a shooting war. The German Nazis stepped across the presumably impregnable protective shield of France: the Maginot Line. In a matter of days *la grande nation* was overrun. The best part of the country became the Germans' armed camp, and a titular French state was allowed to vegetate as a Nazi satrapy under the senile ex-national hero, Marshal Henri Philippe Pétain. Corresponding to the importance of the satrapy, the capital was set up in the small resort of Vichy.

Across the Mediterranean, in Algeria, and in the adjacent protectorates of Tunisia and Morocco, the French government could have offered resistance to the Nazis. It did not do so for compelling reasons. One was the fact that the majority of the European settlers in North Africa, especially in Algeria, were convinced that Hitler was the best thing that could happen to them.

He knew how to handle an "inferior breed," such as the Moslems. Resistance to the Nazis under such circumstances, would have run into sullen opposition from the most influential portion of the population—the Algerian Establishment.

One Frenchman did not resign himself to the "inevitable." His name was Charles de Gaulle, a general by profession. Around him formed a nucleus of like-minded Frenchmen. Within France herself, a resistance developed. It assumed the name of the southern French hilly bush country, *maquis,* because it protected these freedom fighters.

A few Frenchmen in Algeria, too, joined the *maquis,* but most of the *colons* followed Pétain. What was the stand of the articulate Moslems in Algeria? The *beni-beni-oui-oui* sort rallied to the cause of Pétain and Hitler. Any cause was good as long as selfish interests could be safeguarded. A few of them rallied to the cause of General de Gaulle, who represented the "new wave"—a more enlightened colonial policy, a more human approach to the development of the French colonial empire.

Ahmed Ben Bella joined the 141st Algerian Rifles. Subsequently, he served as a sergeant major of the 6th Algerian *Tirailleurs* of the French army. At the time he joined, the horizon seemed to be dark for the Allies. The enemy powers—the Axis of Germany, Italy, and Japan—appeared to have scored in an unequal battle. The Axis formed an armed camp that contained a firepower which threatened to blow its adversaries on the scrap heap of history.

By the time Ben Bella reached the fighting front the situation had changed. The Axis had overextended itself. Its arrogance aroused the resentment of decent people throughout the world. The Allies—and especially the United States—made swift progress in retrieving the original losses. Ben Bella's unit was assigned to the Italian front. There the Allies began their arduous march northward in an attempt to come to grips with the heartland of their foes.

On the Rapido River in the Appenines of Central Italy one of the bloody battles of the war was fought. It was near the small town of Cassino, in the very shadow of the famed Abbey of Monte Cassino on a nearby hill. There, in early 1944, Ben Bella received his baptism of fire. His company commander was wounded, and young Ben Bella dragged him to safety over an endless route of a mile, exposed to enemy fire. Four times the young Algerian was cited for bravery. At the victory celebration in Rome it was General de Gaulle himself who pinned the Médaille Militaire on his tunic.

With such an auspicious beginning, it was Ahmed's fondest dream to become an officer in the French army. He applied for admission in the regular military service. He received no word for a long time, and he considered this wait a good omen. Then the answer came. His application was rejected. He learned later the reason: "Intelligent and dangerous." Dangerous because intelligent, perhaps. Intelligent young Algerians were not welcome in the Military Establishment. Their intelligence would have demonstrated the falsehood of the view that *ratons* were inferior. Now that Ahmed Ben Bella was rejected as a prospective loyal Frenchman what road would he take?

A SPLIT PERSONALITY

Frustrated? That he was. Resentful? That he was, too. And so he would start an Algerian nationalist movement? That he did not do. It had been started a score of years before. Half the movement was serious, the other half was Bohemian. Hadj Ben Ahmed Messali (Messali Hadj, for short), its founder, had been either an eccentric or a man of deep political insights—it was difficult to determine which. His idea of Algerian independence was concocted of a desire to find a basic solution to the *malaise* of Algeria and of a dash of Marxism and Leninism, the mixture being saturated with Montparnasse apéritifs and wrapped into an anticipation of a future Zeitgeist—the coming call of nationalism.

Le colonialisme, c'est le vol, said young people intoxicated with Marxism, their *mot* patterned on Pierre Proudhon's dictum, *la propriété c'est le vol.* It was the colonial infamy which the aroused conscience of man was to crush: *écrasez l' infâme.* Messali Hadj's concept of filling the world with an appreciation of human dignity was romantic and so was the organization he launched, *L'Etoile Nord-Africaine.* Its poetic name gave an inkling of the scope of its program. All of French North Africa was to be included in the program—not only Algeria, the extension of *la mère patrie* into the desert and continent, but also Morocco and Tunisia. The purpose of the program was just as vague and grandiloquent: the protection of the social, material, and moral interests of North African Moslems. As the founder of the movement himself came to see later, this was too unwieldy and extravagant; he therefore transformed the Star into the more practical *Parti du Peuple Algérien*. Tunisia and Morocco should fight for their own stars since they had an easier job before them than Algeria had; for not only did the French consider Algeria to be a part of France and in Algeria, but the Algerian *colons* were devoted to more radical forms of frontier nationalism than in the two adjacent protectorates.

To many cautious Algerians, Messali Hadj's program appeared too unrealistic, even in the form of the PPA. They wanted their fellow Moslems to have more freedom, to be sure. But they belonged to the French cosmos, and no other cosmos existed for them. Full independence for Algeria would mean a nation devoid of resources to keep its people going. Where would Algeria get the investment capital, the technical knowledge, and the worldwide connections that France had. Ferhat Abbas, one of the most respected nationalists, commented: "I will not die for an Algerian homeland because such a homeland does not exist." It was not long before he changed his mind.

World War II created a new set of political relationships. *La grande nation* had been defeated in a shorter time than little Greece had been. The Algerians saw this, and they also realized that the uneasy conscience of the powerful nations was expressed in the Atlantic Charter, which foresaw a free world inhabited by free people. The charter may have been prompted by the cold war fear that the most fertile ground for communism might be colonialism, but no matter—the document seemed to promise freedom to suppressed peoples. Then, too, the Algerians and their neighbors were Arabs, with an educated leadership. Less progressive Arab countries in the Middle East had won their independence—Iraq, Jordan, and others. Why not Algeria?

The war finally entered its last stage. From Africa the Allies applied the lever that unhinged the Axis. The Allies were fighting for freedom—at least, so the world was told—and the Algerian people were not free. Let freedom then penetrate into this land, too. A "Manifesto of the Algerian People" was drawn up calling for "veritable democracy and authentic national life." This was no more than the substance of the Atlantic Charter—

the Allies' blueprint for the future. The drafters of the Manifesto did not say that France would be excluded from Algeria's authentic national life. That did not seem to be conceivable at the time.

THEN CAME SÉTIF

The Nazis' mad dictator was dead; the war was over. May Day of 1945 was a wildly exuberant day for many in northern Algeria. The town's happiness was reflected in the vault of the unflecked azure of the sky. There was a victory parade, and a new flag waved, but it was not the tricolor of France. It was the projected banner of Algeria—red, white, and green. Red represented the blood people had shed for their freedom, white the purity of their purpose, and green was the color of Mohammed the Prophet. The French *colons* of Sétif were enraged and considered this parade a provocation. Did it celebrate their defeat since most of them had supported the Vichy regime? And now the *sales métèques,* the "dirty bastards," dared to flaunt their filthy rag. The gendarmes and the police were called out. At that point the facts of history become distorted and mixed with fabrication. Shots were fired; the crowd went wild and started cutting down the *colons* who happened to be around. Then began a long reign of terror. The Algerian Moslems claimed that as a result of the Sétif "incident" some 40,000 of their people were slaughtered. The spokesmen for the French replied "Preposterous!" France was on the side of the victors, the Allies' honymoon still continued, and it was not expedient to look further into the incident. The world may never know what exactly took place there.

But the chaos of that May Day in Sétif was a traumatic experience for many Algerian Moslems even though they had neither read about it in their newspapers nor heard about it on the radio. News spread by the grapevine, and with it, distortions and exaggerations. The basic fact remained. The *colons* had shown their real faces. They had exhibited their deep contempt for the common people, whose lives were of no importance in their eyes.

Now even Ferhat Abbas, the supercautious Algerian, found that the cause of his native land was worth fighting for. There was indeed an Algeria! Messali Hadj once again changed the name of his organization, this time to *Mouvement pour le Triomph des Libertés Démocratiques.* That name indicated a program and also suggested an open door for an understanding with France. Democratic liberties could be achieved within the political framework of the country which had first proclaimed the right of all men to freedom. But there were also *les durs,* "the hard ones," among the Moslems, who maintained that force was the only language understood in international relations.

Ahmed Ben Bella, the disappointed aspirant for a French officer's commission, was one of *les durs.* He had himself elected a member of the municipal council of his native Marnia. Later he became the deputy mayor. When he learned that he could advance on the political ladder only as the "yes-man" of the French, he rebelled with all his heart. He knew that Algerian liberties could not be obtained without funds, and money could not be had from the moneyless people who were in favor of liberty. The rich Moslems among them dreaded the triumph of democratic principles; that would strip them of their unearned privileges. How was money to be had?

Organisation Spéciale was the name of the fighting body which Ben Bella set up—OS—and thus he became the pioneer of a militant organization. The OS proceeded to declare war upon the French administration. In war, the moral principles of peace do not prevail. What is murder in peace, becomes heroism in war. The peacetime crime of robbing a bank becomes an act of valor during war, if the bank belongs to the foe. The French banks in Algeria had the money the OS needed, therefore the OS resolved to hold up a bank. But—the protective measures of banks against such eventualities were stringent. Also, to rob a privately owned bank would have seemed a common crime. Another move was decided upon.

A ROBBERY AND A TRIAL

The organization was secret and so the number of its membership was not known. But it did become known eventually that, beside Ben Bella, Mohammed Khider and Mohammed Boudiaf played leading roles.

On the morning of April 5, 1949, in Oran, the most important city in northwestern Algeria, the Central Post Office was robbed. The robbers got away with the equivalent of six thousand dollars. They must have been in a great hurry because they left ten times that much money on the floor of the post office.

The robbery seemed to have been the work of three men, but even the most painstaking police investigation could not identify them. Was this really the work of common criminals? The police of Oran had their doubts.

A year passed before the headline news flashed upon the Algerian world. The police had found part of the loot; also the German revolver which had been identified by an eyewitness. Both the loot and the pistol were found on the person of Ahmed Ben Bella. A thorough investigation revealed that he was the national leader of the secret OS. The robbery had not been the deed of common criminals but an "act of war" to secure much-needed funds for the purchase of weapons. Weapons for what? *Les durs* believed that only by force could the great powers be persuaded of the just cause of their victims. Look how the Irish had won their freedom from the British! Observe how the Israelis had forced the world to recognize their independence!

Ben Bella was delivered into the jail of the city of Blida. It is beautiful country, Blida, orange-growing land—and the French called it *souriant*, "smiling." But the Blida prison did not smile at Ahmed Ben Bella. It was just as bleak as if it had been situated in the Siberian tundra.

For two full years Ben Bella languished there while the prosecution prepared its case against him. His was to be a gala trial, aimed not only at one perpetrator of a crime but also at a movement that advocated the freedom of the Algerian people.

In Blida, Ben Bella was not cut off from the world; he was in touch with the portion of the OS that was still at large. How was this possible? He may have had sympathizers in the prison shops through which many of the communications were directed. Also, the jail guards were poorly paid; a little side-money went a long way. When communications passed between the jail and the outside world, many eyes were closed.

Finally, the prosecution was ready for the trial. By that time the authorities had rounded up fifty-six defendants. For some technical reason Ben Bella was tried for plotting against the State and for the illegal possession of weapons—not for the actual act of robbery.

Sympathizers surrounded the courtroom, a defiant and sullen crowd. Into the courtroom marched the accused—the leading actors in the drama. Public approval boosted their spirits; it was public opinion at home and abroad they were after, and not the approval of the solemn-faced judges. Far from being the cowed defendants, they appeared to be the accusers. They entered the court with a chorus of defiance: "To the cause of glory and the *jihad* ["holy war"] we consecrate our efforts in the interest of salvation." The audience chimed in and their Honors, the judges, were incensed.

Ben Bella acted like a *jeune premier,* "matinee idol." The presiding judge had to admonish him that it was he and his companions who were on trial in the Blida courtroom—not the government of France.

The witnesses for the prosecution made their statements, and the court accepted their version of the case. The hour of judgment finally arrived. Within half an hour sentences for hundreds of years in jail were handed out to the accused. Ben Bella himself received a seven-year sentence. He stood before his judges every inch of him still *le jeune premier,* and with a radiant smile, he looked around as if to acknowledge the plaudits of a rapturous audience. With injustice rampant in Algeria, it was an honor to be found guilty.

The convicted men lined up; outside, the people waited to learn the verdict. The leader and his comrades intoned the revolutionary song as they marched out of the courtroom, and they were still singing as they were herded into their cells. The time was March, 1952.

Seven years in jail might have removed the smile from even the most radiant matinee idol. Ben Bella did not stay in prison seven years, nor seven months, nor even seven weeks. A few days after his conviction, visitors entered the Blida jail bearing gifts for Ben Bella. One brought a large dish of steamed groats with meat, *couscous.* In the best tradition of romantic jail deliveries, the dish contained a file. Ben Bella used the tool to good advantage; he filed his way to freedom and vanished into thin air five days after his conviction. Many people must have aided him. Eventually, he turned up in Egypt and then in Algeria's own Kabylia Mountains where the French gendarmes were neither welcome nor safe.

The mills of justice continued to grind—in their slow, detached ways. Retribution had still to be made for the Oran post office robbery. Another trial was held at which Ben Bella was again accused. The witnesses made depositions, and the prosecution triumphed. Ben Bella was found even more guilty than on the previous occasion. All his life he was to serve at hard labor as a penalty for his attempt to fill the treasury of the special organization he headed. Of course, working for his cause in Egypt and the Kabylia Mountains, he was not only out of the jurisdiction of the court but also out of the jurisdiction of Algeria and of the French. The sentence for life at hard labor was handed not to him but to his shadow. It was a sentence *in absentia.*

He rebutted his sentence across the airways, and his *plaidoyer,* "defense," sounded more than self-confident. Triumphantly it resounded over the Voice of the Arabs in Cairo, the strongest and most influential radio station transmitting in the entire Arab Middle East.

ARMS AND THE MEN

"Nationality explosions" were setting the colonial world on fire. The best parts of Asia had belonged to European powers, as did nearly all of Africa. But there was now a new consciousness abroad. Colonialism belonged to the past. It had been challenged by the spirit which had emerged after World War II and by the aggressive voice of the Soviets. Clinging to her colonies, Britain feared that their substance would dissolve in her aggressive hands. It seemed more sensible to establish new relations with members of the Empire. To Britain, India had seemed the pivot of her world position, the hinge of her status. But now, the British felt, an unfree India would be a liability to their prestige in international relations and in trade, and that a free India would be an asset. England decided that the way to keep India was to free India. The signal had been given for the global freedom movements.

France was the second largest colonial power. Would she follow the example of Britain by granting freedom to Algeria? Defiantly, the French government asked: "Would America give up California?" Algeria was as much a part of France as California was of the United States. And that was that.

France, wrapped in the radiant garment of *la gloire*—reflected by her overseas territories—failed to follow the precedent set by the British. Britain could free the colonies because she had been a victor of the war. France had yielded to the enemy without resistance; even General de Gaulle had been little more than the second thought of a small minority. France had been invited to join the victors because she was *La France* and because the other Western powers needed her in their company, not so much for her armed strength as for her strategic geographical span. Victor by invitation but vanquished by actual demeanor, France lacked Britain's self-assurance. However, she had to present at least the semblance of magnanimity toward her dependencies—to satisfy the other members of the Western alliance and to trump the Soviets.

The *Communauté* was thus created, patterned on the British Commonwealth of Nations. It had its own logical structure, a legislature, an executive department, and interweaving strands with the government of France. But it was only a paper logic, intended to impress the people in the French dependencies. While the British Commonwealth was a reality, the French *Communauté* was bogus.

The Algerian Moslems would have been content at first with a role within a French Commonwealth. Nearly all the Moslem leaders were French educated. They felt that they needed the guidance and capital of France, for they were not really convinced of their own ability to assume the burdens of full independence. But *les militants* among the Algerian Moslems were not deceived by the infantile blandishments of the *Communauté*. It was an insult to assume that they would fall for such a bait.

The Algerian Moslems had to face their foes on two fronts. One of these was the awesome power of the State—the French Republic—mortally weak on the mainland, but very strong in Algeria, where its heads were proconsuls who need have no concern about the opinion of the majority of the people. In France herself, the policy of the government, was "Listen," while in Algeria it was: "Command!" and command the French government of the Algerians did.

The other front—that of the European settlers—comprised one-tenth of the population and controlled nine-tenths of the country's exploited resources. It was backed by a Moslem retinue, the privileged *effendi* class, the masters serving the European supermasters. The European settlers, too, were different from the homebody French across the sea. Many of them were descendants of pioneers. They were so assured of their future that they dictated to the government in Paris rather than being dictated to. Many of them were as brutal as the master-race people of Mississippi, or as the South African practitioners of *apartheid,* who considered the complete separation of people and the subjection of the majority to the will of the minority almost as the sacred obligations of a perverse form of religion.

To face these forces, the Algerian Moslems had to develop not only an organization but also a *mystique,* a quasi-religious fervor, a belief that white was not black, as they had been taught. They were to wash their own brains, which had been brainwashed by their masters.

The time had come for the Algerians to abandon their romantic ideas, their Stars of the North and their Manifestoes, their puny parties and atomized movements. A great integration was needed by a bold movement, the very name of which would tell the people what they were supposed to do. There had to be cooperation between the *militants* who worked at home and those who aided them from abroad, especially from the other Arab countries—for in the Land of the Nile the idea of a greater Arab unity was incubating.

Thus was formed the *Comité Révolutionaire d'Unité et d'Action,* CRUA, which spelled out its program in its very title. Ben Bella, the "fugitive" from Algerian injustice, as he liked to call himself, was the head of the External Delegation. There was a delegation within Algeria, too. The majority of the members, both inside and outside, were *les jeunes.* The revolutionary steering committee contained nine members: Ben Bella, Mohammed Khider, Mohammed Boudiaf, Belkacem Krim, Hocine Aït-Ahmed, Rabah Bitat, Murad Didouche, Mustafa Ben Boulaid, and Mohammed Larbi Ben M'Hidi. A few months later the *Front de Libération Nationale,* FLN, was set up by the CRUA. It was to operate through the *Armée de Libération Nationale,* which was formed at the same time. Here at last, was a united front. *Les jeunes* were old enough to know that revolutionary ardor was not enough to win revolutions. *Une tête bien organisée* was the objective—a level-headed organization. Military districts had to be organized, with cadres and supplies of arms. Operational strategy and tactics had to be determined. Lines of communications had to be correlated, and supply lines had to be established with foreign countries. The people's minds had to be organized, too, their ardor sustained and their personal involvement in the national cause assured. At home, France was involved in a chaotic political situation. In Algeria the *colons* continued to assume that there could be no negotiations about the status of Algeria. They were convinced that the *Communauté* met all needs and would solve all problems.

ORGANIZING ARMS AND BRAINS

Algeria was divided into six *villayas,* military districts. No. 1 was the Aurès mountain range, ragged, jagged, impenetrable, ready-made for guerrillas. No. 2, straight to the North of the Aurès, was part of the district (*département*) of Constantine. No. 3 was another difficult mountain terrain, the Kabylia region. Most inhabitants in that area were Berbers: Moslems like the Arabs of Algeria, but not of Arab speech, for they predated the Arabs. However, in the revolutionary struggle against the French, the Berbers forgot their usual disdain of the Arabic Algerians, and the two worked together to overthrow the common enemy. The most heavily populated zone was No. 4, which included portions of the District of Algiers. Ben Bella's own home territory was Villaya 5, which covered Oran and its environs. The huge Algerian Sahara was No. 6.

"Operation Brainwash" was a major part of the master plan of the revolutionaries. "Islam" means submission, and submissiveness was the way of the masses. Their mission in life was to obey; the mission of the French was to command. The prevailing power relationship between the European landowners and their indigenous workers prevented any voicing of the people's opinions. In a society the very nature of which was submission it was considered not only treasonable but also blasphemous to entertain ideas contrary to those of the leaders at the helm. That is why Operation Brainwash was a major undertaking.

Everybody was to play a role; everybody had to be involved. No one was unimportant. The male population was divided into precisely structured units which were to be trained not only in the use of arms but also in ideology. Eleven men formed the smallest group, named *fauj,* brothers in the service of a common ideal. The *ferka,* "section," was comprised of thirty-five men, and the *katiba,* "company," contained 110 fighters for the common cause. Three of the latter groups formed a *failek,* "battalion."

All the people became indispensable and therefore of the greatest importance. Each had to be ready to offer himself to the cause that consecrated their fraternal unity. Nobody was allowed to drift into the nirvana of fatalism. Even the village idiots became somebodies, freedom fighters. Not only did their lives acquire a deeper meaning but the former human ciphers became human values. Millions of people were thus invested with status. The advantage of large numbers was turned to good account while the economic weight of the less numerous Europeans was minimized.

The Algerian War of Independence began on November 1, 1954, and this time its objective was really nationhood. The French called it rebellion, fought by *fellagha,* guerrillas. Besides the rebels' advantage of the *levée en masse,* they also had in their favor their knowledge of the terrain, their own land, which aided them in their plot to baffle the foe.

This War of Independence began with an Egyptian subsidy of $40,000, or so the lore of the revolution has it. But in the years to come the French were to spend about a billion dollars every year on the operations. They weakened their forces within the North Atlantic Treaty Organization, of which they had become one of the most important members. More important than the material items, they represented law, legitimacy, respectability, the continuance of the established order—in other words, they were one of the most highly esteemed established institutions, *la grande nation,* the Republic of France.

For the French it was *la sale guerre,* "the dirty war." If the ragged rebels had shown themselves in military formations by broad daylight, then it would have been a clean battle. Then they could have been mowed down and soon the war would have been over. But that was not the way of the *fellagha,* and for good reason: that would not have been a war for them but an organized mass suicide. The Algerians' strategy had to employ the advantages of known terrain and popular support to outweigh the disadvantages of inadequate arms, amateur leadership, and improvised organization. In other parts of the world the Algerian rebels' strategy had been tested and found effective—in China and in Indochina's torrid jungles. It had worked even under the handicaps of severe cold and extreme heat. Guerrilla warfare suited Ben Bella's plans. He and his fellow *dirigeants* were familiar with the classical conception of that type of warfare, described by China's Mao Tsetung: "When the enemy advances, we retreat. When he escapes, we harass. When he retreats, we pursue. When he is tired, we attack. When he burns, we put out the fire. When he loots, again we attack. When he pursues, we hide. When he retreats, we return. Our strategy is one against ten, while our tactics is ten against one."

The Algerian units hardly ever showed their faces to the French during the day. It was only in the hours of darkness that their embattled countryside stirred with life. Then the Moslems thrust swiftly, so swiftly that the attack was over almost as soon as it had begun. When the cocks crowed their triumphant greetings to the rising sun, the *danse macabre* of the hills and plains had ended. Again placid peasants cultivated their masters' gardens. Were they the guerrilla fighters? Who could prove that? Perhaps some of their hostile neighbors might. Within the next nightfall those neighbors, native Algerians in most cases, were no longer among the living.

The guerrillas could operate only if they had the support of the nearest *mechta*. After a guerrilla attack, the French would wreck that village. To strip the nocturnal landscape of its hidden supply lines, the French relocated the people of entire regions. Their secret services, backed by native informers, introduced a reign of terror. Frequently, French uniforms camouflaged Gestapo tactics, and medieval torture-chamber methods were used to extort confessions. But confession was evidence of the truth of the charges of cruelty. And so people died as much for saying "yes" as for saying "no."

More intelligent French colonial administrators in Algeria attempted to apply "soft" methods. The indigenous people were aroused against the government because they lived a life unfit for human beings, in shacks, on short rations, in the midst of the plenty of nature. Special services were offered to the people. They accepted. What else could they do? And they were killed by the revolutionaries for that, too.

The countryside was an armed camp: army trucks everywhere; military strongpoints in the middle of elegant shopping-centers; helicopters hovering in swarms like hideous, death-bringing new moons in the Mediterranean sky. There were also the pleasant scenes, café terraces where people sipped their apéritifs and reflected how pleasurable life could be in this land gilt by the sun, caressed by breezes. Then a car would drive slowly by—a bomb would burst, a machine gun rattle—again the horrid face of sudden death.

A BRIEFCASE IN A CAVE

A fugitive from justice and an escaped convict, Ben Bella had been hovering along the borders of Algeria for a long time. On the periphery of the country, he was not involved in personal dangers, nor exposed to tortures or to the swift thrusts of the French security services. How important a man was he in the Algerian rebellion? When the fighting ended—and no war lasts forever—what would be his role in the changed scheme of things? A man who is out of sight can easily be dropped from the minds of the people. The answer was given in the Nementcha Mountains.

Under the September sky, those mountains in eastern Algeria might have belonged to the realm of science fiction. They exhibited a desolate landscape where nothing seemed to exist except the gnawed-out rocks, corroded by the pulverising force of the elements. The area was under the command of Bachir Chihani, bold, adventurous, devil-may-care, ready to take great risks and to sustain great losses. The year was 1955, and a good year it was for him. His hammering drives were too much for the French, who quietly abandoned their toehold in his domain.

It was near the *mechta* of Djeurf that Bachir Chihani held a council to deal with top policy matters. That being over, the Algerian commanders faded into the moon-like landscape. Just because it was so like the moon it was possible for hostile forces to thrust quick reconnoitering units into the area. An informer revealed the location of the parley, and a French unit proceeded to poke into the mountain caves. It made a particularly lucky find—a well-stuffed briefcase.

Was it a ruse, a prop in a dramatic trap, or had it been abandoned there through an oversight? The top sleuths of the French intelligence service studied the papers in the briefcase and decided that they contained information of the highest import and that they had been left in the cave either through oversight or because of a panic due to the movements of French troops.

The most significant item in the briefcase was Ben Bella's correspondence with Chihani about the procurement of arms, methods of transportation, and matters of strategy. Even more important was the outline of a project that Ben Bella, from outside the country, had submitted to the revolutionary leaders inside Algeria.

His communique set forth the existing situation: the war required too much blood; however, strategically, it was not going badly. In spite of the enormous disproportion of the strengths of the armed forces, the French had been held on the defensive. They could, however, maintain their hold for a long time; they had a vast regular army in the field. The trouble with the Algerian forces was that they had no pivot. And this was Ben Bella's recommendation: Let the Nementcha region, freed of the French, be the nucleus of Free Algeria. Instead of waiting for the time when an all-Algerian government could be established, let independence come to the country in installments. This would boost the morale of the people, encourage more active aid on the part of other Arab countries, demoralize the French, serve as the proving ground of self-government, and produce a strong public-relations move in international relations.

The find in the cave revealed Ben Bella's importance in the Algerian insurrection. It also prompted the hostile armed forces to regain the lost mountain territory. Yet, Ben Bella's suggestion was not completely unheeded. It was reincarnated in the decisions of the Soummam Valley conference in August, 1956. Ben Bella's platform was the first step toward setting up an independent Algeria while the tug-of-war was still going on, though it did not result in the type of regionally limited independence that Ben Bella had envisaged. The Algerians eventually formed a legislative and an executive organ. The legislative body was the National Council of the Algerian Revolution, CNRA, and it had about thirty members. Ben Bella was not one of them. Real power was to rest in the hands of the five-member Executive Committee of Coordination, CCE, and Ben Bella was not a member of that either. The key man of the executive body was a former student of pharmacy of the University of Algiers, Benyoussef Ben Khedda. The other members were Ramdane Abane, the theoretician of the revolution; Belkacem Krim, a man from the mountains; Saad Dahlab, a spokesman for the peasants and a peasant himself; Ben M'Hidi, the military "genius."

Revolutions usually devour their own children, and this one seemed to have devoured Ahmed Ben Bella while he was working abroad for the Algerian cause. The emphasis is on the word "abroad." The number of fronts in the Algerian war had increased. Now there was also a power struggle among the leaders. Possessing the looks of the *jeune premier,* what could Ben Bella do to become the leading actor in a historic role? Being abroad he could indirectly affect the conduct of affairs.

A STRANGE TRIP TO TUNIS

The "dirty war" in Algeria had become of deep concern to the rest of the Arab world. In 1956, Algeria's two neighbors—Morocco, to her west, and Tunisia, to the east—had become independent. They had been French protectorates whose nominal rule rested in the hands of native potentates. Algeria was not a protectorate but theoretically an integral part of metropolitan France.

It was in the special interest of the leaders of Morocco and of Tunisia—Sultan Mohammed V and Habib Bourguiba respectively—that peace should return to Algeria. As long as there was war, their own countries were endangered. As fellow Arab nations, they could not refuse to give sanctuary to the Algerians, not merely to persecuted individuals but to entire armed units. The French could not tolerate this and felt justified in violating the sovereignty of these neighbors.

Other reasons, too, impelled the two neighbors to wish for the return of peace to Algeria. As a battleground, North Africa was unattractive to native and foreign investments. The three regions had been under French rule and thus had common experiences and interests. Could they not also share a common future? Influential outside forces exerted pressure on the two neighboring countries to seek a solution to the Algerian imbroglio.

This offered Ben Bella a means by which he could stage a dramatic comeback. Should the intervention of the neighbors be successful, he would trump the cards of the participants in the Soummam Valley conference.

It was the plan that Ben Bella, tacitly recognized as the "first among equals," should take a plane from Rabat, capital of the Moroccan sovereign, to Tunis, capital of Bourguiba. In his company were to be Mohammed Boudiaf, Mohammed Khider, Mustapha Lacheraf, and Hocine Aït-Ahmed.

On October 22, 1956, the plane took off from the Rabat airfield. Besides the five Algerian revolutionary leaders, its passengers included nine journalists. It was a DC 3 commercial plane flying the Moroccan flag, chartered from a French-owned line, Air Atlas.

The destination of the plane was Tunis. Awaiting the Algerian leaders there were Mohammed V, ex-prisoner of the French, a national hero of the Moroccans, and Bourguiba, another former prisoner of France. With Ben Bella, also a former prisoner, this was to be a reunion of P.G.'s, prison graduates.

Flying in a northeasterly direction, the plane landed briefly at Palma, on the Spanish island of Mallorca. Taking off again, it headed out to sea, this time in a southeasterly direction. On its way to Tunis the plane reached a point close to the coast of Algeria. It was at that point that the pilot received instructions from French authorities to land at the airport of Algiers, Maison Blanche, instead of the Tunisian capital.

The pilot accepted these instructions and summoned the stewardess into the cockpit. There he asked her to see to it that her passengers should have no suspicion about the detour. Promptly, the stewardess returned to the Algerian leaders and engaged them in animated badinage. Meanwhile, the pilot was filling out the time between the longer stretch to Tunis and the shorter route to Algiers by circling over the sea. At the precise time of the anticipated arrival at Tunis he put down his plane at Maison Blanche.

Meanwhile the route from the airport of Tunis to the heart of the capital was lined by an enthusiastic crowd, shouting *Aljezair Yahia,* "Long Live Algeria." Mohammed V and Bourguiba were on hand to welcome their distinguished guests.

As soon as those guests reached Algerian soil the French authorities detained them. They were in possession of Egyptian and Moroccan passports. Detectives searched them; several objects of interest were found on Ben Bella, including an automatic pistol, a substantial amount of money, and a briefcase the study of which proved to be particularly instructive. It contained a list of the Algerian sources of arms shipments, the locations of parachute drop points, keys to secret codes, and another plan to hold up the post office at Oran.

It took some time before the stunning news of the hijacking of the Moroccan plane reached the prospective hosts in Tunis. The Moroccan Sultan declared that the men's capture was the "most stinging blow that ever had been struck at my honor not only as a sovereign but also as a man." Normally not a man of strong words, Bourguiba called the event an "act of piracy." So outraged was the French ambassador accredited to Tunisia that he resigned his post forthwith. Telephone calls were made to Paris demanding the release of the five prisoners. They were retained in custody.

From Algiers the prisoners were flown to Paris, and that is how Ben Bella was lodged in the Santé. This time he and his confederates were accused of having attempted to demoralize the French army and nation. The charges were shrewdly devised to arouse fear in the population of the mainland. The trial was to be held before a military tribunal and a vast *dossier* was being collected about the accused. Months passed and then years. There was no sign of the trial, but the accused were still confined in their jails.

Nothing could have done a greater disservice to the French cause in Algeria than the kidnaping by plane. Now Morocco and Tunisia went all out to help the rebel cause. The easiest time of it was had by the revolutionary leaders: simply by sitting still they were demonstrating the truth of their allegation that in Algeria it was impossible to negotiate with the French.

THE REVOLT OF THE CLASSES

Ben Bella was kept away from his homeland for an eternity—or so it seemed to him. Because of the madly accelerated events in the modern world, memories about headline figures of yesteryear are short. Were the memories of the Algerian masses short about Ben Bella, too? What image did he reflect on the retina of their recollections?

Before these questions could be answered, however, the revolving stage of history in Algeria exhibited another scene. In that setting the main actors were the *colons,* the wealthy European settlers, with their strongly nationalistic traditions—*Algérie française,* "Algeria is French." Was Algeria really to be French, even though nine-tenths of the population opposed that slogan? Of what importance were the nine-tenths? They were only the people, poverty-stricken, wretched people at that. Real power was in the hands of the Establishment, a small representative body of the great landowners and other magnates, *les pieds-noirs,* "the black feet."

These *colons* observed developments on mainland France with increasing apprehension. Parliamentary democracy was the designation of the French Republic, but democracy there seemed to run amok. Individualistic to the core, French political parties were as quickly formed as they were dissolved. Each deputy carried in his briefcase the accreditation of the Premier. Power appeared to be the sole object of the parliamentarians; the interests of the country were disregarded. Six months—and no more—represented the average life expectancy of a French government.

Weakened by such conditions and also by the war, France was losing her grip on her colonies. In the Far East, in an unequal battle in jungle country against pauperized wretches, France had lost Indochina. *La gloire de la grande nation* was tarnished elsewhere, too. The French military leadership, never having reconciled itself to the republic, continued to be dedicated to the ideals of the *ancien régime*. There were exceptions among the officers, of course, but they were exceptions—no more. The colonial defeats were galling to the Military Establishment.

Was Algeria to be lost, too? How could one win a war against the phantom rebel forces? The native population was aroused to the point where it was conceivable that the majority would rather face death than be ruled by the *colons*. However, the French army in Algeria felt that victory could be had if only the cabinet on the Seine were headed by a strong man. There was one such man in France, the army men believed, the former commander of the wartime Free French forces, ex-Premier Charles de Gaulle.

It was at the height of all these frustrations that the "classes" of French Algeria—the influential civilians and the military—spoke through a mass demonstration on the Forum of Algiers on May 13, 1958, a crucial date in French history. It roared its will across the sea to mainland France: Clean up the mess! De Gaulle is the man to do it! Mainland France bowed to the will of French Algeria, and the general was installed as premier. "Democracy is the keynote of France," said the new man at the helm of France, but it was to be a one-man democracy in which the premier's powers were vastly enlarged. From the premiership he eventually moved into the Elysée Palace as President of France.

The "classes" in Algeria were sure now that they had triumphed over the masses. The *ratons* would be crushed and Algeria would be fully integrated into a rejuvenated *mère patrie*.

De Gaulle's ideas, however, did not coincide with those of the extremist *colons*. A man of vision who could see current problems in historical perspective, he was not sure that the masses could be held on the leash of the "classes." He took a closer look at the Algerian situation. About 90 per cent of the Moslems were illiterate in spite of the *mission civilisatrice* of France for a century and a quarter; the per capita income of the indigenous people was a mere fraction of that of the European settlers; maladies ravaged the people in the midst of nature's plenty. Not "Liberty, Equality, and Fraternity" were written large on the French banner in Algeria but the words: "Disease, Ignorance, and Poverty." A D.I.P. land it was, in truth.

An attempt had to be made to remedy this situation and the general set forth a development plan in the city of Constantine. The civilizing mission of France was to be implemented by the Constantine Plan. The plan provided for schools, industrialization, increased employment, and sanitation. Should it be a success—as De Gaulle had every reason to believe—then the Algerian Moslems' interests would be linked to those of mainland France, the source of venture capital and technical knowledge.

Would the plan solve the Algerian problem? That was the question I asked the official in charge of the execution of the plan some months later. He was a Frenchman from the mainland, and a university professor. He answered frankly to my questions about the Algerian facts of life.

"I would like to pose a question," I said, "which you may be in no position to answer. I'll try just the same. The impression I have gained as a student of history is that political problems seldom yield to economic solutions alone. The Algerian problem is basically a political problem, while the Constantine Plan offers an economic solution. Under these circumstances do you think that it would work?"

The French official observed me for a moment and then replied with an absence of bureaucratic double-talk.

"You are right, I am afraid. Economic projects alone do not solve political problems."

"Why, then, are you attempting to carry out this plan?"

"Because the solution of these problems in Algeria is long overdue. We are trying to trade the plan against time."

"Do you believe that there is a solution for the Algerian problem within the present context?"

"As matters stand now, there is no solution."

Of course, the Moslem leaders might have been dazzled by the plan, for it offered hope that the Moslems might obtain a decent livelihood. Their own followers might have forced them to heed the General's words. Or a conflict might have broken out among the leaders on that score.

What did Ben Bella in his cell think about all this? "Unacceptable. Too little, and too late."

No longer was he in the grim Santé of Paris. His place of detention was now off the Atlantic coast near the estuary of the Charente River, on the island of Aix. And a historic place it was. There Napoleon the Great had boarded the boat that took him to St. Helena where he became Napoleon the Puny in his jailers' hands.

THE UNFORGOTTEN MAN

In jail for an endless term, Ben Bella had not been forgotten. In countless *gourbis*—the mud and wattle dwellings of the Algerian poor—his photogenic face was displayed. Algerians in France were staging demonstrations: *Libérez Ben Bella.* The prisoner had an excellent public-relations liaison man in the person of Maitre Hachemi Cherif, his Moroccan lawyer, who kept the newspapers well informed. Ben Bella himself managed to remain in touch with the outside world.

The Algerian *fellahin* were faithful to their idol. In their villages, life was not as dazzlingly kaleidoscopic as in the Western world. Heroes were not created there just to be discarded in favor of the headliners of later editions of the newspapers. Ben Bella was not only a hero but also a martyr, and his image was not at all tarnished by his long absence from the guerrilla battle line.

ALGERIA GETS A GOVERNMENT

Not long before, the Algerian indigenous people would have been satisfied with the status of full French citizenship. In the intervening time, however, they had learned two lessons. The knowledge that *en masse* they were strong and even invincible was one of these lessons. All along the line they were winning the war in spite of their incredible loss of lives and their limited resources. And there was the second lesson. The spokesmen of the "black feet" were impervious to argument, typical die-hards. One could not negotiate with people of that sort. Algeria must take matters in her own hands.

On September 19, 1958, the Algerian leaders burned their

bridges to the Europeans. They set up a government of their own. It had to be a cabinet-in-exile and therefore provisional. Much depended on the selection of the head of the government. Was he a moderate or a fire-eater? He was Ferhat Abbas, the most moderate of all moderates. He had been the president of the Algerian Moslem Students' Union and the author of a book of political essays in which he wrote: "I served with the forces [during World War II] because I am French and for no other reason. We are Moslem and we are French. We are natives and we are French."

He held various political offices in Algeria and he owned a pharmacy in Sétif. It will be recalled what happened in that town on May Day, 1945. After that, Ferhat Abbas was no longer so French. Barely more than a dozen years later he considered himself an Algerian. There was now the nucleus of an Algerian nation—a nation, however, that could still be induced to make common cause with France, for France had the funds and the skills to help Algeria in the task of nation-building. Ben Bella, still in jail, was named vice-premier of the government-in-exile.

Meanwhile, the "dirty war" became even dirtier for France. In spite of the efforts of an extremely able general at the head of the government in Paris, the French military effort in Algeria turned out to be a fiasco. The thrifty French were throwing their billions into a bottomless pit. It became obvious that money was being wasted on an irredeemable situation: the law of diminishing returns was in full operation. Paradoxically, economic conditions in France were not bad. The "economic miracle" of Europe continued to dazzle the continent. But how long could the spell of prosperity last if vast sums of money had to be used to maintain a recalcitrant offspring? Sensible people on the French mainland agreed that to continue waging a war that could not be brought to any conclusion was the closest thing to madness. The general-statesman in Paris knew that a bold solution in Algeria was inevitable.

The Algerian high command, with its headquarters in Tunisia, knew it, too. Ferhat Abbas was a man of high caliber, but the "Young Turks" in his government found him too conservative, not quick enough to pounce on the opportunities presented by the adversary. All the world could see that French Algeria was bent on its own destruction, for now the French Algerians—the very people who had put General de Gaulle into power—turned against him because he failed to implement their extremist policy. The French generals in Algeria were in open rebellion against the head of their own state. This was the time for the Algerian natives to hit hard, and Ferhat Abbas, the moderate, had not the disposition to do so.

Also, the time had come for a resolute Algeria to decide upon the political line that would free her of the colonial shackles. Was she to follow the capitalist line, or the socialist one, or should she become a communist nation? What should be her role in international relations—East, West, or somewhere in-between? What was to be the relation of the masses to the "classes," whose status would be reduced? And what were to be the economic development schemes—land reform, industrialization?

Some of the Algerians said that the answers would have to be provided by the people themselves—in due time. That was not the view of Ben Bella in his island prison. He kept communications open with his followers at home. Time was too short for prevarication. There was no dramatic showdown among the Algerian leaders, nor open recriminations. The government-in-exile met in Tripoli, Libya, and it was from there that the change of guard was announced. Ferhat Abbas had to step down, and Benyoussef Ben Khedda stepped up as the head of the provisional government. The time was August, 1961.

De Gaulle won his own battle against his former sponsors who had turned against him. French public opinion supported him—there was no other choice. The pleasures and treasures of prosperity were not to be jeopardized. An agreement had to be reached with the Algerians, while safeguarding the interests of the Europeans and, of course, those of all France. Negotiations between the French and the Algerians began on the French side of Lake Geneva, at Evian-les-Bains. This was early in 1962.

TO THE LATECOMERS, THE BONES

From the island in the Atlantic Ben Bella had been transferred to another place of detention, the château of Tourquant, two hundred miles from Paris.

He had been in jail now for over five years. The fate of Algeria was to be decided. "To the latecomers, the bones," says the Latin proverb. Others had exposed their lives to French bullets and torture chambers in Algeria. The survivors among them felt entitled to speak for their countrymen and, eventually, to govern in their names. And now a delegation of Algerians was negotiating with the delegates of Paris to lay the foundations of the new state. Ben Bella wanted to be one of them—more, the head of them. Self-confidence he had in abundance. Also, he claimed, it was he who had launched the rebellion. He had to break out of his isolation, force his countrymen and the French to take account of him. How was a man in detention to do it?

He started a hunger strike. The French government could not afford to let him starve to death. It resorted to the measure of feeding him by force. While Ben Bella was not allowed to leave the château, he was a prisoner *de luxe,* with his own key to his suite. So he locked himself in, to prevent the personnel from feeding him. Thus a strange situation arose. The prisoner locked himself in, contrary to the will of his guards, who wanted to free him. There was only one thing they could do. They smashed the lock, then whisked him into an ambulance which took him to the Raymond Poincaré Hospital at Garches, outside Versailles. While close to Paris, he was still far from Evian. The parley ended without his participation. One of the peace conditions of the Algerians was that he and his comrades should be released. This was in the spring of 1962, and Ben Bella was set free.

What was he to do now? Peace did not come immediately to the harassed land of Algeria. Terrorists within the French Secret Army Organization (OAS) threatened to throw the country into chaos. There was murder by night and by broad daylight, too. Women and children were slaughtered, as well as men. Mere bystanders were shot down in the streets. OAS members made repeated attacks on the life of the French President. "De Gaulle to the Gallows," was the battle cry of the extremists. *Algérie française,* they clamored incessantly.

De Gaulle decided to counteract the agitation of a minority with the will of the majority of the French people. He called for a referendum, which did not include Algeria. It took place on April 8, 1962, and 90 per cent of the ballots favored the settlement which the President espoused. The terror regime of the OAS continued, just the same. There was a series of bloody clashes between the loyal units of the French armed forces and the units that had sided with the terrorists. The OAS suffered a blow when ex-General Edmond Jouhaud—its second in command, and one of the leaders of the 1961 Algiers uprising against General de Gaulle—was captured in Oran and sent to prison in Paris.

Following up the referendum in France, De Gaulle concluded the agreement with the Algerians. They, in turn, submitted it to a referendum on July 1, 1962. The final result was close to six million votes for the settlement and only 16,500 against it. Charles de Gaulle declared the independence of Algeria on July 3.

THE MAN WITH THE BARAKA

He had to go to Morocco first, the erstwhile *jeune premier*. Conditions in Algeria herself were not yet consolidated. Also, the new men of the new nation, the *ministrables*, those of ministerial timber, had to be tested. Public opinion had to be weighed.

Ben Khedda was the head of the government of Algeria. He was one of the nationalist pioneers and had been jailed for eight months some twenty years before. Algeria's only strong civilian organization was the Federation of Labor, the half-million members of which backed Ben Khedda. He also had the backing of the Berbers in the strategic Kabylia region. No less important was the accolade Ben Khedda received from Morocco. Mohammed V was dead and his son, King Hassan II, did not like Ben Bella. "He is a marionette," said the press which Hassan influenced. Ben Khedda found favor in the eyes of the King.

Yet, it was in the capital of King Hassan that Ben Bella first touched Arabic land after his release from the French prison. As he descended the ramp of the plane he still looked the matinee idol, tall, erect, self-confident, his eyes flashing, his smile dazzling people. This was all to the good. But did he have that state of grace which Moslems call *baraka?* Was he a charismatic man, a creature of destiny? *Baraka* could not be obtained in the way one could acquire a college degree. It was "in the genes."

People had heard about his return and there was an endless line from the airport to the center of town to give him an ecstatic welcome. Absent physically for many years, he must have been present in their minds. But these were simple people, who had no personal politics to play. They were mere supers on the stage of history. How was Ben Bella to impress the other leaders in the moment of the great confrontation, when the rivals' eyes, reflecting their real strength or weakness, were engaged in the decisive psychological tussle?

Ben Bella could be sure of the backing of Colonel Houari Boumedienne, the former chief of staff of the Army of National

Liberation, who had been relieved of his top position by the Provisional Executive of the Algerian government. Ferhat Abbas, the first head of the Algerian provisional government, also supported Ben Bella.

The political situation in this Time of Troubles of emergent Algeria was as follows: The Evian Accords had conferred independence on Algeria and had stipulated that there should be an *Exécutif Provisoire* to arrange the elections of the first government of independent Algeria. The Algerian Provisional Government, headed by Benyoussef Ben Khedda, paid no attention to the Exécutif Provisoire. Ben Khedda dismissed the three-man general staff of the Algerian Army of National Liberation on charges of "criminal activity" aimed at frustrating the revolution. The general staff of the army supported the claims of Vice-Premier Ben Bella to political leadership.

Ben Bella decided to call upon the Algerian people to arbitrate in this dispute. He entered Algeria for the first time in many years. He came from Morocco and then moved on to Marnia, the place of his birth. From there he proceeded to Tlemcen, which had played such an important role in his youth. His next stop was Oran, the scene of his first dramatic revolutionary exploit. Everywhere he received a rapturous reception and he oozed that self-confidence which was the external sign of *baraka*. This triumphal tour amounted to an unofficial referendum.

Now it was Ben Bella's turn to present his case. He charged that Ben Khedda, head of the provisional government, was a "usurper." Ben Bella's main strength lay in the National Council of the Algerian Revolution, CNRA, which had originally set up the provisional government, and Ben Bella operated through it. He and his supporters in the CNRA named a seven-member Political Bureau which he headed. He called on all Algerians to rally around the new authority. A brief armed clash took place in eastern Algeria, and there was fear of civil war. Saner counsels prevailed and negotiations began between the provisional government and the dissident faction. Ben Khedda now accepted the authority of the Political Bureau as set up by Ben Bella. The Political Bureau, dominated by Ben Bella, held its first meeting on August 7, 1962. Subsequently, the provisional government resigned.

The first elections to the National Assembly took place on September 20, and about 80 per cent of the voters elected a single slate of candidates that had been nominated by the Political Bureau with the approval of the *Exécutif Provisoire*. Six days later Ahmed Ben Bella was named premier by the National Assembly. There was now one party in Algeria, FLN, the National Front of Liberation, and one leader, Ahmed Ben Bella. On September 15, 1963, he received 99.6 per cent of the votes as the unopposed candidate of the FLN in a nationwide balloting. Five days later he was sworn in as the first constitutional president of the Republic of Algeria.

FACING PRACTICAL PROBLEMS

After Algeria's time of troubles, Ben Bella fell heir to one of the most difficult problems. How was he to turn the remnants of destruction into the building blocks of construction? First, the damage had to be appraised. No two estimates will ever agree on the extent of the damage. Paris estimated that 141,000 rebels were killed during the seven years of war to the end of 1961, against the loss of 17,250 French officers and men, and 51,800 French wounded. The Algerian leaders estimated their dead at more than one million, many of whom had been killed in concentration camps and in the torture cells.

In the wake of the change, about 80 per cent of the million Europeans left Algeria, taking their skills and much of their funds with them. In the first year of Algerian freedom about one-third of Algeria's most lucrative farm export, wine, was lost. On the other hand, when the Europeans had fled from Algeria in July, 1962, they had abandoned about 2,500,000 acres of farmland. In March, 1963, Ben Bella seized the biggest European-run estates under the proviso that the land must belong to those who work it.

What about the *fellahin* who were unfamiliar with modern machines, who lacked the means for food and seed? Ben Bella told them that the answer was the integration of the land. Not, however, under a distant centralized Soviet-style agency but in the hands of the turbaned workers on the former estates. This he called *autogestion,* "self-management." Education received the highest priority and a crash program was launched to put an end to illiteracy. Even cafés and places of public entertainment were turned into part-time schools. Industries, mines, and vacant farms were to be managed under the system of *autogestion.* It was organized on four levels. The broadest of these was the General Assembly of Workers. It appointed the Council of Workers, which, in turn, designated the *Comité de Gestion*. These organs decided work programs, wage rates, and profit-sharing. In this respect Ben Bella copied Tito's Yugoslav communism.

A New York *Times* correspondent reported in October, 1963, that about 600,000 Algerians were working on farms and in a few small factories, restaurants, and hotels run by self-management committees. The outcome, in economic terms, was still uncertain. Money, know-how, and machinery were scarce. *Autogestion* was a logical expression of Ben Bella's almost mystical faith in the Algerian peasant. All over Algeria Ben Bella had it proclaimed: *Un seul héro: Le Peuple*.

Mystical belief in the peasant was not enough. More land had to be available, and more water was needed. Ben Bella's government set out to build high dams such as at Chefia where some 60,000 acres were to be irrigated.

National independence without industrial plants was a farce, Ben Bella held. Countries might be members of the United Nations but they were not really independent as long as they produced raw materials for other nations to turn into finished products which they then had to repurchase at exorbitant prices. The establishment of new plants required capital, technical competence, and good habits of investing. These did not exist in Algeria, and Ben Bella did not reveal much ability to deal with economic conditions. The Golden Age failed to materialize. Unemployment was widespread and the people, though independent, lived worse than before. What, then, was the solution?

"Islamic socialism" answered Ben Bella. What did that mean? Maybe it was just a slogan, a vacuous term denoting nothing more than aspirations. Islam sounds well in a Moslem land, and socialism appeals to people who want to break away from the leash of their former masters. Islamic socialism might mean something more specific, too. *Zakat* is an important duty imposed upon the Moslems by their creed, and it means "helping thy neighbor." Islamic socialism might denote a method by which the community itself would help the individual to fulfill his social obligations. Society—the nation—is in a better position to accumulate capital for socially useful investments than is the individual. There can be no capitalism where capital is absent. Nor can there be free enterprise where shortages of all types prevent economic growth. Leading Algerians referred to one another at political meetings as "Brothers."

In spite of his years in French jails, Ben Bella realized that his country was dependent upon France. The French knew the country, had invested capital there, and had established numerous contacts. Algeria had been woven into the web of the French economic system. He reached an agreement with De Gaulle that provided for French economic and financial assistance, and for joint exploitation of the mineral resources of the Algerian Sahara.

"Algeria has placed herself beside the neutralist and uncommitted countries," Ben Bella had commented at the time of his investiture as premier. "We reject pacts and bloc politics."

ARABISM AND THE MAGHREB

At his inauguration, Ben Bella said "Historically, Algeria is a Arabo-Islamic culture and occupies a choice position in the movement of the Arab people. This is a question of civilization, ethics, culture, and of a way of life."

Centuries ago there was a time when the Arab world formed a cosmic realm—the cosmos of those days. The memory of that empire still haunts the Arabs, and therefore the attempts to bring about such integration as the United Arab Republic. Arab leaders have made fitful attempts to form a comity, but these have proved abortive. Algerians had not shed their blood merely to be submerged in an amorphous unit. They had been separated into compartments by the accidents of history, by geography, by ideological differences, and above all, by entrenched interests. Today thirteen Arab countries extend over thousands of miles, covering millions of square miles, from the Atlantic to the Indian Ocean. Ben Bella had to take his people into the Arab League. That was an expected ritual. The League is a loose organization where homage is paid to the presumed integrated interests of the member nations.

Closer to Algerian interests are those of the Maghreb, the Moslem sunset land comprised of Morocco, Algeria, and Tunisia. "Algeria is an integral part of the Maghreb," Ben Bella intoned another ritual. Then he continued: "The Maghreb constitutes an historical and economic unit that is viable and coherent. Its reconstruction and reunification are imperatives that will impose themselves sooner or later. Beyond national differences and international contingencies the Great Maghreb will be built up slowly but surely, because it will be demanded by the masses."

Maybe so, but Ben Bella himself will not demand it, nor will King Hassan II of Morocco, nor Habib Bourguiba, the President of Tunisia. There is no more justification for a Maghreb than there is for the integration of Canada and the United States. Or for that matter, for the unification of the Latin republics of South America. The economies of the three countries of the Arab Farthest West are competitive—not complementary. Their ecologies are different and so are their growth potentials.

"Algeria has an African calling," Ben Bella said. "She intends to participate in the construction of African union and unity within the framework of the large political and economic groupings." In the fall of 1963, two of the Maghrebi countries, Algeria and Morocco, were at each other's throat. Was it because the contested area in the desert was expected to contain iron ore? Or was it because either one or both governments needed their people's backing and never was it more readily forthcoming than in war?

Africa was absorbed by the spectacle of Algeria's fight for independence. No country in Africa had shed as much blood for its freedom as Algeria. Ben Bella received a great ovation in mid-1963, when the Organization of African Unity was formed in Addis Ababa. What were the chances of African integration? We have seen an aspect of it in Nkrumah's history. On the map Africa is, indeed, one continent, but that is only on the map. The same map shows North Africa separated from southern Europe by the Mediterranean. Yet that sea is not a chasm but a link. It has held civilizations together throughout the aeons of history.

The southern portion of Algeria trails off into the Sahara Desert, fanning out into the torrid regions of half a dozen other countries. Beyond that desert, people look different, nature looks different, and there is, indeed, a different world. North Africa's history is millennial. The history of Africa, south of the Sahara, is today's history for Western man. Less than a century ago the map of that Africa was a void. The sea links Ben Bella's Africa with Europe, while the desert—the dry ocean—separates it from the rest of Africa. Two worlds on one map are not likely to meet on equal terms.

THEN AN EPILOGUE

It was Ben Bella who drew up the Constitution of the sovereign nation of Algeria. All power was delegated to the National Front of Liberation, the sole party of the country. It was accorded the right to choose the supreme legislative body, the National Assembly, and the president of the country. There was much opposition to the party, some from Ben Bella's earliest fellow workers and some from Berber groups. Ferhat Abbas, the country's first provisional president, called it "Fascist" and resigned from his post as the speaker of the assembly. The Berber Algerians objected to the heavily Arab orientation of the Ben Bella regime. The Berbers are Moslems, as are the Arabs of the country, but they speak a different language and have distinctive ways. All differences had been set aside during the war because the ultimate goal had been important, but now the times had changed. The strongest opposition was in the restless Kabylia mountain region. There, in the fall of 1963, representative men of the Algerian Front of Socialist Forces, composed largely of Berbers, set up armed resistance to Ben Bella. The most important leader of this group was Hocine Aït-Ahmed, the same man who had helped to organize the Oran bank robbery. He was one of the "historic chiefs" who had aided the onset of the 1954-62 war of independence. Like Ben Bella, Aït-Ahmed was a member of the external forces of the National Front of Liberation. He had been on the plane that the French had intercepted, and he had spent all those years in jail.

The Constitution was submitted to popular referendum and was accepted by an overwhelming majority. Algeria, as we have seen, became a one-party State, and Ben Bella, being the only candidate, became the first elected President of the Republic of Algeria. When he selected his cabinet members, the names of the best known early fighters were missing from the slate. Was Ben Bella jealous of the other "historic chiefs"? "Napoleon," the "potentate," "Battista," the "Fascist," Aït-Ahmed was to call his former comrade-in-arms. The highest position next to Ben Bella was held by Colonel Houari Boumedienne, defense minister and army chief. Ben Bella sounded the keynote of his administration in the first lines of the Constitution he fathered: *Révolution par le peuple et pour le peuple.*

A PRISONER AT LARGE

Ben Bella's home and headquarters were in the Villa Joly, a secluded modern apartment building perched on the Algiers hillside. He occupied an eight-room air conditioned flat on the top floor, which he shared with a cook, a butler, and visiting relatives. Ben Bella is unmarried. (At one time it was said that he was interested in the twenty-two-year-old sister of King Hassan II of Morocco. Then hostilities broke out with that country.) The apartment was tidy, its furnishings undistinguished. But it had a magnificent view, looking down upon the Bay of Algiers.

Years of prison life had not lessened Ben Bella's dynamism in the least. On the contrary, they seemed to have helped him accumulate new and almost inexhaustible reserves of energy. On a typical day—in the fall of 1963—he was observed going through a grueling routine. Early in the morning, with half a dozen of his immediate staff in his apartment, headed by Cabinet Director Hadj Smaine, they discussed the day's business. Appointments ran from 9:30 to noon, with visitors often staying longer than their scheduled time. A New York *Times* correspondent reported that the American Ambassador, William J. Porter, who speaks Arabic and French, was the most welcome diplomat.

At noon, Ben Bella suspended appointments, took the elevator downstairs, and began his daily public appearances. One day he might visit a cluster of farms, confer with foreign farm experts, and familiarize himself with the problems of an individual *fellah* family.

On other days he would visit projected industrial plants, discuss problems with managers and labor union leaders. He found time to participate in the dedication of a mosque. Mid-afternoon might bring an interview with a foreign journalist over small cups of strong black coffee at the Villa Joly, followed by a cat nap. Then came a flurry of decree signing and other paperwork. By 5:30 he was downtown at his big official office for meetings with his cabinet and staff.

At 8:30 Ben Bella was back in the Villa Joly for a family dinner with his mother, a lively old lady who dressed in the traditional garb of her native Marnia, veil and all.

Other relatives might drop in. Frequently, the President paid a surprise call on some old friend from conspiratorial days. By 1:30, having given the local and French papers a thorough reading, he was asleep.

Acting quickly and impulsively on his whirlwind tours, he would distribute praise and blame. Occasionally, he handed promotions to those who worked beyond the call of duty, and demoted laggards. He exhibited little patience with slow-moving bureaucracy. Most of the time he retained his charm, his eyes and teeth flashing.

THE INFLUENCE OF THE PRISONS

Not only his actions but also his *Weltanschauung,* his outlook on life, were affected by the years he spent in prison. In his "cell universities" he had fallen under the spell of two teachers, philosophers both, and both French, one of a previous generation, the other a contemporary. The philosopher of another generation was Henri Bergson. From him, he had learned that while knowledge is vital, its profitable use depends largely on the person's intuition, bearing in mind that it has to be adjusted to the eternal force of life, the *élan vitale* that sweeps onward in response to the innate evolution of existence.

The contemporary philosopher from whom Ben Bella had also learned much during his confinement in jail was Jean-Paul Sartre, the existentialist. From him, the President of Algeria had learned what he likes to call the basic facts of life—which is his own somewhat simplified interpretation of Sartre's philosophy. Each individual is alone in this world and it is of the greatest practical importance that he should be fully aware of this fact. The singularity of each detached existence must be related to other lives so that the welfare of one person should not be the undoing of others. It is not because people like one another that life is an uninterrupted exercise in coexistence but because they cannot live in a vacuum.

Ben Bella's prison life could have been a stultifier. It is that for people who arrive in jail because of their inability to adjust to the everyday norm. Ben Bella had the choice either to lapse into the torpitude of degraded existence, in which case he would have become an "un-man," or to rise to the challenge and soar beyond his everyday capacities. In prison he had had an opportunity to deepen his knowledge of the world and, above all, of himself. There he had been able to test his own strength and to reach the conviction that he had a mission in life. Shriveled as a prisoner's life may become, Ben Bella had not let himself become a "ghost at sunrise."

On the contrary, his life in jail had released concealed springs of dynamic energy. After his liberation he discharged this unused energy into his work as the maker of supreme decisions for his country. He learned to trust his insights and intuitions, to turn them into decisions, and he learned that he was endowed with *baraka,* which prison universities can activate, but not generate, because it is "in the genes."

Fate placed many handicaps in the way of Ahmed Ben Bella, above all during his prison years. These handicaps could have thwarted the ambitions of even very dynamic men. But Ben Bella did not let himself be overtaken and surpassed. He was nearly always at the crucial point at the crucial moment, a man of startling self-assertiveness. Few contemporary developments parallel his success in maintaining his grip on his people.

The most important question, however, still remains to be answered. He did full justice to the building of his own career. Will he do equal justice to the monumental problems of building a nation whose productive forces were eroded by one of the most dismal of wars? The answer to this question will depend not only on him. It will also depend on the future of France, for Algeria's fate is still closely linked to that country. Above all, the success of Ben Bella's endeavor is predicated on the ability of his own people to follow him on the paths of peace as they followed their leaders on the byways of war. Ben Bella named his country the "Democratic and Popular Republic of Algeria." History will judge him on his ability to turn this designation into a reality. Will he be able to give Africa a democratic and popular republic of Algeria?

3

Jomo Kenyatta: The Scholarly Convict

The country around Lokitaung seems to have been torn out of the inchoate mass of the world plasma long before that fatal day when Mogai, Ngai, Mwene-Nyaga—the Divider of the World and Chief Deity of the Kikuyu tribe of the British Crown Colony of Kenya—breathed life into it. The contorted hills surrounding the desert station of Lokitaung appears to be the result of a sudden petrification in the midst of the awesome travail accompanying the birth of the cosmos. The only sign of the twentieth century in the Northern Frontier Post is an unmetalled road that twists out of the gloomy horizon and disappears at what seems to be the end of space.

No better site could have been found for a prison camp than this Lokitaung, which was fenced in by a swamp, named Lotagisi, from which arose the fumes of death. Lake Rudolf, with its brackish water, was at a distance in the East, and it was said by some who had never seen the lake that birds straying into the exhalations from Lotagisi dropped into the burning waters of Lake Rudolf. But the very name of the latter was linked to tragedy. A Hungarian explorer had christened it after the popular Crown Prince of Austria-Hungary. Prince Rudolf was later to die a tragic death at Mayerling by his own hand, taking with him his young inamorata, a beautiful member of Vienna society.

The Lokitaung prison camp was surmounted by bare-ribbed hills that further accentuated the desolation of the place. Standing guard over it, the hills dropped away and left this narrow rift in the middle of the distorted landscape.

Was the prison camp really in the midst of nowhere, and if so why was it there? Because the borders of other worlds required watching. To the northeast spread the extreme southern marches of Ethiopia. To the west were the southern portions of the Sudan—known then and for some years more, as Anglo-Egyptian Sudan. Lokitaung kept an eye on these distant boundaries over which smugglers tiptoed stealthily.

Lokitaung was closer to the distant stars in the nocturnal sky, whose blue-black luminosity covered this tiny atom of the cosmos with a shroud of silence, than it was to the surrounding countryside. This silence was broken only by the hyenas, whose howling sounded like the anguished wailing of the world burnt alive. Lokitaung was close, too, to the sun, that tropical life-giving torturer that sank its deadly shafts into helpless human flesh.

It was not a town, this Lokitaung, but merely a crossroads post for a few heads of Kenya Rifles, who kept an eye cocked too, toward the poorly demarcated frontier in the North. It was also hell for a few subordinate government clerks, the guards, and the prisoners. For the latter, this was the end of the road from which there was no return to life. For the government people posted there, it was Equatorial Siberia.

KOMAU WA NGENGI

One of the prisoners was Jomo Kenyatta, alias Johnstone Kenyatta, alias Komau wa Ngengi, a burly figure, heavily bearded, with prominent almost Mongoloid cheekbones, beetling eyebrows, eyes cowering in deep sockets, strong teeth displaying a wide gap between the two center incisors. His dark eyes were his most striking feature, eyes which were sometimes veiled almost lifeless, and then again athrob with life. An anthropologist might say that he had the face of a criminal, a typical example of Lombroso's sinister *l'uomo delinquente*. But, Kenyatta himself was an anthropologist, a scholar of note in Africa, the author of a classical work, *Facing Mount Kenya,* a man of deep insight, highly respected in the world of science.

He had been sent to Lokitaung because his accusers felt that death on the gallows would have been too merciful for him. He would have been subjected there to only one agonizing moment, and then the kindest of fates, the end of all suffering, would have saved him. In this prison post, however, years of myriads of seconds stretched into an infinity of frustration. Inhumanity fenced him in on every side. Nature's unrelenting forces gnawed at his nervous system, exposed as he was to the blinding glare of the sun whose fire created an earthly inferno. Here rain did not fall—

it seemed—ever, and if by some miracle it did, it was a deluge.

The inhumanity of man for his fellow man was a constant spectacle. Prison mates, free of the conventions of civilization, sank to the level of savages and lived in never-ending abhorrence of the very traits that were their own hallmarks. The frustration of inactivity imposed upon the prisoners, brought here by their overactive natures, found its outlet on prison mates. Worse than the poison of the scorpion was the hatred the convicts felt for their fellow prisoners, whose very faces, mannerisms, and enforced ways of life were intimately known and therefore detested in the enforced proximity of the detention pen.

The prisoners had been sentenced to hard labor, but what labor could they perform in the middle of this vast emptiness, lacking tools and adequate guidance, serving no purpose? That is why the prisoners' hard labor was to hate one another, and this they did with a heat as intense as that of the tropical sun. But the sun itself restrained the prisoners' hands and it was the occasional breaths of fresh air released into the valley of the accursed from the far-away mountains that stirred the desire in frustrated men to assert themselves aggressively. They began to pummel one another with murder in their bloodshot eyes, their only wish being to see the juice of life squirt from the bodies of their victims, because only this sight could soothe their raw nerves.

Kenyatta appeared to be an old man in the midst of much younger people. The traditional respect for age—for the tribal elder—was absent in this camp. Nor did it afford him any protection because he had brought fame into this prison, he, a scholar, symbol of the freedom of his tribe, the Kikuyus. He was knocked about and lost his spectacles. He could not see well without them, and in his helplessness, he was exposed to more cruel punches.

The fight over, the prisoners settled down, gloating over the wounds they had inflicted and ignoring the bruises they had received. After the sun had baked all energy out of them, they sank back into deep apathy. But when that distant chill arose from the mountains, filling them with renewed desire to live, they sought to kill again.

The guards were just a little better than the prisoners—but not much better. Even if they had not been ill-tempered by nature, they would have become so in the middle of this void. Filled with the frustration of their occupation, a frustration compounded by the cruelties of tropical African nature, they tried to find release by making their prisoners' lives even more unbearable.

Jomo Kenyatta had few chances to pursue his scholarly interests in his desert jail. The government officials of Nairobi, capital of the colony, about four hundred miles away, had far more urgent matters to deal with than to comply with his requests for books. Besides, the prison compound had no post office. The heavy trucks that carried the provisions could not be overloaded with books for the prisoners.

In the spring of 1953 Kenyatta entered the jail for seven seemingly endless years. Did he do anything during that time? Nothing that made a real contribution to the life around him, to the broader world of Kenya, to the wider universe of Africa. Or should we say that he did make a contribution? As a free man in one of the freest of all countries, Britain, he had learned many skills. One of them was cooking. It was a hobby then—only sometimes a necessity—but now it became a vocation and a mission. He became a prison cook. This work filled him with satisfaction because it provided him with a goal in life. While he detested many of his fellow prisoners, it gave him much pleasure to know that he made their lives more tolerable by providing them with good food.

Younger men might have been broken by seven years in prison, but not Jomo Kenyatta. He was made of a particularly strong fiber. This he had demonstrated when, in his own forceful way, he had challenged the established order and brought down on his head the wrath of Her Majesty's officials in Kenya.

A CHANGE OF PLACE

With the usual time off, his prison term was over in 1959, but he was not released. Considered a danger to the security and peace of the colony, he was transferred to another place of detention in the village of Lodwar. The place was more desirably located than Lokitaung, even though it was closer to the Equator than the prison camp. Lodwar was less arid, and it was flanked by the Ngapo Hills.

Kenyatta was assigned a small government cottage for his enforced residence. He even received a monthly allowance of £9, most of which he used to buy newspapers and books. These, however, were screened in Nairobi before he was allowed to read them. In the village itself he was permitted to move about freely. A small plot of land was placed at his disposal on which he could putter, and the authorities may have hoped thus to divert his attention from politics. But Kenyatta took scant interest in his piece of land and his attention was not diverted from Kenya. He knew his name was being hailed by the native people of Kenya as a symbol of freedom and independence.

In Lodwar he could get books readily, but he was allowed to read only "innocuous" ones. It is interesting to note his intellectual taste within the limitations imposed on him by his jailers. The study of religions appealed to him greatly, above all, the philosophy of non-violence. (Because his accusers had linked him to one of the most violent tribal uprisings, that of the Mau Maus, the motive behind his studies has been questioned.) Hinduism was one of the subjects he chose to study. Did he do so because he was enthralled by the apparent success of India's Great Soul, Gandhi, in securing the independence of his people? Or had he been moved by the many Indian settlers he had met in Kenya; people who had wanted to and did help him more than his fellow Africans? It had been Hindu Indians who had helped to finance his defense at his trial.

Whatever the reasons, Kenyatta was greatly impressed by one of the Hindu classics, *Bhagavad Ghita,* "Song of the Blessed One," a paean to non-violence. In that epic poem, Lord Krishna, the beloved figure of the Indian pantheon, expressed what Gandhi thought was the essence of the Hindu creed—adherence to the life-sustaining doctrine, *bakhti yoga,* "loving devotion," fused with *katma yoga,* "resolute acts of piety." It is within ourselves, Lord Krishna proclaimed, that we find fulfilment.

> *The dust hides the mirror,*
> *The smoke hides the flame,*
> *The sight of the outer eye*
> *Blinds the insight of the soul,*
> *Behold me, thy true self,*
> *With the spirit's eye.*

Wars solved no problems, Lord Krishna chanted. On the contrary, by running counter to the very essence of life, they created additional problems. Wars spread death, and death could never solve the problems of life.

Although Kenyatta was nominally a Christian, during his imprisonment he was more interested in Islam and Hinduism. Islam had been spreading swiftly in tropical Africa. Kenyatta wanted to know the reason why. It was one of the aggressive mono-theistic creeds, bent on expanding its influence and saving souls, sometimes against their will. Kenyatta preferred religions that were more tolerant of other creeds—Buddhism, Confucianism, and Hinduism.

He noted the many similarities between Buddhism and Hinduism; these religions seemed to him to present the same basic ideas. Both creeds held that the universe was filled with the divine spirit, God being everywhere, which is a form of pantheism. Both creeds held, too, that suffering was the price man had to pay for the knowledge he extorted from nature—a knowledge that enabled him to employ nature for his own uses. But man was also cursed with another aspect of knowledge—he was the only living creature that knew about his own inevitable end. Naturally, he ignored the when and how of his terminal point, but this uncertainty be-came a cause of constant torment. Man's good deeds were often motivated solely by a desire for an end to suffering after his death. To Kenyatta's understanding, some of the Eastern creeds encour-aged nobler motives. Eastern religions offered the hope that worldly suffering would eventually be extinguished by the purifi-cation of all life—the achievement of the state of nirvana. This idea seemed to appeal to Kenyatta.

In Confucianism, Kenyatta was enthralled by the picture of the Great Family of mankind in which men were brothers and no one turned a hand against his fellow man. Confucius had en-visaged the future world as a community of all men in which rulers would be chosen for ability and wisdom. In that world, mutual trust and peace would prevail.

These beliefs appear to have buoyed his spirits because Kenyatta once told a lawyer who called on him that he felt almost like a Hindu. A European doctor reported after a visit, "He is cheerful, except when he gets depressed because of the heat." And another visitor observed: "He is the man with the most striking personality and charm."

Meanwhile Kenyatta was described in the outside world as a terrorist, the former leader of "criminal thugs" bent on thrust-ing Kenya into a regime of "primitive and debased tribalism." In 1960, the governor of Kenya, who was an enlightened man, de-scribed Kenyatta as "A danger to public security."

Yet to millions in Kenya, this prisoner at Lodwar was a towering personality, the symbol of an emerging nation. He would become the first head of his independent nation, some people said, while others jeered. Kenyatta had spent so much time in jail that an entire generation had grown to manhood without ever having set eyes on him. During his detention, Africa had been overtaken by the "nationalism explosion," which its enemies said had spread like a "rash," a "hysteria," a "forest fire." In spite of the feeling of self-confident supremacy among the white-skinned people in the White Highlands of Kenya, that colony, too, began to feel the change in the political climate. When the time came, it was the leader of the "criminal thugs" who became the first prime minister of a non-colonial Kenya. Jomo Kenyatta's rise from prison to power was unique. Let us look at his unfolding and evaluate him according to our own best lights.

THE WHITE HIGHLANDS

First we must look at Kenyatta's background, particularly that part which unfolded in the White Highlands. Kenyatta was born into the Kikuyu tribe (he says that the correct spelling of this name is "Gikuyu"), and within its strange framework he grew into manhood.

Kenya is unique, British settlers have said, and unique it is indeed, especially its coreland, north and northwest of Nairobi in the direction of Mount Kenya.

An airplane passenger, shaking off drowsiness as the craft prepares to land, might be startled to observe from the window that he has been whisked to the Swiss Alps, for the Kikuyu landscape does remind one of the Alps—of Switzerland, northern Italy, and France. There is a difference, though, in that Mount Kenya is 17,000 feet, higher than the highest Swiss peak. In spite of the fact that Kenya straddles the Equator, her glaciers inch their ponderous way into the sizzling heat.

The green carpeting of this mountain region is similar to that of the Alps. The German name for this picturesque meadow-land is *matten*, the green grass "mats." These fields are verdantly beautiful, exuding that ozone-filled freshness which intoxicates all lovers of high hills. These are the White Highlands of Kenya, an area of some 16,000 square miles—the size of Switzerland—another interesting coincidence.

A dramatic feature of the country is indicated by its name—Kenya. According to one view, Kenya is a Bantu word which means "ostrich," describing thereby the juxtaposition of white glacier and dark rock one finds in the Highlands. Others say the word is derived from *Kilinyaa,* White Mountain.

The dark skin of the tropical African, anthropologists say, is due to his adaptation to the climate. All Kenyans, including the Highlanders, are dark-skinned. Why are their skins not lighter? Perhaps because the tall mountains have been their homes for only centuries and not for geological ages. Furthermore, the Kikuyus have been thoroughly mixed with Africans from both the plains and the bush.

THE FIRE-SPITTING SNAKE

Jomo Kenyatta burst into international fame because of the presence of white-skinned people in the White Highlands in the midst of black Africa. The whites had been there only from the beginning of this century, a much shorter time than had Kenyatta's tribal forebears. The whites had come because of the "fire-spitting snake." Superstitious natives gave that name to the railway built by the British government from the port of Mombasa on the Indian Ocean to Lake Victoria in the African heartland. The rails revealed a new world that had barely been ruffled from the day of creation.

The line had been built across the Highlands, a difficult undertaking in those parts. There the rainfall was adequate, feeding the lushest grass, the climate invigorating, and health conditions good. This news had spread quickly in the white world, and the "grass rush" to the White Highlands had begun.

Colonies often attracted the failures of Britain, men who were unable to adjust themselves to the competitive life of the West. Kenya became a "place in the sun for shady people." In the same vein, men called it: "God's own paradise; and the Devil's own problem." But the Kenya Highlands attracted also enterprising and respectable white men. The white intruders started dislocating the natives.

Most of the natives had used the Highlands for pasturage. But the whites needed the area for farming. Consequently, they started crowding out the native population, reducing the blacks to peonage. Out of a total of 16,000 square miles, they set apart some 12,000 square miles for themselves and it was this area they turned into a white reservation where the natives were out-of-bounds. The White Highlands was overrun by white people, who numbered about 60,000 by the middle of the twentieth century.

Approximately 4,000 white men were to own about a quarter of the arable land of Kenya, while millions of the natives—some eight million today—had to be content with inferior soil, or no land at all. Intruders, the respectable whites felt the need of rationalizing their ruthlessness. And so it came about that they claimed they were carrying the extra load, the white man's burden.

THE KIKUYUS

Today there are about 1,200,000 members in the Kikuyu tribe, and it was to the burning problems of his fellow tribesmen that Kenyatta first addressed himself.

It would be impossible to delineate Kenyatta's career without sketching his tribal background. He thinks he was born at the beginning of this century, while the British believe it was earlier. At any rate, the white influx had not yet started on a large scale, and he was reared according to the ancestral ways. His grandfather, he says, was a *morathi,* a seer and magician, a man of wisdom, who could foretell the future and provide the people with charms.

Kikuyu society was based upon group loyalties that clustered around the family and the clan, members of which were interdependent and were thus expected to provide mutual aid. A democratic society, the government was not in the hands of hereditary chiefs or the nobility. Wisdom came with advancing age, the tribesmen held, and thus the elders ran the tribes.

People were fitted into the tribal scheme so that everybody had his place. This insured a measure of security and peace of mind. The tribal children learned through experience—the best of schools—to adjust themselves to the hazards of life. Upon reaching the proper age, they were initiated into the adults' circle. The ceremonies were ponderously solemn so as to leave a deep impression of their covenanted duties upon the minds of the young people. They had to demonstrate their endurance, too, because the initiation was painful—circumcision, not only for boys but also for the girls. The neophytes had to take their tests with fortitude to be considered worthy of membership in the tribe.

The young men were required to demonstrate their doughtiness as warriors. Jomo Kenyatta recalls that as a young man he was provided only with the tribal weapon of those days—bow and arrow. When the Mountain God failed to bless the land and a shortage of food plagued the country, it was the warriors' task to replenish the tribal larders. They did this by pouncing upon their neighbors, the nomadic Masai tribe, whose ancestors must have come from afar because they spoke a Hamitic language, mainly used along the Mediterranean coast. The Kikuyus were settled agriculturists, except when they were hungry.

Religion played an important part in the Kikuyus' lives. Ngai, the Divider of the Universe, was their chief god; his lofty abode was on Mount Kenya, the Kikuyu Olympus. A practical people, the tribesmen turned to him only when they wanted to ask a favor. The tall trees which symbolized the high mountains that dominated Kikuyu life, were the native shrines. When there was trouble, people attempted to bribe Ngai into complacency by offering him the scent of roasted ram. In turn, the tribesmen expected Ngai to recognize their efforts by sending them rain. There were no tithes to pay because there was no organized clergy.

Ancestors had to be pacified so that they should not feel impelled to leave their ghostly abodes and haunt the surviving kin. The practice of magic, adapted to the countless problems of everyday life, was common among the Kikuyus. There was a magic for love, for hatred, for the fertilization of the soil, for healing, and for purification.

Few taboos surrounded the sexual life of the natives. An African variety of bundling was an established practice and helped to relieve basic desires, while keeping young people "clean" for the solemn act of mating. A social requirement was filled by the establishment and respected institution of polygamy. Since there was a surplus of girls in the tribe, this custom enabled young women to get husbands.

The world of the Kikuyus was peopled with hideous *orogi*, evil persons who practiced witchcraft, masters of black magic and poisoning. The lot of these people was awesome. First, they were formally ostracized by the community, and that itself was tantamount to death. Then they were dragged to a spot that would be declared contaminated, where they were covered with banana leaves. At this point the tribe called upon their kinsfolk to disown them. The relatives then set fire to the leaves. Because of the leaves the victims could not see their executioners and so could not return as ghosts to haunt them. After the horrid death of the black magician, the tribe would arrange festivities.

Special ceremonies attended court procedures. Sacred oaths were employed to ferret out the truth. A goat was brought into court and the litigants were summoned to break the animal's bones, while reciting the oath: "If the property I am claiming is not mine, let my limbs be smashed to smithereens, just like the bones of this goat. If I am claiming more than what is due to me, let my family group be crushed like the bones of this goat."

THE LIFE OF A LONELY BOY

Where was Kamau wa Ngengi born, the future Jomo Kenyatta? He does not know the place any more than he knows the date of his birth. His parents lived in Ichaweri and that may have been his birthplace. His grandfather, the *morathi*, bequeathed his calling to his grandson, Ngengi. He also left him some calabashes, the insignia of his office. At an early age Jomo was orphaned. Is it possible that his grandfather was put out of the way by wrathful tribesmen because he had failed to bring them rain?

It was a primitive world in which Jomo lived. His house was the usual circular hut, the walls made of wood and the roof of straw. The fireplace was in the center, and the sleeping bunk in the rear, where the household animals were kept. The animals had no worse quarters than men.

Each day Jomo drove a small herd to the pasture and then back to the village for the night. When he was hungry he would steal food. He was a skinny child with a winning smile except when he was cross. Then, his temper would explode in a titanic outburst and he would storm from the village and conceal himself in the bush.

He had heard about the big city, Nairobi, where life was exciting and opportunities great. From where did this village lad get his immense ambition? He was different from other boys, and his horizon was not restricted to his hamlet. One day he left his herd, vanished out of sight, and turned up in Nairobi. He offered himself on the overcrowded job market and his winning smile paid off. He got a job as a kitchen helper for which he received his meals and a bunk. His white boss, J. Cooke, called him "John the Chinaman." The young fellow could spin a yarn as if he had been an old China hand.

In Nairobi he contracted a spinal infection. It was a serious ailment and it might have been fatal, but the Nairobi people were able to help the "little Chinaman." He required surgery and it was performed by a European physician. Europeans treated the natives badly, but they did their best to save the young Kikuyu's life. That made an impression upon the boy.

In Nairobi he found himself between two worlds—Africa and Europe. He was too young to draw conclusions from his bi-polar life but he did know that he preferred the ways of the West to those of the bush. Physically, he was in a Western city, but he had to make his way there intellectually, too. The magic of his grandfather's ministrations would have been of no avail. He needed a different type of magic—a European school, where he could learn the skills necessary to get ahead in life. He wanted to leave the House of Bondage.

He decided to enter a school of the Pharaoh, and he gained admittance to the Presbyterian Mission School north of Nairobi, one of East Africa's best schools. Strangely enough, he made his way slowly up the educational ladder. Plodding was not his nature, and so he worked well only in subjects that were of personal interest to him. As part of the school curriculum he also learned handicrafts.

He completed his courses and received a certificate of attendance which opened the door to the atrium of the civilization that both attracted and repelled him. Perhaps he had a precognition of East Africa's need: to be attracted by the West in order to repel it. In Nairobi there was a shortage of young natives to perform minor public chores. Europeans expected better positions from the colony than such inferior jobs. That is how Jomo became an inspector of water supplies in the Public Works Department of Nairobi Municipality, but his heart was not in the work and he performed his chores with indifference.

He wanted to learn from the West but not to be absorbed by it. He no longer wore the skin garment of his fellow tribes-men—although he assumed it again later during his time in England. He had always been possessed by an urge to look different, this unconventional man who sought to adapt himself to the conventions of the West. A beaded belt had distinguished him from others to such an extent that fellow Kikuyus referred to him as *mucibi wa kinyata,* "the belt with the beads," and that is another explanation of the origin of his adopted name.

THE WHITE HOUSE AND THE RED EMPIRE

"Make the world safe for democracy," the call had issued from the White House of Washington during the Great War. These words may have voiced a propaganda slogan, addressed to the Western world, without any thought that the underdeveloped areas might be listening in. But many young people took the words literally, and Jomo Kenyatta was among them. "Oppressed people of the world, turn against your colonial masters!" These words were addressed directly to the colonies, and they were heeded, too. They came from the Kremlin in Moscow.

To many Britishers the Kikuyus did not look like people who would understand those declamations from the White House and the Red Realm. But the Kikuyus were different from the low-landers. Their divinity was perched on a higher mountain peak than that of any other tribe. Their climate was more stimulating than that of the enervated people of the plains. Their thinking was more aggressive and it was attuned to the words that issued from the White House and the Kremlin. Many of the Kikuyus doted on those words.

Some of the Kikuyus shared the opinion that the time had come to begin the process of emancipation. Where did one begin it? Kenyatta believed that it should begin in a hut where there were children and a teacher. There was some education for the natives in the colonies, mostly imparted by the missionaries, but few youngsters participated in that education. Now a group of natives decided to establish the Kikuyu Independent Schools Association. It was a declaration of educational independence. In that association, three years after the end of the Great War, Kenyatta began to play a political role. Still another step was taken in the educational field. The Kikuyus founded the Kenya Teachers College at Githunguri, of which Kenyatta was to become the principal.

The founding of the Kikuyu Central Association led to a further assertion of independence. Its aim was to regain the land from whites. Built into this aspiration was also a political motive, the desire for political self-expression. Thus, gradually, Kenyatta had become a *homo publicus*. He launched the first Kikuyu journal, *Muigwithania,* and was editor-publisher. He visited his tribal brethren and the regions of neighboring tribes, talking to the traditionalists as well as to the new generation interested in new ideas. He was admitted to the councils of the elders. South of the mountains, near Narok, he stayed for a time in the Masai's country, where he learned about their tribal ways.

IN THE LAND OF THE FOE

Kenya contained a sizable group of East Indians, enterprising people who played important roles on the east coast of Africa as traders. There were more Indians in Kenya than Europeans, and they were not happy with their plight. They were being discriminated against, and handicapped on many fronts. In spite of that, their numbers increased. Some of the Indians thought that by aiding the Kikuyu to wrest privileges from the British, they, themselves would benefit. They supported the Central Association of which Kenyatta was the general secretary. Kenyatta testified to the Hilton Young Commission on the land question. His Indian sponsors then aided his travel to Britain to testify further on Kenyan problems and to petition the government for permission to run native schools. He was accompanied on this trip by a prominent Indian attorney, Isher Das.

During his first visit to the West, Kenyatta established contacts in a strange new world. For instance, the League Against Imperialism, a Communist group with its headquarters in London, courted his attention. Thus his interest in the Soviet Union was aroused. He paid a quick visit to Moscow. On his way back he made the acquaintance of several prominent Communists in Berlin. He attended the International Negro Workers' Conference at Hamburg, where he played a modest role. He met a rising star on the Negro firmament, George Padmore, with whom he later worked in a Pan-African group.

Communism offered an arsenal of solutions for colonial problems. The solutions were easy to apply and worked miracles, according to the Communists. Kenyatta seemed to be impressed, but he was realistic enough to know that if a Kenyan was to be useful to his people he must find solutions that would prove acceptable not only to his own people but also to the British. And those were not the Communist panaceas.

He would have liked to tarry in Britain. But how could he support himself? There were occasional jobs for him, but they were too sporadic. He appeared in a film, as a native chief, with his friend Paul Robeson, the American singer and actor. It was called "Sanders of the River," a work by Edgar Wallace, the most successful mystery-story writer in those years. Also he gave lectures, sometimes on highly exotic subjects, as, for instance, the tradition of female circumcision in his native land.

Kenyatta had been away from home for eighteen months, and that, his Indian backers found, was about enough. Short of funds, he returned to Kenya. But the memory of his stay in Britain lingered in his mind.

His native land, Kenya, was a special problem. It had come into existence in a haphazard way, as had many other portions of the British Empire—created in "moments of absent-mindedness."

Kenya's neighbor to the south, Tanganyika, had belonged to Germany and as the result of a mandate, was now part of the British Empire. The British were to train the people of Tanganyika for self-government. To the west lay another British territory, Uganda, a protectorate. It would make sense, Colonial Office bureaucrats in London thought, to merge these three possessions as had been done in South Africa with Transvaal, Orange Free State, and the Cape. This, however, was not done.

In 1931 Kenyatta returned to Britain and stayed there for the next sixteen years. The reason for his visit was to testify before a parliamentary Joint Committee on Closer Union in East Africa. Again a representative of the East Indians accompanied him to London. This time Kenyatta was to testify not merely for the Kikuyus but also for the other tribes. He was now a "representative" of East Africa, a man able to think in terms of the indigenous population and also in terms of the possibilities open to the Crown, a man who straddled the two worlds—the West and Africa.

He was too articulate and politically oriented to suit some of the British who had African interests, and so they thwarted him. On a technicality he was ruled out-of-order to appear before the investigating body. Another body, however, was ready to listen to him and to his Indian escort. Named after its chairman, Sir Morris Carter, it became known as the Carter Commission, and was authorized to inquire into the land problem of the colony. The Africans complained of having been deceived by the whites. Thus the White Highlands had become a live issue. The commission listened to the two Kenyans but did little else. It recommended a few minor reforms in landholding and sanctioned the existing inequity.

The world did not know it then but was to learn later that the year 1931 was a crucial point in British history. Circumstances had forced Britain to devalue her currency and to go off the gold standard. A nation with a devalued, weak currency could not easily play a major role in world affairs. In Ottawa, the Dominions of Britain signed agreements with their mother country turning them into fully independent and sovereign nations. The British Empire was about to be dissolved. In England, a new government headed by Ramsay MacDonald, a Labourite, took the helm.

THE STUDENT AND THE SCHOLAR

The Labour party appealed strongly to Kenyatta. It had the usual party wheel horses, of course, but it also had a group of eager young intellectuals who wanted to know more about the Empire and who became deeply interested in the "new men" of the undeveloped areas. Kenyatta appealed to them. They found that he had a keen mind, a profound knowledge of conditions in his country, and a sense of humor. He was good at the ping-pong game of small talk and also at the fast play of diplomatic tennis. He made friends quickly even in the higher echelons of the Labour party. The fabulous team of scholars Beatrice and Sidney Webb were among his acquaintances.

The British have a strong affinity for the exotic and the eccentric, probably because convention plays an important role in their lives. Kenyatta was welcome even in aristocratic drawing rooms. He soon learned that the more exotic he looked, the more his drawing-room rating soared. On special occasions he donned his tribal skin garment in which he struck a particularly impressive figure. Also, he cultivated the use of an exotic English.

His friends helped him to secure a steady income. Teaching was in his blood; he was given a post on the faculty of a Quaker college in Birmingham. He also found a home in a Quaker household of that city. While teaching he discovered the weak points of his knowledge. Before he could instruct further he would have to learn more, and so he decided to return to London. There he became both a student and a research scholar.

The London School of Economics and Political Science, a part of London University, was a creation of Sidney Webb, and its interests were close to those of the Labour party. In the course of time the school became so closely associated with one of the towering intellects of the party, Harold Laski, that it might well have been named the "Laski School," after that remarkable political scientist. This was unjust to other excellent faculty members whose accomplishments seemed to fade in the dazzling light of the Laski record.

Bright young people from the British colonies in all parts of the world, especially Africa and Asia, were particularly attracted to the London School of Economics. There they found a congenial atmosphere and a spirit of understanding that made them feel at home. A great number of colonials who studied at the school eventually came to play important roles in the history of their countries. One of these was Krishna Menon, who became the No. 2 man of independent India for a long time, ranking right behind Prime Minister Nehru.

Kenyatta matriculated at the London School of Economics. The liberal policy of the school enabled him to work for a graduate degree even though he had no undergraduate diploma; the school authorities had decided that regulations could be waived in the presence of unusual competence. The African International Institute helped the impecunious Kenyan to defray the costs of his education. That institute had been established by the former governor-general of Nigeria, Lord Lugard, one of Britain's great empire-builders.

London University had long been a center of the study of African anthropology and languages. One of the notable scholars in the field, Bronislaw Kasper Malinowski, was professor of anthropology at the university. Although his special field was the sexual life of savages, particularly in Melanesia, he was also learned in the way of other primitive societies. Kenyatta, who had an intense interest in these subjects, became one of Malinowski's disciples, and through him he learned of the Kikuyus' importance in Africa's tribal society.

Here was an important group of people in a significant area, yet next to nothing was known about them. They were important because few tribal societies lived in as close contact with the whites as did the Kikuyus. The whites in their midst looked at their tribal neighbors as if they were people from the moon. Very few whites ever attempted to master a native language, and the remarkable customs of the indigenous people aroused their revulsion more than their curiosity.

Here, then, was a gap in the field of anthropology which should be filled. A study should be made of the Kikuyus' tribal political system, sectarian practices, ideology, and general way of life. The university was fortunate to have Kenyatta, a native Kenyan, bent on scholarly work. Would he undertake to open Kenya's Kikuyu tribal life to the world?

Kenyatta did undertake that task and produced the pioneering volume *Facing Mount Kenya: The Tribal Life of the Gikuyu.* It was the product of a tribesman who was able to look at his own native ways of life with the detachment of an outsider. Lord Hailey, director of the African Research Survey and author of *An African Survey,* which is considered a classic, called Kenyatta's work the best study in its field. Malinowski himself characterized it as instructive, inspiring, entertaining in a variety of ways and for a multitude of readers. "It is one of the first really competent and instructive contributions to African ethnography by a scholar of pure African parentage," Malinowski continued.

Throughout Kenyatta's academic career Malinowski was in touch with him. For several years he had the Kenyan in his discussion class. "He was thus associated in research and discussion," said Malinowski, "in original contribution and extempore critical activity with a number of brilliant, experienced and highly competent young scholars, many of whom had done their own terms of field work, and all of whom had had years of previous academic training. In this group he was able to play an active, indeed, creative part, giving us illuminating sidelights, inspired by the inside knowledge of an African but formulated with the full competence of a trained Western scholar."

Kenyatta's work was thus accorded accolade by leading scholars in the field. Yet, his book was not only the work of an anthropologist. Underlying all its factual statements was an intensely felt personal testimony. In this book he proved conclusively his ability to straddle the West and Africa, the one presumably advanced, and the other backward. Many phases of Occidental life attracted him, else he would not have tarried so long in the West, but in his book Kenyatta revealed a measure of nostalgia for the security that people enjoy within the womb of tradition. In a traditional society, people are in closer communion with the forces of nature; they have their established places in society. On the other hand, the ever changing values of the West leave the people insecure because they do not know whether it is worth preserving values that are cherished today and discarded tomorrow. Thus, they become disturbed and almost schizophrenic.

A PEREGRINATING SCHOLAR

Through his contacts with the London School of Economics Kenyatta obtained an appointment as lecturer in anthropology at the Workers' Educational Association, an organization sponsored by the Labour party. Britain's Trades Union Congress, TUC, was backing the Association. Kenyatta went on the lecture circuit. Mostly, he spoke about his native Kenya and the problems of the indigenous population of Africa. Often he criticized Britain's role on that continent, and his English audiences took his criticism in their stride—mostly. His line of argument was logical enough. Africa contained more wealth than people imagined, not only in natural resources but also in human faculties. The continent had limited purchasing power because it had been exploited. Were it not exploited it would produce higher profits not only for the blacks but also for the whites. Africans could produce more if they were allowed to work for themselves—not for others. Britain could get more out of Africa as a friend than as a master.

Occasionally, he was heckled, which indicated that his audience responded to him. He was lightning-quick at repartee—almost too quick for some stodgy people—and frequently he fended off the sharpest shafts with a joke. "Never did he say more than what he wanted to say," was a typical comment, "and that is an art, you know." Judging from his sophisticated Western platform technique it would have been hard to guess the speaker's tribal background.

The English paradox impressed Kenyatta greatly. There he was in Britain, twisting the lion's tail to his heart's content. "Agitator extraordinary" was one of the nicknames he earned. Had he said that the British Empire was decrepit, senile, and ready for the scrap heap, only the hecklers would have objected. An amused smile would have been the most critical reaction to his words. However, for a similar utterance in his native Kenya he would have been placed behind bars. Freedom of speech, an accepted privilege in Britain, was a serious offense in the colonies. Britain was a sanctuary where the colonials could air their views without restraint.

Kenyatta's horizon was not limited to the welfare of Kenya. A fellow anthropologist, Prince Peter of Denmark, acquainted him with an interesting phase of adult education.

From him, Kenyatta learned about Denmark's *Folkehöjskole*—Folk High School, with the emphasis on "High," beyond the academic, hence national and even spiritual. From the Prince he learned, too, that the purpose of the Folk High School was the realization of the pure national soul by enlightenment of the uneducated mass. This enlightenment included purification of the language through the elimination of foreign elements. Originally, the movement had served to consolidate the agricultural revolution; in recent times, it has been directed primarily to the sick souls of *la dolce vita*.

In London, Kenyatta also became concerned with the freedom of all Africa. Italy had annexed Ethiopia (Abyssinia). This aroused not only many Africans but also a great number of Europeans who felt that Italy's dictator had attempted to set the clock back. Africa was to move toward greater freedom, not to a higher degree of colonization. In Britain there was support for the International African Friends of Abyssinia Society, of which Kenyatta became the secretary. Among his fellow workers were other distinguished Negroes, including John Payne, the actor, and Dr. Joseph Doakye Danqah, of the Gold Coast, who was to make his name in that colony.

The Society sought to raise the alarm over this resurgence of imperialism, which it considered another aspect of the struggle between light and darkness and in which the light-faced Fascists represented darkness and the black-faced Africans the hosts of light. The Fascists' creed that brute strength outweighed moral values would make many converts, the Society believed, unless decent people raised their voices in vigorous protest.

The Soviet Union intrigued Kenyatta, as it did other colonials. His first visit had been very short and during a particularly difficult period in the history of that country. What did Russia look like now, in the late thirties? To many people she seemed to be the champion of the common man, fighting off the Fascists who represented the eternal attempt of the old to hold the new at bay. He had to see "new Russia." On this visit Kenyatta continued to cultivate the acquaintance of the noted American Negro singer, Paul Robeson. It is believed—although it cannot be confirmed— that in Moscow Kenyatta took courses in Marxism-Leninism, as interpreted, naturally, by the Soviet strong man, Stalin.

Apparently the Soviets made no special attempt to win Kenyatta over. The Kremlin was deeply concerned by the tidal wave of fascism that was threatening the continent. Fascism proclaimed the day of the Military Man. Soviet Russia undertook to line up the non-Fascist parties against the Fascist danger. These were the days of the Popular Front—all forces opposed to the extreme right must be united. Kenyatta was critical of the British whom the Soviets were wooing now.

From Russia Kenyatta, friendly to the Communists but not a Communist himself, returned to London and to his Labour friends. Apparently, he could not tear himself away from England. He was attracted by the white man's life, by the many educational advantages, by the opportunities he had to popularize the cause of Kenya. He had a strong desire to visit his native land, but the cost of the trip was high. Meanwhile, the international horizon continued to darken. The madman in the German Chancellery decided to probe the weaknesses of the democracies. War broke out and Kenyatta was forced to remain in Egland.

"JUMBO" AND ROMANCE

Friends helped him to get out of London where the Blitz had demolished whatever chances he may have had to make a living. Again it was mainly the people in the Labour party who gave him a helping hand. They found a place for him at Storrington, a village in Sussex, about forty miles from London. There he led the diversified life of a teacher, a farmer, a cook, and of a Romeo.

To his new neighbors Kenyatta became known as "Jumbo," and he entered into the spirit of the small town. Being an outgoing jolly good fellow, his neighbors took a liking to him. "His eyes were usually alight with laughter," a local woman recalled, "rather than afire with zeal during those years of the war." Jumbo was one of those fellows whose leg could be pulled. In return, he gave as much as he got, and people liked this game.

Jumbo got along well with London refugees from the Blitz, sophisticated people speaking the language of high-class Englishmen. He was as well educated as any of them, and his knowledge of English literature was broad. The late composer, Sir Arnold Bax, another wartime resident of Storrington, became Kenyatta's close friend. One of Kenyatta's favorite poets was Rudyard Kipling, the bard of British colonialism, and Jumbo liked to recite his poems to Bax. Also he liked to recite from the writings of Hilaire Belloc and from Shakespeare's *Othello,* which seems to have been his favorite play.

Storrington was small, but the tasks that confronted Kenyatta were large. He had to make a living and carry on his self-education. When things began to quiet down he continued on the Workers' Educational Association circuit. However, to fulfill the immediate needs of the British people was more important than to disseminate information about Africa. Food was what Britain needed above all, as the enemy's submarines sought to isolate the country from its sources of supply. There was a shortage of farm hands and so Jumbo began his food-producing career as a hired helper on a farm. It was one of those old-fashioned patches of land which were vestiges of old England—a non-mechanized farm. Working in a tomato house was his next assignment. For his own needs he raised vegetables and cooked his own food, the neighbors spread the word that Jumbo was a "superb" chef.

Earlier in London, he had met Edna Grace Clarke, a fellow teacher on the Association circuit. Now since she worked as a governess near Storrington, the African farmer-scholar and the English teacher-governess had occasion to see each other. The difference in color of the skin was no obstacle to either of them. She was a gentle creature, quietly handsome. He was irresistible; when he turned on his charm, she responded. Were the Storrington farmers surprised to hear that Grace and Jumbo got married? Their inbred English habit of not showing surprise made it easier to accept the newlyweds. The wedding took place in the midst of the war. The year was 1943.

They had no money, but Kenyatta could work, and he made a living, although he was poorly paid. Then the child came, a boy. A few of the neighbors thought that Kenyatta's true feelings would be revealed by the name he would bestow upon his offspring. But he did not even consider such a tribal name as "Burning Spear." The boy was named Peter, the rock upon which the Christian Church had been built.

THE END AND THE BEGINNING

The war was over, at last. What would the peace mean to Kenyatta's Kenya, to all Africa, to all the underdeveloped countries of the world, to the majority of mankind in the new one world? The victorious powers had pledged themselves in the Atlantic Charter: "They [the Allies] respect the right of all peoples to choose the form of government under which they wish to live."

What was the form of government under which Africans, for instance, wished to live? Under the government of white people? One fact the war had demonstrated beyond any doubt: the color of the skin was a sign neither of superiority nor of inferiority. In record-breaking time the yellow-skinned Japanese had swept the white-skinned Europeans out of their lairs. The weakness of white colonialism had been exposed. The Soviets now proclaimed the expected "liberation" of the "oppressed peoples."

Above all, it would no longer be necessary for Negroes to apologize for the color of their skin. The number of the colored people—yellow or black—in this world was far greater than that of the whites. Sophisticated Negroes began to speak of the brotherhood of the people of color, of the "African personality," of négritude. Were they to move eventually toward a color discrimination against the whites? "Blackism," "black power," "black Zionism," said the extremists among the whites.

Kenyatta, too, heard the call of Pan-Africanism. The economically backward natives of the continent would progress more rapidly if their forces were united. So he took part in the process of integration. It had to be *in partibus infidelium,* in Great Britain, the center of African awakening. There he found fellow fighters, including the Gold Coast's Kwame Nkrumah, and the doughty George Padmore. In the latter's words Pan-Africanism "rejected both white racialism and black chauvinism. It stood for racial coexistence on the basis of absolute equality and respect for the human personality." In England he took a prominent part in founding the Pan-African Federation, which aimed at coordinating the political activities of the various African Negro organizations. He became the Federation's first president.

The first congress of the Federation was opened by the Lord Mayor of Manchester in 1945, the miraculous year of liberation and dreams. "We affirm the right of the colonial peoples," the Declaration of the Congress stated, "to control their own destinies. All colonies must be free from foreign imperialist control."

And this was proclaimed in the country exercising the greatest "foreign imperialist control." Kenyatta's contribution to the debate was subdued. Many years of resistance in Britain had schooled him to beware of overstatement. Extremes and pyrotechnics were not to be evident in his remarks. He approved the final declaration of the meeting, which called for action but not violence, for socialism but not communism. In the same year he published a pamphlet, "Kenya—Land of Conflict," in which he ventured some second thoughts and was less reticent. Revolution might be necessary in his homeland, he wrote, if the white settlers failed to heed the lesson of the times.

RETURN TO THE HOMELAND

The time had come now for Kenyatta to make the decision which Nkrumah, too, was facing. Should he stay in Britain, which he enjoyed and where he felt at home, or should he return to his country and fight Britain from there. In England he would have worked for Kenya's freedom as a propagandist and a free man. In

Kenya he would face arrest and jail for similar activity. Yet Kenya needed him. Who else could launch the freedom campaign? He needed all his energies for his work and yet wanted also to keep his wife and child out of trouble. As Kenyatta returned to Africa he left behind his wife, Edna Grace Clarke, and his son, Peter. (Years later the son became a student at King's College, Cambridge.) Kenyatta would provide for his family as well as he could from Kenya. It was in 1946 that he returned to his homeland after an absence of sixteen years.

Organization was the magic cure for social ills. Kenyatta was convinced of that, and therefore, he brought into existence the Kenya African Union—KAU—of which he became the president. The Kikuyus formed the nucleus of the Union, but it was not a one-tribe organization. Kenyatta obtained much of his support from the Luo and from other tribes. He was a spellbinder; he attracted as many as 30,000 people to his public lectures. What did it matter if most of the tribesmen did not understand his language? More powerful than the language of the tongue was that of the heart.

The fate of Kenya lay in the hands of Britain, but there was now a Labour government in London, several members of which he had heard speak at the London School of Economics. These men were Fabian socialists, as Kenyatta himself appeared to be at the time. They all believed that the forces of history followed their own laws and that—in the long run—gradualness was inevitable. But people must not be held back from keeping up with history's gradualness. In the case of Africa that meant that the native population should be trained for self-government. The first step for Kenya should be the establishment of a legislative council. The details were to be worked out. Democracy should rule the council—no stratification of the tribes but a representation of all the major ethnic groups. This sounded good to Kenyatta and his audiences. How would it sound to his Labour friends in London? It did not sound good to them at all. Power seemed to have had a strange influence on the liberal Labourites.

Naturally they had to take into account the power-parallelogram which Kenyatta seemed to have overlooked. The government of Britain was powerful, but it was located in London. On the other hand, the white estate-owners were in Kenya. What could the parliament of the motherland do in the face of the opposition of a small lobby in Nairobi? Send troops to crush the settlers?

There is every reason to assume that Kenyatta continued to believe in the propagation of his ideas by non-violent means. But that was not the view of some of the Kikuyus. Mwene-Nyaga, the god on top of Mount Kenya, was theirs and not the white man's, and the usurpers' encroachment made him shroud himself in wrathful silence. It was his people's mission to oust the infamous poachers. The white man's cattle were waxing fat; the Mountain God's sacrificial animals were growing lean. For the defense of the tribal divinity, secret organizations began to thrive on the mountain slopes. One was the *Dini ya Msambwa* (Religion of the Spirits), another the *Watu wa Mungu* (People of God). They all took the pledge to oust the white man from the mountain "mats." Nothing was gradual in their approach or their intention.

Jomo Kenyatta was forced to increase his demands on the white men, but he refused to follow his followers to the brink. Now he insisted that Africans should be represented according to their numbers, and not by their economic importance. Thus democracy would prevail. The Africans should also strive for the benefits of better housing, better health standards, and better sanitation, from which would ensue an increase in the black man's life span. Irrespective of the pigmentation of his skin, a man's work was worth his wages and therefore let there be no differentials in wage. Full ownership rights should be restored to those who had been defrauded of their ancestral heritage, and so let there be a land reform.

THEN CAME THE MAU MAU

So quiet were the Kikuyus until then that only specialists took note of them. Under the title of "Kikuyu," the *Encyclopaedia Britannica* had merely this to say: "A Presbyterian mission station north of Nairobi, Kenya colony, in eastern Africa. The Kikuyu reserve is the habitation of the Kikuyu, one of Kenya's principal tribes. It is a forest region which is subjected to cultivation by the natives" (1947 edition).

Suddenly, in 1947, the word "Kikuyus" blazed forth on the front pages of the newspapers. It was in that year that the world began to hear about the Mau Mau, a name which denoted a hideous, bloodthirsty, and sadistic terrorist organization. Its members were known as Mau Maus.

Much is still unknown about the Mau Mau. Its very name

is subject to diverse interpretations. Some say that it is a distortion of the word *uma,* meaning "Go Home." Others say that it means *muma*—"oath," a word in the Swahili language, the *lingua franca* of East Africa. It may have been composed of the reversed initials of the Union of Africa Movement. A more fantastic interpretation refers to weird initiation rites at which cats may have been disemboweled—"miaow." Then there is the inevitable Kikuyu Princess, daughter of Muumbi, legendary founder of the tribe. Finally, the word may actually mean nothing.

But the substance of the organization meant a lot to the British and the white settlers. Said Britain's colonial secretary, Olyver Lyttelton: "It is an unholy union of dark and ancient superstitions, with an apparatus of modern gangsterism." "Nostalgia for barbarism" was another designation.

There were also those, mainly Africans, who thought it was a variant of "uninformed nationalism," referring to those Africans who believed that to carry influence in the power relations of a power-mad world required the exercise of terror. Some of the Kikuyu leaders must have been aware of recent applications of this principle. They may have recalled the way the Irish had gained their freedom. Think of the Phoenix Park gunmen! And Israel? Think of the Irgun and the Stern Gang! In India, too, violence exploded at the time of the partition, even though it had been headed off temporarily. Violence it was that finally forced the Dutch out of the Indonesian archipelago. And so on.

The Mau Mau fitted into the occult Kikuyu tribal ways— the initiation ceremonies and the awful oaths. Midnight was the time of the initiation, and the ceremony was impressive. The neophytes passed through an arch of twigs and leaves. Circlets of grass were placed on their heads and around their necks, while loops were placed on their wrists. A slaughtered goat's warm blood was poured into banana leaves mixed with handfuls of earth. Each person, holding a stick, dipped it into the mixture as the oath was taken. The blood and earth mixture was then passed around the neophytes' heads seven times. There was magic in that number. Sometimes the initiated took seven sips of the blood, bit into a piece of the meat seven times or circled around the sacrificial object seven times. Occasionally the goat's eyes, removed from their sockets, were placed on either side of the receptacle for blood and earth, or the intestines of the sacrificial animal had to be tasted. The nocturnal darkness was relieved by a shaft of dim light from a torch. The neophytes had to pay an initiation fee of three pounds, a large amount.

The authentic text of the oath was never revealed. It was from memory that a turncoat Mau Mau quoted it to a British court: "If I am asked to deliver the head of a European and I refuse, the oath will kill me. If I am summoned any time during the night and I refuse to go, the oath will kill me. If I reveal any Mau Mau secrets, this oath will kill me. If I see anyone stealing European property I will not tell of it. Instead, I will assist him to hide it. If I refuse the oath will kill me. If the members agree to do a thing, whether good or bad, and I refuse to obey, this oath will kill me."

Mau Mau drumhead courts-martial were held to punish traitors. One such trial was described by a suspected terrorist to a British court. In imitation of the wigs worn by English judges, the Mau Mau "judge" wore a white cap. Occasionally these judges managed to lay their hands on authentic judicial robes which they then wore. Among the paraphernalia of the court was a rhinoceros whip to carry out sentences of flogging.

To get the British out of the Highlands was the Mau Maus' aim, and terror was their weapon. Head of the terroristic "army" was "Field Marshal Sir" Dedan Kimathi, who also dubbed himself the "Popular Prime Minister of South Africa" and the "King of Africa." He seems to have been one of those eccentrics who join exotic movements in order to work off their obsessions while cloaked in the mantle of the respectability of public-spirited causes. He was denounced as a sadistic murderer whose forest gangs perpetrated uncounted atrocities.

The Mau Mau armory included not only modern weapons but also primitive tribal instruments of murder and torture, such as the *simi,* a double-edged short sword shaped like a scythe, the *rungu,* a nail-studded wooden club, and the *panga,* a heavy knife. Victims of a *panga* murder were sometimes sliced into small pieces. All members of a murder detachment were obliged to participate in the assassination so that all should be guilty, if detected, and none should be able to "sing." The dead person's eyes were frequently removed so that his ghost should be unable to identify the killers. Most of the Mau Maus' victims were fellow Africans.

On October 22, 1952, Kenyatta and five other leaders of the KAU were detained and charged with "managing" the Mau Mau movement. In other words, they were accused of being the wirepullers, the "intellectual accomplices." It was then that terrorism erupted in full fury.

The British took counter-measures—in most cases, counter-terror. No money or time was wasted on legal trimmings. Suspected Mau Mau gangs captured in the forests were hanged on the spot. The British required the natives to tell on their neighbors or else. . . . They also devised their own loyalist oath for the natives: "If I have never taken a Mau Mau oath I will never take one, or let this oath kill me. If I am forced to take it, I'll report and confess to the authorities, or let this oath kill me. . . . I am and always will be a loyal subject of Her Most Gracious Majesty, Queen Elizabeth."

THE TRIAL AND THE OUTCOME

Kenyatta and his co-defendants had to stand trial in Kapenguria, a small place outside of the Kikuyu country, north of Mount Kenya, instead of in the colonial capital, Nairobi. The choice of the trial location handicapped the defense. It had no railway or any other adequate form of transportation; documents and the requisite law books were hard to come by. The population of that area was the Nilo-Hamitic tribe of Suks. They did not belong to the Kikuyus, and were assumed to be totally indifferent to Kenyatta's fate.

The defense was headed by a British barrister, assisted by lawyers from Nigeria, India, and the West Indies.

The choice of the English counsel was not very fortunate. He was Denis Nowell Pritt, holder of the Lenin International Peace Prize, author of such publications as *Russia is for Peace,* and *The State Department and the Cold War,* in which he sought to show that the United States favored war. Whether or not he was a Communist was beside the point. He conveyed the impression that Kenyatta placed his trust in Communists.

The case was tried by an all-white jury. The prosecution produced two witnesses who claimed that they had been present at an oath ceremony over which Kenyatta himself presided. The defense charged that one of the witnesses was known as a compulsive liar and that the other, too, was a perjurer. It was for the application of the ideals of Britain that Kenyatta, not a Mau Mau member, was fighting, his defense contended. In his political struggle he never used anything but legal means. He repeated the substance of his political creed: "True democracy has no color distinction, and it does not choose between black and white. . . . We are not worried that other races are here with us in our country, but we insist that we are the leaders here, and what we want we insist we get."

As to the substance of the criminal charge: "He who calls me Mau Mau is untruthful. I do not know this thing Mau Mau. . . . KAU [of which he had been president since 1947] is not a fighting union that uses fists and arms. We hold to the old saying that he who is hit with a *rungu* returns, but he who is hit with justice never comes back."

Kenyatta's backers claimed that the White Highlanders' public relations was responsible for pulling off one of the most fantastic propaganda jobs in recent years—creating the image of a murderer out of the ingredients of a character which combined scholarship with benignity. Even well-informed people were under the impression that Kenyatta himself was a Mau Mau gangster.

On April 8, 1953, Kenyatta was sentenced to seven years' imprisonment. Then his calvary in Lokitaung began. Three years later an African policeman in the service of the colonial authorities captured the Mau Mau "Field Marshal" who was then executed. The campaign of terror was terminated. The figures were compiled. How many people had participated in the campaigns? What were the casualties?

British Colonial Secretary Alan Lennox-Boyd estimated that the number of active Mau Maus was never more than eight thousand at any given time. Others guessed that the campaign was conducted only by a few hundred people. The Mau Mau killed about 2,000 people, mostly fellow Africans, "traitors." Fewer than a hundred whites were killed, and this number included members of the security police. The official figure of the Mau Mau dead was 11,503, and more than 60,000 suspected members had been jailed. The contradiction between these figures and the British estimate of active Mau Mau members has never been dispelled.

Sir George Erskine, the British commander-in-chief of this Kenya campaign, diagnosed the ailment. "There is no military answer to the Mau Mau," he said. "It is purely a political problem of how Europeans, Africans, and Asians can live in harmony."

The British now worked out a plan to open the 12,000 square miles of White Highlands to native settlement and agreed to underwrite $49 million of the cost. Native farmers were to be taught to improve their soil.

Kenyatta, even in jail, remained the *bête noire* of the British authorities. The colonial secretary described him as the "African leader of darkness and death." The Archbishop of Canterbury used his case as an illustration of obscurantism. KAU, now headed by Walter Odede, was outlawed.

Meanwhile, Africa awakened from its slumber and the Dark Continent was illuminated by the new dawn. Even for the die-hard White Highlanders of Kenya it became impossible to halt the onrush of events. New African generations began to appear on the political scene. Educated in the West in the spirit of the West, they wanted to see their countries freed. Twenty-six year old Tom Mboya, general secretary of the Kenya Federation of Labor and founder of the People's Convention Party, appeared as a representative of the "new African," conscious of his rights and ready to work for their realization.

The British could no longer resist the pressure to open the Kenya legislative council to Africans. The Africans elected to the council launched a major campaign in 1958 to have Kenyatta released. Public clamor in his favor continued. He had nearly served his full sentence anyway, and, finally, the British government was persuaded to release him from prison. But he was to be kept in enforced residence in Lodwar. The year was 1959.

London was host to the Kenya Constitutional Conference in January, 1960, and the continued detention of Kenyatta became the major issue there. Three months later the Kenya African National Union, KANU, was formed to take the place of the outlawed KAU. Kenyatta was elected president of the new organization.

The days of the colonial regime were numbered. Everywhere in the area new African countries were in the making. British Africa could not be 90 per cent free and 10 per cent enslaved.

The British decided now to speed up the transfer of power to Africans. The voting rolls were enlarged, and seats in the legislature were appointed by race: a certain number each for Africans, Europeans, Indians, and Arabs. Elections were held on February 28, 1961. The Kenya African National Union won the majority of the African seats, nineteen, against twelve for the Kenya African Democratic Union, headed by Ronald Ngala. "Freedom and Kenyatta" was the battle cry of both parties.

About this time Kenyatta was transferred from Lodwar to Maralal, closer to Nairobi and, therefore, to politics. The restrictions on him were relaxed and he was allowed to have a press conference. He had been under detention since 1953. Was the world to see an elderly man broken by long detention? On April 11, the "new" Kenyatta was revealed to the world. The *Times* of London, which had treated Kenyatta as an outlaw, wrote about him on this occasion:

"For three hours he faced questions from more than fifty journalists with a sharpness and agility that many Western politicians might envy, dispelling once and for all the illusion that he is an old man who wants nothing better than to spend his last years in peace."

In that interview Kenyatta declared himself against all violence, including that of the Mau Mau. A "pack of lies" he called the reports that sought to link him to terror. In the Kenya of the future, he declared, there would be a place for Europeans alongside the non-whites.

Kenya wanted Kenyatta, of that there could be no doubt. From Maralal he was transferred again, this time to Kiambu, still closer to Nairobi. Would the next transfer be to the capital of the Crown Colony and would he become a free man there?

The agitation for his release was continued not only by KANU, his party, but also by KADU, his opposition. The British saw that no further progress could be made in Kenya if Kenyatta were not free. They released him on August 21. After all those years he once again faced his people. At a vast public meeting in Nairobi, 30,000 Africans gave Kenyatta a delirious welcome and thundered their approval when the vice-president of KANU called him a "second god."

He may have been that to his people, but not to the British, who kept him from holding public office. "Kenyatta and Kenya," the agitation continued. Before the year was over the British passed a law that came to be known as *Lex Kenyatta,* which opened the doors of the Nairobi Legislative Council to him. A seat was found for Kenyatta at Fort Hall, in his beloved Kenya mountains, and in January, 1962, he was returned to the legislature. A month later the Kenya Constitutional Convention met in London to decide on the principles of the new Constitution. In April a transitional coalition government was set up to prepare the way for full independence. Both Kenyatta and his political rival, Ngala, became ministers of state. Sir Patrick Renison, the governor, was the head of the administration.

Full independence was not now far distant; the agitation for it continued relentlessly. The Kenyans' aspirations were expressed in a Swahili word—*uhuru*, "freedom." It was what *freedom* meant to Ghana, *merdeka* to Indonesia, *indépendence* to the former African colonies of France. Political meetings began and ended with it, and were peppered with it. *Uhuru* became the pass-key to all locks, the solution of all problems, the magic word.

UHURU

Brilliant young people were the *uhuru* salesmen. The pug-nosed, boyish looking ex-Oxford scholar, Tom Mboya, was outstanding among them. "He has the most fabulous retentive memory," one of his professors had said. He formed sentences so perfectly rounded that they cried out for the printer's ink, and he could ooze charm from all pores. He knew how to obtain quick results; he had become the trade-union boss of Kenya at the age of twenty-five. But his opponents scoffed: "A glib fellow. Give him a bowler hat and an umbrella, and what have you got? A black-skinned Britisher." Spreading the gospel of *uhuru,* combined with his own fame, Mboya criss-crossed Asia, Africa, and the United States. He appeared to be the St. Paul of the triumphant new creed.

Spreading the new gospel with him was Joseph A. Z. Murumbi, a man of eccentric ethnic mixture, part Masai and part East-Indian from Goa (then a Portuguese enclave on the subcontinent). British schools in India provided him with his Western education. A hybrid Britisher, he had served as an official in Somalia. A political tactician, he also considered himself an expert in foreign affairs. An intellectual, he was proud of his library of several thousand books.

Then there was that other political operator and headline-smasher, Oginga Odinga, an older man, who would stand on his head to catch public attention. Some people said that his earthy humor made a greater impression on Kenyan tribesmen than Mboya's Oxford-nourished intellectualism. But, then, intellectuals are convenient targets of criticism everywhere.

All in all, this was a strong team of impetuous men who had trained themselves for competitive work toward their mutual goal: freedom. Were they preparing the political ground for themselves? Definitely, they were; and many others besides them aspired to the highest position to be had in a free Kenya. And what about the "god," Kenyatta? Were they ready to shunt him aside? Yes, they were; but not after Kenyatta emerged from his imprisonment. When he appeared among his people, Mboya, Odinga, Murumbi, and all the others fell back, forming a line behind the people's choice.

Two more steps were to be taken yet before Kenya would be declared independent: general elections were to be held, followed by a probationary period during which an African government would rule with British guidance—and then full independence.

Before the general elections could be held the two main parties, KANU and KADU, had to agree on the Constitution. The main difference between the two parties was expressed in their designation: KANU stressed the "national," KADU the "democratic," meaning regional. Kenyatta held that the new country would gain strength through unity. His opponent, Ngala, head of KADU, maintained that Kenya could not be centralized because the regions of the country were too different in their ethnic structure, ecologies, mores and folkways. Kenyatta feared the centrifugal tendencies inherent in a tribal structure. Kenya, he believed, could not afford to be fragmented into a cluster of miniature states, each of which followed its own tribal ways: should there be decentralization, a central government could not even be formed. It was best for the country if the ministers were chosen for their ability, and not on the ground of their tribal affiliation. In a decentralized country would the Masai, for instance, accept a Kikuyu as the national government head? What about the Turkana people in the northern Rift Valley, and the Luo in the Lake Victoria country, and Taita tribesmen, in the hills, the Samburus, a pugnacious breed, around Lake Rudolf, and the Giriama, near Mombasa? And what about all the forty-eight major tribes the British had counted? Kenyatta wanted not only freedom but also *uhuru na umoya*, "freedom and unity."

Finally, a compromise was formulated. Kenya was not to become a group of states under a weak federal government that was charged only with the conduct of defense and foreign affairs. It was to consist of seven regions, the jurisdictions of which extended to local matters, such as health, education, and the roads. The federal government would have final authority in cases of disagreement. These were the regions: Nyanza, Rift Valley, Coastal, Central, Eastern, Western, and Northeastern.

The general elections were held from May 18 until May 26, 1963. They lasted nine days because access to the polling places in the gashed Rift Valley, in the hills, and on the dusty plains was difficult. Then the returns were counted. Kenyatta's KANU won the absolute majority, sixty-four seats in the House of Representatives, against the forty that had been gained by KADU in coalition with the APP, African People's Party.

Baba wa Taifa, ecstatic Kenyans hailed Kenyatta—"Father of the Nation." Five times in succession his women admirers uttered the *Ngemi,* the trilling sound of triumph with which mothers announce the birth of a male child, and also a cry of triumph to proclaim the arrival of a man of destiny. No greater honor could be conferred on a man.

Thus the solemn day arrived on which Malcolm McDonald, representing Her Majesty's Government, transmitted the seal of office to the ex-convict, His Excellency Kenyatta, the Prime Minister of Kenya, the same man whom a previous governor of the colony had denounced as an "agent of darkness and death."

The government Prime Minister Kenyatta set up consisted of KANU members. It included young Mboya, as Minister of Justice, and Oginga Odinga, Minister of Home Affairs. Further conferences took place in London to iron out the wrinkles in the Constitution and to strengthen the fabric of the State. By the end of 1963 the British were persuaded that the time had come for Kenya to gain full independence.

UHURU DAY

Kikuyu tribesmen were gathering around their sacred fig tree. Seventy years before, the tribe's legendary prophet, Mugo Kiburi, had foretold that the tree would fall on independence day. And, indeed, tribesmen from the rugged mountains reported that the tree was near collapse, for it had been struck by lightning as if in divine support of Kiburi's prophecy.

Eighty delegations converged on Nairobi from all parts of the world. That of the United States, headed by G. Mennen Williams, Assistant Secretary of State for African Affairs, included a galaxy of stars—Walter Reuther, the labor leader; James Baldwin, author of best-sellers; Sidney Poitier, the actor; and Harry Belafonte, the singer.

The Queen of Britain was represented by the Duke of

Edinburgh, her husband. The roster of three hundred honored guests included the barrister, D. N. Pritt, who had defended Kenyatta in 1953. It included also "Field Marshal" Mwariama and a number of other former Mau Mau "Generals," wearing their khaki uniforms and caps. More than five thousand prisoners were released, including 1,500 members of the Mau Mau, terrorists in another day, freedom fighters now.

It was midnight, December 11, 1963. A quarter of a million people filled the vast Uhuru Stadium of Nairobi, which covers 940,000 square yards near the edge of one of Kenya's famed game parks. Blazing floodlights turned the night into midday. The British flag was fluttering in the nocturnal breeze. Then, suddenly, the lights were switched off and the world was plunged into darkness. The night composed itself for a few seconds, then the lights were switched on to reveal that the Union Jack had been lowered for the last time after sixty-eight years of British rule. It had been replaced by the national flag of Kenya, black, red, and green. The band struck up the national anthem of the youngest of all countries: *Mungu Nguvu Yetu,* "O God, Our Strength." At that moment "political power in Kenya," reported the New York *Times* correspondent in Nairobi, "slipped from the grasp of its 55,759 whites and was taken up by its 8,365,942 Africans."

On that day, the ex-convict became *Waziri Mkuu wa Kruanza wa Kenya* (The First Great Minister of Kenya). And he told his people, "I have snatched you out of the lion's belly."

Kenya became the thirty-fifth African territory to gain independence. She became the hundred-and-thirteenth member of the United Nations a few days later. Also Kenya became the eighteenth member of the British Commonwealth. In spite of the fact that Kenyatta had been the prisoner of the British for about nine years, he concluded a military agreement with them under which the United Kingdom was to retain 4,500 troops in the country for eighteen months. Now the British were protectors; not oppressors.

KENYATTA AND HARAMBEE

Kenyatta had his office in the Ministry of Public Works for the time being. Lights were burning there late into the twilight hours. His home was at Gatundu, some thirty miles north of Nairobi. It was surrounded by a farm of fourteen acres. In that house he lived with the latest of his four wives, a young Kikuyu girl, Ngina, "as shy as a dove." He had many children now. The youngest, Mohoho, was born in 1964.

Kenyatta, the statesman, had little time for dallying at home. He knew the problems *uhuru* entailed. He was familiar with the Equatorial climate, the enervation it caused and the sluggishness it induced. Many of his countrymen believed that freedom was synonymous with the Golden Age—free land, free food, and lots of time for play.

Kenyatta launched a campaign of education to make his people realize that better housing, better food, and more schools were not gifts from the gods on top of Mount Kenya, but that they were the products of hard work. So he told his people that *uhuru* was not a magic chant and that he could help them only if they helped themselves. He thrust the challenge upon his people in the form of another Swahili word: *Harambee*—Let's get going!

There was much work to be done. Three of four Kenyans still lived in the most primitive mud huts, and only 7 per cent of the people had full-time paying jobs. There were only three practicing lawyers in a country the size of Texas. There was a scarcity of schools and teachers and of hospitals and physicians. And Kenyans spoke thirty-six different languages.

To make *harambee* a reality he needed loans. His studies at the London School of Economics stood him in good stead. He conducted negotiations for loans from a dozen different sources. He had a Six-Year Development Program drawn up as a "crash measure." Some of its objectives were the equitable redistribution of much of the country's arable land, the tripling of the farm output, and the placing of every child into school. The program was to cost $280 million. Of this amount some $77 million was needed to settle 50,000 to 75,000 African families by 1970. The financing came from Britain, the British Commonwealth Development Corporation, the International Bank for Reconstruction and Development, and West Germany. The assistance program of the United States was started with $21 million in funds and technical aid. About a million acres of the White Highlands were to be reserved for Africans.

This brought up the question of the minorities. Kenya had a conglomerate of non-Africans, including 176,000 Asians of Indian, Pakistani, and Goan descent, who were shopkeepers, carpenters, mechanics, etc., as well as 34,000 Arabs, whose ancestors had moved into East Africa centuries before, and 66,000 Europeans, the so-called whites.

The whites, we have seen, had formed the "master race." They called the African men "boys," even though they were grandfathers. In turn, they expected Africans to call them *bwanas,* "masters." Under the British regime the whites had certain rights as, for instance, the monopoly to raise coffee. They were the owners of the lushest lands. And this is what Kenyatta said to them and to the other non-Africans: "We are all human beings and we all make mistakes. And we can all forgive. That is what we need to learn in Kenya. Where I have harmed you, I ask forgiveness. We must put the past behind us." Then he told them: "We want you to stay and cooperate to make Kenya great. We must trust each other."

At the same time, he sounded also a sterner note: "Anyone who still wants to be called *bwana* should pack up and go, while others, who are prepared to live under our flag, are invited to stay."

Prime Minister Kenyatta gave to the whites of the new nation two years to decide whether they wanted to become citizens of Kenya. Unless they chose citizenship they would be permitted to stay only as aliens, with fewer rights. But he appointed a white man, Bruce Mackenzie, his Minister of Lands, and charged him with the task of dividing the freed land among African farmers. "The success of Mr. Mackenzie's efforts," according to the New York *Times,* "will determine whether the Britons who have farmed Kenya's productive coffee, sugar, and cotton plantations will remain or will continue to pack and leave."

What about the Africans? Former Mau Maus and others had learned to batten on poor and rich alike. Some of them had remained in the bush, criminals posing as patriots. "Kenya is free now," Kenyatta said, "and there is no need to hide or fight." Parcels of land might be theirs and they were assured an amnesty. Out of their hiding places came the tribesmen, their hair plastered with red mud, the Mau Maus' fighting badge. But more came out than had gone in before the declaration of independence, for some of the Kikuyus of independent Kenya vanished into the bush, only to reappear immediately as claimants of land and their people's gratitude. Most of these alleged freedom fighters claimed they were field marshals or at least generals. Not one private was found among them.

Although it was too early yet to know, it appeared that the precedent created by the Mau Maus might survive. Some of the Kenyans found Kenyatta not sufficiently dynamic, not a son of the revolution about which they had dreamt. Reports began to reach the outside world about a new terrorist group exacting terrible oaths from its members. *Kamau Maithori* was the name of the society, which gave the impression that it was a Mau Mau offshoot. Did it represent an incipient danger or was it one of those fringe groups which arise in the wake of great transformations? The world has yet to learn.

A disgruntled group of soldiers rose in arms against the Kenyatta government early in 1964. Similar uprisings occurred also in the neighboring countries of Tanganyika and Uganda. Armed units of the former rulers, the British, were called in. The rebellions appeared to be mere brush-fires. Were there to be more of them or were they only the symptoms of the "teething ailments" of infant nations? Then there were the restless Somali tribesmen in the northeastern part of Kenya. They demanded union with neighboring Somalia.

Could these new countries in East Africa prosper? The British had set up an East African Common Services Administration, which provided for the joint control of the post, telegraph, railways, and harbors of Kenya, Tanganyika, Zanzibar, and Uganda. It cut costs, increased efficiency, and worked reasonably well. Would it work under *uhuru?* Would the re-introduction of joint controls appeal to the leaders of the other countries, to self-willed Julius Nyerere of Tanganyika, to lone-wolf Apollo Milton Obote of Uganda, and others?

Would it be a good idea to go a long step further and establish a political federation? Tanganyika and Zanzibar provided a model in that part of Africa. What would the people of these countries say about this plan? Would they like to have their newly acquired nationalism diluted in a federation with neighbors when they found it hard to reconcile the conflicting interests among their own tribes? There were so many urgent problems and so little time in which to find the solutions. Kenyans and other Africans had not wanted freedom merely to have their own flags and national anthems. *Uhuru* to the Kenyans meant more of the good things of life. Kenyatta had to step lively.

THUS SPAKE ZARATHUSTRA

Kenyatta had descended from the mountains, like Zarathustra, with the message: "Human beings are entitled to humane treatment . . . even though one's epidermis is dark, since the words,

'All men were created equal,' did not refer merely to the lighter hue."

To his people, Kenyatta appeared to be cloaked in the raiment of the Prophet. While they could not speak to him during his years of isolation, their pulses raced when they heard his name. "Educated" people may derive their loyalties from the headlines, but simple people are capable of abiding loyalties.

Kenyatta's case was different from those of others who had come *de profundis* and ascended to the peak. Even though jail was their fate, too, theirs was an honorable lot because they were political prisoners. Kenyatta had been charged with being the mastermind of a terrorist gang; he had been tried for being an accomplice in murder. Abhorred by decent people, he was a "criminal," and "bestial" was the term the whites applied to his deeds.

Longer than any of the other men mentioned in these pages he lived with his shame. He survived the ordeal, and emerged from his imprisonment unbroken, more self-confident in himself, and more radiant in his people's eyes. And this after years of detention in the leper house. And lo, the leper was glorified in the pure air of the mountain peaks; the heralds carried his fame to all parts of the globe.

The other graduates of jail, his fraternity brothers, were strong men. He was older than they, and much stronger, too. Kenyatta was stronger because he had lived with a shame for so long, a shame that became his pride. He was stronger because he remained loyal to his convictions. He had years in which to meditate upon his fate and to think about the White Highlands which he was not allowed to see.

Had he been a weaker man he would have conceived the deepest hatred for the white masters who confined him to Inferno. There was no such hatred in his heart because he knew that weaklings alone gave way to hate. He was strong and that is why, as Prime Minister of Kenya, he took his nation into the British Commonwealth.

Kenyatta lived among the British for many years. He admired the democracy they practiced at home, but he detested the autocracy they exercised abroad. However, he noticed that they were uneasy about their double standard. His belief in the basic honesty of the British was kept alive, and he came to admire their best qualities.

If Kenyatta was not to be pulverized by fate he had to remain an optimist. And he kept on being one even when his expectations of a change in his fortune appeared to be impossible. Above all, he had to believe in his own star, the one that guides the men of destiny. There was that sign on his forehead, too, the sign of charisma, the sign of the man who dares to risk his fate on a throw of the dice, because he knows that he is right, and is confident that he will win.

Invested with the seal of his high authority, Kenyatta surveyed his past and had reason to be content with what he saw. At the peak of his career, he looked at the Promised Land. This new Zarathustra—like the *Übermensch* of Nietzsche, the Superior Man—proclaimed the dawn of a new age. He proclaimed the Age of Man, where all men were to be equal at birth.

Kenyatta was determined to make the practice fit the theory. What was the use of being created equal if the expectancy of life was so different? Yes, *uhuru* meant more food, better dwellings, and longer life.

The Prime Minister of Kenya was familiar with the felicitous phrase of the "revolution of rising expectations." He knew, too, that the rising expectation was no longer sufficient in this fast-moving age. People no longer have the patience to wait for the slow maturation of their hopes. Today the world wants to be on the threshold of fulfilled expectations. What will be Jomo Kenyatta's role in seeing these expectations fulfilled? The answering of this question is bound to be the greatest test of Prime Minister Kenyatta and of the other famed statesmen who have made their way from the jail to the peak.

4

The Man From Tunisia: Habib Bourguiba

Nature is kind to Tunisia. The country has no harsh extremes, except its Saharan south. The Mediterranean enfolds it in its embrace, as it curves southward, past the towns of Sousse, Sfax, and Gabès. This is not the land of heaven's angry moods—no tornadoes, hurricanes, volcanoes, or earthquakes.

How does human energy respond to nature's caresses? North Africa may have been the abode of Homer's *lotophagi,* "lotus-eaters." In such a climate man may only want to sit in the sun, and intoxicate himself by inhaling the air. Yet, this had also been the home of the "Anglo-Saxons" of antiquity, the Carthaginians, who had fairly burst with energy.

And who are the people of this land today? They are an ethnic hodgepodge, as people are everywhere, but here perhaps even more so because of the sun, the sea, the caressing climate, the location, and history. The people of today are the descendants of the conquerors and the conquered of many centuries. The Romans called them barbarians because they were ignorant of "civilized" speech, which to the Romans meant Latin and Greek. The barbarians became "Berbers," a people that shared with old Egypt a basic Hamitic tongue. To Americans these people came to be known as the natives of "Barbary." Tunisia at the time we are talking about was a French protectorate.

Avenue de France was the name of one of the thoroughfares of its capital, Tunis; it was intersected by the Avenue de Paris. "France" and "Paris" represented both a boast and a feeling of nostalgia in this North African metropolis. The nostalgia was the reason that the terrace cafés were frequented by so many of the French officers and government people who reveled in the salty air wafted inland from the sea. Under the multicolored parasols the Frenchmen may have been thinking about the surly climate of their Normandy and Picardy, thus being torn by a conflict between their homesickness and their apprehension that they would have to leave the African sky as soon as their tour of duty was over. It may have been because of these emotions that they were imbibing habit-forming doses of apéritifs.

An affluent-looking Moslem occasionally entered the terrace, placed his heavy frame on the wicker chair, and made an awkward attempt to imitate the Frenchmen's nonchalance. He failed to notice that when he was served, the normally submissive smile of the waiter of the Café de la Régence appeared to be less servile.

The streets of the urban junction were crowded with the diversity of North Africa, a dramatic juxtaposition of two worlds, the one somnolent, and the other one wide-awake, the East and the West. Veiled women floated by, trying to make themselves invisible as they proceeded to the nearby department store, Bon Marché. Panting asthmatically, the porters, *hamar,* were carrying loads heavy enough for small carts. Bleary-eyed drivers, urging their apathetic donkeys to move faster, were moving toward the *souks,* the bazaars. The tributary streets were lined with trees which peered down at garden plots that were partially hidden behind gold-tipped grilles; the flustered leaves of the trees curtsied to exotic plants that did not conceal their haughty belief that they were gorgeous. The purifying rays of the sun washed the stones of the walls with the hue of gold-tinted snow. The colors were immaculate: the purest gold, the purest snow, reflecting the pure azure of the celestial canopy.

A well-dressed European finished his drink at the café on this spring morning, then, walking slowly, he headed for the military jail. That grim building stood close to the intersection of the Avenue de Paris and the Avenue de France. A guard eyed him closely from behind the slit of the *lucarne* of the heavily framed gate. The European identified himself: he was a member of the French Chamber of Deputies, and he had the official permit to visit a prisoner. He was a well-known *homme de politique,* one of the luminaries of the legislative body in Paris. He was Gastone

Bergery, deputy of Seine-et-Oise, later to become the French ambassador to the Soviets and to Turkey. He was a prominent attorney, and an advocate of a more liberal policy toward the overseas protectorates and possessions of France.

INFERNO IN PARADISO

As much as life outside the jail appeared to be the reflection of Paradiso, so the interior mirrored Inferno. How could anything be so dismal in this luminous Mediterranean world? Ascending a spiraling wrought-iron staircase, encrusted with slippery filth, the Parisian deputy nearly lost his balance. He held his breath; the air of the jail reeked with a disinfectant that was losing its battle with the smell of the latrines. The pale corridor-walls were mottled with fungus patches. As the deputy progressed toward the center of the building, heavy gates opened and closed with a clangor that seemed to shake the world.

The prisoner whom the noted Parisian was about to see was a Tunisian attorney, and a Moslem political figure, Habib Bourguiba. In his mid-thirties, Bourguiba seemed much older here in the deep shadows of the jail. Those who had known him would have remembered him as an impressive figure, although of short stature. He had a Roman emperor's profile, and his pale eyes used to pierce his interlocutor with an imperious gaze. Particularly the strongly chiseled nose invested him with that haughty air, and the heavy-set jaws bespoke determined will power. Serious when at work, young Bourguiba had always been ready for fun. But now the visiting deputy could barely conceal his shock. Before him stood a *clochard,* a "bum," heavily bearded, hair disheveled, his skin scarred—the result, no doubt, of nocturnal bouts with vermin. Could this man be the elegant Habib Bourguiba, the conscience of awakening Tunisia? The year was 1938, a landmark in human history, a year of the horsemen of the Apocalypse who were riding mankind toward the doom of World War II.

A FRIEND OF FRANCE

Bourguiba had been the head of the Tunisian political organization, *Neo-Destour,* "New Constitution." The summary of his program was brief: "We love France so much that we want to be her

friends and partners. We are no longer children—to be protected."
Then he supported his argument: "Under this arrangement, not
only France but we also will be better off. The best arrangements
benefit people all around."

The French *dirigeants* in Paris and Tunis challenged this
view. The Tunisians lacked the ability, so Paris said, to govern
themselves. An independent Tunisia would need a veritable armory of human skills and a treasure-trove of funds, both of which
it lacked. The universe of the French pivoted on the order then
prevailing and it appeared to be inconceivable that it should be
changed. Bourguiba's ideas were subversive, therefore his proper
place was behind bars.

Bourguiba's ideas did make sense, Deputy Bergery thought.
The Tunisian politician was familiar with the problems of his
native land, and France would benefit by having him at the helm.
In a rapidly changing world, the values of which were exposed to
a constant barrage of questioning, the Tunisian protectorate arrangement could not last for long. Tunisia was Paradiso for the
wealthy Europeans, *colons,* but for the majority of the people,
disease-ridden, illiterate, and poor, it was Inferno. It did make
sense to Deputy Bergery that commensurate with the increase of
Tunisia's welfare, the prosperity of France would also wax.

Although as a result of this visit Bourguiba was not freed,
the French deputy's call upon him in the jail did not pass unno-
ticed. Before then Bourguiba had been merely one of the *sales
métêques*—"dirty foreigners"—to the French prison guards. Now
it seemed that he was a man of some importance. Several bespoke
his intervention after his liberation—for a promotion or a better
post. Buoyed by the upsurge of his prestige, the prisoner assured
his guards that he would give favorable consideration to their requests. For the time being, he was assigned to a less noisome cell.

HIS COUNTRY AND ITS PEOPLE

For centuries Tunisia had developed impressively, and then again,
for long periods, it had declined shatteringly. Tunis had been the
site of Carthage, then the "Africa" of Rome; then the abode of
the Vandals, and finally, the Arabs' midway house. Later it became the vortex of chaos, lorded over by anarchistic governments
headed by piratical gangsters. Toward the end of the nineteenth

century, France took over control of Tunisia as a protectorate.

Although purged of its autocratic power, the reigning family, presumably of Cretan origin, was retained. The title of the nominal sovereign was "Bey." He had an "army" of his own, a band of musicians. He also had a cavalry unit to serve as his escort at parades. His "artillery" had one cannon with a booming voice which used to usher in the Moslem holidays and announced the coronation of a new Bey. There were real Tunisian army units, too, but these were commanded by the French. The sovereign's only duty was to sign the decrees which the French issued in his name. If he could not write, so much the better. Then his signature was scrawled by a French scribe. But the Bey's official title was *possesseur du royaume de Tunisie.*

The Arabs engulfed this region in the early Middle Ages, depositing their creed—Islam—their Arab way of life, and hosts of problems. They were the only conquerors in this much-conquered area that were able to knead the inhabitants of the North African littoral into their own likeness. The Berbers were Islamized and the differences between them and the Arabs became slurred. All but a tiny fragment of the inhabitants of the Tunisia of today speak Arabic. In years to come, independent Tunisia was to join the Arab League.

About 90 per cent of the Tunisians were Moslems before World War II. At that time, the country had a population of 2,500,000. Fewer than 10 per cent were Europeans, and they were mainly French and Italian. (By 1964 the population explosion had boosted the total figure to about 3,500,000).

Islam means "submission," and that was related to Allah's will. Waves of conquerors sweeping across North Africa exacted submission to their own wills, too. The last of the conquerors were the French, coming late in the nineteenth century, and they were a European breed that did not follow the Prophet's precept to submit to a higher will. The French conquerors knew only submitters. The Tunisians were to submit to the will of the French Third Republic, as were their neighbors to the west, the Moslems of Algeria and Morocco. These three countries formed "The Farthest West"—Maghreb, the Land of the Setting Sun. The world ended there because it was the farthest outpost of Islam. Beyond that there was the darkness of the sea and of unenlightened non-Moslems.

One of the Tunisians who at first submitted to the will of the French was Habib Bourguiba. From them he learned to worship the new god—the nation—while paying lip service to Allah.

THE BOY WHOSE NAME WAS HABIB

"Habib" means "The Beloved One" in the Arabic tongue. It was in Monastir, one of the Mediterranean picture-book towns, that Tunisia's Simon Bolivar—the freedom-fighter hero—was born. The year was 1903. Monastir is not actually situated on the edge of the sea, and for good reason although no lovelier sea could be fancied. But the Mediterranean attracted seaborne gangsters preying on maritime trade, and the pirates of yore were also in the habit of raiding the larders of the coastal towns. Many of these were therefore built inland a short distance from the dangerous sea. To make it even more secure, Monastir was surrounded by sturdy walls with embattlements and towers from which sentries could look out for the landing of pirates.

The real name of this child from Monastir was Habib Ben Ali Abu ar Rgaybah (the short-necked one). It was Gallicized into Bourguiba, and the change of the name was significant. He was a child of a Moslem family that had turned its face toward the West. Habib was the last of eight children of a petty officer in the French army stationed in the Tunisian protectorate. His father, Ali, also had some landholdings, and he was an ambitious man. Only people of his ilk made common cause with the French. Habib seems to have inherited his father's drive.

A petty officer's income was meager. Father Ali knew that Habib was not the type of boy who could spend his time and life in a *souk* hammering at tin plates. Nor did Ali relish the thought of seeing his son serving as a "native" in a Tunisian regiment. In order to smooth Habib's way to a richer life, Father Ali had to help him win a *certificat d'étude* from a recognized French school. He had to sell some of the olive trees of the family. It was at the age of five that Habib was sent to school in Tunis, and he lived there in his eldest brother's house. It was there that he acquired his primary and secondary school education.

Sadiki College, named after a former ruler, was his secondary school, a "biracial" institution, partly Moslem and partly European, where the language of instruction was French. It trained many of Tunisia's future civil servants. He was there when the Great War broke out, and even a teen-ager could perceive that life then was not a bed of roses in the flower-bowered Tunisian villas.

There was a shortage of food and clothing. Habib developed a primary infection in his lungs. He was convalescent for two years in the mountain town of Le Kef, the Sicca Veneria of the Romans. There he acquired the habit of reading endlessly—a habit to which he returned many times in his life, and especially during his numerous stays in jail.

One of the books made a very deep impression on the teen-ager, opening up entirely new vistas in his thinking and, eventually, launching him on his unique career. The title of the book was *La Tunisie Martyre*, written by Sheik Thaalbi (sometimes transliterated from the Arabic as "Thaalibi"). Habib had assumed that heavenly forces ordained man's fate, and that was in accord with his creed. Part of the eternal scheme appeared to be the rule of the French in Tunisia. The country had a ruler of its own, to be sure, but he was merely a puppet, "protected" by the French. Hence the name: Tunisian Protectorate.

Thaalbi's book convinced him that the Tunisian scheme of things was neither eternal nor in the people's interest. On the contrary, the French were in his country to protect their own interests at the expense of the local population. They were not only the rulers of the country but also the owners of its natural resources on the ground, underground, and in the adjacent seas, as well as the owners of the banks, the commercial establishments, and of the few industries Tunisia possessed. Tunisia was martyred by France.

Sheik Thaalbi followed up his *Martyred Tunisia* with an appeal to the native population and with the organization of what he hoped would become a mass party. He founded a newspaper, *As Sawab* ("The Correct Line"), which set forth a program of action for the future. In place of the subordination of the native Tunisians to the Europeans, coexistence between the French and the Tunisians should be established, a process of mutual intellectual and professional fertilization.

The foundation of the new order, as Sheik Thaalbi envisaged it, was a Constitution. And so he founded the *Destour*, "Constitution," movement, which was to work for the realization of his ideals. With the aid of the French as partners, the Tunisians were to be given a chance to arrange their own lives according to their own best lights.

After his recovery, young Bourguiba entered the Lycée Carnot of Tunis, a French school to which came Europeans, Frenchmen, Italians, and Jews. The competition at school was especially keen. Bourguiba saw this as a challenge. He wanted to convince the Europeans that a Tunisian was in no way inferior to them.

During his days at the Lycée, Bourguiba fell under the influence of two of his teachers and of a dissolute genius. A mathematics teacher, a M. Perrachon, became one of his idols, proving to him that working even with the most abstruse mathematical problems could be made exciting. The other teacher was a M. Picard who taught him to turn his thoughts to an understanding of man's mental processes. The combination of mathematics and philosophy would enable him to see problems in the clear light of logic, unencumbered by the misty atmosphere of inherited traditions and sentimental attachments.

The dissolute genius whom Habib worshiped was republican Turkey's post-World War I founder, Mustafa Kemal, whom his people were to call Atatürk, Father of the Turks. There had been an Ottoman Empire, center of the Moslem world, ruled by a Turkish dynasty, a Leviathan in looks, but a jellyfish in substance. The Great War smashed the Ottoman Empire, which was then dismembered and its fragments picked up by a large number of succession states, haters of the Turks. Kemal aroused the Turks to resistance against their despoilers. The heart of the former empire, inhabited by the Turks themselves, was all he wanted to salvage. He did not care about the vast peripheries, inhabited by Armenians, Arabs, and Greeks. He did save the heartland of the Turks.

Then he started a massive movement of political education, for he had come to power amidst a fantastically backward Oriental despotism, sunk into the miasma of indolence and fatalism. He shook that country awake, presenting it with a set of new values, energizing its limp body, and turning it into a model of political, social, and economic rejuvenation. Never had the Middle East seen anything like that. If Turkey could change her ways so drastically why could not other Moslem countries do likewise? Habib Bourguiba had daydreams of his becoming the Father of the Tunisians. These thoughts came to him when he was barely more than a boy. His ambitions were limitless. But the limitations imposed by the French on the potentialities of a Tunisian "native" were great. Could he remove some of those limitations by acquiring not only a fund of knowledge but also the self-confident ways of life of the rulers of his native land? Yes, Tunisia was a martyred country but he did not hate the French. On the contrary, he admired them. They were strong and self-confident. But they did not know the "right line."

LA VILLE LUMIERE

He finished his studies at the Lycée but he wanted to continue his education. In Tunis there was only a Moslem university. Attached to the Great Mosque, its program was religious. Bourguiba was eager for a secular education, and a Western education at that. Especially in his studies, his French was now better than his Arabic; Arab technical terms were little known to him. There was only one place where he wanted to make his intellectual home— *la ville lumière,* "the city of light," Paris. One of his brothers, Mahmoud, helped him to continue his studies in the very center of Paris, his universe.

Ecole Libre des Sciences Politiques of the University of Paris became his alma mater. He was greedy for knowledge, and so he studied philosophy, psychology, literature, and—for good measure and for the sake of a career—the law. He would become an attorney.

As so many other young people of his generation in the underdeveloped parts of the world, he was attracted to Marxism. French politics was in constant turmoil then—government followed government—*cartel des gauches,* "left-wing groups" such as the Socialists and Communists, played their spectacular roles. Bourguiba, who attended many evening sessions of the Chamber of Deputies, was intoxicated by the poetic flow of French oratory. He had the impression that there were almost as many political parties in Paris as there were deputies. The Communists attracted him, as they did many of his contemporaries, for they had a ready remedy for every social ill. He was particularly attracted to their simple solution of the colonial problems—*debout les damnés de la terre,* "arise the damned of the earth," meant the colonial slaves, too. He sat in the audience at many Communist meetings in the building of the Mutualité, but he never was drawn to join the party. This was only one of several political periods in his life.

Public finance interested him greatly, and at school he covered himself with laurels in that subject. In those days he could not have foreseen that he would one day be able to turn the knowledge he thus acquired to his advantage.

He was galvanized by the theatrical and social life of Paris. He loved the theater, perhaps because it encouraged his day-dreams—he could identify himself with those on the stage, and he pictured himself surrounded by admirers. He could nearly always get free tickets to the French national theaters, the Odéon and Comédie Française. He liked the former even better than the latter, because it was situated on the Left Bank of Paris, not far from his quarters, and also had an open-air library. Between the acts he could rush off to browse among exciting books. He had learned to absorb information at a prodigious speed.

He had a room in the Hotel St. Séverin, on the sixth floor. That it was a walk-up did not matter. It was next to the Place St. Michel, and that did matter very much. The very center of Parisian student life was the legendary "Boul' Mich." Around the corner was the Montparnasse, the center of Bohemia's bubbling life in the mid-twenties. Not a religious Moslem himself, young Bourguiba liked to experiment with apéritifs—whenever he found a Croesus to invite him—on the terraces of de Café de la Coupole. He also liked to frequent the *boîtes* of the Parisian golden youth. He became a thoroughbred Parisian, shrugging his shoulders in the French way, spitting out words, as if in anger. Where was his home: in Tunis or in Paris? A popular couplet sung by the darling of the Parisian music halls of those days, Josephine Baker, provided the answer: *J'ai deux amours, mon pays et Paris.* And, indeed, he had those two loves, his own country and the city of light.

Girls were attracted to him and he to them. His virile looks, his rapid-fire conversation, his sparkling personality were appealing to feminine acquaintances. Moslem girls did not frequent Montparnasse cafés—hardly any. But he felt quite at home in the company of French girls. That is how he met Mathilde Lorrain, the French girl who was to become his wife. He was still a student when she had a son, to whom they gave a name that was not French at all. The newborn baby was named Habib Kemal. Beloved he was to his parents, to be sure, and they anticipated the realization of his middle name too, Kemal—"Perfection"—after his hero, Atatürk.

RETURN TO THE HOMELAND

Bourguiba was the kind of young man who would have liked to keep on studying in France. Now twenty-four years old, married, and the head of a family, he had to make a living. He could have acquired the qualifications of an attorney. But the competition would have been keen: Frenchmen did not often go to a Tunisian with their litigations. He could not have made a living with the court cases of Arabs in the national capital. Most of the Arabs there were Algerians, anyway, who preferred to entrust their litigations to attorneys of their own kind. Also, most of the Arabs in France were poor devils, itinerant peddlers, poorly paid unskilled factory workers, and miners. What little money they made they remitted to their penurious families in Africa.

The only alternative for the Bourguibas was to go to Tunis—home to him and a new country to his wife, Mathilda. At home his chances of having a law office of his own were better. Also, he was still very much interested in politics, for which his stay in Paris had whetted his appetite. Sheik Thaalbi, the founder of *Destour,* was fading out of the picture, unable to keep step with modern life. Soon he was left far behind, vanishing into political obscurity. Tunisia needed a political movement, *Destour* or something else. Bourguiba felt his muscles bulging, a task was to be performed, a gap to be filled. He had not only the training but also the ambition.

August 23, 1927, was the day on which the Bourguibas—Habib the elder, Mathilda, and Habib junior—were to leave Paris. It was a difficult day to leave the French capital. How were they to take their belongings to the railway station? The taxis were on strike in protest against the execution of two men across the Atlantic, in the United States of America, in the city of Boston. For years France and much of the rest of the world had been aroused by a criminal case involving two American anarchists of Italian birth. The taxi drivers protested against the scheduled electrocution of the two men on that day. They had been convicted of a common crime, but many people believed that their political beliefs were the cause of their electrocution. The two men, Nicola

Sacco and Bartolomeo Vanzetti, were executed at the appointed hour, in spite of all the strikes and protests. Somehow the Bourguibas managed to reach the railway station and, eventually, Marseilles, where they took boat for Tunisia.

Back in his homeland, Bourguiba settled down. It was in line with native custom that his wife vanished out of sight, neither heard nor seen. He was a man of parts, versed in many fields. But he had no job, perhaps because he was "overqualified" in the midst of the underqualified people who held the good positions. Although a product of French education and an admirer of the spirit of France, he could not hold his own against the Europeans who had social advantages over the native sons.

He found employment at last as apprentice to Maitre Citrier, a French attorney; his task was to prepare summaries of court judgments. He had to work ten hours a day, Saturdays included, and he was provided with only a scratchy pen for his penmanship. Salary: six hundred francs a month, the equivalent of twenty-four dollars. His heart could not be in such chores, and he proved a poor apprentice. After a few months he was sacked.

The law partners, Maitres Pietra and Samama, hired him next. This job, too, was poorly paid, but this time Bourguiba dared to stipulate that he must have the right to accept certain cases for his own account. These were the cases of the poor *fellahin,* the peasants, who could not afford to pay the fees charged by established attorneys. However, this position did not last long either.

Finally, Bourguiba was enabled by a kin to open a small office of his own. It was situated at 158 rue Bab Souika in a Jewish section in a northern suburb. The majority of his clients were poor Jews who admired his French eloquence and low fees. At last he could eke out a modest living.

THE ARCHEOS AND THE NEOS

Habib Bourguiba continued to be interested in politics. The closer he looked at the Tunisian problem the more clearly he saw that colonialism was the foe. At the same time, he realized that an underdeveloped country like Tunisia needed the support of a stronger power. He favored France, the one country that was familiar with Tunisia's problems and whose civilization he liked. He had learned at the University of Paris—and through his attendance at left-wing meetings—that the economic foundations of colonialism were weak. The mother country could derive benefit only from being a real mother, and not a stepmother. He knew that in this day and age it was the wages that created the purchasing power of the large masses of people and not merely funds spent by the employer for the cost of production. Hence, the more adequate the wages, the greater the purchasing power and, ultimately, the profits. France had failed to maximize her potentialities in her dependencies by keeping the wages abnormally low. Also, the psychological impact of this policy was harmful. France applied a system of double standards; she was not faithful to her own liberal traditions. North of the Mediterranean, on mainland France, was the land of freedom and of light, while south of it lay the land of oppression and of darkness. France's own interest demanded that this distinction should be removed.

Among the seminal books Bourguiba had read was Julien Benda's famous treatise, *La Trahison des Clercs,* "The Treason of the Intellectuals." In Tunisia, too, it was true. Tunisia's small band of intellectuals had failed to assert their influence. They seemed to be happy by being unhappy; they were a lot of complainers, not creators. They appeared to be afraid that by working for the increase of the knowledge of the masses they would see their own monopolistic position and profits wiped out. It was the *Destour* that gave the intellectuals their Wailing Wall, that permitted them to bemoan the sterility of the colonial administration while failing to take notice of their own barrenness. "Unproductive," impatient young Tunisians complained when speaking of *Destour.* They referred to them contemptuously as *archéos,* "primitives," and referred to themselves as the "moderns," *néos.* The *archéos* moved slowly, cautiously, hampered by vested interests, represented by the "old turbans," reactionary landowners, mired in the past. Bourguiba and the other *néos,* on the other hand, wanted to provide the movement with a broader base. The people meant to them not only those who talked glibly about politics but also the simple peasants, *fellahin,* who were trying to see the interests of their own families within the context of an emerging Tunisian nationalism.

The importance of the press for the dissemination of political ideas had impressed Bourguiba in France. There every political shading had its organ. *Sawt At-Tunisi (La Voix Tunisien)* was the only political organ of the native majority of the protectorate, and Bourguiba started working for it in 1930. It had an angel, a wealthy landowner, Chedly Khairallah, upon whom Bourguiba prevailed to turn the weekly into a daily newspaper. There he would comment upon the political events of the day. It was in the column of that newspaper that "Bourguibism" first emerged.

Bourguibism took issue with the two then prevailing points of view. One of them said that France had a mission in Tunisia, a *mission civilisatrice*. She had the investment capital and the technical knowledge which the Moslem Tunisians lacked as yet. The supporters of this view held that it was going to take time before North Africa could catch up with the most advanced nations of Europe. Meanwhile, it was in Tunisia's interest to be able to fall back upon the resources of France. At the same time, it was in the interest of France to help the native population get the most out of its economic potential.

The upholders of the opposite view maintained that the only mission of France was to get out of Tunisia. It was in the very nature of colonialism to exact much from the native population and give back little. As long as France was the "protector," the economic life of the country was bound to languish. Once the French were gone the urgent needs of the country would serve as stimulants for the creation of a modern state.

Bourguibism took the stand that Tunisia needed the French as much as the French needed Tunisia. It believed in the peaceful coexistence of the *ci-devant* dependencies and their European masters.

La Voix Tunisien was an organ of the *Destour* and not even a large dose of Bourguibism could rejuvenate it. "Angels" were acceptable to Bourguiba as long as they kept in the background, but he did not want them to meddle with politics. He left the paper, and in November, 1932, he founded a new journal of opinion, to which he gave the name *L'Action Tunisienne,* "Tunisian Action." Gone were the days when he was satisfied merely with letting the Voice of Tunisia be heard. Now the time had come for deeds. He still adhered to his view of integration. "The Tunisia we mean to free will not be for Christians, or Moslems, or Jews," he wrote. "It will be a Tunisia for all of them without distinction of religion or race who wish to have it as their country and live in it under the protection of its laws."

These were noble ideals and Bourguiba meant no harm to anybody—not even to the 90 per cent of the population, the Moslems. But the French thought otherwise; the very idea that Christians, Moslems, and Jews should be of equal standing appeared to be subversive.

The top French official in the protectorate was Marcel Peyrouton, the Resident-General. He was a man of strong democratic leanings and of liberal views. But how could his personal views prevail against the demands of his official position? His position required that he should safeguard the interests of the people of power, the 10 per cent, against the 90 per cent. As a liberal he realized that Bourguibism made good sense, and would be of great benefit for France—in the future. But he lived in the present. And he also realized that as the people at the bottom, the Moslems, rose in the scale, the people at the other end of the scale would be lowered. Eventually they would reach a balance, and that the *colons*, the influential residents, did not want. In other words, Bourguibism might subvert the established order; Bourguibism was subversive. Criticism in native newspapers was repugnant to the protectorate authorities. On May 31, 1933, publication of Bourguiba's newspaper was suspended by the French.

THE CALL TO ARMS

"Divide and Rule" had been the policy of the Romans in that part of Africa over which M. Peyrouton now ruled. The Resident-General decided to split up the *Destour*. He was successful at first, but very unsuccessful in the long run. The *archéos* and the *néos* could be encouraged in their differences until, according to the plans of the Residency, the *Destour* would shatter in a storm of controversies. This might have happened if it had not been for Habib Bourguiba, who had learned from the French how to deal advantageously with policies that were based upon emotional manipulations instead of on the logic of events.

The time was the early spring of 1934. France was surrounded by Fascist or right-wing countries: Hitler in Germany, Mussolini in Italy, and a right-wing government in Spain (soon to be engulfed in civil war). Tunisia had to be ready for any contingency. The Resident-General had torpedoed the old *Destour*, and thereby he, inadvertently, forced the militant youth to create a more dynamic organization.

The executive committee of the *Destour* met on March 2, 1934, in the village of Ksar Hellal, in the district of Sousse, a lovely silk and olive oil producing center near the Mediterranean. Little publicity was given the meeting, in which an historic split occurred. The young militants bade the tired *Destour* good-bye and formed their own organization, *Neo-Destour*. After that the *Vieux-Destour*, as it came to be known, waged a losing fight and languished, while *Neo-Destour*, on the other hand, began a spectacular ascent. *Neo-Destour* was the political movement of the provincial petty bourgeoisie—hoping to reach the peasants, too— against the passive nationalism of the people of the bazaars and of the urban professionals. The chairmanship was assumed by a Dr. Materi, who was little more than a figurehead. The secretary-general was Habib Bourguiba, and he was a dynamo.

This was viewed as a declaration of war by the French in the Residency and by the influential, self-assured *colons*. Particularly vocal against the *Neo-Destour* were the local Europeans of Italian descent. Living under a French regime they felt it their duty to distinguish themselves as pro-protectorate, "more Papal than the Pope." Get rid of *les meneurs*, they said. If it were not for propagandists the *fellahin* would lead happy lives.

Bourguiba happened to be in Monastir, his hometown, when the authorities found him and placed him under arrest. He was shipped into the Sahara region, in the southern-most portion of Tunisia, a place called Bordj-Lebeuf, where there were neither railways nor adequate roads. In this suffocatingly hot place he was detained *pour se rafraichir*, "to cool off."

He lived in a tent, which seemed to be ablaze during the heat of the summer days. Then the desert played its tricks at night, and the temperature slid to the freezing point. Also, he suffered acutely from attacks of dysentery. Between bouts of ill-health, he managed to have letters smuggled out of the tent. He continued to behave like a political leader even in that tent.

Inadvertently, his jailers performed a notable service for their detainee. Despite his periodic intestinal troubles, his health, on the whole, improved; the dry desert air strengthened his lungs.

THE POPULAR FRONT

Bourguiba spent twenty months in this Saharan camp. These were endless months of endless humiliation and yet, also, of never-ending hope. Sometimes it seemed to him as if the French authorities wished to put him to death by exposing him to the merciless elements. At other times, he thought he saw some new hope in a French government which had suddenly emerged, but the government would usually submerge before anything could be done. He himself could not give up hope altogether.

On June 4, 1936, a Socialist government was formed in France. Headed by Leon Blum, an intellectual aristocrat and a political democrat, this was a new kind of government, the Popular Front, in which all the political groups, except the extreme right, were to be represented. The Communists, too, were included in the government. "No enemies to the left," was the motto of the Popular Front. The enemy was fascism in whose deification of war and of the warlike nation the Popular Front saw an imminent and grim danger. Across the Rhine, German youth was chanting: "Today the nation belongs to us and tomorrow the entire world."

The Popular Front professed belief in a liberal policy toward the colonies, reaffirming the eternal validity of the Declaration of the Rights of Man. Because men were created equal, all men were to be treated as equal. Such enlightened views had been forcefully expressed in the front-page editorials of the Socialist daily, *Le Populaire,* from the pen of Leon Blum himself. One of the first acts of his government was to order the release of Bourguiba from his blazing hell.

That was an auspicious beginning. But would the Popular Front government heed the words of Bourguiba about the new relationship of Tunisia and France? He asked for the "replacement of the despotic regime by a constitutional one permitting the people to participate in power." The prospects looked bright.

Leon Blum's views could not have been more enlightened, but, though he was the premier of France, he was still the prisoner of the conditions prescribed for him by the presumed power of the forces at work in the world. Soon the enlightened West and the Fascist powers might be engaged in a test of strength. One could not set the stage for that sort of struggle by abandoning one of the most strategic regions controlled by the West. Then, too, the premier's power represented only one side of the parallelogram; the *colons* of Tunisia represented another side. Those Europeans in Tunisia were as determined as they were strong and ruthless, and they seemed to favor fascism. With France threatened on her flanks by mortal dangers, Blum could not afford to irk any potential allies. Bourguiba and his followers were sorely disappointed but the Popular Front could be of no help.

READY FOR STRUGGLE

The merry-go-round of French politics swept a succession of governments into view. Governments came and governments went; the Tunisian situation remained the same. The *néos* were becoming impatient. "The Tunisian people are ready for the struggle," Bourguiba proclaimed.

Of this declaration the French authorities took notice. First, they arrested two *Neo-Destour* leaders, Dr. Ben Slimane and Salah Ben Youssef, the former because of his position, and the latter because of his outspokenness. The *Neo-Destour* followers were alerted, and they demanded the arrested men's release. Disorders continued.

A strike was proclaimed, and a huge demonstration was held. The day was April 5, 1938. The police fired into the crowd and a hundred people fell. Bourguiba laid responsibility at the doors of the French Residency. The latter accused the Tunisian *meneurs*, the "political agitators." The latter were rounded up and jailed. The most prominent of those apprehended was Habib Bourguiba. He was lodged in the Tunis military jail, where we had encountered him before. This time he was to be detained for more than five years. This is where we saw him at the beginning of the chapter.

He was in jail when World War II erupted. Again the ancient foes, Germany and France, were at each other's throats. Riding on a tidal wave of incomparable strength, Germany swept over France in 1940 in a matter of days. She took Paris in that effortlessly superior way that might have impressed onlookers as if men from the planet Mars had suddenly descended. A puppet government was set up in the small watering place, Vichy; its chief, Marshal Pierre Pétain, hero of World War I.

Bourguiba, in his jail, was not insensitive to the dramatic impact of these events. Now it had become clear to the entire world that the strength of France, mistress of a huge colonial empire, was not invincible, that perhaps it had been based upon fiction. Would the people of the colonies be able to capitalize on this exposure of weakness?

North Africa, too, became a theater of war. There the Axis powers, headed by the Germans, made an effort to sever the jugular vein of the West, the important Suez Canal. Should they succeed in reaching it, the heartland of the world, the Middle East, would fall under their rule. For there they would control, as if by a global hinge, the adjacent areas of Africa, Asia, and Europe. They would control the world's great lifelines, Suez and the Straits. They would hold the center from which operated all-weather global aviation. Above all, they would have what they needed most, the Middle Eastern oil. Meanwhile, the Japanese were bounding westward with giant strides. If the war machines of the East and West were able to effect a junction the world would belong to the Axis powers.

Since he was fighting the French himself, the Tunisian patriot should have regarded the Germans as his potential allies. And yet it was at the height of Axis triumphs that Bourguiba confided to his followers in a message smuggled out of the prison: "Germany will not win the war. This is the truth staring one in the face."

Because North Africa was now a theater of war, Bourguiba was transported to the mainland across the sea which was now the *mare nostrum* of the Axis, its own "lake." Now began his career as a peregrinating prisoner. First, he was taken to Marseilles. He was lodged in the Haut Fort St. Nicolas until the late fall of 1942. Then he was taken to Fort Montluc, at Lyons. Then to the small village of Vancia. There the Germans laid their hands on him. He was needed for their global scheme. His next prison was in Chalon-sur-Saône. Then he was taken to Nice on the French Riviera. He was placed under detention, but there, in line with the spirit of the place, he was held in a "jail de luxe."

Europe was, for the Axis, *Festung Europa*. France was in fetters. But within the country there appeared an internal front of patriots, known as the *maquis*. Outside of the country, a small cluster of Frenchmen had rallied around General Charles de Gaulle, leader of Free France. Suppose the Free French did achieve their goal, the liberation of their country, what would happen to the overseas dependencies? Bourguiba recalled how disappointed he had been with the Popular Front. Yet he did not hesitate to take his stand alongside of the Free French and against the victorious Axis: "On my responsibility and over my signature, if necessary," he wrote to his followers in a letter smuggled out of the jail at Nice, "give to the militants my order to enter into relations with the French Gaullists in Tunisia. . . . Our help to the Allies must be unconditional. . . . It is a question of life and death." Then he added peremptorily: "It is an order I am giving to you and do not question it."

His followers did not question his order. However, the Germans, his captors, were in a better position to issue orders. Their next order was that he should be transferred to Rome. He was lodged in the Palazzo Piacentini, where his neighbor was another Arab, Amin al-Hussaini, the former Grand Mufti of Jerusalem. The latter was not only a free man in Axis lands but a respected collaborator. He was to influence his Tunisian fellow-Arab to make common cause with the Axis. He prevailed upon Bourguiba to speak over the Bari Axis radio station in a program beamed to the Arabs. Bourguiba did speak, criticizing colonialism, but not declaring himself in favor of the Axis. "Our country is passing through one of the most difficult periods of its history," he said. "It is the theatre of fatal events, a prey to colonial greed, and the object of foreign covetousness."

Years later, the French held this speech against him.

This was not, however, the commitment the Axis sought. It wanted him to set up a Tunisian government-in-exile. This he did not do. On the contrary, he sought to strengthen his links with the French underground. "When it is darkest the stars will emerge."

It was in Tunisia that the Axis war machine was smashed. The United States 2nd Corps in North Africa distinguished itself in these battles, first under the command of Lieutenant General George S. Patton, Jr., and later under Major General Omar N. Bradley. A quarter of a million Axis soldiers and very large supplies of arms were captured. The Free French assumed administration of the Maghrebian littoral under the Committee of National Liberation. Two French generals played leading roles in it at first, and then only one. General Henri Honoré Giraud was the commander-in-chief of the fighting forces, while General Charles de Gaulle, co-president of the committee, was permanent chairman of the National Council of Defense. De Gaulle eventually pushed out Giraud, and years later he reached the presidency of France.

What happened to Bourguiba in the meantime? The records are so badly blurred at this point that it is impossible to straighten out the tangle of events. The Bourguiba version is this:

In the face of the Allied attacks in Europe the Germans placed an airplane at his disposal to enable him to retreat to the Reich. He refused it and exhibited his hostility to the Axis with increasing boldness. "He made contact with the Gaullists," according to the official version, "and wrote 'For a Franco-Tunisian Bloc,' which was clandestinely distributed by supporters of the *Neo-Destour* to the Allied forces as they entered Tunisia."

In this pamphlet he is alleged to have written: "A new world will come the day after this victory. The Allied nations have solemnly promised it. Our first duty is to aid them in winning the war, and the best way of helping them is to form a bloc with struggling France."

According to the official version, Bourguiba was back in his native land on May 7, 1943, a few days before the Axis forces were pushed into the sea. We do not know how he got there, and he has never divulged his secret. The Allies had not brought him there. Had he been placed on a German plane in the last moment and deposited in Tunisia? There is no evidence to support this hypothesis. He was lost in the shuffle. He could not help the Allies at a time when Tunisia was a major battlefield. After liberation the main conflict was between the two embattled French generals, De Gaulle and Giraud. Neither of them could even think of bringing Bourguiba or the *Neo-Destour* into the picture. They replaced the nominal Tunisian ruler Sidi Moncef Pasha, denounced as a collaborator with the Axis, by Sidi Lamine, another nonentity. And there the matter was to rest.

Bourguiba was accused of having been an Axis collaborator. General (later Marshal) Alphonse Juin took over interim control as Resident-General of Tunisia and ordered an inquiry into Bourguiba's wartime activities. According to one version, reports revealed to Juin that Bourguiba had been hostile to the Axis and so he closed the prosecution. According to another version, proceedings were dropped against Bourguiba because of the intervention of the "American Consul General Doolittle." Why an American consular official? How did he intervene? The details are missing.

North Africa had been cleared of the Axis; the time was propitious for the Allies to launch the final assault of the war on the core of Hitler's fortress Europa. As dramatically as the Axis had overwhelmed the continent, the Allies subdued the Axis. And Bourguiba reiterated his belief: "A new day will come after this victory. The Allied nations have given their solemn pledge."

THE NEW DAY

The surrender of the German Reich was unconditional; Germany became the ward of the Allied powers. The weakness of the French political system had been revealed during the war, as had the weakness of France itself. Only the strong were entitled to rule the weak. And the French were not strong. Were the Tunisians weak? The majority of them were afflicted with disease, ignorance, and poverty, the heritage of the *mission civilisatrice* of France. But there was now a nucleus of a middle class, French in education, French in their attachment to the idea of the *patrie,* but Tunisian in their application of the lessons learned from France.

Also there was a new alignment of power. As so often in the past, the victors had fallen out among themselves. The cold war had begun; the democratic countries of the West faced an overconfident Soviet Union. "Free World," the West called itself. The cold war presented the Communist world with an incomparable launching site for its attack on colonial "protectors." Hundreds of millions of people lived in subordination of the colonial masters. Could the world be called free if the majority of peoples were unfree? That was the question Bourguiba kept asking, and so did other Bourguibas all over the world.

Yet, pro-West was written all over the program of the *Neo-Destour.* Supported by the small middle class of French-educated youngish people, the program was also backed by the only mass organization Tunisia possessed outside of the *Neo-Destour.* That was the UGTT, *Union Générale des Travailleurs Tunisiens,* the labor-union organization, with some 60,000 members. Its leader was fiery Ferhat Hached, who was also a leader in the *Neo-Destour* movement.

The labor-union movement in Tunisia was a transplant of the French *Confédération Générale du Travail,* which had been infiltrated by Communists and eventually taken over by them. The Communist party of France was the only one in that country to call for the liberation of the colonies and protectorates. It was playing politics, no doubt, but to Tunisians and other "natives" its words sounded like the words of the Prophet.

Not so, however, to Habib Bourguiba. He realized that neither France nor the leader of the Western coalition, the United States, could afford to have all or even part of strategic North Africa fall into Red hands. To him the world of communism was a House of Bondage, and he led the UGTT out of the CGT, aligning it with the international free trade-union movement, strongly anti-Communist and pro-West. Bourguiba never opposed France. On the contrary, his orientation was strongly pro-French. But he did oppose what he considered the misinterpretation of the civilizing mission of France.

Meanwhile, in France a new Constitution was framed. The Chamber of Deputies of the Third Republic was renamed the National Assembly of the Fourth Republic. Little odds and ends of the political system were cleared up. But the foundations of the republican *ancien régime* did not change. The legislature was king, and within that legislature every single deputy was a sovereign. The membership of the political parties remained fluid. Every deputy hoped to be *ministrable* one day—to obtain a cabinet portfolio, and if he did not, then he turned against the government in power. The old pre-war game continued—a new cabinet in every six months, on an average. The permanent government officials carried on the routine work, of course, but one could never be sure of the higher level decisions.

In Tunisia, residents-general came and went, almost as often as the premiers in Paris. Liberals at home in many cases, they became hidebound conservatives in the protectorate. Power was in the hands of the influential European minority for which the sun had stopped on its appointed course. Tunisia was a French protectorate and a French protectorate it was to remain. Scraps of meat were to be thrown to the "snarling native politicians" but nothing more.

The French did not recognize Bourguiba as the spokesman of the Moslem majority. They kept alive the *Vieux-Destour*, which they employed in their policy of divide and rule. Because of his alleged wartime activities, Bourguiba continued to live under a shadow, free to move around in the protectorate, but not to leave it.

Meanwhile the United Nations had been established, the conscience of all mankind. The League of Arab States had been set up, too, to speak for the Arab world, once a mighty force in the history of man, but now weak because of generations of misrule by Turkish and Western masters. It attempted to speak for all the Arab nations in the entire world.

The United States became the uncontested leader of the non-Communist world. An ex-colony, it appeared to be sympathetic to the colonial world. Convinced of the justice of the Tunisian cause, Bourguiba wanted to establish direct contact with the United Nations, the Arab League, the United States, and other friendly powers. He wanted to leave Tunisia. But he was under surveillance and he knew it. Legally he could not leave Tunisia.

So he left her illegally. Tunisia is not a large country, but her coastline is long. From times immemorial smugglers have been carrying on their nefarious trade along the North African coast. One moonless night in March, 1945, from a beach near Sfax, Bourguiba sneaked out of Tunisia in a smuggler's boat. The boat headed for Faroua, in the Tripolitanian portion of the adjacent Kingdom of Libya, another Arab country. The British were still in command there, and had he fallen into their hands, they would have turned him over to the French. Bourguiba followed unconventional routes across the desert, traveling on camel back and on foot. It took him fully a month before he reached his final destination, Cairo.

At long last he reached the headquarters of the Arab League and could feast his eyes on the Nile. Even though he was now a fugitive from the French, his reputation as a pro-Westerner had preceded him, and the welcome accorded to him was far from cordial. Disappointed, Bourguiba turned westward, visiting Switzerland, Belgium, and other Western countries, trying to convince people that a friendly Tunisia was vital for the strength of the Western world. He spoke of a "friendly compromise with France," leading to the election of a constituent assembly in Tunisia and the establishment of a democratic government. "All this will not happen in a day, and a dramatic gesture by France . . . creating a climate of confidence will facilitate the solution of all the secondary difficulties."

He had been abroad for a long time, the traveling salesman of Tunisian freedom. Finally, it dawned upon the new resident-general of Tunisia, Jean Mons, that Bourguiba at home would be less conspicuous than abroad. Bourguiba was permitted to return to Tunis on September 9, 1949. But he could not accomplish much at home. Also traveling was now in his blood.

Bourguiba was off again six months later, and this time he

traveled around the world, "talking Tunisia." In Paris he was closeted with the minister of foreign affairs, Robert Schuman. The French minister announced that the objective of these talks was "to conduct Tunisia to the full flowering of its riches and to lead it to the independence which is the ultimate goal of all the territories of the French Union."

Tunisia and France had entered into negotiations that would last for years. Bourguiba wanted internal autonomy in those days, leaving the defense and foreign affairs of Tunisia to France. How far could the French go in extending such privileges to Tunisia and to other overseas possessions? There were the Europeans in Tunisia and elsewhere, holding on to their privileges and considering the natives an inferior breed.

A French "Union" had been created to encompass France and her overseas dependencies. The Union had a general legislative body in France, but the ultimate decision lay with the government in Paris. Arrangements were worked out in Tunisia, as elsewhere in the French overseas realm, for the "natives" to become members of the local government. However, there were French "advisers," and the government itself was headed by a Frenchman, the resident-general. The Tunisian members were mainly the *beni-beni-oui-oui* type, members of the pasha and *effendi* class, large landowners themselves who wanted a Tunisian gloss over the semi-feudal status quo under which they flourished. This was not Bourguiba's solution.

All kinds of interesting things were happening to Bourguiba in his globe-trotting crusade. He was contacted by another crusader, an American, Irving Brown by name, an overseas representative of the American Federation of Labor. It was Mr. Brown's mission to strengthen the anti-Communist wing in the international labor movement, and this he did with the zeal of the convert. He invited Bourguiba to the convention of the AF of L in San Francisco that was scheduled for September, 1951.

Bourguiba flew to San Francisco on September 18. He spoke to the delegates, as did President Harry S. Truman, whose message to the convention was read. Bourguiba developed his idea of the importance of Tunisian independence for the cause of the free world. The Voice of America transmitted his message to North Africa. The French government was puzzled. Bourguiba was fighting for a cause which France considered not to be in harmony with her own interest. France and America were allies. Why had an American labor organization given Bourguiba a platform from which to speak?

His peregrinations over, Bourguiba was ready to return home. The *Neo-Destour* had not been inactive during his absence. It was under the command of Salah Ben Youssef, an unregenerate anti-colonialist, who did not believe in any kind of coexistence with France. He believed that a good France was a France on the other side of the Mediterranean. An independent Tunisia would have to be charged with the conduct of her own defense and foreign affairs. Otherwise independence would be a farce. He also believed that the capital investments which Bourguiba believed were to come from Paris could be obtained from Tunisians themselves. Ben Youssef and Bourguiba represented two antithetical views. What reception would Bourguiba be given on his return home?

There was now a French-Union government in Tunisia headed by a "native" figurehead under the French resident-general, Mohammed Chenik, a stand-in for Bourguiba, as all the world knew. Again Bourguiba was given a hero's welcome upon his return to Tunis at the completion of his globe-circling tour.

By now Bourguiba had learned that he and the French meant two different things when they spoke of independence. To the French it meant a glittering array of Tunisian ministers, equipped with de luxe offices, and limited power. This would keep the "natives" quiet, leading lives in which they had all the glory and no work. The work was to be done by the French "advisers."

Bourguiba was interested in glamour and glory, too, but he was more interested in work. He wanted to be the real power in an independent Tunisia and not merely a figurehead. His organization needed strengthening. Perhaps under the influence of his American experience, he was moving closer to the UGTT, the labor federation. The leader of the movement, the dynamic Ferhat Hached, was a man who knew and could not forget that most Tunisians were afflicted with malnutrition. He also knew that the nominal independence which the French protectorate officials had in mind would do little to raise living standards.

Ferhat Hached was ready to cooperate closely with Bourguiba. It was precisely this cooperation which the European minority dreaded. The *colons* set up an organization of armed thugs with the bloodcurdling name of "Red Hand," which was to keep the Bourguiba–Hached–*Neo-Destour*–UGTT coalition in line. One day the thugs waylaid the labor leader. It was only a few days later that the police found his dead body. The police ledger recorded the perpetrator of the crime as "unknown." This was an *accident d'Etat* which often occurred in perilous times.

The assassination of the labor leader may have saved Bourguiba's life. Until then he was carefree in his movements. After the murder, he became more careful. Furthermore, it was no longer so easy to get a prominent person out of the way, for an international scandal would have erupted in the case of another "accident of State."

The Tunisians were unwilling to stand aside for the Red Hand, and terror was answered with counter-terror. Many Tunisians began to think that violence was the only language the protectors understood. The freedom fighters' self-defense organization sprang into life, and the Tunisian landscape was besmirched with blood. The usual contingent of brigands and mercenaries employing patriotism as their cloak began to flock to the hosts of freedom fighters.

PRESSURES AND COUNTER-PRESSURES

French governments came and went but the Tunisian problem could not be solved. Pressures were applied on the government in Paris from many sides. The politically sophisticated segment of French public opinion realized that the time of procrastination was over. The protectorate was an anachronism. France could remain an influential power in Tunisia only as a friend, not as a master. Other members of the North Atlantic Treaty Organization were also interested in the Tunisian problem. Tunisia's Bizerta was an important naval base. The Tunisian imbroglio played into the Communists' hands: "Freedom" in the Western world looked like that, Moscow's propaganda sneered. The United States was particularly unhappy with events in North Africa. The "natives" there charged that America's weapons, destined to protect liberty, were used against the freedom fighters.

What was Paris to do? Eventually, Bourguiba's demand for domestic independence was accepted by the French government as a starting point. Tunisia's ultimate fate was to be determined by the ballots. However, the subdued voice of Paris was one thing, and the roar of the influential Europeans in Tunisia was another thing. The Tunis Residency was exposed to the full force of the local nabobs and not to the wish of the Paris government. On January 13, 1952, Salah Ben Youssef secretly left Tunis in order to confer with Arab and Asian leaders over the placing of the Tunisian issue before the Security Council of the United Nations.

Bourguiba summoned the *Neo-Destour* to a Congress. On January 16 the Tunisian French authorities banned the *Neo-Destour*. Its Congress was to be convoked on the following day. In the morning of January 18 Bourguiba heard the familiar knocks on his doors. It was the gendarmes. "This is the last time that you are going to arrest me," he told them.

Again he became a peregrinating prisoner, pulled up from one place, deposited at another one. Why all the changes in his places of detention? The French authorities may have played this game so as to head off his contact with his followers. Or they may have entertained the hope that less competent rivals would wrest the leadership from his hands during his protracted detention. In the isolation of exile he may be forgotten. Again the authorities failed to see that fame was not measured among illiterate people by the yardstick of front-page headlines. The longer Bourguiba was away from home the more he, the martyr, became a living legend.

First he was taken to Tabarqua, on the Mediterranean Sea, close to the Algerian frontier. Then he was taken to the remotest point in southern Tunisia, in the pre-Saharan region, where the sun was a huge ball of scorching flame in the summer, and the sand was like ice by night. His next place of enforced residence was the forsaken island of La Galite in the Mediterranean, where he spent months in what he called "solitary confinement." From there he was taken to the storm-tossed island of Groix, off the coast of Brittany.

He had plenty of time to think and to read during his long detention. He took a liking to Voltaire and read him endlessly, learning passages of his writing by heart. In years to come he used quotations from Voltaire for many occasions.

Meanwhile the political mills were grinding. M. Chenik was deposed from the premiership. The United Nations General Assembly was "seized" of the Tunisian case. France declared that the world body was not competent to act in a domestic matter. The UN, however, did consider the case of Tunisia and urged France to take steps leading to the independence of the protectorate. Meanwhile Bourguiba was deposed in a château sixty-five miles south of Paris. And then came a startling development in *l'Affaire Tunisie.*

In the summer of 1954 the French again had a new government, this one headed by Pierre Mendès-France. He was quick to see that the days of the colonial empires were numbered and that Tunisia was ripe for self-government. He also realized that the only man with whom he could negotiate on this issue was the prisoner of France, Bourguiba. He motored down to Bourguiba's de luxe place of detention, Amilly, and there the Premier and the prisoner had a cordial talk. The result of this was a momentous announcement: France was ready to proclaim internal autonomy for the country. And it was to be without strings. Bourguiba hailed the agreement as a "decisive and substantial step along the road to the restoration of complete Tunisian sovereignty."

But it was not yet the solution. Mendès-France ran into the opposition of *les durs*—"the hard ones," in France and in Tunisia. The extreme right attacked him because he was of the Jewish faith. Because of his attempts to help the French overseas territories he was called *"Mendès-Russe,"* not Mendès-France. He had to resign the premiership in February, 1955. His successor at the head of the government, Edgar Faure, however, continued the negotiations with Bourguiba, who was now allowed to move to Paris where he took residence in the Hotel Continental.

Bourguiba returned to Tunis on June 1, 1955, and again he was accorded a hero's welcome. On June 3, 1955, the agreement was signed under which Tunisia gained internal sovereignty. The French resident-general was replaced by a high commissioner. France retained control of the Tunisian army and diplomatic service, and a French general was to act as the minister of defense. Tunisia was to remain in the French currency bloc and France had the exclusive privilege of providing financial assistance and technical aid to the new country. The French of Tunisia acquired the status of "privileged foreigners."

The nominal head of the state at the time was Sidi Mohammed, an impressive-looking man of truly royal bearing but of limited intelligence who could barely sign his name. He was probably one of the last rulers to have court jesters and dwarfs. His great passion was to brew potions, just like medieval alchemists, and from a mezzanine alcove built specifically for the purpose, he liked to watch the world go by on the main street to the bazaar. The protocol being over, he descended from the dais on which his throne stood, embraced Bourguiba, and hailed him as the "father of his country." In turn, Bourguiba hailed the ruler as the champion of Tunisian independence.

A LITTLE LESS AND A LITTLE MORE

"Bourguiba betrayed his country," was a charge now leveled against him by one of his closest collaborators. It was none other than the secretary-general of the *Neo-Destour* since 1952, Salah Ben Youssef, who had been abroad so as to escape the heavy hand of French retribution in Tunisia. He returned to Tunis on September 13, 1955, and attacked Bourguiba. He called the agreements recently signed with the French a series of backward steps. A protectorate Tunisia had been and a protectorate it was to remain, he charged. A country whose army was headed by a general of the French was not independent. And what fool could speak of sovereignty in the case of a so-called nation the foreign affairs of which were conducted by foreigners?

Ben Youssef was now the leader of *les dures* among the native Tunisians, and he proclaimed his intention of leading the country to full independence: provided, of course, that he could line up a sufficient number of *Neo-Destour* delegates to support him; also provided that he had the armed force to contest the leadership of Bourguiba now supported by the French armed forces.

The *Neo-Destour* Congress met at Sfax on November 15, and a vote was taken to settle the question of Tunisian leadership. All the world could see that Bourguiba was the man of destiny of the new nation, the man with the *baraka,* the charismatic leader. It was to him that the masses of Tunisia looked for their salvation and not to the sullen Salah Ben Youssef. The vote was overwhelmingly in favor of Bourguiba. His opponent was ousted from the party. Ben Youssef disappeared from sight, turning up finally in Cairo where he launched a propaganda campaign against his former comrade-in-arms. For a time he directed a guerrilla campaign against Bourguiba by remote control. But then a new development took place which stripped his movement of its rationale.

Domestic independence was not sufficient for Bourguiba. The French, no longer in the saddle, had to sign another set of agreements. The signatures were affixed on March 20, 1956, and the seventy-five-year-old protectorate of France ended. Tunisia became sovereign in foreign affairs and defense. At the national elections five days later Bourguiba's pro-Western National Front won all ninety-eight seats in the Constituent Assembly.

Then came July 25, celebrated now annually as Republic Day. The year was 1957. A year before, Bourguiba had hailed the nominal ruler of the country, Sidi Mohammed al-Amin, as the fighter for Tunisia's freedom. Now he denounced him, his family, and his predecessors as people who "lived in ignorance and had only one aim: to safeguard their regal position." The Bey, his three sons and one daughter were escorted from the royal residence. Thus ended a dynastic rule that had begun in 1705 under Hussein ben Ali, who was presumed to have been a resident of the isle of Crete. And thus began the reign of Habib Bourguiba, Prime Minister, President of the National Assembly, Minister of Defense, and Minister of Foreign Affairs. Coincident with the deposition of the Bey, the Republic of Tunisia was proclaimed. Again with unanimity, Bourguiba was elected chief-of-state. He remained the president of the *Neo-Destour*. Conferred upon him was *L'Ordre du Sang* ("Order of Blood") and *L'Ordre de la Confiance en Diamants* ("Diamond Order of Confidence"). His people eulogized him as *Le Combattant Suprême.*

THEN THE CONSTITUTION

The Constitution of the new nation was proclaimed a few weeks later, on June 1. It had been drawn up by the constitutional committee of *Neo-Destour,* in constant consultation with the President of the new republic. It consists of ten chapters, divided into sixty-four articles. The Third Chapter of the Constitution deals with the Executive Power and it was tailor-made for Bourguiba. A candidate for the presidency of Tunisia must have an unbroken Tunisian descent for three generations, being born of a Tunisian father and grandfather. (No mention is made of the nationality of the mother: Bourguiba's son has a French mother.) The President is elected for five years. His period of office "cannot be renewed more than three times consecutively."

The president of the Republic draws up the general policy of the country and supervises its execution. He selects the members of the government and they are responsible to him (not to the legislature). He has the right to address the National Assembly either in person or through messages. He has the right of the veto which, however, may be overridden by a two-thirds vote. He ratifies treaties, declares war, makes peace, makes civil and military appointments. He has the right of pardon. The president is *le commandant suprême*.

The Preamble of the Constitution states that the Tunisian nation is "free, independent, sovereign. Islam is its religion, Arabic its language, and the republican system its regime. . . . We, the representatives of the Tunisian people, meeting in the Constitutional Assembly . . . are determined . . . to remain true to the teachings of Islam, to the ideals of the Union of the Great Maghreb, to membership in the Arab family, to cooperation with the African peoples in building a better future and to all peoples struggling for justice and freedom."

Thus the Tunisian Constitution expresses not only the solidarity of Moslems, of the Arabs, of the Africans, but also of all the developing countries. This embraces all mankind with the exception of the developed countries. True to his French upbringing, Bourguiba likes to express his policies in sweeping statements. He described the basic policy of his regime in the following words: "It means our freedom, our personality, and our dignity."

"FATHER OF THE COUNTRY"

In an address President Bourguiba delivered in a military school at Funduk-Jedid on March 15, 1963, he said: "I am not only Supreme Commander of the Armed Forces, but also Father of the Nation."

One of the national holidays of the country is June 1, his return from exile. The Tunisian national anthem weaves his name into a patriotic paean:

> *For our glorious fatherland*
> *We have shed undying, precious blood,*
> *All hardships we gladly stand,*
> *So as to free our verdant land.*
> *Sweet is the fight when victory is sure*
> *When shedding the yoke we had to endure.*
> *Fire we face staunchly and with heart light*
> *Cherishing the spirit of Habib, our Great Guide.*

Now Tunisia was ready to go into business. Independence was not an aim in itself. It was the means by which human beings could lead more human lives, so that they should evolve from their condition of D.I.P.—disease, ignorance, and poverty—to H.A.K.—health, affluence, and knowledge.

Bourguibism meant accelerated internal development, on the one hand, and pro-Western orientation in foreign relations, on the other. It was pivoted—in Bourguiba's formulation—on the fulfilment of two integrated conditions. One of these he described as a matter of sentiment, a disinterested civic sense which related private interests to those of the public welfare of all Tunisians, of Arabs, and of even larger circles. He described the other condition as technical competence. "Our ideal is to act in such a way that civic sense and technical competence are developed equally." The City of Allah, the New Mecca, consists of two parts, with a broad thoroughfare between them. Technical competence is the function of one side, a twentieth-century field for the cultivation of farming, industries, trade. It does not exist for its own material benefit, but in order to enhance ethical and moral human values.

"If we are to place our nation on democratic foundations while associating each citizen with the responsibilities of the State, and if it is agreed that we must raise the technical standards of our people so as to wage a successful fight against underdevelopment, then, we must not forget that in the first place we must train our people's civic sense, which is an extension of the moral sense," Bourguiba proclaimed.

POLICY AND ACTION

These policies were to be implemented. The harsh word "investment" answered the call for the elimination of D.I.P. But who would invest in Tunisia? The local nabobs were not in the habit of risking their capital on untried industrial and trading ventures. Their money was invested in land, the value of which was bound to increase as the population continued to grow. Also they hoarded their capital in the form of gold, jewelry, and in the safe deposit vaults of American and Swiss banks. In the past, French capital investments had served the purposes of the Europeans. But Bourguibism was predicated on the continued investment of French capital—and technical knowledge—in Tunisia.

At the end of one year of independence, investments had declined by 50 per cent. In successive years, annual investments averaged only 6 billion dinars (the official rate of the dinar was

$2.38, but sold for much less on black markets) against a minimum of 20 billion needed to preserve the existing living standards.

A 1 per cent increase of living standards would have required a 27 billion dinar investment. The actual investment amounted to no more than one-fifth of this minimum. There were 6,700 salaried European-trained public employees in the country when it became independent. Within a short time only some seven hundred of them remained, outside of the thousand or so teachers whose prospects of finding jobs in France were extremely bleak. Technical skills evaporated. The native Tunisians had never been taught how to install water meters or to get electric current flowing.

Free enterprise cannot flourish on depleted private resources. A National Planning Council was established in order to accumulate a stockpile of funds that could put the public sector of the economy into motion. A development program was projected, encompassing ten years. Foreign capital was encouraged, especially in "blue chip" currencies, such as the dollar. The United States risked unusually large funds in Tunisia. American government aid of all kinds between the end of World War II and the fiscal end of 1961 amounted to $300 million. In 1963 alone the United States committed $60 million to Tunisia. Add to this the direct military aid from America, and one may see that Bourguibism was, after all, the quintessence of Western orientation.

Industrialization is not a prominent feature of colonies, yet industrialization is considered equivalent to independence. Tunisia's "industries" under the protectorate were European-owned. Outside of that there were the bazaar handicrafts. Eloquently, Bourguiba encouraged his people to turn their minds to technology. Schools were opened to implement these exhortations. But it takes years before ancient traditions are extirpated and new ways of life are grafted onto the character of nations. Only "inferior" people soiled their hands with factory work in Tunisia. Superior people went into politics, public administration, and law. Many people in Tunis could solve intricate legal problems but where was one to find a plumber?

Aggravating the situation was the population explosion. The increase of the population was 2.9 per cent a year. The mortality rate was falling and life expectancy rising. There were more mouths to feed, and so there was less food than ever. The Tunisian dinar was sliding downhill on foreign black markets, always an indication of the economic ill-health of a country. Free Tunisians were worse off than they had been under the French. Bourguiba had to run three times faster to remain at the same spot. The laws of economics defied both *baraka* and charisma.

SOME IMPROVEMENTS, TOO

Of course, the picture was not all black; there were some grey spots, too. We have seen that already in his youth Bourguiba was a great admirer of Atatürk, the creator of modern Turkey. From him he learned the seminal importance of education. Bourguiba allocated $20 million for education in a typical year. The traditional Koranic schools retained their places for the time being, but they were to be nationalized and their standards raised. The schools were as good as the teachers, and teacher training occupied a pivotal point in Bourguiba's plans.

Islam permitted a husband to have four wives, if he could support that many, but the institution of polygamy is an almost dead institution in the Moslem world. To support several wives requires greater affluence than is at the disposal of a *fellah* or a nomadic tribesman. Urbanization created additional problems. How was one to accommodate a multiplicity of jealous wives in a one-room slum abode? The Western world equated monogamy with the modern way of life. Bourguiba's idol, Kemal Atatürk, outlawed polygamy, and one of the first measures taken by the President of Tunisia was a similar ban. Since the religious *archéos* equated the spirit of Islam with polygamy, the new law was viewed as nothing short of blasphemy. Unperturbed by the concern of the traditionalists, the Tunisian government went ahead with its plans. The hold of traditions had been loosened.

Under the protectorate, modern law had been introduced in Tunisia. But the French did not dare to tamper with the contentious issues relating to a person's family status. It was up to the religious courts to deal with them. Bourguiba took another bold step when he integrated these courts into the national judiciary system.

The incidence of sickness was high in the protectorate, as it was in all underdeveloped regions. Infant mortality was especially high. The Tunisian Republic launched a major offensive: government regulations reduced the price of medicines; subsidies were granted to physicians who were ready to serve in backward regions away from urban centers. Due to these measures, epidemics were all but eliminated.

Westernization means not only education and sanitation, but also militarization. While more money was spent on schools and public health than ever before, relatively even more money was spent on arms in the name of defense. Tunisia spent five times more on arms in a typical year than on schools.

The peasantry of Tunisia formed three-quarters of the population—the backbone of the country. A very large number of the cultivators lived below the subsistence level under the French. Under the regime of Bourguiba the share of the national income of the peasantry was less than 40 per cent—hardly an improvement. Independence gave Tunisia a president, and a National Assembly filled with Tunisians, but it did not give the majority of the people better food rations.

The *New Statesman* of London summarized the conditions in Tunisia on January 12, 1962: "In the last financial year . . . five times as much money was spent on defense as on education, eight times as much as on health, and twice as much as on agriculture. Yet this is the country where 42 per cent of all deaths occur in the first year of life, where there are still 2.5 hospital beds for every 2,000 people, and where a population increase of 66 per cent in twenty-five years has been accompanied by an increase in food production of a mere 25 per cent." And the *Economist* of London: "The Bourguibist doctrine that there is a third way between colonial subservience and intransigent nationalism has been undermined."

NEO-BOURGUIBISM

In the beginning there was Bourguibism. It meant free enterprise, laissez-faire, capitalism. It entailed native capital accumulation, land development, an accelerated rate of industrialization, and consequently, higher living standards. It was classical economics transplanted into the twentieth century—Adam Smith brought up to date.

Sufficient capital accumulation—we have seen—failed to materialize; few foreign investments came to North Africa. Help from France, America, and other sources was insufficient. Still Bourguibism retained its label, its trade mark—capitalism. And this in spite of varying shades of collectivism in most of the developing world—Chinese super-communism; Nehru socialism; Sukarno's mutual-help socialism; Nasser's Arab socialism; the Baath socialism of the Levant; Israel's Mapai socialism; and so forth.

As years went by and capitalism failed to produce an affluent society, the economic aspect of Bourguibism underwent a change. In this second stage it became tinted with the teachings of John Maynard Keynes. Capitalism, yes, for Bourguiba had to remain true to Bourguibism, but when the mechanism of the free economy began to falter, the nation had to apply correctives by using the social forces of the government. Keynesian economics was to justify Bourguiba's faith in his adherence to capitalism.

Economic conditions in Tunisia failed to respond to repeated doses of Keynesian economics. Neighboring Algeria had become independent and had proclaimed her place in the vineyards of Arab socialism. Did the neighbor prosper under socialism? Far from that. But by that time socialism had become a magic word in most Arab countries and elsewhere in the newly freed nations of the colonial world.

Was there another reason for this trend toward socialism? Possibly, there was. America was a crusader not only of a politically free world but also of capitalism—free enterprise. Across the Atlantic, socialism and tyranny were equated. The government that acted for the people was seen as an instrument of oppression. Authority—no matter how benevolent in the beginning—could not but turn malevolent in the end, many Americans held. The fabulous readiness of the United States to help repentant sinners return into the fold became a mid-twentieth-century legend. But one had to become a sinner first in order to qualify for American largesse. A capitalistic country was virtue incarnate and therefore not a sinner. Not being that, it was not entitled to American windfalls. Bourguibism had to fall from grace.

This was the birth of Neo-Bourguibism which was almost as different from the original Bourguibism as the *Neo-Destour* was from the *Vieux-Destour*. It was in a basic policy address to the National Council of the *Neo-Destour* on March 2, 1963, that President Bourguiba unveiled the main features of Neo-Bourguibism.

"We are going in the direction of socialism," he said. If this statement did not startle his audience the following one did: "Destourian socialism, which is at the basis of our action, does not differ in its objectives from Soviet, Chinese, or Yugoslav communism. Only our methods of action differ. The socialism practiced in our country is periodically revised in the light of experience, obstacles, and failures." Originally, foreign-owned Tunisian land was to be nationalized against compensation. Then came the change in Bourguiba's mind. Former foreign landowners were to receive no indemnification.

The Soviet, Chinese, and Yugoslav communisms he named were the children of revolutions. What about Destourian socialism, this Neo-Bourguibism? Obviously, the President of Tunisia did not want to revolt against his own regime, and so he added: "We do not like spectacular gestures termed 'revolutions' which often are no more than so much dust thrown in one's eyes."

The *Neo-Destour* set the major policies that were to be implemented by the government. Bourguiba was the head of the party and of the administration. *Le Neo-Destour c'est moi,* he could have said, adding, *et l'Etat c'est moi, aussi.*

The name of the top-governing body of the *Neo-Destour,* originally called "permanent praesidium," was changed to "Political Bureau." That had been the name of the leadership of the Communist party of the Soviet Union. It remained the designation of the leadership in other Communist countries.

This change has not been noticed by the outside world. Bourguibism becoming Neo-Bourguibism was as if the Board of Directors of General Motors had become the Politburo of General Motors. An incredible transformation. But it did happen in Tunisia.

FOREIGN AFFAIRS AND BIZERTA

Because of *l'Affaire Bizerta,* Neo-Bourguibism also entailed a change in foreign affairs.

At the time Tunisia gained her independence, she agreed to let France retain several military bases on her soil. Four of them were in the deep South, out of sight, and therefore, no eyesores. One of them, however, was in the heart of a population center, the naval base at Bizerta, probably the best natural harbor of the southern Mediterranean littoral.

Even though Bourguiba was the best-known "Westerner" of the Arab world he could not help becoming the foe of the West in the Algerian conflict. The Algerians were fighting for their own freedom, as he had been. The Algerians were Moslems, as was he, and spoke Arabic, as did he. He could not close his ears to a call for help from his Algerian neighbors. He opened his country to Algerian refugees and turned his eastern borderland into a sanctuary for the freedom fighters of his fellow Arabs. The French, unable to tolerate this, bombed the Algerians' sanctuary in Tunisia. Bourguiba retaliated in July, 1961, by demanding that the French evacuate the Bizerta base. This the French refused to do. Bourguiba reacted by having roadblocks set up at the approaches of the Bizerta naval installations, so as to paralyze the forces of France. The French retaliated by airlifting troop reinforcements and strengthening the besieged garrison. This was provocation to the Tunisians, who opened fire on the planes. The French command alerted Foreign Legion units, which started to occupy areas adjacent to Bizerta. More than that, they moved on the city of Bizerta itself. The battle raged for three days; about a thousand Tunisians were killed.

The case was taken to the United Nations. Sixty-six member-nations adopted a resolution recommending France to open negotiations with Tunisia on the basis of evacuation. Thirty-three members abstained, among them the United States and Great Britain. No government gave its support to the French view espousing the status quo. In an address to the National Assembly on October 4, 1963, Bourguiba said: "We had told our martyrs that they must accept the supreme sacrifice, but that victory lay at the end. And today, I give thanks to Allah: my promise has been kept." Eleven days later the French started the evacuation of Bizerta.

In spite of Bizerta, Bourguibism had meant close cooperation with France. "We owe our education, our access to modern culture, to France," Bourguiba had said in his National Assembly speech. "So is it not normal that the success of a young State, fashioned by French presence over a long period, should give France cause for pride? . . . Older Tunisians know that this has been my way of looking at things for the past thirty years. Some used to think it a mild form of madness: friendship with France, but on one condition—the end of French domination. One had indeed to be naïve to believe this seriously. Well, it is now a reality, since French forces no longer tread my country's soil and oppression has departed for ever."

Neo-Bourguibism would maintain this close association with France. The President of Tunisia could not turn against his past. But, Bizerta had revealed the friendly interest of other countries: the entire Communist bloc voted for Tunisia, against France; the Chinese Communist press attacked French "imperialism" on the Bizerta issue. Bourguiba paid tribute to the friendly countries supporting the Tunisian cause. He paid special tribute to the United Arab Republic, and its head, President Jamal Abdel Nasser. "The Egyptians had accused me of being a puppet of the West and so on. But in our time of trial, Jamal Abdel Nasser sent me a message conveying his support and offered Tunisia various forms of assistance, including an unlimited supply of arms. The Tunisian people must never forget this."

Neo-Bourguibism has moved closer to the "non-committed" world, closer to the developing nations and to the Communist countries. Early in 1964 Bourguiba recognized the government of Communist China and an exchange of ambassadors followed. This was a dramatic illustration of the nature of Neo-Bourguibism in the foreign field.

THE BARAKA OF BOURGUIBA

Past sixty, "Father of the Nation," Bourguiba showed few signs of the years of turmoil. He was the creator of independent Tunisia, as much a nation-builder as his idol, Atatürk, the Father of the Turks. He had manipulated the French into giving him half a loaf, then took the other half and gave it to his people. With infinite cunning and perhaps even wisdom he had manipulated the French into surrendering their power. "The messenger of the Prophet," graybeards intoned, and the people assented. *Time* magazine called him "an authentic political genius."

He and he alone spoke for the Tunisian people. He had spoken for them in Tunis, in Paris, and a million miles from nowhere, in the Sahara and on lonely islands. His voice was muted but his image was not dim. It was more vivid than if he had been present.

The *Sturm und Drang* of creating the nation was over, but not that of nation-building. Independence was not the ultimate goal—it was the halfway house. The goal was a seat in school for every child, food for every mouth, decent clothing for every back. His problem was that which the changing world situation has forced upon the head of every State new and old: would Tunisia turn to the East or the West, or stay in-between; what would be her relationship vis-à-vis France; how to meet the aspirations of the Arab world for an all-embracing identification mark; when to take her place as part of the *Maghreb?*

The more towering a person in his people's eyes the more towering are his problems. He and nobody else has the *baraka* and the charisma. The others may have the rank and title but not the invisible power which is a special blessing or curse of heaven. People on those lonely heights can have no close collaborators. Bourguiba has acolytes who take orders from him but not associates. What other Tunisian does the world know about? What other political leaders do the Tunisians themselves know? Is one of them, by any chance, Sadok Mokkadem, foreign minister for a time, who, therefore, should be known? But he never had the *baraka*. As soon as he was established, Bourguiba relieved him of his post and shipped him off as the ambassador to Paris. Does the world know much about Mongi Slim, president of the General Assembly of the UN during its sixteenth session in 1961–62? It was a conspicuous position and an inconspicuous function. Mongi Slim was the "alter ego" of Bourguiba, but not his *éminence grise*. Is Bourguiba selfish, keeping potential rivals out of the way, loath to share the headlines? Of course he is. Otherwise he never would have become the Father of the Nation. No grass grows in the shadow of the mighty oak.

A little stockier than before, his face was still handsome, his dark eyes inquisitive, his hair gray, a mocking, sardonic smile freshening his somber face. Before the National Assembly, before the general public, he was the quintessence of elegance, a fashion plate, eau-de-Cologned, very distinguished-looking, the picture of a stage ambassador, and not of a struggling politician who had been in and out of jails.

He gave every indication of loving to speak in public, and he did it well, forcefully, weighing the impact of every word with effortless ease, propelling his words past the gate of fleshy lips, the lower one protruding as if screening the words before they left the portals of his mouth. He acquired the habit of accentuating important passages of his speeches with quick jabs of his left hand, as if he were underlining their importance. The words accompanied by these swift thrusts were "italicized." "A forceful speaker," foreign newspapermen reported, "whose mannerisms fascinate the masses."

It was also reported by the grapevine that Bourguiba was seldom "in conference," which would have indicated a give-and-take of discussion, even of debate. The Tunis *on dit* said that he was nearly always giving—advice, directives, orders.

Some people said that when speaking in Arabic he was a little less fluent than in French. Was he thinking in French, and translating his French words into Arabic? An indiscreet visitor claimed he heard him counting in French; people count in the language of their thoughts. Tunisian officials, however, scoffed at this notion. On the contrary, they said, the President spoke French with a slight Arabic accent. The impartial umpire was inclined to conclude that, at best, Bourguiba was bilingual.

Having got used to the life of a peregrinating prisoner, how did Bourguiba live? The Tunisian state sequestered the numerous palaces of the former Bey, and they were turned over to the head of the Republic. The Beys of the defunct regime lived in Oriental splendor, and Bourguiba, the most ardent exponent of the West in the Arab world, continued to live in Oriental splendor. It was said of him that he could sleep in a different room of the presidential mansions every single night of the year.

Remarks were passed on the splendor of his ways, and they reached his ears. He reacted to them strongly. "People are talking about my palaces," he said, "and doing so they do damage to the prestige of the Head of the State. The President of the country must have frequent direct contacts with the people and so he must have proper accommodation wherever he goes. Besides, the buildings are old, rearranged residences in most cases, as for instance, in Le Kef and Sfax. These underhanded accusations are being spread against a man who sacrificed his youth and almost gave up his life to the national cause, as if he had diverted public funds to his own use. Am I to live in a hovel because there still are mud huts in Tunisia?"

To which Bourguiba's critics had a ready answer, strictly off the record. A head of State should be housed properly, even in luxury. But as long as there were so many mud hovels in Tunisia what was the sense of spending so much public money on the "rearrangement" and upkeep of so many beylical mansions? Was it necessary for a Bourguiba to wrap himself in the mantle of splendor, an insulating factor in a country of hovels? While nobody expected him to live in mud huts he would have been closer to his people if he had seen fit to forego the splendor of the *ci-*

devant ancien régime. Republican institutions thrive best in a republican setting.

"BOURGUIBA EN PANTOUFLES"

A Western-minded man, Bourguiba lives in the midst of the Arab world, which originated in the East. The family lives of Western statesmen are newspaper items. Not so, however, in the East. This applies, up to a certain point, to the private life of President Bourguiba—his "life in slippers." And this is so in spite of the fact that he married a French woman.

She remained in the background while he was all over the world, becoming a public image and a world statesman. Mathilde Lorrain's name was changed to Moufida when he entered history. Her portrait was shown in the United States on one occasion, when she accompanied her husband to Washington in May, 1961. She was an elderly woman by then, short, stoutish, stylishly-gowned, her eyes concealed by dark glasses, keeping mum. It was a State visit and they were guests of President and Mrs. Kennedy. The American eulogized the Tunisian as a "distinguished world statesman, who fought for freedom and principle."

America did not know then that Moufida and Habib were at that time only "public relations mates." They were living separately and a few months later they were divorced. Not long thereafter President Bourguiba married for a second time, this time to a Tunisian lady.

The wedding ceremony took place on April 2, 1962, the anniversary of Bourguiba's return to Tunis seven years before. The scene of the marriage was one of the royal palaces, the floors of which—according to newspaper accounts—were flower-strewn. The new wife was Mme Wassila Ben Ammar, sister of Mondher Ben Ammar, secretary of state for social affairs. She, too, was short and plump, just like the first wife. For Wassila, as for Habib, this was the second marriage. She was forty, he was nineteen years older. It was a happy day for Bourguiba who—again according to newspaper accounts—"wept with joy." No less happy were the 429 political prisoners who were released on that day. (Incidentally, this was an indication of the comparatively large number of political prisoners.) The school-children were happy, too, because Bourguiba's wedding day was declared a national holiday and schools were closed.

"Her friendship with the President began," Tunisian newspapers reported about the bride, "when she helped him in the war of independence." This, too, was a Western touch. There is no record of women playing a part in Tunisia's struggle for independence. And, certainly, it could not be called a war. Sophisticated Europeans remarked that the newspaper comment reflected patriotic rationalization in the spirit of the West.

It will be recalled that Bourguiba had a son, Habib Kemal. In the spirit of the West, his name was changed to Habib Bourguiba, Jr., and he was called upon to play an important role in Tunisia. Only half-French, he appeared to be *plus français* than the French, debonnaire, *bon vivant*. Like his father, he was a law graduate of the University of Paris. He learned English and served at the Tunisian Embassy in Washington where he was reported to have been on good terms with President Kennedy. He had been Ambassador in Rome and in Paris, and headed special missions for his government to the Far East, to Africa, and to South America. In 1963 he was elected mayor of his father's home town, Monastir. He was then thirty-six years old.

Later that year, he was appointed to act as secretary at cabinet meetings, to serve as liaison between the President and the National Assembly, functions which were previously performed by Abdullah Ferhat, principal private secretary to the President. "Bibi," as his intimates called the younger Habib, was given the title of Secretary-General to the Presidency of the Republic. He was also to have responsibility for the Department of Youth and Sports, the Department of Tourism, the National Office for Artisanship, and the Information Department. Each of these was an equivalent to a ministerial post. All of them together amounted to deputy-premiership. Was "Bibi" groomed to follow in the footsteps of his father? Was a Bourguiba dynasty in the making in the guise of a presidential succession? Few people in Tunisia asked this question and even fewer could provide the answer.

"MES PRISONS"

Bourguiba was in jail and under surveillance so many times and for so long that it will be well to recapitulate the periods of this phase of his life.

He was imprisoned by the French in the years 1934–36.

Again he was kept in jails by the French in the period 1938–43.

He was arrested again by the French in 1952 and placed under surveillance at Tabarka in January; imprisoned at Remada in March; placed in "solitary confinement" on the Ile de la Galite in May, remaining there until 1954. Then he was placed under surveillance until his final release in 1955. Out of a total of twenty years of political *Sturm und Drang* Bourguiba spent some twelve years in a variety of detentions. His captors were the very people whom he admired and whose way of life he sought to emulate. One would think that he would conceive a deep dislike, if not hatred, toward his jailers. This he did not do. During all these years in jail he did not change his ideology and he continued to admire the jailers. Withal he remained faithful to the goals that had landed him in prison, and those were the self-determination of his people and their full independence.

He learned much in jail—as did all the others in similar positions. He read a lot in his prisons—and so did the others. He matured much in his places of detention—but so did the others. He read less of Marx, than the others, and less of Nietzsche.

His orientation in his jails continued to be French. Many—and perhaps most—of the authors he read were French. He relished not only the thoughts of that cynical and yet immensely humanitarian genius, Voltaire, but also his words. He enjoyed every sentence he read. In jail he became more addicted to the French language than in freedom. His case confirms the general observation. With men of Bourguiba's ilk—political prisoners motivated by social impulses—long stays in jails accentuate their dominant traits. Extraneous circumstances in his jails were excluded, together with the hurly-burly of life, and only the essential factors remained.

In Bourguiba's case, too, long absence did not tarnish his fame. On the contrary, the less was heard of him through the public media the more he was in the minds of the people. Had he been physically present, people would have noticed the flaws. Since he was absent, he was perfect. This may be one of the reasons he has also kept away from the crowds after independence.

He was hailed by many as the *Mahdi*, harbinger of happy tidings, a worker of miracles. He was not that. Conditions became worse for most Tunisians after independence than they had been previously. But that was not Bourguiba's fault, for the conditions after independence, and not the conditioner of independence, impelled wealth and skills to flee Tunisia, Bourguiba's own Western orientation was of no avail, and at first, it prevented him from employing the balance-of-power policy of emerging nations. Later, he rectified this flaw in Bourguibism. Then began the era we called Neo-Bourguibism, and it may yet produce better results than the previous phase did.

Bourguiba was at first not particularly interested in the Arab *mystique* which gained such a strong hold on the area from the Atlantic to the Indian Ocean. But he could not escape the influence of the *genius loci* of the region, and so he tried to reconcile his own Western orientation with Arab integration. He gave sanctuary and active physical support to Algerian fellow-Arabs who were fighting the very people whom he admired so much— the French. Paradoxes were compounded. It was his Western-mindedness that made him help his anti-Western friends. Bourguiba and the Algerians wanted to be free to follow the example of the very civilization they fought. Engaged in this paradoxical policy, Bourguiba had to cross swords with his own ideological parents. His motivating force was the spirit of nationalism that had been unleashed by the philosophy of the West.

The West kept Bourguiba confined for a dozen years, we have seen. In the solitude of his confinement he had the best opportunity to engage in a dialogue with the West. The Occident spoke to him through the seminal literature he read. When he emerged from the jails of the West he was more a Westerner than when he had entered them. The old adage says: *Plus ça change, plus c'est la même chose.* In Bourguiba's case it should read: *Plus c'est la même chose, plus ça change.*

5

The Island Cosmos of Indonesia's Sukarno

The captain of the tramp steamer was in no hurry. Besides, the leisurely rhythm of his operations was dictated by the limited power of his asthmatic craft. It was a K.P.M. ship, *Koninklijke Paketvaart Maatschappij,* but there was nothing royal about this old boat of the Dutch Navigation Company which had been exiled to service in the Outer Islands of the Netherlands East Indies. The cargo was heavy and the native hands at the ports of call were slow. Destined for many islands, the vessel carried food, passengers, and mail. Each item of the human freight wore an identification tag. Banished by the Dutch masters of the islands, they were Indonesian exiles.

The stately pace of the ship was four knots an hour. Its name? Probably *Kaimana,* or *Merauke,* or some other outlandish array of letters, barely legible on the corroded hull that was half-submerged in the equatorial waters. The human cargo consisted of about a dozen young men. And they had names by which to call one another—and not merely numbers. Yet these young people were bound for their prison graves. Just now, however, they were surrounded by the vastest imaginable freedom, cradled by a sea, the blue color of which was tinged with gold. Here the sky appeared to extend the horizon, not to enclose it. Lounging on the deck, the young people inhaled deep breaths of the spicy scent wafted to them on the caressing western breeze.

For days they had been sailing the Java Sea, calling at ports that bore such languid names as Surabaja and Semarang. At every anchorage the Dutch police came aboard to take a census of the prisoners. That was a humiliating performance. Then the boat began to move again. What men lacked in courtesy, nature made up. As the vessel skirted each island the palm trees fringing the shore seemed to curtsy deeply to the exiles.

Thus the ship cleaved its way into the Flores Sea, a body of water that is peppered by countless islands. The old tub continued to call at more ports with intriguing names—at Makassar, at Bonthain, at Baubau in the Gulf of Bone. The ship was delayed at the latter port for several days, for the pumps had to be repaired. Into the infinity of space the infinity of time was fused. Again the boat steamed away, breasting the waves almost imperceptibly, so slowly did it proceed. In time, it reached the Banda Sea, in the direction of the rising sun.

Suddenly, the world encasing the steamer underwent a change. The Banda Sea seemed to be in a tantrum. It was behind a misty curtain of sand that the passengers saw the jungle shaking, whipped by a fury that portended the approach of a typhoon. The water was no longer blue but a wrathful brown, and it leapt up in great spouts across the battered bow of the ship.

As suddenly as they had come, these periods of fury yielded, and nature revealed one of her more relaxed moods, as if she had become wearied of the hysterical acrobatics. Again the brown sea had turned to blue, and the waters were at their normal serenity.

In a few more days, the boat reached the broad expanses of the Arafura Sea where islands no longer perforated the placid azure water. There the leaden weight of the equatorial sun flattened even the ripples of the sea into calm unruffled surface. They were navigating at the very limits of two worlds, in waters that separated the farthest East, New Guinea, from the farthest West, Australia.

One day they sighted Cape Walsh, the keen-edged promontory of Frederik Hendrick Island. Now they were enveloped in the brooding silence of the easternmost shores of the Netherlands East Indies—New Guinea. There they finally found their way into the mouth of the Digoel River.

The waters of the stream were a dirty brown. The human freight and the remaining cargo were transferred to a boat of shallower draught. As it inched its way against the insistent current, the boat was swaddled in the steamy air which appeared to oppress the entire world. An impenetrably solid wall of poison-green jungle safeguarded the interior beyond the shore.

At various places the boat stopped at rotting planks that served as landing places. There the people aboard witnessed living scenes out of Joseph Conrad novels. Skeletal bodies of authority came striding out of the bush, accompanied by emaciated porters.

A majestic bearing marked the European officials of a trading firm who supervised the unloading of western consignments. The porters who shouldered the freight moved with the resignation of human beasts of burden. Slow-moving lips inquired about the anticipated return schedule of the boat. Then, as majestically as they had come, the officials faded into the bush, followed by their porters.

The boat was tied up for a night at a tortuous turn in the river. All night long the young men who were to be exiled "behind the back of God" heard sounds that must have kept awake the first men of creation on the first day of their lives: the cawing, churtling, gurgling, hissing sounds of birds, reptiles, mammals, and insects pursuing their difficult existences in a jungle where one life could be maintained only at the cost of the death of another.

And so the boat reached its destination at the end of the world, in Dutch New Guinea, at the Digoel concentration camp. Boven Digoel it was called officially, reserved for the administratively *gestraften,* as the Dutch termed them, the "punished," the people who were sent here for indeterminate stays without the benefit of trial. The Dutch considered them subversives, although the kinsmen and friends of these people called them patriots who had rebelled against the colonial system. These exiles were men who had fought for the freedom of Indonesia, those three thousand islands that straddle the Equator over a distance of three thousand miles.

Even though it was a maximum security camp, the prisoners were neither locked up in cells nor restricted in their movements. Where could they go? They would have been ground to dust by the rapacious forces of the jungle. Even if they had come upon a native settlement, the chances are that they would have been destroyed. Even more dangerous than the hostile forces of nature were one's fellow human beings.

On the ship's manifest the name of one of the exiles was entered as "Soekarno." That was the Dutch version of the name known in contemporary history as Sukarno. (Most Indonesians have only one name.) For many years the history of the three thousand islands was linked with that name. So was the history of one of the most populous of all nations—some hundred million people—Indonesia.

Sukarno had been arrested on December 29, 1929. And

what was the charge against him? Fomenting a rebellion against the government of the Netherlands East Indies that was to have taken place early in 1930. Caught in the Dutch police dragnet were three other young Indonesian accomplices: Gatot Mangku-pradja, Supriadinata, and Maskun. All four were leaders of the P.N.I.—*Perserikatan Nasional Indonesia,* "Indonesian National Organization," which advocated non-cooperation with the archipelago government—à la Gandhi in India. Sukarno had founded the organization two years before.

For eight months the men were kept in the prison of the city of Bandung. Then the trial began, on August 18, 1930, and it lasted four months. Its highlight was Sukarno's speech of defense which was an accusation: *Indonesia Menggugat,* "Indonesia Accuses," in which the accused turned accuser and indicted Holland for misappropriating, during three hundred years, the wealth of the three thousand islands.

The judges convicted Sukarno to four years of penal servitude, the longest term meted out to any of the defendants.

A YOUNG MAN AND AN AMBITION

His year of birth was entered on the manifest as 1901. "Alias Abdul Rahman," the document indicated, and that was a common Moslem name: Abdul—the servant of Allah, and Rahman—the Merciful, one of His ninety-nine attributes.

Sukarno was now twenty-nine years old but looked even younger. He was well built, of medium height, with a strong, heavily structured face that reflected his many moods, stormy and benign in turn. He had dark eyes, flashing, searching, quizzical, moody. He strode, rather than walked, halting impetuously, turning around suddenly, facing his interlocutor with a laconic statement. He could be imperious as well as submissive, a consummate actor, now an exile. The length of his enforced stay might depend upon a bureaucrat's mood in Batavia, administrative center of Netherlands East Indies, on the island of Java. The bureaucratic mood, in turn, might be influenced by the display of the proper amount of contrition this Sukarno exhibited. But how had young Sukarno become a maximum security risk?

The place of his birth was Surabaya, an important port city in Java. There the inhabitants had a window not only on the thousands of islands of the archipelago but also on the rest of the world, because there one could behold the ships of all the major maritime nations.

His father was a school supervisor. His mother was a Balinese. While most of the Indonesians are Moslems, the Balinese are mainly Hindus. Sukarno says that his mother was of the Brahman caste. Centuries ago the people of the archipelago received their religion from Arab traders and that is how Sukarno happened to be a Moslem. The followers of Islam on these islands have been in contact with too many faiths for too long a time to maintain unqualifiedly the monolithic traits of Mohammed's creed. Indonesians are inclined to be more eclectic than the people from whom they acquired their faith.

"My ancestors were poor peasants," Sukarno told his audience on one of his visits to the United States. Americans like to hear about important people with humble beginnings, and Sukarno must have been aware of this fact. His ancestors were, probably, not poor peasants, but members of the lower nobility. His father was a man of erudition and of no common intellect, the type of man who under a stultifying rule would be inclined toward brooding introspection. Yet he was not doing badly compared to the other natives. His monthly earnings amounted to about ten dollars, and that was about three times higher than the average in the island realm.

Sukarno lived under the roof of his paternal grandfather in Eastern Java for reasons upon which he refuses to cast light. There he attended the village school. Most of the native children did not go to school at all—they were needed at farm work on the fields. Other children completed their studies in the village. Not, however, Sukarno. When he was twelve, he was sent to a Dutch school, one that was open only to better-class natives. This fact alone casts doubt on Sukarno's peasant origin, which seems to be a piece of romanticism for American consumption. The child was given the name of Kusno. His father's name was Sostrodihardjo. Years later Kusno changed his name to that of a stalwart hero of Javanese mythology, Sukarno.

It was in the house of a paternal friend that young Sukarno first became acquainted with the Indonesian malaise. The friend, Hadji Omar Said Tjokroaminoto, was a strange mixture of a devout Moslem, zealous nationalist, and ardent Marxist. His devotion to Islam was attested by his prenomen, "Hadji," indicating that he had undertaken the devoted Moslem's arduous pilgrimage to the holiest of all shrines in Mecca. "Said" in his name articulated his family's claim to descent from Mohammed the Prophet.

Religion is an all-pervasive influence to a devout Moslem, expressing secular as well as spiritual aspirations, the only worthy objects of communal loyalty. For this Said nationalism was not an isolated attachment but formed part of his faith. Indonesia's earliest religio-nationalist movement, *Sarekat Islam,* was founded by this family friend. To most religious people Marxism appears to be Satan's own guise. Did not the founder of this school of thought believe that "religion was the opium of the people?" Marxism appeared in an entirely different guise to young Sukarno's teacher who was in the habit of pointing out that already some twelve centuries before the birth of Marx, the Prophet Mohammed was preaching the principles of Socialist economics. Thus Sukarno was initiated into an ideology in which Marxism, Islam, and nationalism were fused and confused.

Said Tjokroaminoto detected great promise in the young man. It was he who paid for Sukarno's education in an urban secondary school that normally was attended only by children of Indonesia's Dutch officials and by the sons of native officeholders of senior rank. Sukarno could not bear the thought of being second in his class. His keen-eyed schoolmates called him *djago,* "rooster," king of the barnyard. Under the influence of the paternal friend, a critic of Dutch rule, young Sukarno refused to accept the version of life as presented to him by his teachers.

Holland which ruled over the archipelago was democracy incarnate in the European homeland; in Indonesia it was the very embodiment of autocracy. The two parts of the same kingdom were thus two different worlds. Virtue in one became crime in the other. In the history of man's attempts to be free, the Netherlands had played a leading role. It had fought the Spanish-Habsburg autocracy. But in the school which Sukarno attended, the students were told very little about the exploits of William of Orange. The history textbooks represented the world as an unchanging phenomenon in which Indonesia's place was eternally fixed.

But change was in the air—even though not in the books. Young Sukarno obtained reading matter of the kind Dutch youth studied in the Netherlands. Thus he was introduced to the growth of democratic institutions in Europe. A clandestine native student organization, *Jong Java,* "Young Java," appealed to him and he became an active member.

POLITICS AND ENGINEERING

Having completed his secondary studies, Sukarno matriculated at the Institute of Technology of Bandung. In that enchanting mountain town, Dutch officials had recreated a miniature "Holland" in the hills, with fine public buildings, homes and stores, cinemas, a theater, and even a race course. The officials boasted that the Malabar Station on the nearby Pengalengan Heights was the most powerful radio post in the world. Bandung was also an administrative center, seat of the Priangan Residency. Thus, without leaving his native Java, Sukarno had moved from the Orient to the Occident, for the spirit of the West pervaded the intellectual climate of this mountain town.

The occupation young Sukarno had selected for himself was that of the West. There were few colonial possessions richer than the archipelago in raw materials for which there was a worldwide market: rubber, quinine, tin, oil, and spices. The people of the islands could have become rich. But they were poor, among the poorest in the world, with the lowest per capita income. Many of the fat Dutch burghers were, on the other hand, very rich. That was the rule of the game. Western countries were wealthy, their colonies were poor. In the West there were many factory chimneys to turn raw materials into finished products. In the colonies the air was fresh and there was poverty. The spirit of the West called for factories. Let smoke pollute the air, and let there also be high living standards. Learning about the growth of democracy was fine, but democracy in the modern world was nourished by air pollution.

Sukarno prepared himself for the calling of a civil engineer, a man whose mission it is to build bridges, roads, and ports. He was motivated by the desire to break out of his Oriental isolation and to enter the twentieth century. He as well as the century were now in their early twenties. World War I had unleashed the torrential energy of a new type of nationalism. It was not merely a political but also a religious phenomenon. The nation had become the godhead before which the world prostrated itself. Man acquired his full stature through the nation. Sensitive to the changing moods of life, Sukarno was among those who heeded the call of the nation.

This call was reinforced by the machinations of the Soviet Union. Powerful radio stations urged the need for change on the underprivileged areas of the world. *Debout les damnés de la terre,* "arise the damned of the world"; the underdog was to get on top of the top-dog. Knowing little about the operation of communism in Russia, young rebels interpreted it in accordance with their dreamy idealism.

"General Study Group" was the name of the clandestine political organization young Sukarno organized at the Bandung school. There, too, he continued to be the "rooster." Members of the group bent their energies to study the structure and functions of modern nationalism. They also read the books of Marx and Engels, and paid close attention to Lenin. They, too, became convinced that "imperialism was the last stage of capitalism." The forces of history were not unbending, they learned. The Dutch had not been masters of the archipelago from the beginning of time. The dynamism of historical institutions was changing in proportion with the ebbs and tides of the ideas by which they were animated.

Sukarno was concerned about the enormous variety of the Indonesian scene. There were thousands of islands and, it seemed, almost as many dialects and customs. And these differences were maintained because each island was like an organ in a body that had no coordinator. Let there be one language on the thousands of islands and there would be one nation. Sukarno liked simple formulas then as well as later, formulas which unsophisticated people could comprehend. The simpler the formula the greater the number of people attracted to them. "One people, one country, one language," was one of his axioms. "Indonesian nationalism needs one tongue." This simple formula led years later to the adoption of the national language, *Bahasa Indonesia.* It is based on Malayan, enriched by the vocabulary of other tongues.

Ideas are plentiful and anyone can produce them, Sukarno learned. Organization was the strength of the Western world, and the lack of it was the cause of Oriental weakness. Nobody should be able to say that young Sukarno was a poor organizer. In a cooperative effort he helped to set up the *Partai Nasional Indonesia,* PNI, a secular political body. In Indonesia, we saw the temporal and the religious were intertwined. The political party was infused with spiritual values. Allah's eyes rested not only on the mosque but also on the assembly hall.

The eyes of the Dutch intelligence also rested on political organizations. The young rebels had learned several tricks from their European counterparts, and one was the use of pseudonyms. That is how Sukarno became Abdul Rahman, the Servant of the All-Merciful One. In the penumbra of the underground, the active mind of the engineering student continued to spin the web in which the Dutch were to be entangled.

"The spoken word is evanescent," said the Latin proverb, "while the written word is permanent." And that is how the *Fikiran Rakjat* began—the "People's Thought," which was largely Sukarno's interpretation of what people should be thinking. However, political thoughts at variance with those of the authorities were signs of subversion.

Another strand of "subversion" was woven by young Indonesians studying in Holland. There they learned about the revolt of the Netherlanders against their Spanish masters and there the Prince of Orange was a national hero. To some of the young Indonesians in Holland the Dutchmen appeared to be the latter-day Spaniards in Indonesia. They formed an organization to which they gave the bland title, *Perhimpunan Indonesia,* "Indonesian Association." To that they attached a revolutionary slogan, *merdeka,* "freedom," which was to be the battle cry of another generation. Leader of this movement was Mohammed Hatta, who used the pseudonym "Hafil."

"BEHIND ALLAH'S BACK"

This is how young Sukarno was transported into the steaming jungles of Netherlands New Guinea, at Digoel in 1930. And that is how "Hafil" Mohammed Hatta and another young rebel, Sutan Sjahrir, were taken there, too. Sukarno's sentence was largely dependent on how much "contrition" he would show. Would the jungle be able to "brainwash" a young man who had seen the light and could not help following it?

What was Digoel like? It was truly behind Allah's back, where the excess energy of young hotheads was to be drained off by isolation and malaria. The camp consisted of two parts: Tanah Merah, which was the administrative center, and Tanah Tinggi, five hours canoeing up the river. There was more life at Merah than at Tinggi and it was there that the K.P.M. boat dropped Sukarno. Then the ship made a quick turnabout as if afraid of the evil spirits that seemed to haunt the place; the steamer would not be seen again for months.

The camp administration left the *gestraften* to their own devices. Guards were superfluous in a place that had no gates. The exiles could "escape" into the jungle, where hunger, thirst, insects, wild beasts, and Stone Age natives would take care of them. As a protection against the sun and rain the political prisoners had the right to build huts for themselves. For this they needed only branches of the trees and corrugated iron. They helped one another. In their own villages and towns such neighborly help was customary, known as *gotong royong,* "mutual help." The camp contained several hundred exiles.

They were afforded a chance to work for the administration, if jobs were available. For every day of work under the tropical sun they got forty cents. This enabled them to improve their prison diet. Normally, their calorie intake was insufficient, their worst foes were the mosquitoes. Although Indonesia is the world's largest supplier of the cinchona bark, from which quinine—a specific medicine against malaria—is made, the camps had not enough of it on hand.

Oppressive living conditions produced serious cases of neurosis, including the "amok" psychology—exiles running wild, flinging themselves on one another, jumping into the muddy stream, to the immense delight of the crocodiles, or vanishing into the jungle, to be lost to sight forever. Political prisoners in other parts of the world, separated from freedom by barbed wire, knew this as the "barbed-wire disease." To persons afflicted with it, the faces of fellow inmates become objects of intense hatred—always the same faces, hungry men, hungry for food and sex, for companionship and for mental stimulation.

For a young man of overactive intellect the temptation was great in the Digoel camp to explore the environment. The region contained vast areas in which time seemed to have stood still, where people lived as they had lived thousands of years before. Neither the "colonial exploiters" nor anyone else had ever penetrated into that interior. Could it not be therefore a bucolic life in which simple people lived in simple communities where the normal appetites of humanity could be satisfied by the fruits of an overabundant nature? Yes, indeed, there were simple people with simple tastes in the interior. Some had a taste for the flesh of their neighbors. They were not only hunters and food-gatherers but head-hunters, cannibals. It was neither feasible nor desirable to engage in anthropological exploration in these last remaining reservations of pre-civilization.

There were primitives up river, though, who were not head-hunters, although they were far from friendly. Some of the exiles visited them from time to time. They were known as the Kaja-Kajas, and if primitive life was like that, the exiles begged to be excused from this earthly paradise. In the Kaja-Kaja settlements as many as a score of people often occupied a single room. Women of the Kaja-Kaja settlements nursed piglets at their breasts. The people lived in the midst of a cacophony and stench which gave the exiles second thoughts about bucolic life close to nature.

A HISTORICAL LESSON

"The Digoel camp enabled me to think more clearly." There was plenty of time for that. Books were censored and so were the letters. But both books and letters did reach the exiles. Luckily for political prisoners, people who apply for jobs as guards are not among the most alert people. Their backs were turned on what was going on much of the time because they were indifferent or just lazy. Never before had Sukarno had the chance to learn so much about the historical background of Indonesia.

The impression young Indonesians obtained in their schools contained a historic distortion. Indonesians at one time were the masters of an empire which extended far beyond their archipelago into Malaya, into portions of Cambodia, and even into parts of the Philippines. This Shrivijaya empire flourished centuries before the Christian Era.

It was not the only demonstration of Indonesian statecraft. There was also the Madjapahit empire, nearly two thousand years later, flourishing for centuries, fanning out into the Southeast Asian mainland, and extremely successful in overseas trade, too. History spoke of other Indonesian ventures of statecraft. No, Sukarno found, he was not of an inferior breed. What, then, had enabled a tiny nation at the other end of the globe to create a colonial empire of thousands of these islands?

He saw the view he had held as a student confirmed, for

there was only one explanation, and one only. Organization was more important than area or population. Entombed in his green inferno, sleepless in his jungle grave, Sukarno had an eternity of time to survey the condition of his country. The very name Indonesia released a chain of thoughts in his mind. It was from the Indian peninsula that his people had got Buddhism and Hinduism. Then came Islam from another portion of Asia, spreading across the archipelago in the trail of Arab traders.

Again Indonesia could learn from India and the Arabs. First and foremost, from India. The hundreds of millions of people of that subcontinent had an organization, the Indian National Congress Party. It was a mass organization. It comprised all political views, right, left, center, and did not dissipate its energies on extraneous issues. It was organized for one purpose only: independence from British rule. And it had a spiritual leader and a symbol, a man whom his people called Mahatma, the "Great Soul"—Mahatma Gandhi. Indonesia, too, needed such a mass organization and also a Great Soul. Would he, Sukarno, be the man?

And how was it that Islam followed in the wake of trade? Because the Arabs were God-intoxicated people, spreading the teachings of the Prophet even when buying spices. They must have been dedicated people, and whatever organization he would be able to establish would come only if he devoted all his energy to his cause. But he must first be free. And to be free he must convince his jailers that he was reformed. To do that he must dissemble his thoughts, for as soon as his thoughts were acceptable, he himself would be acceptable into the society of free men. There he would be free to engage in his missionary work—to organize and to become—who knows?—the Great Soul of his organization. He learned in his exile that Indonesians had been able to create and to operate large empires. Why should they not be able to run their own country?

Sukarno's apparent change of heart was noted by the authorities. They had kept him under observation for signs of a possible relapse, but he exhibited no such signs. They saw Sukarno as a reincarnated man who had become convinced that his subversive ways were of use neither to himself nor to the people of Indonesia. And, one day, Sukarno was told to make his preparations to leave on the next K.P.M. boat.

Witnesses to his self-abasement might have said: "Sukarno is an opportunist." Freedom for Sukarno, however, was merely an interval between two periods of detentions; before long he would be back in enforced residence. But during the short time of his freedom he made an attempt to form a party.

The party he had in mind was a popular movement with a very broad base. He started his organizational work and soon had—in his estimate—some 20,000 followers. Mohammed Hatta, free now, too, did not agree with him. Hatta thought that before the gates could be opened to the masses there must be a professional élite—the framework, the "cadre." Revolutionary techniques needed specialists who would be the recruiters of a mass organization. Hatta concentrated on organizing an élite, and now he claimed that he had about a thousand followers.

Sukarno held that conditions in Indonesia were different from those of other colonial areas. In India there was an educated native élite. In Indonesia there were only a few educated individuals but not a group; in a year no more than four young people were graduated from secondary schools—in a colonial empire of tens of millions of people. In the absence of an educated middle class there must be a strong will. And that Sukarno's was. He had an idea that he could sway the masses with the intensity of his feeling, inspire them with the feeling of their own importance, and turn them into articulate, political-minded individuals. He could talk to the masses more readily than to the intellectuals.

Soon he found that he could not reach either the masses or the élite, because he was surrounded by the secret police. Informers had infiltrated his mass movement. Before he could turn his ideas of organization to practical account, he was apprehended again. Once more he was aboard a steamer of the K.P.M. The year was 1933, and now he was to be entombed in "green mansions" for good.

FIRST FLORES AND THEN KEMPEITAI

For nearly all of the next nine years Sukarno remained in detention. This time the boat deposited him at Endeh, on Flores island of the Lesser Sundas. He does not seem to have manifested the requisite amount of contrition because he was soon transferred to a maximum security place of detention, the town of Bencovlen, on the southwest coast of the island of Sumatra.

Here he lived between the Barisan range in its jungle vestment and the malarial coastal plain. He became personally acquainted with the colonial paradox of Indonesia. The residency of Benkulen, in which he was detained, was particularly rich in colonial wealth, not only rubber and spices, but also extensive plantations of coffee and tea. Within the residency there was the Rejang-Lebon district, rich in silver and gold. Since this Outer Island was so rich, why were the people so abysmally poor? Because wealth belonged to the colonial exploiters, and not to the workers. He had already learned that the solution was *merdeka* and *merdeka* only—"freedom."

Years passed, and Sukarno remained a human cipher. No longer was he to cause any trouble to the Dutch. A pall of silence descended upon him and even his name may have been forgotten. These must have been years of torture for Sukarno. What could a political prisoner do for endless years of detention? He would think a lot about the future—because he would not have become a revolutionary politician if he had not been an optimist. Also, he could obtain a vast erudition through his appetite for books. But Sukarno was not an intellectual—anything but that. He was a practical-minded man who, however, shared a failing of the intellectual in that he believed that he could sway people to his views. Although not an intellectual he had to read or be completely lost in apathy. He read books about prominent statesmen and how they had succeeded. He was interested in the unfolding of the national sentiment in the West, too, and particularly in the history of the arduous road of Germany and Italy to nationhood. He liked to study the biographies of nation-builders: Garibaldi, Cavour, Mazzini, and above all, of the man to whom he was most attracted, although he disliked his philosophy, Germany's Iron Chancellor, Bismarck.

STRANGE PEOPLE ARRIVE

The prisoners did not know when the war broke out in Europe— at least they did not know it for sure. The name "Pearl Harbor" must also have been nebulous. They heard that the armored hosts of Hitler had swept into the Low Countries and that Holland had ceased to exist as an independent nation. That was of deep interest to the political prisoners. Indonesia was thus no longer anchored to her step-motherland. But the Dutch of Indonesia were still the masters. Even without the backing of their motherland they could maintain their control.

According to the legend, transmitted from generation to generation, King Djoyoboyo of Java had made a prophecy many centuries before that the islands would be oppressed by the white race for a long period. But, in due time, alien yellow-skinned men from a distant land would appear in Java and these aliens would drive out the whites. Power would be seized by the yellow-skins but they would not long be able to hold it. After a hundred days they, too, would be vanquished. And then . . . what then? The happiest of all endings. Power would be restored to the Indonesians themselves.

The yellow people came in the wake of the events at Pearl Harbor where the maritime power of the American giant seemed to have been destroyed. The yellow-skinned people erupted from their island fortress, Japan, and there was no containing their ex· pansion. With a miraculous display of energy they overran hun· dreds, perhaps, thousands of islands, swept southward on the Asian continent and conquered an empire that now appeared to be one of the largest the world had ever seen.

One day these yellow men predicted by good King Djoyoboyo appeared also on the island of Sumatra, and on Java, and on hundreds of other islands of the vast Indonesia archipelago. These little people behaved like giants; they appeared so suddenly, and so decisively did they round up the tall Netherlanders, treating them like dirt. The Japanese had piercing voices and they meant what they said. They were the Greater East-Asia Master Race.

The Japanese had a grand design which they proclaimed to all the world. They, the supremely skillful organizers, would work together with all the people of Eastern Asia and lay the foundations for mutual prosperity. This design they called the Greater East-Asia Co-Prosperity Scheme. Most of East Asia had been taken and now they were expanding also into Southeast Asia.

They brought with them the *kempeitai*, their dour secret police, whose voices were not only piercing but also demanding, and they demanded the whereabouts of a man by the name of Sukarno. For years the name of Sukarno had not appeared in public print, and he seemed to have been relegated into obscurity. But the Japanese knew that his name was enshrined in the hearts of many Indonesians whose loyalties did not depend upon this morning's headlines. The Japanese had learned that more than any other fighter for the rights of Indonesia Sukarno was respected by his people. So they needed to talk to him. When they found him, they did not smile, indeed they appeared to be very angry. And angrily they told him that he was free, that they wanted him to help his people—his own grand design—and that the best way for him to do so was to bring the Indonesians into Japan's Greater East-Asia Co-Prosperity Scheme which now was also the Greater Southeast-Asia Scheme.

What was Sukarno to do? He and his friends considered the Dutch their No. 1 foe. The Japanese were Asians, like themselves, and there was reason to be proud of their story. They had proved to be stronger than the strongest of the arrogant European colonial powers. The Japanese themselves had felt the heavy hand of the West. Now they asked the help of their fellow Asians.

However, there was also an "on the other hand." The Japanese were members of an alliance which the Western world knew as the Axis—an alliance with Germany and Italy. Germany was led by a lunatic, Adolf Hitler, who was constantly raving about the "superior" blood of some European races. He was also maniacally convinced of the right of the strong to rule, a Fascist who had established the state as a new god. Italy was under the thumb of the Fascist Benito Mussolini, not a fanatic madman, to be sure, but a big-mouthed mountebank who ranted about the wonderful accomplishments that war could bring to man. Also Mussolini believed that the people in Africa were inferior creatures. Not many years before he had imposed his rule on the Ethiopians. The Japanese, too, believed that might was right and that the strong had the right to oppress the weak.

The offer of the Japanese, however, may have been made in good faith, so reflected some Indonesians. Also, first things first, and so—some Indonesians said—"Let's clear out the Netherlanders first." To show their good faith the Japanese quickly trained an Indonesian armed militia, called *Peta*. Sukarno was impressed. Japan also permitted the Indonesians to established *Putera*, a semi-autonomous organization, the Center of People's Power.

Some of the Indonesian patriots said that the Japanese were no better than the Dutch and, above everything, were Fascists. Merely by looking at Hitler one could see what kind of fanatic he was. Best known among the patriots who reasoned thus were Sultan Sjahrir and Amir Sjarifuddin, and they refused to collaborate with the Japanese. Instead, they vanished out of sight and out of reach of the Japanese.

Sukarno became the president of the Japanese-sponsored *Putera*. The dour-faced secret service men told Sukarno that the Japanese Emperor wished to honor him. They flew him to Tokyo where he was admitted into the Imperial presence, which was also the Divine presence because the Emperor was God. Facing the stony-faced God and His stony-faced retinue, Sukarno received the accolade. He was invested with the Order of the Sacred Treasure, Second Class. Had the Japanese been quite sure of their collaborator they might have conferred on him the Sacred Treasure, First Class.

DOUBLE, DOUBLE . . .

The year was 1945 and the Japanese had overestimated their strength. Carried away by their easy victories, they overlooked the most elementary considerations of logistics. Or perhaps it was in the very nature of their sudden victory that they overreached the limits of their strength. In the West the Fascist armies were also on the run. Suddenly, everything seemed to move into reverse. The Japanese were quick-witted enough to know that if they were to salvage any part of their newly acquired empire they must do so with the cooperation of the native population. They were ready to grant Indonesia independence.

"Every Japanese will understand," Sukarno said when it was all over, "why I worked with the Japanese. We turned the tables on them."

This they did so successfully that the Japanese were crushed; the prophecy of King Djoyoboyo, but for the exact number of days, was totally vindicated.

It did not take Sukarno long to convince his people that he collaborated with the Japanese only to design the destruction of the yellow-skinned people. As quickly as the Japanese came, they were out. But the Dutch were not back. Sukarno deserved his reputation as a master politician. However, many questions remained to be answered in a short time. Was Indonesia ready to take the reins? How strong were the Dutch? The war was over, and a new war was on—the cold war between the United States and the Soviet Union. How would these two countries react to a change in Indonesia's status? Sukarno knew the Soviets' reaction, but he was not sure about the United States. What about the Dutch and the English who had armed forces in the vicinity? Hasty action could jeopardize the chances of the future.

Sukarno can act cautiously—sometimes. By nature he is a diplomatic poker-player. It was he and Hatta who signed a cautiously worded proclamation, published on August 17, 1945: "We, the people of Indonesia, herewith proclaim the independence of Indonesia. All matters pertaining to the transfer of power, etc., will be carried out effectively in the shortest possible time."

He had taken a big step, but he had avoided the proclamation of a republic. Independence, after all, was conceivable within a Netherlands Commonwealth—à la Britain. And now he was waiting for the consequences.

They were not late in coming. "They" were the British. Why not the Dutch? Because their shattered small country was in no position to act quickly. The British sent armed forces to occupy key points on the main islands. "Imperialists of all countries unite," commented an Indonesian newspaper. "You have nothing to lose but your principles."

The British were followed by a single battalion of Dutch soldiers who were to subdue tens of millions of people of hundreds of islands. Then came the stolid and unsmiling NICA, Netherlands Indies Civil Administration, as unsmiling as the Japanese had been, but much taller. Also, the administrators were white. The legendary Indonesian King had not foreseen such a turn of events.

Sukarno made no move. The Dutch and the British had played out their roles; they counted no longer. The Soviet Union was opposed to "colonialism," besides she was still licking her wounds. There was now only one outside power that mattered— the United States. Neither the British, nor the Dutch, nor the newly created United Nations could decide the fate of Indonesia. Sukarno knew that Washington must be watching for the reaction of his people.

Not in vain had Sukarno studied mass psychology in the solitude of his jails. His problem was how to counteract the disparate interests and the fissiparous tendencies of a vast archipelago spread over an endless ocean area. There must be a unifying interest that could be expressed in a common policy, perhaps in a slogan that might summarize the aspirations of the tens of millions. Such an expression must be not only simple but also forceful, compelling.

Sukarno is a complex person, and his ability to feel his way intuitively is, of course, the hallmark of the man of destiny. Here practical-mindedness and lack of sophistication were assets.

Though he could not construct a paragraph that might explain Indonesia's problems, he knew that one word was all that was needed to relaunch the program which could help his country: *merdeka*, "freedom."

The uncanny insight of the man, Sukarno, is reflected precisely in this ability to perceive the strength of the simple. He will not look for complicated expressions when simple words will suffice. "Freedom," to many of us is a hackneyed word, one that people no longer can get excited about or read significance into. But if the person who utters the word *merdeka* is an Indonesian, that can be quite another matter—especially if that person has listened to Sukarno explain in a speech lasting a full hour the meaning of freedom. Sukarno may not add anything startling to an understanding of the word to a Westerner. But to the Indonesian he weaves a magic spell and releases emotions that thrill the listener.

MERDEKA

Merdeka to a simple islander meant everything he wanted it to mean. It meant more food and also a higher standard of living, school for his children, and hope for a better work opportunity, and it meant a little more of the pleasures of life. Lastly—and only in that order—it meant what one calls "human dignity." In the scale of immediate values, food is a million times more important than the dignity of oneself as an individual.

The word did catch the imagination of some people. Anyone could have seen that who observed the thousands—not thousands but tens of thousands—hanging on the words that fell from the lips of Sukarno. The majority of his listeners could not follow what he said. Their dialect and his literary language belonged to different worlds. But his intentions and their aspirations belonged to the same cosmos, and that was what counted. Sukarno knew that Washington knew, and what Washington knew the Western Allies' foreign policy was to learn, too. They knew that the "free world" espoused by the West could not be burdened by millions of slaves.

THE END AND THE BEGINNING

There are a few simple natural laws in international relations. Natural Law No. 1 says that no power vacuum can be tolerated in strategic areas. Indonesia is a strategic area. Should it turn into a power vacuum an aggressive power is bound to move in. Of course, to itself no nation appears an aggressive power.

Then there is Natural Law No. 2, which states that a power vacuum in a strategic area may be desirable under certain conditions. It is desirable if two powerful nations keep each other in balance. It is more desirable than filling in the vacuum when the "filler" is an aggressive and highly dynamic power. A country with strong financial resources hopes eventually to assert its economic influence in the area.

In addition to these Natural Laws there is an axiom, which says that a free world filled with too many unfree people becomes something of a paradox. Indonesia as the unwilling colony of the Netherlands was bound to be such a paradox and an embarrassment to the leader of the free world—the United States.

This was another power situation which Sukarno weighed and found to his liking. He knew, of course, that Washington could not afford to advance too far in making its influence felt in the region, but he also knew that no power was more effective than the invisible pressure of the United States. That is why he signed that irrevocable proclamation, the Declaration of Independence, without being at all sure that he and his people were ready to implement the words.

The Dutch were quite sure that Sukarno made the greatest mistake of his life by signing his name to the Declaration of Independence. They could not be budged from their belief that the Indonesians were lacking in administrative gifts, completely unorganized and unorganizable people, sunk into the sloth of their tropical paradise. They admitted that even if the Indonesians had their intellectual élite, the usual frustrated literati, they were not "illuminati," merely poor imitators of Demosthenes, mass-producing purple-patched phrases in their intoxicated eloquence. For all their eloquence, the literati could not operate computer machines. The Indonesians, the Dutch summed up, were floundering in a dreamworld of *malesh*—"let Allah's will be done."

On the other hand, the Indonesians had their own opinion of the Dutch. They recalled the days when the little Japanese supermen had herded the tall Dutch "undermen" into concentration camps. When the Dutch showed their dejection in the presence of Japanese arrogance they lost face. Also, the Indonesians recalled how long it had taken the Dutch to produce a single battalion for the occupation of the three thousand islands after the war. Above all, they knew about the cable the presumably victorious Dutch—members of the Grand Alliance—had dispatched to the supposedly defeated Japanese, requesting the vanquished to keep their grip on the islands until the victors, erstwhile defeated, reappeared in the archipelago.

As to themselves, Sukarno had not been the only one to read about the notable history of the Indonesians and, especially, of their ability, demonstrated time and again, of holding not only their own land but also vast foreign territories.

This was then the situation when the Dutch returned, and the British brush-fire brigade was relieved. The Hollanders found that in their absence Sukarno and Hatta had signed a Declaration of Independence. The returning Netherlanders refused to recognize it, but they realized the obligations of the new colonialism that had been defined by America to suit the conditions of the cold war.

Merdeka could no longer be ignored. The Dutch, therefore, proclaimed that there should be a commonwealth, to consist of the Netherlands and of Indonesia. The latter would become a federation, consisting of several states the most important of which was to be the Indonesian Republic, comprising Java, Madura, and Sumatra. Then the States of Borneo and of East Indonesia. In making this plan the Dutch recalled how they had played one native ruler against the other. Again they would play the game of "divide and rule." The new nation would be linked to the Netherlands through the Dutch-Indonesian Union. The Dutch had the administrative knowledge, the Indonesian leaders the spellbinding eloquence. It was clear what ultimately would be the outcome of the association. It would be something like the Anglo-Egyptian Sudan of those days—all "Anglo" in substance and only part Egyptian in appearance.

PRESIDENTS AND PUPPETS

Sukarno was the president of the Republic, Sjahrir the premier. "Puppets," that would be their roles as the men in The Hague cast them. What could these natives of the far-off islands know of the mechanics of government? Besides, government involved economic power, and that was in Dutch hands.

The Dutch had assumed that the pomp and circumstance

of power would satisfy Sukarno and his colleagues. The latter would be bespangled with the highest offices of the State, so high, in fact, that no one would expect them to do any work. What an ideal combination for people who surely had lost the taste for work in jail.

Little did the authorities in The Hague and in Batavia understand the psychology of former inmates of jails. They did not know that only static persons went to seed there, while the dynamic ones recharged their energies. Sukarno and his colleagues wanted to man the ship of state; they did not want merely to be carried in it. Both sides were talking different languages and so the Dutch-Indonesian conferences about the implementation of previous agreements broke down. The Dutch now set out to regain what they appeared to have lost. But the Indonesians were not ready to take their fate lying down. Their Japanese-trained armed forces were in readiness and military action began. Used to colonial conditions, the Dutch regarded the action of Sukarno and his fellow leaders as acts of subversion. Since the temporary republican capital was Djokjakarta, the Dutch launched a surprise attack against it on December 18, 1948. They removed Sukarno, Hatta, and other leaders from their government offices and placed them under arrest.

Sukarno was again on his way to a prison camp, once more on Sumatra. He was placed under detention at Prapat, on the shore of Toba Lake. From there he was transferred to an island off the South Sumatra coast—to the Isle of Bangka. Here more than in many other places, he could again observe the wealth of Indonesia and the cause of its people's poverty. For here the Dutch were in full control of the world's largest tin mine while the miners owned only tattered clothes.

Meanwhile powerful forces interested in the settlement of the Indonesian problem began to assert themselves through the United Nations. There the Soviet Union struck the posture of a knight in shining armor hastening to the rescue of immaculate virtue imperiled by colonialism. Such a role was, of course, to be expected of the Soviets. On the other hand, the United States could not afford to let the situation deteriorate to the point where the emergent Communist party of the islands might be able to stage a coup. The White House, too, had to assert its anti-colonialism. Due to outside pressures, in February, 1949, reinforced by the reassertion of public opinion, the Dutch released Sukarno and his colleagues from their jails. At the same time they evacuated the republican capital.

A few months later a cease-fire agreement was signed. Sovereignty was finally transferred to Indonesia at the end of the year. There was created the Netherlands-Indonesian Union, a sort of Commonwealth, with the Dutch Queen its symbolic head. The U.S.I. was composed of sixteen states of which the Republic of Indonesia was the strongest. Some of the others were East and South Sumatra, Bantam, Pasundaw, Bangka, Billiton, East Java, Madura, the various regions of vast Borneo.

Sukarno must have signed the agreement with tongue in cheek, for the Indonesian federation struck him as a monstrosity devised to further the aims of the Netherlands. Now that he was in the saddle he knew what to do. Fifteen states voted the next year to dissolve their petty governments and to merge with the Republic of Indonesia. The existence of a new nation—the Republic of Indonesia—was proclaimed on August 17, 1950. Sukarno became its first president, and Mohammed Hatta the vice-president. Eventually the bonds between the Netherlands and Indonesia were dissolved. The United States of Indonesia gave place to the present Republic of Indonesia, a unitary state. So the Dutch lost their colonial empire in Southeast Asia. The only region they retained was Western New Guinea, a tremendous area in which civilization had come to a halt in the Stone Age. Economically it meant nothing to The Hague—more a liability than an asset. But it was salve to wounded pride. Through it the Dutch retained a toehold in the Far East. The people of New Guinea were not of the same racial stock as the inhabitants of the other islands.

Apart from that region, colonialism had been routed from Indonesia. The arrangement left a bitter taste in the mouth of the Netherlands. Under their breaths, the Dutch blamed the United States for having ousted them from their ancestral heritage. They were members of the Western alliance, of which the United States was the head, and their criticism therefore had to be subdued. The time would come, they prophesied, when the powers in Washington would rue the day that Indonesia had been left to Sukarno's tender mercies.

TIME OF TROUBLES

Events followed one another precipitately in Indonesia, and only their nature can be indicated here. In his prisons Sukarno seems to have paid scant attention to economics, the dismal science. On the other hand, he left his jails with countless undelivered orations in his head. From his readings in Marxist literature he did not become familiar with the British Fabian philosophy of making haste slowly. Otherwise he would have learned that great leaps in history lead to great disasters. Nor did he learn that oratory was no adequate substitute for blueprints of the future. It helps us to understand his actions more if we bear in mind that oratory is his forte and that he tests his policies against rhetorical slogans.

From his readings in prison he became acquainted with the economic interpretation of history, a heritage of Marx. The wielders of economic power were, according to Marx, wielders of political power. As long as the Dutch controlled the vast natural resources of the islands, real power belonged to them. Sukarno stripped the Dutch of their power by harassing them into a despair that resulted in their abandoning their strongholds and leaving the islands. Did he have substitutes for the owners and the managers he thus ousted? There were substitutes for government officials but not for technicians. Austerity was to be expected in the interregnum between the rule of the alien classes and of the indigenous masses. He convinced himself and his enthusiastic audiences that abundance eventually would come to every member of the vast Indonesian national family.

A father image he did not want to become—he was not old enough for that. Also fathers on some of the islands were dumped into the human scrap heaps, unused and unwanted. He became the "brother" of Indonesia's tens of millions—Bung Karno, Brother Karno. He was strong, invincible, the man of destiny who had tackled and defeated the arrogant men of the West. No longer was the Occidental to throw his weight around. Brother Sukarno was to feed his people—at first with words and later with food. The words provided the psychological fuel with which Indonesia's people were to charge into the performance of their superhuman tasks.

He is in his element when unfolding his governmental philosophy, while guiding his people by the hand toward the light which will illuminate a fabulous world of abundance. Let us follow his oratorical habits and lines of thought. They will reveal to us, Sukarno, the people's tribune, the New Man of Indonesia.

"Brothers and Sisters," he begins his speech. He clasps all the tens of thousands of his audience to his chest. There they find comfort and security. A hearty glance cast on the enthusiastic crowd establishes that rapport which makes everybody feel warm. Over and over again he repeats the same phrases, as if he wanted to hypnotize his hearers. Were he to repeat the alphabet people would be swept off their feet just the same. He coins names which he invests with the magic of mystery: "Manipol" and "Usdek" are his magic words. "Political Manifesto" is Manipol, first enunciated in his seminal address on August 12, 1959, Independence Day. It was eventually adopted by the People's Consultative Assembly as the nation's basic policy. "Usdek" is formed of the initials in Indonesian of the words denoting the main concepts of national policy: "1945 Constitution," "Indonesian Socialism," "Guided Democracy," "Guided Economy," and "National Personality."

Here are a few examples of Sukarno's oratory:

"This world today is a revolutionary ammunition dump. This world today holds revolutionary electric power. This world today is 'loaded with revolution.' It has never before happened that the history of man has gone through such a revolution as at present—so strong and so tremendous, so wide-sweeping and universal—a revolution of humanity which surges, flashes, thunders in almost every corner of the globe."

"Wake up people who suffer from revolution-phobia. We are in the midst of a revolution, and not just a small revolution, but a revolution greater than the past American revolution, or the past French revolution, or the present Social Revolution. One year ago I explained that this revolution of ours is at the same time a national revolution, a political revolution, a social revolution, a cultural revolution, and a revolution in man. Our revolution, I said, is a five-faceted revolution, a multicomplex revolution, a revolution which is a summing up of many revolutions in one generation."

Manipol and Usdek are the implementation and consummation of all these revolutions.

"That is why people who are charged with the realization of the Political Manifesto-Usdek, but who are not fully convinced or who are not able to implement the Political Manifesto-Usdek should be retooled. But you, from among the people, you too are not free from shouldering responsibilities. People who have become conscious should actively contribute their energies to the realization of the Political Manifesto-Usdek. Those of you who are not yet conscious, who do not have the slightest understanding of the Political Manifesto-Usdek, and understand even less about the realization of the Political Manifesto-Usdek, must be indoctrinated."

Note the hypnotic effect of repetition. He does not explain the meaning of the "Political Manifesto-Usdek," assuming that everybody knows it. (They do not. Personal interviews informed me about that.) "Political Manifesto-Usdek" cannot really be explained any more than the mystery of religion. It is to be taken for granted, a magic term, endowed with miraculous powers which are possessed by Indonesia alone among all nations because she has Bung Karno.

At least at two points of the above passage the critical listener might expect Sukarno to be explicit about the responsibilities he wanted the people to shoulder. He never is, for one must have faith in the "Political Manifesto-Usdek." Then all will be well. Bung Karno is the only one conversant with the full meaning of those magic words.

"My philosophy" is another recurrent theme in his speeches. He has derived much of his philosophy from philosophers whose names he mentions but does not quote. This "name-dropping" exercise may convince his enthralled audience that Bung Karno is in constant communion with people of previous generations who paved the way to his supreme understanding.

"My philosophy is composed of nationalism, religious belief, and Marxist historical analysis. . . . I admire what is positive in all great men: Jesus Christ, Marx, or Adolf Hitler." He is fond of mentioning the name of the pre-World War I French Socialist leader, Jean Jaurès. In one single speech he once dropped the names of Aristotle, Renan, Gandhi, Lenin, and Sun Yat-sen. He quotes sentences in the original German, English, Dutch, and French, which his countryfolk audiences cannot be expected to understand. Understanding these sentences is unimportant; comprehension of Sukarno's many talents is. Constantly he employs tautologies, such as the "multicomplex" revolution which people would find ludicrous if they understood him.

Sukarno is no more specific when he is supposed to speak about bread-and-butter problems as, for instance, in his much-publicized "Address of Counsel" to the First Plenary Sitting of the National Planning Council. In that basic address he fell into the much-traveled groove of praise for a "national economy," as against a colonial economy. "Our economy was a colonial economy during the colonial period," he said, "and we must change this colonial economy into a national economy which is clean of imperialism, clean of blood-sucking exploitation by outsiders."

Then the constant refrain:

"Our revolution is a 'telescope revolution,' a revolution which is telescoped. Yes, I said, a political revolution, an economic revolution, a social revolution, a cultural revolution, yes, I said it is even a revolution in man's ideas: a multicomplex revolution"— his favorite term.

THE SCIENCE THAT IS REALLY DISMAL

There is no richer ex-colonial area in the world than Indonesia, with all its rubber, tin, petroleum, trees, and spices. The Dutch did exploit it, to be sure, taking out much, giving back little. That was in the nature of the colonial administration.

How has the average Indonesian fared during the years of Sukarno's administration? The Indonesians have a name for their average man, their own "John Doe." They call him Marhaen. So what about this Marhaen, the man in the street? Has he seen the benefits of Sukarno's Manipol-Usdek? Is he better off now that the Dutch are gone?

During the last decade the average per capita income of Indonesia has declined, and at the outset it had been the lowest in the world. Other poor countries, India, for instance, starting from a slightly higher base, have seen an improvement of the per head income. During the last few years most Indonesian industries have been operating at only half their capacities. Rubber trees have become overaged and sterile. While the population of the country has increased 30 per cent in the last two decades, rice production has risen by only 10 per cent. Today Indonesia is one of the world's largest importers of rice.

The consumer price index increased by about 1000 per cent between the declaration of independence and 1963. A catastrophic currency inflation has taken place, with all the black markets and other attendant ills. The gold and foreign exchange reserves of the country have been exhausted. The national balance of payments has become worse. Money printing presses have started working overtime.

In 1964 one dollar, which sold at the official rate of forty-five rupiahs—the Indonesian currency—cost 1,250 rupiahs on the black market. Government funds were spent on such extravaganzas as the 1963 Games of the New Emerging Forces held in the Indonesian capital. The games cost $30 million which could have been far better spent on rice for underfed school children.

Ambitious plans remained pious hopes. Sukarno had little to report under the heading of "Industrial Production." He could report mainly the extraction of bauxite, tin concentrates, and petroleum, at the same level as under the rule of the Dutch.

Even the most sluggish Asian countries had started to improve their economic conditions by working on the basis of plans. It was only in 1961 that Sukarno gave his approval to an Eight-Year Development Scheme. He gave no sign of grasping the significance of the order of priorities to improve the country's economic plight. How strong can a country be whose people are poorly fed? Sukarno's eloquence will never fill the stomachs of his people. And when the stomach becomes too empty, the mind may refuse to follow even the most loftily soaring words of a leader.

In one important field, however, Indonesia was moving ahead. Sukarno attempted to carry out a "crash program" in education, with the aid of United Nations' teams of experts and Western specialists. There was an immense amount of work to be done in that field. The policy of the Dutch had been to deny higher education to native Indonesians. There were only two Indonesian "natives" enrolled in 1920 at a domestic university. (There were a few of them studying abroad.) It was only in 1919 that the first technical college was opened in Indonesia. The first law school opened its doors in 1924, and the first medical school in 1926. The number of Indonesian college students studying at home rose to more than 50,000 by 1960. Education between the ages of six and twelve was declared compulsory, and in the twenty years until 1961 the number of elementary school students rose from two million to more than nine million.

REVOLTS EVERYWHERE

The nation was still young when revolts flared up in many places. Some of them were of the flash variety, while others smoldered for years. Their causes were too numerous to provide simple explanations. One was the problem of the "three thousand islands." How does one govern thousands of islands, separated by long distances, inadequately linked?

The problem of Java was one of the causes of unrest. It is indeed a tight little island, with the largest concentration of population in the world. Two thirds of the population of the Republic live on Java, which produces the largest contingent of officials. On the other hand, Sumatra produces 60 per cent of the Republic's revenues. To the Javanese the island of Java is Indonesia. Inhabitants of other islands resent this attitude. Revolts flared up on the Outer Islands, especially on Sumatra and Celebes. A typical example of these revolts was that of the Minangkabaus, on Sumatra, not far from Padang. However, these people are unusual in that they claim that they are descendants of the conquerors who awed the world under Alexander the Great, whom many Moslems know by the name of Iskander. There are some two million of the Minangkabaus, indicating that the great Macedonian's stalwarts must have been a fertile lot. The Minangkabaus have other claims, too. They say that their ancestors were the conquerors of all of Sumatra. More than that, their region cradled the culture of the Malayans.

No sooner had this revolt sputtered to a halt than the attention of the Sukarno government was drawn to the outbreak of another revolt in another part of vast Sumatra. This time it erupted on the opposite coast of the island, near Palembang, in the region of the Musi River. More serious were the outbreaks on Java itself.

Indonesia—we have seen—is a predominantly Moslem country. The Dutch imposed the rule of the hated "infidel dog" on Allah's people. But now the Dutch were gone, and Allah's people were in the saddle. But were they? Sukarno himself pays lip service to God. But as head of the State he did not want to share his power with Allah. Religious zealots in Java—and elsewhere, too—had other ideas about independence. Indonesia was to be a religious community dedicated to the service of the All-Merciful One. The Republic was to be a theocracy. Upholders of this view were swayed by religious leaders who hoped to be exalted into higher positions in a Moslem Commonwealth. *Darul Islam* ("State of Islam") was the backbone of the zealots' rebellion, and their operations extended into the very heart of the mountainous districts of central West Java. Some of the leaders and followers of *Masjumi* ("Council") and *Nahdatul Ulama* ("religious teachers"), two political parties, were zealots whose "religion" was terror. It took many years before this rebellion was crushed.

Then there was the Indonesian Communist party—PKI—
which believed that independence meant extreme radicalism.
Communism had triumphed in the country with the world's largest population, China. Party discipline was the forte of the Communists who were also well supplied with funds. Sympathetic to
Marxism, Sukarno was not unsympathetic to communism as an
ideology, though he was naturally unsympathetic to the idea that
the Communists should wrest power from him. He came to grips
with them, defeating them. Then he made his peace with them for
reasons we shall see.

The very nature of the fragmented archipelago was a cause
for revolts. Transportation between them was utterly inadequate.
Even in the age of the airplane only a few islands had been linked.
How could the central government deal with political brush-
fires, flaring up at one place one day and two thousand miles and
two thousand islands away next week? Such islands could be em-
bargoed, of course. But what if they were able to sustain themselves on their own production?

Democracy was an integral part of the Western creed Sukarno wanted to adopt. The prosperity of the Occidental countries had been nourished on their parliamentary institutions.
Twice he tried to conduct parliamentary elections and twice—he
declared—fiasco was the result. Politically uneducated delegates of
politically ignorant electorates could not be expected to be able
to adopt the institutions of the Western world. Thus it was that
Sukarno adopted the concept of "guided democracy."

GUIDED DEMOCRACY

"The assemblies of the people," Sukarno said, "should not be
twisted into political battlefields, the scenes of wasteful and never-
ending debates."

He also said that the "soul, character, and personality of
the Indonesian people should mold its political system."

Indonesia has a folk institution which should become the
foundation of a new system to take the place of the discredited
parliamentary regime, he said. The folk institution is known under its indigenous name as *gotong royong*, "mutual aid." That is
what Sukarno called "guided democracy." Also, guided democracy
is "Manipol-Usdek"—we are back again in the company of the
magic words. Socialism is the pivot of the system. In other words,

it is a cooperative undertaking under the benevolent eyes of the government. In Sukarno's eyes, Socialism is equivalent to "social action," action motivated by the spirit of *gotong royong* and not by the greediness that was seen in individuals during the period of capitalistic exploitation by the Dutch. Democracy and Indonesian socialism will terminate *l'exploitation de l'homme par l'homme*, a phrase Sukarno likes to repeat endlessly in French to his mass audiences.

His guided democracy, Sukarno has said over and over again, is the "sublimation of the American Declaration of Independence and of the Communist Manifesto." At other times he has said: "There are in existence three large groups of revolutionary powers in Indonesia: Moslems, nationalists, and Communists." He frequently introduces the Moslem element. "With the blessing of the One, Supreme God," he starts off important state documents.

To guide democracy Sukarno established a complicated structure. The power pyramid was to be headed by himself. Then, he appointed a ten-man "inner cabinet." He further appointed a forty-five-man supreme advisory council, comprising delegates of the "accepted" political parties, of regions, and of occupations. The latter included also the armed forces. A seventy-seven-member National Planning Council was to devote its attention to economics. To top this off he designated a 261-member legislature, half the membership of which was drawn from nine political parties. The other half, plus one, was drawn from the functional groups, such as farmers, laborers, intellectuals, youth, women, and religious leaders.

These organizations were to be the "guides" while Sukarno himself was to be the Supreme Guide. Why did he fail to establish an outright dictatorship? Because the impression was created under this system that democracy was in operation. Also, it enabled him to keep honor- and office-hungry politicians under close control. Within the groups he had a chance to use his favorite device of divide and rule.

"There is a lot of guidance in this system but no democracy," critics say. As to "mutual assistance," Sukarno at the head of the guided democracy pyramid is Bung Karno, the beloved brother figure.

Sukarno selected a presumably able army leader as his chief-of-staff: General Abdul Haris Nasution. While overwhelming the general with honors, Sukarno keeps him on short leash. The army is well supplied with funds and honors, to keep it contented and constantly on the alert to serve Sukarno.

The Communists were shown their places once before by Sukarno. Today he uses them for his purposes, but they could cause him much trouble if he were to antagonize them. In Indonesia the poor have become even poorer under the Sukarno regime, but the Communists must keep quiet about this. By consulting the Communist leaders, Sukarno keeps them under constant surveillance and feeds their egos with the belief of their importance.

Several times conditions in Indonesia have reached the point where one could see no solution for the country. The system should have collapsed. But it did not. There would have been anarchy on countless islands, but the country pulled through because of the feeling of national unity that was based, primarily, on the glittering oratory of Sukarno and the belief that he will produce a saving formula. And, Sukarno is everybody's brother. Furthermore, people close ranks in the face of an imminent and present foreign danger, and Sukarno always saw to it that there should be such a peril.

AUX ARMES, CITOYENS

First there was Dutch West Guinea, which the Indonesians call West Irian. We have seen that it is a primitive area which it would have been in the interest of a developing country to shun. Sukarno converted the Irian question into a policy of major importance to his regime: West Irian should be joined to Indonesia.

"We have been strengthening ourselves," Sukarno said, "in order to face the Dutch in all fields, and we feel now quite strong to take all measures necessary in order to unfurl our beloved red and white flag on West Irian's soil."

Year after year Indonesia took the issue to the United Nations which patiently referred it back to the contending parties. Then, suddenly, in 1962, the Netherlands expressed their readiness to hand over West Irian's administration to Sukarno's regime. With the acquisition of West Irian, Sukarno was expected to run out of bugbears. Also, the maintenance of this territory would burden Indonesia's shaky economy with additional deficits. This diplomatic "victory" was thus to precipitate Sukarno's bankruptcy.

After West Irian's transfer to Indonesia, Sukarno did seem to be embarrassed, but he had had his way. The Dutch were out of all of Indonesia.

At about this time, several units of the former British Empire decided to federate themselves. Malaya, Singapore, Sarawak, and North Borneo (renamed Sabah) adopted the name of Malaysia.

"Malaysia is a state under foreign control politically, economically, and particularly militarily," the Indonesian government declared. "As a result it is becoming a base for foreign domination in Southeast Asia and for subverting our economy and security." He issued an "action command" to "21 million volunteers" to crush Malaysia.

Here was, then, the substitute for West Irian, the new *bête noire,* and Sukarno appeared again as the savior of his nation. This was the time for all good Indonesians to come to the aid of their country.

Sukarno was not doing too badly on another front of the international field, either. He learned that poor countries could alleviate their poverty by playing on the jealousies of the rich nations, especially of the two greatest world powers. In one form or another, Indonesia received funds from foreign countries in large installments. Most of this money came from the Soviet Union, perhaps a billion dollars. In surplus agricultural commodities Sukarno's country received about $300 million from the United States. Smaller sums were obtained from West Germany, France, Britain, Italy, and the International Monetary Fund. Indonesia received no funds from her former mistress, the Netherlands. That was an expression of the profound distaste of the two nations for each other. The relation of Britain and France with their former colonies was different. These two ex-imperialist nations provided the bulk of the foreign funds of their former charges.

SUKARNO IN SLIPPERS

We have observed Sukarno in public life, on the forum and in the presidential palace, as a nation-builder and an aspiring nation-developer. What was he like in his private life? We know that he was one year younger than the twentieth century. How did he look in his early sixties?

He appeared different in slippers at home in the palace of

Bogor, the former residence of the Dutch governors-general, thirty-five miles out of the capital, surrounded by one of Asia's most beautiful public parks and zoological gardens. The place was known as Buitenzorg under the Dutch, and that means "Care-free"—*Sans Souci*. In this setting Sukarno, too, tried to relax.

At home he appeared without his sartorial trade mark, the black fezlike headgear, *petji*, which he exalted into the national hat. He was bald and that made him look older. He wore spectacles with dark, heavy rims, and that did not make him look younger, either. When relaxed, the wrinkles of age showed more clearly in the telltale region of the neck.

The dividing line between his public and private lives was nebulous because, being a thoroughbred politician, his life on the platform overlapped his life in the easy chair. He liked to be surrounded by subordinates and disciples to whom he could reminisce about his past and at the same time clarify his own thoughts by carrying on a monologue about affairs of state.

He was particularly fond of describing what he called the "heroic age" of Indonesia's struggle for *merdeka*. He liked to embroider his role in history by explaining that he had outwitted the Dutch by appearing to be naïve enough to fall for their traps while actually he was catching them in the coils of his plans.

Sukarno no longer had the leisure to continue the habit of reading he had acquired in his prisons. This is, at least, what he told his hearers, but the reality was different. He simply lacked the patience. Reading books could not be the preoccupation of the head of a state with nearly a hundred million people beset by billions of problems. Although he read few books now, he often talked about those that had made the greatest impression on him. He told the correspondent of the New York *Times*, C. L. Sulzberger, that the number of his favorite authors was large. He mentioned particularly Marx, Engels, and Thomas Jefferson, in the same breath, as if they had been kindred in spirit. He also mentioned Gandhi, who did write some books, as well as China's Sun Yat-sen, who was not known to have written books. Sukarno said that he had been particularly impressed by the writings of Jean Jaurès, the French Socialist leader who was killed at the outbreak of World War I. Sukarno was especially impressed by Jaurès' writings about the use of a citizens' militia in lieu of a professional standing army.

In his long monologues Sukarno spoke of the political leaders to whom he gave credit for having influenced him. It was a strange group, encompassing the entire political spectrum from the ultra-red to the ultra-violet, from the most extreme left-wing to the most extreme right-wing. On the one hand, he admired Yugoslavia's Marshal Tito, a Communist. He also admired Portugal's Premier Antonio de Oliveira Salazar, a Fascist. And he expressed admiration for India's Nehru, who called himself a Socialist.

In his younger days Sukarno liked to think of himself as a latter-day Leonardo da Vinci, an engineer, an architect, a painter, and the practitioner of many other skills. He had prepared designs of mosques, churches, and even of a prison. He lost his taste for that when in power. He did some paintings, but by the time he reached his sixties he liked to display only one of them, a Balinese woman. In his younger days Sukarno had been a caricaturist and an illustrator—which became mere nostalgic memories.

As Sukarno reached his sixties he became increasingly tradition-minded, and his hobbies reflected that attitude. He reached the conclusion that nations, especially young ones, must have traditional distinguishing marks. India had such traditions, especially the *Wayang Purwa,* shadow drama of puppets cut out from leather. As a boy, Sukarno liked to draw *Wayang* heroes on his slate. The stories are derived from the ancient Indian epics, *Mahabharata* and *Ramayana,* recitals of the complicated dynastic struggles of the Pandavas and Kauravas. Sukarno adopted one of the main characters, Gatutkaja, as his main hero, representing justice, courage, and strength. As the head of the state, Sukarno enjoyed taking his guests, his collaborators, and foreign diplomats to these shows, which lasted sometimes all night long. The diplomats were dying of fatigue, not understanding the language and not interested in the fantastic plot. But protocol did not permit them to leave the show until their host, the head of state, rose. And he did not rise until the wee hours. He claimed that these endless plays refreshed him.

Sukarno started collecting paintings, folk art. He came to hold the view that his countrymen had latent artistic qualities which could be coaxed out of them by encouraging grass-root "geniuses." It was his plan to lay the foundations of a National Folk Art Gallery.

Even in his early sixties Sukarno liked to dance. Being a thoroughbred politician he gave dancing a political undertone.

Western dances were being introduced all over the world, including Indonesia, and Sukarno did not like what he saw. He considered it part of the patriotic education of his people, to turn to the traditional archipelago dances, especially to the *Serampang Duabelas,* a regional dance of the island of Sumatra.

Sukarno is said to have been a good shot as a youngster. Then, one day, he shot and wounded an eagle. His companion caught the bird and broke its wings. "I could never forget the eyes of that eagle." That was the end of his hobby as a hunter and even as a fisherman.

As the years passed by, walking became the only sport in which he indulged, and there was plenty of space for that at Bogor. Walking, he was also talking to his subordinates, meditating, planning his future speeches and actions. The Indonesians have a word for these talking exercises—*musjawarah,* clarifying thoughts through talks. He claimed that physical exercise stimulated his mental faculties.

But gradually the aches and pains of age began to affect him. He developed a kidney ailment. Perhaps it was not as bad as he made it appear. Immensely public relations conscious, did he employ this method to keep the people interested in him? Or was he merely hypochondriacal? Sometimes as many as seven doctors were in attendance at the same time. He underwent surgery at the hands of a team of Chinese physicians from the mainland. And that was not bad public relations for the Chinese Communists.

How good a family man was Sukarno? The presidential palace in Indonesia is not the counterpart of the White House, the greatest of international showplaces. His first wife, Fatmarvati, lived an isolated life in Jakarta, the second Bogor shared the president's palace. From time to time Sukarno has let himself be photographed with his second wife, especially when dancing the *Serampang.* The world learned that her name was Hartini and she appeared to be much younger than he. Wrapped in highly decorative garbs, she looked a pretty woman.

Only seldom did the world hear about the children of Sukarno—the offspring of his previous marriage. His son, Guntur, (Thunder), was approaching twenty early in 1960. And then there were the three girls: Megawati (Cloud Girl), sixteen, Rachmawati (Blessed Girl), fourteen, and Sukmawati (Soul Girl), twelve. Little was heard about their mother. Gossip maintained that she had refused to give a divorce to Sukarno, so that he had two official wives at the same time. But then, this was nothing unusual in the Moslem world where the permissible maximum for wives was four if their husband could support them. There was no question about Sukarno's ability to support two wives.

THE ITINERANT STATESMAN

Traveling was one of Sukarno's great passions, which he indulged year in and year out. When traveling, his private and public lives were fused. He let his public relations people tell his countrymen that it was upon the advice of his doctors and for reasons of his health that he was abroad so much. The public relations people did not explain how traveling with all its ceremonial obligations and speechmaking was more relaxing than the Bogor easy chair. Nor did they explain how it came about that the huge variety of the thousands of islands failed to offer the kind of conditions that Sukarno's ailments required.

Sukarno went off on one of his trips when all was quiet at home—and that was seldom. He went off also when conditions were ripe for an outbreak, when a revolt flared up or when it was over. When he came back Indonesia was still there, for conditions always righted themselves somehow. His detractors mumbled under their breaths that they righted themselves because he was not around.

Sukarno's travels were combined with government business. Sometimes it was easier to find him thousands of miles from home. To take just one instance, he was on a State visit in Tokyo when he was urgently needed for a top-level conference on the Malaysian issue. He was found there by the Attorney-General of the United States, Robert F. Kennedy, dispatched to the Japanese capital by President Lyndon B. Johnson.

The Indonesian President became a passionate traveler for various reasons. The "eternity" he spent in detention under the rule of the Dutch must have been one of the main reasons. Staying in one place for years became associated in his mind with "imperialism." On the other hand, moving around the wide world became the corollary of *merdeka,* "freedom."

He also liked the pomp and circumstance of State receptions, the honor guards, the sight of the banner of his country, the red horizontal stripe over the white stripe, and the playing of the national anthem, *Indonesia Raya* ("Great Indonesia").

He liked to show his strongest side, his ability to deliver orations in several languages. He appeared to be at his best when his cheeks became slightly flushed with the pleasure of keeping his foreign audiences enthralled.

Above all, he liked to collect decorations and honorary degrees along the route wherever he went. He pinned the decorations on his military tunic, which he wore on official occasions. His desire for academic recognition was another psychological compensation of the potential intellectual turned into a politician and still yearning for the Paradise Lost of his early youth.

This was the harvest of honorary degrees and decorations in one single year, 1956:

Honorary degrees of doctor of laws at every stop: one from Columbia University, New York, another one from New York University, still another one from the University of Michigan, Ann Arbor, and one more from McGill, in Montreal. An honorary degree of Doctor of Technical Sciences from the University of Technical Sciences in West Berlin. Then to show his impartiality, honorary degrees in the Soviet Union and the Federal Republic of Yugoslavia. Also, a number of decorations: The Lenin Medal as a "champion of peace" (when Sukarno made warlike noises in connection with West Irian); the Grand Yugoslav Star; the White Lion medal, Czechoslovakia; Gold Medal, Austria (both of them the highest decorations in those countries); and the order of the Grand Knight of the Order of Pius IX, from the Vatican.

And this in 1958: The Grand Collar of the Order of the Southern Cross, Brazil; Collar of the Order of San Martin, Argentina; Grand Order of the Chrysanthemum, Japan (the highest medal of honor); Medal of Resistance, First Class, bestowed upon him by President Ho Chi Minh of the "Democratic Republic of Vietnam"; also the Medal of the Grand Cross of Santiago, Portugal; and another papal medal: Gold Medal of the Consecration of Pope John XXIII. Also additional honorary degrees, this time from the universities of Prague, Istanbul, Warsaw, and Rio de Janeiro.

THE SUKARNO ENIGMA

Detention camps and the endless horizon of Indonesia helped Sukarno to survive even the most cataclysmic tidal waves of politics. More ailments have been visited upon Indonesia than on most developing countries. It has been ravaged by economic contre-temps of all kinds and sizes, by lack of clear-cut plans of politics and economics, by a series of civil conflicts, by governmental inef-ficiency, and by bureaucratic bungling. Sukarno survived all these tempests and became the "great Leader of the Revolution, Presi-dent, and Commander-in-Chief," which became his official titles.

And what about the explanation of this strange phenome-non? It seems again that years in prison bring out the most im-portant character traits of the victims. In the case of Sukarno, imprisonment brought out a trait that has enabled him not only to survive malarial detention camps but also political cataclysms. In his prison camps he learned to fend for himself against the tropical cruelties of nature, the death-bearing mosquitoes, and the other dangers of the breathtakingly beautiful "green mansions" of nature. Opportunistic by his own nature, no doubt; but his op-portunism was sharpened in the midst of circumstances that en-dangered his very life.

After liberation he faced dangers no less than those with which he had been confronted in his jails in New Guinea, Su-matra, and the other prison islands. He fell heir to chaos, to a political jungle in which again he had to fend for himself. Oppor-tunism became the keynote of his policy. Since the last word can-not yet be written on his life, it is impossible to say whether he has not outsmarted himself.

Sukarno's strength has been sharpened by his uninhibited belief in himself, a belief that was rendered even keener by his survival in his jungle graves. He does believe that he is endowed with *baraka,* the Moslems' state of grace. He believes, too, that the Indonesian globe revolves around him and—strange to say—it does. He is skillful in the dagger-game of politicians and also in the art of the political boss. Thus, he is the best of friends and the worst of foes. The rewards he offers are rich and the penalties he metes out are heavy. He is not a bloody tyrant—at least, not as far as the world knows. In one word, he is president and founder of Indo-nesia, its incarnation. Although never uttering the phrase, he acts as if he believed *L'Indonésie c'est moi.*

After having looked at the Guide, let us note some of the traits of the guided ones. In the face of a more sophisticated audi-ence Sukarno might have become a failure. But his audience is not sophisticated. The Indonesians learned from their previous mas-ters, the Dutch, to respect authority. And here is a paradox. Sukarno has been benefiting from the rule he execrates—that of the Hollanders.

The Indonesians are products of a generous nature—which can become cruel, too. On the whole they are delightfully genial, inclined to be kind, and they are romantic. They can be aroused, of course, and several times they have been stirred up in recent years. Sukarno, who knows how to handle his genial people, reminds them constantly that it was he who suffered for them. Then he tells them that he created their country. Victory in West Irian was his handiwork and, of course, he will win in Malaysia, too. Against the hideous terrors of men and nature Bung Karno stands in the breach. His people see him in the glittering light of his self-confidence and oratorical prowess on the platform and not in the dull glare of his bungling in Merdeka Palace in Jakarta. They feel their stature growing because Sukarno's majestic presence fills the universe. There was Allah and there was Mohammed. And now there is Bung Karno upon whom the blessing of Allah and of the Prophet rests.

With Bung Karno's aid, Indonesia's man in the street, the proverbial Marhaen, has ceased to be a native member of an inferior breed. He has become the citizen of a large country with nearly a hundred million people, living in happy expectation of his national apotheosis on thousands of islands. Marhaen, too, feels that he is a soldier in Allah's army, in the *jihad*, "sacred war," against all the vicious colonialists of the world. This undersized and perhaps underfed Marhaen has become a man of stature, due to Sukarno's work as the Guide. While food is important in Marhaen's life, his heroic posture is no less important, for it sustains his morale, which was all but crushed by the Dutch imperialists. Endless repetitions may characterize Bung Karno's speeches, but they do have a hypnotic influence on Marhaen. And that alone is a remarkable feat.

Meanwhile the facts of life in Indonesia cannot be overlooked. Even the most romantic citizen of the country will discover one day that oratory is a poor substitute for food. Luckily, you thrust a stick into the fabulous Indonesian soil and out of it sprouts a tree of delicious fruit. But romantic people, too, have their boiling point. What will happen to Sukarno and to Indonesia when the temper of the guided ones begins to boil?

"Intelligent, moody, dynamic, vain, energetic, sensitive,"

C. L. Sulzberger of the New York *Times* described him. "An artist, an idea man, not an administrator." Yet it was not an artist but an administrator that Indonesia needed. A talented, attractive people, the Indonesians had more than their share of artists: have they not revealed their supreme artistry in the way they have managed to survive even under the Sukarno regime?

6

His Beatitude Goes Into Exile

The prisoner was in the custody of the chief of police of the British-ruled Seychelles, Major Trevor Williams, who was escorting him to Mahé Island, a tiny dot in the immensity of the Indian Ocean. The distinguished prisoner was none other than the Archbishop and Ethnarch of Cyprus, His Beatitude Makarios III. He had been brought here from another British-ruled island, Cyprus, in the eastern Mediterranean, thousands of miles away.

Archbishop Makarios III, head of one of the oldest autocephalous Greek Orthodox churches, ranked immediately after the patriarchs of Constantinople, Alexandria, Jerusalem, and Antioch. Ancient privileges had conferred special rights on His Beatitude. He had the right to carry the imperial scepter, with the image of the globe, instead of the Pontiff's staff. He had the right to wear a cope of imperial purple, a prerogative which his ecclesiastical predecessors had shared only with the Byzantine emperors. Like them, he had the unique privilege of signing his name in red ink.

As the Archbishop of Cyprus, His Beatitude was not the subject of a higher ecclesiastical authority. The Ecumenical Patriarch of Constantinople of the Holy Orthodox Catholic Apostolic Eastern Church is merely a *primus inter pares*. The heads of the self-governing—autocephalous—churches, of which there are thirteen at present, are Supreme Pontiffs in their Sees. It was for historic reasons that Makarios III ranked higher than the heads of the churches of countries with far larger populations.

Even now that he was a prisoner, the Archbishop carried the scepter, the symbol of the most exalted authority. He was not alone in his captivity. His fellow prisoners were three other Cypriots: Bishop Kyprianos of Kyrenia; Papastavros Papaagathangelou, a priest; and Polycarpos Ioannides, secretary to the Bishop of

Kyrenia and former editor of the Greek language Cypriot newspaper, *Ephemeris.*

The four men had been flown in a Royal Air Force plane from Nicosia, the capital of Cyprus, to Mombasa, in Kenya. There they were transferred to the frigate H.M.S. *Loch Fada,* for the final lap of the voyage, from East Africa to the Seychelles, a distance of about twelve hundred miles. Now they were approaching Victoria, the tiny capital of the Seychelles, on the island of Mahé.

As the boat approached the landing stage, the prisoners rose from their benches. Now one could see that His Beatitude was a tall man, appearing even more so because of the *kalimafchi,* the ecclesiastic stovepipe hat, he wore. He was well groomed in spite of the long voyage, beautifully cassocked in his dark *raso,* the garment of his rank.

Even though his face was unlined, he did look somewhat older than his forty-three years, perhaps because the back of his head was touched by early frost. There were silver threads also in his pitch-black beard. He looked pallid, perhaps because of the long ocean trip. The contrast between his dark garments, beard, and hair and the paleness of his face was striking.

His eyes, hands, and lips were his most conspicuous physical features. His eyes were dark and deeply set; they seemed to probe suspiciously. His eyebrows appeared to slope downward and outward. His hands were small for so stately a man, but they were well shaped, manicured, elegant. It may have been the blackness of his beard that accentuated the redness of his lips. Had he not been a Prince of the Church one would have said that his lips were sensuous. Walking erect, with born dignity, he looked every inch a prince. In a stage aside, an English official whispered with irreverent admiration: "The fellow has presence."

Why were His Beatitude and his three companions prisoners of the British? Because the majority of the people of Cyprus, Greek in speech and Greek Orthodox in religion, was in revolt against the colonial authorities of Her Most Gracious Majesty, Queen Elizabeth II, of Great Britain. Makarios was their leader as Ethnarch and Archbishop. The Greek people of the island wanted *enosis—*"union"—with Greece, which they regarded as their motherland.

Bishop Kyprianos was described by his jailers as leader of the "most fanatical extremist wing of the fighters for *enosis,*" the Kyrenia Group, of which Ioannides was also one of the leaders.

Father Papaagathangelou was charged with inciting the Greek nationalistic Cypriot youth to violence through his prominent role within PEON—Pan-Cyprian National Organization of Youth.

Some time before, terror had erupted on Cyprus; the British accused His Beatitude, who was both the secular and religious leader on Cyprus, of making common cause with the Cypriot Greek terrorists. The bloody acts of the revolters—the gory details of which were disseminated mainly through the English press—shocked the Western world. And so it came about that the British deported the Archbishop and his companions to this tiny island far away in the Indian Ocean. The prisoners arrived on Mahé on March 14, 1956.

THE LAND OF THE LOTUS-EATERS

The boat made fast at the pier. Major Williams turned to the member of the captive group who carried the symbol of highest authority, the scepter, and asked him a question. The Archbishop answered him curtly, in a completely colorless voice. He spoke good English, slowly, somewhat too precisely, but with a pronounced accent, softening the harshness of the language by inserting an occasional *"e"* between two consonants, aspirating his *"h"* in a heavily guttural tone. The way he spoke to the English officer nobody would have suspected that on his own island and in his native Greek language he was a spellbinder, his voice soaring with an ecstatic assertion of his people's rights.

In front of the captives rose a scene which travelers have described as the most glorious land- and seascape of the world. The iridescent horizon framed a group of serrated mountains, jagged and stark, the edged peaks clearly etched against the flood of green and orange lights that irradiated the eastern skies.

The prisoners set foot on Victoria, the capital of the Seychelles. As much as they saw of it at this nodding acquaintance, the tiny town looked pleasant enough. They probably noticed that many of the houses glistened like white marble, and later they learned that they were made of coral that had been hewn into square building blocks.

They were driven to an attractive house on the outskirts of Victoria. It was the country residence of the governor and commander-in-chief of the islands, Sir William Addis, C.M.G., and its name was Sans Souci. It was their place of detention.

Sans Souci was not only the name of the dwelling, but also the expected way of life of the prisoners during their enforced residence. They were supposed to live without care as far as the lot of their native island, Cyprus, was concerned. Their needs were taken care of, and while enjoying the bliss of this earthly paradise they were to forget about the problems of the world.

The four detainees had never been tried by a court. Their detention was an administrative measure. They were to be kept on the island at "Her Majesty's Pleasure." Thus the period of their detention would depend upon events in Cyprus.

A PRIMITIVE PEOPLE

The Seychelles consist of ninety-two islands and all of them add up only to 156 square miles. The largest of them, Mahé, on which Victoria is situated, comprises fifty-five square miles. Many of the islands bear French names, recalling that they were first colonized by the French. The names of some of them are exotic, as for instance, Félicité, Silhouette, Curieuse. Steamers from Mombasa to Bombay normally call at Victoria every four weeks. Bombay is about 2,100 miles away; Mombasa somewhat more than half of that distance.

What about the people of this small archipelago? They represent an ethnic cocktail: mainly Africans and Creoles, and a smaller number of Indians, Chinese, and Europeans. The population of the Seychelles is estimated at 42,000, and about one-fourth or one-third of the residents live in Victoria or on its outskirts.

Speaking about his experience on the island, Archbishop Makarios summarized his appraisal of the inhabitants: "They are primitive, very primitive people." They speak a language of their own, the base of which is French, and into it have been grafted words and expressions from Bantu, Hindi, English, and a little bit of everything else. This language has never been reduced to writing.

"There were therefore no local newspapers on the islands," says Archbishop Makarios. "There were no radios, let alone television. The Seychelles people have never seen an airplane. The people assumed that we were vacationers."

And how do the people live on the Seychelles? Their employment opportunities are limited. Coconut and copra are their most important products. Next in importance is the production of cinnamon leaf oil, cinnamon bark oil, patchouli oil, and vanilla. Mangrove bark and turtles are collected on some islands, and guano deposits are worked.

Spring is eternal on these islands, and the influence of vast expanses of water keeps the climate moderate. Because the Seychelles are so far from the world its "surplus people" cannot emigrate, and that is another reason why the unemployment rate is so large. People in such an environment tend to be carefree and even apathetic. Constantly they appear to ask the question: "What's the use of moping?" And they provide the answer: "Let's drink and dance." And drink they do whenever they have the chance. *Bacca* is the name of the searing brew of sugarcane which they fancy helps them to forget. And then they dance the *moocha,* the rhythms of which work the dancers into a state of ecstasy. Thus people become lotus-eaters.

The "Seychelles way of life" may have been a reason of the Archbishop's long voyage. The British were apprehensive about his excess energy. They thought that he might be affected by the islanders' torpor under the Seychelles sun. So far from home, he might lapse into a state of lassitude and be forgotten. Out of the sight of his people, the Ethnarch would also be out of their minds. The Archbishop thinks that the British might have had another motive, too.

The Archbishop had his political opponents at home. His absence from Cyprus would give these people a chance to dent his prestige and present themselves as potential new leaders. Eventually, this might lead to a power struggle between Makarios and his rivals. This struggle, in turn, would weaken the Cypriots' fight for *enosis.* Meanwhile the British would draw up a plan giving the islanders a measure of self-government.

"LIFE WITHOUT CARE"

Makarios does not complain about the treatment accorded to him and his companions on the Seychelles. Sans Souci, the governor's summer residence, was the type of place to which one could quickly get accustomed. True, the humidity on the island was often high, and the captives were not used to it, but it was pleasant to spend many twilight hours in the garden. But one could not spend all day doing nothing. Political prisoners, being active and articulate people, usually catch up on their readings and make their plans for the future. Many of them evolve new reading habits, discover new authors, develop more sophisticated philosophies, and sharpen their intellectual powers in preparation for the tests they may have to face after their return to their homelands.

There was no adequate public library in Victoria. As we have seen, no newspapers were published on the islands. A request for a book was first screened, and because the Seychelles had no air connection, it took ages before an order arrived. Foreign newspapers no longer contained any "news" by the time they reached their destination in Sans Souci.

However, books the detainees had to read—mainly the kind that was "harmless" from the point of view of their captors. Books about religions, philosophy, and history were the Archbishop's choices. Who were his favorite philosophers? The giants of antiquity, of course, and particularly Zeno, teacher of the Stoics. Why Zeno? Because of his close links to the Christian ethics, which he adumbrated, and perhaps, also because of his place of origin. Zeno, too, was a Cypriot. The highest good in life to the Stoics was virtue. Makarios accepted this view. "Live consistently with nature," Zeno taught, and Makarios agreed. Banish impatience, passion, and unjust thoughts, the Stoics besought people, and Makarios shared this view. Patience, the Archbishop says, is his motto. And the following is his maxim: "In good fortune learn moderation; in bad fortune learn to be prudent." This he learned from one of the Seven Wise Men of Greece, Periander.

Even though a Prince of the Greek Orthodox Church, Makarios had long been interested in Eastern religions, and especially in Buddhism. "Life is suffering," the Buddha said. And what conclusion was man to draw from this? To be resigned. Suffering was not the lot merely of the individual—a hardship placed on his shoulders by God—it was the fate of all mankind, the universal human lot. It is not merely a negative quality. It should draw people together, because it was universally human. And at this point Makarios turned back to the Stoics: "Bear your suffering stoically. Be a man." Suffering is the price man pays for his higher spiritual status.

History was another field Makarios had the time in Sans Souci to explore. British history, at first, and later the history of America. His captors could not withhold British history books from him. And he learned a lot of "subversive" lessons from those books. A real man must fight for his freedom. The British did.

They even committed regicide. They became prosperous and great when they asserted their right to freedom against their oppressors. The Cypriots have learned from the lesson taught to them by the British.

Were his captors going to withhold from him the books about American history he requested? The writings of Jefferson, for instance? And the history of the American revolution? They would have liked to do so, probably, but they must have thought about the consequences. Makarios had been studying in the United States and had contacts there. What would the American newspapers say if they learned that the British were engaged in censoring American history? So the Archbishop got his books about the War of Independence in America.

He must have read them closely, for they provided many an argument he was to use in years to come. And they were telling arguments, the British had to admit. He quoted Jefferson, too, particularly "A Summary View of the Rights of British America." The parliament in London had no authority in the colonies, the sharp-witted American said, and "the only bond with England was that of allegiance to the King." That is, it would have been so if the British had not been so sluggish. Would they learn their lesson in the twentieth century—a lesson they had failed to learn in the eighteenth?

Makarios probably spent more time with newspapers and magazines, which he usually read in the later hours. They kept him on his toes, even though the news the captives received was dated. Books might have put him to sleep. Even today the Archbishop reads books because he has to. But he is still a passionate reader of periodical literature. In the race for the attention of the cleric and the politician it is usually the latter that wins. The periodical literature is the record of the events of today, and Makarios has always been more interested in today than in yesterday.

But one cannot fill all free hours with reading. A man as active as Makarios craved more dynamic occupations. He had been the leader of the Cypriot Greeks. Were they now leaderless? He wanted to keep in touch with his followers. He wanted to, indeed. but how? His correspondence was censored. Besides, in the Seychelles it took ages for an exchange of letters to be consummated. Even if he had been able to elude the vigilance of the authorities how could he have kept his fingers on the pulse of the events? He could not do it, and evidently his people realized it. Yet, the calculation of the British that he would be replaced by one of his rivals in Cyprus failed to materialize. He had his rivals, of course. The Cypriots are passionately political-minded, and they seldom agree on political issues. But they did agree on the basic policy of *enosis* and also on the fact that Makarios was their leader, no matter how far away from home he was. The British could have tucked him away on the other side of the moon, and it would not have mattered. By this time the Archbishop had become a legend.

There were four detainees in Victoria and Sans Souci was a lively household. Four Greeks represent at least five divergent political views—and these Cypriots were Greeks. They had been exiled because they were Greeks. Yet their views were divergent on many issues, some of them trifling and some of them basic. And so they quarreled a lot. Then they made up. Then they quarreled some more. Sometimes they were not on speaking terms. That was a symptom of the "barbed-wire disease." But they needed the company of one another, and so they made up again. When the end of their imprisonment finally came, each of them went his own way. Comrades in adversity, they drifted apart in freedom. That, too, was to be expected.

Let us leave the four prisoners on that pin-point island in the Indian Ocean and look at that other island whence they had come. The role of Makarios cannot be fully appreciated without a searching look.

THAT OTHER ISLAND

Cyprus has been in history as long as some of the most historic parts of the Middle Eastern world. Situated in the eastern Mediterranean, it attracted attention and greed in the earliest recorded times. Its strategic value is attested by the fact that no conqueror of the region overlooked it. Per square mile it has witnessed more invasions than its famous neighbors. Egypt, Turkey, and the Levantine coast. It is a compact little island of 3,572 square miles, densely populated by about 600,000 people. Its contemporary problems are due to the composition of the population: 485,000 Greek-speaking people, who consider themselves Greeks and are members of the Greek Orthodox Church; and about 100,000 Turks, who are Moslems. The rest are Armenians, Jews, and Maronites, these latter in communion with the Roman Catholic Church, but with their own Levantine liturgy.

The location of the island provides the explanation of its history. It is a mere forty miles south of Turkey (the mountains of which are visible from Cypriot mountain tops); sixty miles west of Syria, the Levantine heart of the Arab world, and 240 miles north of Egypt. The island is situated in the most pivotal region of the eastern Mediterranean which, in turn, has always been one of the most strategic areas in the world. Select almost any period of human history, and Cyprus is nearly always in the fulcrum, from the days of spears and arrows to the days of the nuclear bomb.

Strategic location is only one of the reasons that the importance of Cyprus is completely out of proportion with its size. The island has minerals which have been coveted from the earliest times. The very name of Cyprus seems to have been derived from *kypros*, "copper." The island also has iron pyrites, asbestos, and chromite.

Cyprus is situated along the most important invasion and defense lines of the eastern Mediterranean region. It was needed for offense no less than for defense. An ideal place to assemble and organize armed forces, it was no less ideal to give the armies a rest, to reorganize them, and to provide them with a sanctuary. In this latter respect Cyprus may be compared with Great Britain, protected by her broad water-filled moats. With this exception: the moats of Cyprus are even wider. And this other exception: that in spite of them the strategic importance of the island was so great as to invite an endless series of invasions.

History usually begins with fables, of which Cyprus has more than its share. The Greeks of classical times held that it was out of the incredibly blue waters of the Cypriot seas that the foamlike white body of Aphrodite rose. Nor did Christian legends overlook the island. The famed monastery not far from the birthplace of Makarios contains the thaumaturgic ikon of the virgin which tradition considers the handiwork of St. Luke.

The long series of invasions began with Tethmoses III (Thutmose) of Egypt, of the Eighteenth Dynasty (*circa* 1500 B.C.), who needed islands to strengthen his lines against the Levantine coast and to secure a launching board for his own plans. And then came the other conquerors: the Assyrians, who turned the island into their protectorate, the Egyptians again, and then the Persians. Alexander the Great swept into the island on his way to world conquest and immortality. After him came the Ptolemaic dynasty of Egypt. The island became a Roman province in 58 B.C.

Christianity did not overlook the island. Paul visited it, in the company of Joses the Levite, whom history knows as St. Barnabas. The two of them are said to have converted the Roman governor of Cyprus. Thus the island was the first Christian-ruled region within the Roman Empire. After St. Paul came St. Mark.

When the Roman Empire became too unwieldy because of its vastness, it was divided into East and West in 395 A.D. The East became the Byzantine Empire, speaking Greek. It was this empire which ruled over Cyprus for seven hundred years, the usual interruptions apart. It was during those centuries that the people of the island became Greek in speech and traditions. That was the starting point of the "Cyprus problem."

Arab invasions provided the strident counterpoints to the cacophony of history on Cyprus. The invaders established themselves on the nearby Levantine coast, which has remained Arab to this very day. The crusaders came next and obtained a foothold on the island. The most legendary of them ruled over Cyprus for a year, England's Lionhearted Richard I. He sold the island to the Knights Templar, who, in turn, transferred it to Guy de Lusignan, the titular king of Jerusalem. There was a brief interruption again, as the Genoese occupied Famagusta, one of the main towns of Cyprus. The rule of the French Lusignan dynasty lasted for three hundred years. Then came the Venetians, who had become the great power of the region, and finally the Turks in 1571. During one of these "time of troubles," this small island of Cyprus was divided into ten different countries which were, naturally, warring with one another.

For three centuries the Ottoman Empire ruled over the island, and it provided the Turkish population of the island. During the first two centuries of their reign, the Turks came as the rulers—officials, tax collectors, police—and in their wake came the settlers. Thus close to one-fifth of the inhabitants were Turks.

Turks and Greeks became proverbial enemies. Following different ways of life couched in the ideologies of their antithetical religions, both of them are proud people. The Greeks are proud of their tremendous heritage as godparents of the civilization of the West. No less proud, the Turks were the fabulously successful "master race" of the Middle East, architects of a nearly global civilization.

The Turks had overextended themselves and had failed to provide the foundation of a peaceful empire. Spectacularly they had ascended, and no less spectacularly they had sunk into the mire of an Oriental despotism that was kept alive by the jealousy of the great powers who were apprehensive that the Ottomans' demise might precipitate a major conflict. Gradually, the most aggressive and dynamic of the Western powers, Great Britain, began to shoulder the burden of the Turkish sultan.

The pressure of Britain on Turkey was great. In 1878 the sultan in Constantinople "leased" Cyprus to the British. Nominally, the Turkish sultan remained the sovereign; in reality the British were the rulers. They became the masters of Cyprus both *de jure* and *de facto* when World War I broke out. The Ottoman Empire sided then with the enemies of Britain. The British government offered the island to the Greeks during the war. There was a condition attached to this offer. The Greeks were to aid Serbia, invaded by their Bulgarian neighbor. The Athens government failed to act in time and the offer lapsed. Cyprus remained under British rule.

The Greek population of the island resented the British regime. They were considered "third class people," natives, an ethnic group of inferior breed. Cyprus, as we have seen, did belong to the Greek-speaking Eastern Roman Empire for seven centuries. That empire was pivoted on Constantinople. The Ottoman Turks extinguished it, as they extinguished also much of the civilization of the Greeks. For centuries there was no sovereign country by the name of Greece.

The Turks devised special methods to rule over the minorities which, in fact, formed the majority of the population. One of the important minorities were the Greeks. Others were the Armenians, the Greeks, Kurds, Jews, Arabs, and many others.

The "Church" and State were not separated in the Ottoman Empire. The head of the State was also the equivalent of the Supreme Pontiff. He was both the sultan and the Caliph, secular potentate and presumed successor of Mohammed the Prophet and, therefore, supreme leader at the prayers. He was called the *Padishah,* and that meant "Foot King," because he had the right to place his foot on the prostrate bodies of all other kings. His title was "Emperor of the Mighty Emperors; Refuge of Sovereigns; Distributor of Crowns to the Kings of the Earth; Keeper of the Two Very Holy Cities; Governor of the Sacred City of Jerusalem; Terror of the World; Master of Europe, Asia, and Africa; High King of the Two Seas; Shadow of God on Earth."

Since the religion of the Turks was Islam and since religion and secular authority were not separated, how were the non-Moslems governed? The Turks devised a special system for their non-Moslem subjects. They set up non-Moslem communities, called *millets*. This designation is significant. It means both "religion" and "nation," revealing the fact anew that the Ottoman Turks could make no distinction between the secular and religious authorities, which overlapped. The Greeks of the Ottoman Empire were organized in the Rum Millet, and "Rum" is a distortion of "Roman," derived from the name of the Eastern Roman Empire, the Byzantium of yore.

Within the *millets* and also in the Rum Millet authority was vested in religious heads, thereby copying the governmental system prevailing among the Turks and other Moslem subjects of the empire. We have seen that Cyprus has an autocephalous church organization, one of the oldest in the Eastern Christian world. That means that it is not subject to the direct authority of the Patriarch of Constantinople, or of any other extra-insular religious authority of the Greek Orthodox Church.

The system of the *millets* expired after the Turks lost control of Cyprus. Now the British ruled over both the Greeks and the Turks. But the hold of the tradition continued. The Archbishop of Cyprus was the primate of the Church, and to him the Greek-speaking people of the island were looking for leadership. That is how Archbishop Makarios became not only the religious head of the islanders but also their political leader. The grip of traditions is not loosened quickly in that part of the world.

And what did the Greek-speaking people of Cyprus want? They did not dislike the British, as decent "imperialists" as one could find anywhere. But they did dislike imperialism, and they were opposed to their being treated as a colony. They wanted to practice that very same democracy which their own ancestors transmitted to the world. They wanted to have the parliamentary system which the English themselves introduced to the West. At home the British were democratic, in Cyprus they were autocratic.

The Cypriots helped the British and their Allies during World War II. Cypriot soldiers distinguished themselves in fighting the Axis dictators in North Africa, in Crete, in Syria, and eventually, in Greece. If they were good enough to lay down their lives for the cause of democracy, as represented by the British, they were entitled to its benefits.

The Greek-speaking people of Cyprus observed the spectacular "nationalism explosion" all over the world. They saw how the people of Asia and Africa were freeing themselves from the thralldom of their colonial masters. If the people of the subcontinent of India could do it, why not they? All over Africa people who had never had a national life of their own became independent and were warmly greeted in the United Nations when their delegates took one of the seats reserved for the representatives of sovereign nations. Why not Cyprus, too?

What did the Greeks of Cyprus want? Did they want a government of their own, a flag, a national anthem, a seat in the General Assembly of the United Nations—appurtenances of sovereignty? No, they felt Greek and wanted to join Greece. They wanted *enosis*. Had they ever been part of Greece? No, never of Greece, but of the Greek-speaking Eastern Roman Empire in the distant past. Cyprus is much farther from Greece than from Turkey, Syria, or Egypt. The distance between the nearest points of the two countries is more than five hundred miles.

Yet, the Greek-speaking people of the island wanted *enosis*. But the British did not want it, and the Turkish-speaking Moslem Cypriots did not want it either. The British did not want it for the same reason that they wanted the island at the time they acquired it. And that was the reason of Tethmoses, too, and of the Phoenicians, of the Assyrians, of the Persians, of Alexander the Great, of the Romans, of the Crusaders, and of all the others. And that reason was the incomparable strategic location of the island. The British wanted to retain Cyprus very badly. And that is why Archbishop Makarios was exiled to the Seychelles islands. And now we can return to the story of his life.

THE BLESSED ONE

Makarios means "Blessed One," but that was not yet the name of the infant born on August 13, 1913, whose fate it was to become an exile on an Indian Ocean island. His name at birth was Michael Christodoulos Mouskos. The meaning of the second name is "Servant of the God." Greek parents gave their children such names so as to set them apart from their Turkish neighbors. Mouskos means "fragrance" in Cypriot Greek dialect.

It was in the southwestern corner of the island that the future Blessed One was born, in the town of Ano Panayia, in the

District of Paphos. St. Paul was supposed to have visited the place, and the truncated granite column which people call "St. Paul's Pillar" still stands there. He had been tied to it and flogged.

The father of Archbishop Makarios, Charalambos Mouskos, did not look any different from the other peasants, wearing his baggy pants, *vraka,* as he tended his small plot of land, his olive trees, a small vineyard, and about a hundred goats. Certainly he was far from being well-to-do, but he was not poverty-stricken, either.

The mother of the future Archbishop was a simple peasant woman. She died when Makarios was still very young, and the neighbors have no recollection of her. Charalambos Mouskos married a second time, another peasant woman, the Archbishop's stepmother; she is still alive. He has two brothers and two sisters, the latter married.

The father wanted young Michael to help him on the farm, to become a peasant. The boy helped to tend the goats, but he was not much good on the farm. He was a smart child. Some of the oldsters in Ano Panayia remember how he became known as the "little deacon" because he liked to gather five or six boys after church and chant Gregorian psalms and "bless" his congregation.

Not far from the Archbishop's place of the birth is the Abbey of Kykko, one of the venerable institutions of the island, dating back to the early twelfth-century rule of the Byzantine Emperor Alexius I Comnenus. This largest and wealthiest religious institution of Cyprus, high up in the Troodos mountains, at an elevation of some four thousand feet, contains the famous *Eleousa,* "The Compassionate One," the miracle-working ikon of the Virgin and the Child. The peasants believe that it has the power of producing rain, their most constant need. It is an important place of pilgrimage, especially at times when the sluices of heaven prove to be sluggish. At the age of thirteen Michael became a novice at Kykko.

Why the choice of ecclesiastic vocation? Kykko had much to do with that, the Archbishop says today. He also says that his father was quite unhappy over his choice. The farm was calling out for the hands of the young people. The young boy was not interested in his father's humdrum life. His choice of the monastery may have been induced by a negative consideration, rather than by a positive one. He did not want to become a peasant. Was he looking for higher status in the monastery?

The Greek islanders' attitude toward clerics is ambivalent. The priests, as we have seen, are recognized spokesmen of the Greek people on Cyprus. People are Greek not only because of their speech—which is a dialect resembling that of Arcadia, the center of the Pelopponesian part of Greece—but also because they belong to the Church that calls itself Holy, Orthodox, Catholic, Apostolic, and Eastern. On the other hand, members of the clergy seldom till the soil and therefore they are costly. Even today setting eyes on a man of the cloth is not considered a good omen, and the peasants touch their sex organs so as to avert the evil eye.

For the next six years the boy Michael was linked to the abbey, at first as a novice. In that capacity he had to perform work for which he did not care particularly, doing the chores left to the youngest members of the community, attending to agricultural and pastoral work. The abbey had extensive estates on which he could employ the aptitudes inherited through work on the farms. He stood the tests and the barriers standing in his way toward more distant goals were gradually removed.

It was the Abbey of Kykko that sent him to the Pan-Cyprian Gymnasium—secondary school—in the capital of the island, Nicosia. And it was on a Kykko Monastery scholarship that he proceeded to Athens, where he was matriculated at the Theological College of the University of Athens. Meanwhile, he was ordained a deacon in 1938.

He remained in the Greek capital for eight years, part of which was during the occupation of the capital by the Germans and their Italian and Bulgarian satellites. World War II and the enemy occupation wrought tremendous havoc in Greece.

Makarios shared the privations of millions of Greeks during those endless years of trial. The meat, wheat, and flour which the Greeks normally imported from abroad, could not be obtained. On the other hand, there was limited demand for the olives, currants, and sponges they produced, for the importing nations maintained strict wartime austerity programs. But Makarios survived these vicissitudes as did millions of Greeks.

As a student of theology his contacts with the occupying forces were limited. He does not appear to have expressed political opinions that might have caused him trouble. He was not detained by the Axis soldiers, nor was he tortured, as were so many Greeks.

While at the University of Athens, he branched out in his

studies. He entered the law school of the university. What goal did he have in mind? He says that his main interest was centered on the canonic law. And why was that so? Probably because of conditions in the clergy on his native island. Most members of the clergy were not highly educated. In order to get a thorough education one had to have the drive of Makarios. He saw that the island offered great opportunities to clergymen with superior education. He may have been thinking of becoming the head of one of the insular bishoprics.

It was in the year of 1946 that he was ordained a priest, receiving the ecclesiastical name under which contemporary history was to know him, the Blessed One, Makarios. The record says that he had become a member of the teaching staff of the Abbey of Kykko. He never completed his law studies.

TO THE UNITED STATES

In Athens and at home Makarios established valuable contacts with the outside world. Almost coincidental with his ordainment, he was awarded a scholarship by the World Council of Churches for futher theological studies, and so he left for the School of Theology of Boston University, reaching Boston in time for the beginning of the 1946–47 academic year.

He matriculated at Boston University under the name of Makarious Christodoulos Kykkotis. The different spellings in his first two names are due to differences in the transliteration of the Cyrillic original. He selected the name "Kykkotis" because of his connection with the Abbey of Kykko.

He had a limited program in the academic year of 1946–47, and the courses he took were not for credit. He was only an auditor. This may have been his way of testing his capacity to study in a foreign environment and not in his native language. He took the following courses: New Testament; Church History; Public Address; Organization, Administration, and Supervision of Religious Education. Two courses were theoretical, while the other two were practical.

During the next academic year, 1947–48, he took the following courses for credit: Pauline Studies; New Testament Introduction; Life and Teachings of Jesus; Background of the New Testament; Studies in the Fourth Gospel; Problems in the Gos-

pels; Systematic Theology I; Church History I and II; Principles of Religious Education; Organization, Administration,
and Supervision of Religious Education.

This program would indicate that he was considering
a career in the field of religious education or administration.
He took a total of twenty-six semester-hours credit during the
year. How was he doing in his studies? Very well, indeed. He
was a B+ to A− student.

Dr. Edwin P. Booth was the professor of Historical Theology at Boston University, and he has the most favorable recollection of "Mr. Kykkotis."

In the church history lecture room, Professor Booth told
me, "Kykkotis" always sat in the front row and gave his most
concentrated attention. "I have never forgotten the quietness, as
well as the steadiness, of his eyes as he watched me. As we went
over the early church's evolution, we found ourselves deeply
involved in history and our own positions would, temporarily,
be in the background. Among all the students that I have had
over the years, granted all our differences, none impressed me
more than he did.

"I well remember the day when I was lecturing and he,
as usual, was sitting in the front row, when a knock came on
my classroom door. Mr. Paul Harrington, Superintendent of
Buildings, entered with a cablegram for the then Mr. Kykkotis,
informing him of his election to his bishopship. He quietly rose
and, bowing to me, left the classroom. This election marked,
of course, the end of his studies with us."

Years later, His Beatitude Archbishop Makarios visited
Boston University, presenting it with valuable ancient manu-
scripts. On many occasions in Cyprus, he received visitors from
his American alma mater. "The warmth of his friendship over
the years has been amply attested," Professor Booth said.

It was not only theology Makarios learned in Boston.
He also became closely acquainted with the modern type of
nationalism. He found secular and religious emotions fused in
the nationalism of Americans. He was impressed by the quasi-
religious reactions of the people of the United States to the
rendering of their national anthem and the raising of the flag.
Also, he observed the stimulating impact of national loyalty in
stirring up political action.

He maintained contact with influential Americans of Greek

descent and with Greek-American societies. It was within the concept of Greek nationalism, as developed through his contacts in America, that his own feelings about Cyprus became further clarified. He could not be proud of the cultural heritage of that part of Cypriot life that was based on the traditions of the Lusignans, Venetians and Turks. But he was immensely proud of the cultural heritage of Greece, which appeared to him—more than ever against an American background—the great awakener of man's capacity to launch his career in the most varied fields of the sciences and arts, the sum of which represented humanity's intellectual history.

Strangely enough it was in Boston, and not in Athens, that he detected that extra throb of his heart at the sight of the flag of Greece, the blue and white colors of which entranced him. He did not try to suppress his emotions at Greek-American social meetings when the band struck up the *Ethnikos Hymnos,* "Hymn to Liberty," the Greek national anthem.

He learned other things, too. An expert in "socialization," he became a past master of it in his new American environment. He knew that noble deeds were not enough—they had to be noted by the right persons. Word of his activities in America reached the press of Cyprus, and he was a much sought-after speaker at the service clubs.

Life in Cyprus was leisurely in comparison with New England. The Mediterranean sun, the blueness of the sea, the lassitude of lingering sips in cafés induced people to find enjoyment in the stagelike setting of life. New England was different. There Makarios—always quick to learn—became acquainted with another dimension of life: the potential depth in each individual, unexplored and often undetected, containing the most precious treasures of unprobed possibilities. He learned to reach down into his own capacities, bringing forth the values that one can find only in those depths.

The relaxed social ways of America appealed to Makarios. He could become a "gay blade," too, on occasions, and an admiring bevy of attractive young women found that "Mac," as they came to call him, was a "doll," who had the "cutest smile." And could he smile? In all Boston there was not another young man with his happy flashing smile. With the process of Americanization went also the related process of standardization. American convention frowned upon his beard, which most of the admiring girls may have liked but which the folkways scorned. And off went the glistening beard of Boston University's pet, "Mac," at least for a time.

Greek Orthodox priests need not be celibates. However, bishops and higher ranks have to be unmarried. Makarios was now thirty years old and unmarried. Was he expecting a call to one of the bishoprics of Cyprus?

THE BISHOP OF KITION

That call did come, as we have seen, while he was a student of the School of Theology of Boston University. The ancient see of Kition (Citium) fell vacant. This was the birthplace of the founder of the School of Stoics, Zeno, whose philosophy Makarios shared. For many years the See had been without an effective religious head. Long after the official hours the light was still burning in the study of Bishop Makarios. The finances of the See, when he took it over, were in the red, but it did not take him long to turn to the use of black ink. He was a man of practical good sense, a competent administrator, and a highly convincing speaker.

By this time the great independence explosion in Asia had begun. Britain was out of India and India had been considered the very pivot of the British empire. The subcontinent was now the home of new nations—of India, Pakistan, and just off the shore, of Ceylon. Soon the revolutionary fire was to spread to other parts of the underdeveloped continents—Africa and Asia. Louder and louder became the clamor of the Cypriots for union with Greece—*enosis*. Also more insistent became the voice of the Turkish minority on the island against the union. And the British needed Cyprus more than ever as their last toehold along their imperial lifeline leading to the Commonwealth countries.

Because of the traditions of the Greek Orthodox Church on the island, the clergy could not refrain from political action. No sooner was Bishop Makarios elected than he took political matters in hand. In the autumn of 1949 he visited Greece, where he had important talks with the prime minister and other officials about the handling of the Cyprus question by the Greek government. Bishop Makarios was now chairman of the Ethnarchy Office and it was in that capacity that he organized a "Pan-Cyprian Plebiscite" in January, 1950. The Greek-speaking population was to decide whether or not it wanted to have union with Greece. It was a completely informal plebiscite, not authorized by the British government. Churchgoers simply signed their names in a register in the vestibules of their places of worship. They were asked the question: "Are you or are you not in favor of *enosis?*" Ninety-seven per cent of the voters were in its favor. And what was the answer of the British: "This so-called 'plebiscite' has no standing in law." And as far as the British were concerned, that was that.

THE ETHNARCH OF CYPRUS

The Archbishop of Cyprus is, at the same time, its Ethnarch, spokesman of the ethnic Greeks. The literal translation of the word is "governor of the province or people." That the archbishops had been, in a limited sense, under the rule of the Turks, but not under the British. Still there remained the Ethnarchy Office, and the Greek-speaking people continued to consider the archbishop their political spokesman.

Because of this role of the archbishop, he is elected by the people. Makarios II, the Ethnarch and Archbishop of Cyprus, died in the early fall of 1950, an old man. Who was to follow him?

There were two candidates for the office. One of them was Bishop Makarios and the other one was Bishop Iakovos, the Metropolitan of Derkon, not a Cypriot. The Cypriot Greeks are no less political-minded than the "mainland" ones. Politics is in their blood. After all, politics itself is a Greek word.

The political lineup in Cyprus followed the modern trend—right and left. Makarios was on good terms with the Greek government, which was considered right-wing. He was also on good terms with the United States Embassy in Athens, which many Greeks considered extreme-right-wing. His opponent was backed by some of the left-wing Cypriot trade unions. The Metropolitian was not a left-winger by any means, but he was not "compromised" through contacts with the Athens government and the American Embassy, as was Makarios.

Qualified to vote were adult males falling within the purview of property qualifications. They were members of the Greek Orthodox Church. Because of the property qualifications the candidate of the right-wing had a decided advantage. The election took place in October, 1950, and Bishop Makarios won. Was it a landslide victory? On the contrary. He won by the skin of his teeth—with a majority of a couple of hundred votes. Thus Michael Christodoulos Mouskos became His Beatitude Makarios III, Ethnarch and Archbishop of Cyprus, a Prince of the Church in one of the most ancient sees of Christendom.

The work of Archbishop Makarios in ecclesiastical matters is very little known. Very much is known about his work as the Ethnarch of Cyprus. Judging by the following record it would be a miracle if he had the time to work in the ecclesiastical vineyard.

Enosis was his main concern, as it was the chief problem of the Greek-speaking Cypriots. Recent history had shown that the great colonial nations were less impressed by arguments than by the show of force and of strength. Young people were the most ardent supporters of the idea of union with Greece. One of the first tasks of the Ethnarch-Archbishop was to aid the establishment of the Pan-Cyprian Youth Organization, PEON. Also, he organized many meetings and mass demonstrations through which he tried to take the message of *enosis* to the most remote places in the hills.

One of the first tasks of Makarios III was to pay another visit to Greece, where he renewed contacts with the government, the foreign ambassadors, and King Paul. In 1952 he went on an extended tour of Egypt, Lebanon, and Syria, informing the coreland of the Arab world on the problem of Cyprus. From Syria he proceeded back to Athens where he tried to persuade the Greek government to appeal to the United Nations about Cyprus. The United States was not in favor of such an appeal since it threatened to disturb the unity of the Western alliance. The appeal would have implied criticism of the main pivot of the European Western alliance, Britain.

Makarios returned to Cyprus and there he sent a protest to the Committee for Non-Self-Governing Territories of the United Nations against Britain's omission to submit political information on Cyprus. Makarios made it clear that the Cypriots were determined to fight for their freedom.

In October, 1952, he went to New York, where the Seventh Session of the General Assembly of the UN was taking place. Cyprus not being a member of the world body, Makarios could not take the floor. But he was seen engaged in earnest conversation with chairmen of various committees and with delegates of friendly countries. He also visited many American cities. He was given the freedom of several American cities, including Detroit. He founded branches of the organization, Justice for Cyprus, appeared on television and the radio, gave press interviews, and appealed to President Eisenhower and the Congress, advocating freedom for Cyprus. He also met political leaders and senior officials of the State Department in Washington.

On his way back to Cyprus he visited London and Athens, where he conducted press conferences. For the first time the British press gave wide publicity to his statements, thus breaking the silence it had maintained on the Cyprus question and the Archbishop's stand.

On his return to Cyprus he was accorded an enthusiastic welcome by the people. He addressed a letter to Sir Andrew Barkworth Wright, the governor, asking him to promote the application of the right of determination for Cyprus by recognizing the 1950 plebiscite or holding a new one. He gave a fiery speech before a large mass meeting in Nicosia, pledging the people's will to struggle to a victorious end and reaffirming their determination to have recourse to the United Nations. He addressed a petition to the secretary-general of the United Nations in August, 1953, requesting the inclusion of an item on the "application of the right of the people of Cyprus to self-determination" in the agenda of the Eighth Session of the General Assembly.

Since it was necessary to have the petition sponsored by a member-state, Makarios paid another visit to Athens in February, 1954, and persuaded the Greek government to place the Cyprus question before the United Nations. And, indeed, the prime minister of Greece, Field Marshal Alexander Papagos, submitted a petition to the UN, calling for the application of the principle of self-determination to the people of Cyprus.

The pro-Western bloc of the United Nations was loath to come to grips with this problem. All three countries in the controversy—the United Kingdom, Greece, and Turkey—were members of the North Atlantic Treaty Organization. The United States, as leader of the alliance, was reluctant to bring a "family quarrel" into the open.

The Archbishop turned up again in New York in the autumn of 1954, so as to attend the Ninth Session of the General Assembly of the United Nations. This time the Cyprus question was discussed but no resolution was taken on its essence. Makarios was a highly interested observer.

Next, the Archbishop turned up in another part of the world, in the mountain town of Bandung, on the island of Java, in the Republic of Indonesia. There representatives of African and Asian nations assembled. Many of them had recently gained their independence. They met in the Indonesian town in order to discuss the common problems of the underdeveloped countries. For long the white man had been carrying his "burden," and now the time seemed to be propitious to relieve him of his heavy load. The Afro-Asian nations represented by far the largest part of humanity; they wished to have their say in world affairs. Makarios had many talks with leaders of the African and Asian nations on the question of self-determination for the Cyprus people. On his return from Bandung he again visited Athens and Cairo where he had talks with the Greek and Egyptian governments.

THEN THE EXPLOSION

Then the uprising started which made the name of Makarios headline news throughout the world. The time was April, 1955. The Cypriots called it "revolution." The British denounced it as a "revolt." It was to last for four years; the world was to hear a lot of the Archbishop and Cyprus during that time. Much blood was shed and bitterness engendered.

In spite of its history, it is hard to associate Cyprus with bitterness and bloodshed. It is a lovely island, this "Aphrodite land." What could be lovelier than the Mediterranean countryside when nature bursts into new life? Could anything be more soothing to frayed nerves than the first shy blossoms of the almond on the Kyrenian coast, or the riotous colors of the cyclamen and the cystus in the hills? What could be more pleasant than the perfume of the citrus groves? Even the starkness of the Messaoria plains is softened under the blue southern sky.

The world used to know the Cypriots as gentle souls, the sun of the Mediterranean reflected not only on their cheeks but also in their hearts. They are quick to laugh—Archbishop Makarios, too, has a flashing smile—to drink and sing, and they love to chat. They fill their cheap-priced, popular cafés, chatting, laughing, sometimes quarreling, too, drinking, smiling, talking politics, and playing their favorite backgammon game. Their tempers are violent, however, when brought to the boiling point. And this is what happened now.

Archbishop Makarios continued to make every effort to reach a *modus vivendi* with the British. Self-determination was the motto. If the Cypriots could only express their true voice, *enosis* would no doubt be established. He had conferences with A. T. Lennox-Boyd, the British secretary of state for the colonies. But he also had other irons in the fire.

The Pan-Cyprian Youth Organization was alerted, the conscience of the younger generation, dedicated to the cause of union with Greece. Members of this youth group were made to take a sacred oath: "If I disobey my oath I shall deserve every kind of punishment as a traitor and may eternal contempt shame me."

The trouble started in the town of Limassol; it took the form of a demonstration against the refusal of the UN to come to grips with the substance of the Cyprus case. The British military had been alerted, too, and the young demonstrators found themselves surrounded by armed troops. As the temperature of the mob rose, the young people began to hurl stones. The military ordered the demonstrators to disperse; the young people stood their ground. Another demand, and another refusal. The soldiers fired, and three youngsters were wounded. This was the beginning of the revolution that landed the Ethnarch in the Seychelles. *Enosis* had its martyrs.

A fighting organization sprang into existence, and the world was to hear much about it in years to come. It was the EOKA, *Ethniki Organosis Kyprion Agoniston,* "National Organization of Cypriot Struggle." Who were its leaders? After investigating the organization, the British announced that the *spiritus rector* of EOKA was the Archbishop-Ethnarch himself. It was he who procured the funds and the arms. It was he who had first organized the resistance, keeping the Greek Cypriots in a state of alarm, disseminating the seeds of hatred against the British rulers and the Cypriot Turks.

Makarios said then and has reiterated it countless times: "The uprising was a most unfortunate event, because I am against violence and do not want bloodshed." And he repeated over and over again: "Our struggle has never been against the British, whom we like, but against colonialism."

The British now called upon one of their ablest proconsuls to solve the Cyprus puzzle. He was Field Marshal Sir John Harding, former chief of the Imperial General Staff. He was appointed Governor of Cyprus and Commander-in-Chief of the armed forces there. He appeared to be a worthy successor of Britain's empire-builders and empire-savers, a man of iron, in character and looks, undaunted and undauntable. Would he be able to stop the bloodshed and bless the island with peace?

He was not able to do so. Armed units of EOKA continued to roam over the entire countryside. The EOKA forces consisted of two types of fighters: the rural guerrillas and what the British called the "urban terrorists." The guerrillas were the country people, part-time peasants and part-time soldiers, operating by night and dissolving into the lovely countryside by day. The "terrorists" were all kinds of people, idealists and realists, people who were ready to sacrifice their lives for a national cause which was also their religion. But there were some who gloated over gore, who liked to rationalize their sadistic nature with the call of an idealistic and quasi-religious cause. The beautiful Cypriot countryside resounded with the shattering impact of plastic bombs, the clatter of the machine gun, the swish of the knife. Corpses became a common sight in the streets of towns and on the highways and byways of the island.

The Archbishop himself was in the Ethnarch's palace. Was there a common command for the activities of the armed men? People spoke in hushed tones about the commander-in-chief of the *enosis* underground. Most of the time they referred to him as Dighenis, a famous name in the lore of the Greeks. The word means "twice born," and the original Dighenis was a Robin Hood, a villainous hero of Greek epics. The original Dighenis had also been known as "the King."

Who was this modern King of the patriotic outlaws, the fighting arm of *enosis?* His real name was George Grivas. Born in Cyprus under the British rule, he had become a naturalized Greek. He was not a young man, for he was now in his fifties, but he was a hardened military man who had fought the Axis in Greece during World War II.

The British knew about him and were combing the countryside from sea to sea in search of him. Cyprus is not a large island; yet the British could never find him, although during all this time he apparently remained on the island, conducting operations. Did he maintain contact with Makarios? The Archbishop denied this. While Makarios was in the Seychelles the British claim to have discovered the diaries of Grivas, with frequent references to the Ethnarch whose rather obvious code name was "Mac."

The terrain favored Grivas: the maze of hills that are almost impenetrable in spots, the deep gashes in the sun-scorched mountain slopes which shoot off in trackless spurs. On one occasion a British platoon searching for Grivas swept past his hideout. On another occasion, a pile of bottles of yogurt, to which he was partial, almost gave him away. While the British were patrolling the village of Kholarakes, Grivas hibernated there. It was not only the ruggedness of the island that protected the legendary Grivas, but also the character of the Cypriots. They were loyal to the field commander of their fight for freedom, and also they feared his retribution. Those who were not for *enosis* were deemed to be against it, and the EOKA fighters made short shrift of them.

THE TURKS ALSO ROSE

Even if the British had wanted to grant self-determination to the Cypriot Greeks, there was also the problem of the local Turks, who made up about 18 per cent of the population. *They* did not want to join Greece. That country was hundreds of miles away, while they could sometimes see the peaks of the mountains of Turkey. The Turkish inhabitants were satisfied with British rule. If it was to be ended they wanted *taksim,* the partition of the island into Greek and Turkish regions. There was precedent for this on the subcontinent of India, where India and Pakistan had been formed, and also in the former Palestine, from which Israel and a part of Jordan had been carved.

To counter EOKA the Turks set up their own self-defense organization, TNT, *Turk Nudafa Teskilat,* "Turkish Defense Force." The counterpart of Makarios among the Turks was a physician, Dr. Fazil Kutchuk. He told me at the time that the Turkish Cypriots could not consent to *enosis* under any circumstances. Throughout the years, he said, the Greeks of the island had been pushing the Turks into the corner, advancing from positions of strength to positions of greater strength. Should Cyprus become part of Greece, the Greek Cypriots would have their Turkish neighbors at their mercy. The Greeks had a deep-seated hatred of the Turks.

The Cypriot problem was entangled now even more than before. The Turks of the island were against the pro-Greeks, who in turn were against the British and, even more violently, against their "loyalist"—anti-*enosis*—fellow Greeks. Turks began to move from sections of the towns in which the majority was Greek. In Nicosia, particularly, the exodus was from the south side to the north, past the arterial roads between the Famagusta Gate in the east and the Paphos Gate in the west. Greek lawyers no longer dared to attend trials at the law courts, which were in the Turkish quarter of the island capital.

The conflict between the two communities now spread to the mainland, Greece and Turkey. In Constantinople Turkish mobs descended upon the Greek quarters, looting the shops, setting fire to churches, and wrecking Greek dwellings. The police was called and it arrived in due time—after the damage had been done. There was a demonstration in front of the Turkish Embassy in Athens.

Bloodshedding became a habit; it looked as though the lovely island would be turned into a shambles. There were worried consultations among the members of the Western alliance. How was Cyprus to affect the North Atlantic Treaty Organization, of which all the three countries involved in the conflict were members? A way out had to be found.

The situation was further complicated by events in the Middle East. Egypt had nationalized the Suez Canal, and two major Western powers with the chief interest in the canal, Great Britain and France, decided on action. More than ever, the British needed Cyprus, their last toehold in the region. It was the launching pad of their airborne forces to the Suez Canal. The United Nations stopped the British and the French. Just the same, the strategic importance of Cyprus was demonstrated anew.

THE FIELD MARSHAL AND THE ETHNARCH

The governor of the island, Sir John Harding, wanted to justify the expectations placed on him. Since Makarios was the *spiritus rector* in British eyes, he and he alone was the person to stop the violence.

The Archbishop replied that not he, but the British, were responsible for the violence. Let the authorities in London produce an acceptable solution and the bloodshed was bound to end. A typical proconsul, Sir John did not wish to have this sort of dialogue. His demand was categorical. "We have asked for a clear statement on violence and this is what we got." Again he called on the Ethnarch to stop the bloodshed, and again he received the same answer. "To come to grips with Makarios," the Field Marshal grunted in anger, "is like trying to come to grips with quicksilver."

"Quicksilver" was one of the more flattering designations applied to Makarios. A respectable journal of opinion in London summarized English public attitude in these words: "An ambitious cleric, a parcel of Athens politicians, and a handful of hooligans in Nicosia are responsible for the terror."

The Field Marshal made another try. This time he called on Makarios to denounce the EOKA terrorists. Since he was a prince of the Church and in the service of the Prince of Peace the Archbishop could do at least this much. However, Makarios rebutted: "To condemn EOKA would involve the risk of exposing myself rather unprofitably."

What was the meaning of this cryptic statement? Was this another dodge? Or was His Beatitude the prisoner of the extremist dogma of the nationalists? The wolves were howling and he had to howl with them or else they would get rid of him. Was the leader of the Greek-speaking islanders being led by the terrorist "hooligans" to whom the London newspaper had referred?

The deadlock had to be broken, and the British came forward with what they called a "positive" plan. Its substance was summarized in the words: "Self-determination in principle for Cyprus." This was one of those ambiguous statements which may have meant something or nothing. The reply of the Archbishop, spokesman of the supporters of *enosis,* was unambiguous: "We have plenty of principles ourselves. We need an implemented plan." And he produced one.

First, he said, there should be an elected legislature in Cyprus, and the Greek-speaking people should control the majority in it, commensurate with their numerical strength. It was up to this body to make the ultimate decisions. Meanwhile, the British should relinquish police authority with no delay. Also, they should proclaim full and total amnesty for all political prisoners.

Now the British decided on "positive action." In their appraisal of the Cyprus tragedy, the Archbishop was at the root of the trouble; he would therefore be removed from the Archepiscopal palace. The farther away he was the better it would be for the island. He should be detained at a place where he could not get in touch with his "henchmen."

Makarios had an "ear" in Governor Harding's palace, and he realized he had to make a move before the British could act. He decided to fly to Athens. With that plan in mind he showed up at the Nicosia airport on March 5, 1956, and headed straight for the Athens plane that was ready to take off. Before he could reach the plane he was accosted by British secret service men. He was to emplane but not in the craft bound for Athens. He took the plane for Mombasa, in Kenya.

The *Times* of London summed up the official British opinion: "The Archbishop was so deeply committed to cooperation with the terrorists that he could not or would not condemn violence. His silence positively condoned it."

Known as the "Thunderer," this respected organ of Great Britain did thunder: "Makarios is a double talker."

Not all the respected press organs of British public opinion agreed with the Thunderer. Another highly respected British publication, the *Economist,* commented: "Experience shows that the deportation of recalcitrant nationalist leaders creates more trouble than it settles."

THE ECHO OF THE THUNDER

How were the Greeks of Cyprus to react to the official kidnaping act? The mysterious and elusive Grivas now spoke from his concealment: "The deportation reveals the desperate difficulties of Governor Harding."

And who was to carry on the affairs of the Church during the absence of the Archbishop-Ethnarch? It was carried on by the Ethnarchy Council, which consisted of three bishops and the Abbot of Kykko. Under Grivas the fighting forces of EOKA stepped up their operations. There were more corpses in the narrow alleys of the towns and in the lanes of the rural areas. The dead bodies were mostly Greeks who had been killed by fellow Greeks, the outcome of a ghastly "dialogue" between the "loyalists," comparatively few in number, and the numerous revolutionaries. There were also the corpses of the guerrillas killed by the British security forces; the corpses of Greeks and Turks, felled in a violent communal warfare; the corpses of British service men; and those of accidental bystanders, not only men but also women who had done no more than go on their daily shopping tour. The island was engulfed by a reign of terror. Shady elements crawled out of their hiding places—as they do nearly always on such occasions—and the route of their march was marked by senseless slaughter.

The Ethnarchy Council made a solemn declaration: "There can be no negotiations until His Beatitude is back." The crude posters of the EOKA demanded: "Release Makarios." Thousands of miles away Makarios was closer to his people than if he had been in the palace of the Ethnarch in Nicosia. Far away, he was the best propaganda for EOKA and *enosis.*

Makarios had been on the isle of Mahé for three months when the Governor of Cyprus went to London for further discussions about the future of Cyprus. The chief of the British Imperial General Staff, Sir Gerald Templer, visited Ankara to ascertain the views of the Turks on this issue. The problem was now to find ways to protect the interests not only of Britain but also of Turkey. The British government decided to send Lord Radcliffe to Cyprus as a peacemaker. He was to make recommendations for a new liberal constitution for the island, including safeguards for the interests of all the communities. The Radcliffe Constitution was then presented to the exiled Archbishop by a British delegation. He rejected it.

Shortly afterward EOKA announced that to help achieve a settlement it had ordered the cessation of hostilities. The Governor replied that members of the EOKA might surrender with their arms within three weeks and decide whether to be evacuated to Greece or to remain in Cyprus. In the latter event they would be detained during the emergency but would not be tried for any terrorist offense unless the government had evidence that they had committed a particular act of violence. EOKA rejected this offer and violence was renewed. One of the victims was the United States vice-consul in Nicosia.

There was no longer any sense in keeping Makarios on the Seychelles. Even though absent for months, he had remained the symbol of *enosis;* any plans for the future would have to be submitted to him. It was on March 28, 1957, that the Archbishop and his fellow detainees were released. Thereafter, not much was heard about the three companions while the name of Makarios was heard over all the world.

The "vacation" of Makarios was to end. His neighbors in the little town of Victoria actually thought that he and his fellow

exiles were tourists. When the local people learned about his proposed departure they visited him to express their regret. It was a
pity, they said, that he was leaving them. Was he not happy on the
island? Would he return, to resume his vacation? Some of his visitors were pressing him for an answer: Was there a possibility for
him to come back? And he answered: "I don't consider it impossible."

THE RETURN OF THE NATIVE

The earliest boat for Mombasa left on April 16, 1957. The name
of the ship was *Olympic Thunder,* a tanker, and it belonged to
the fleet of Aristotle Socrates Onasis, the Greek shipping magnate.
Makarios was released from the Seychelles with a reservation: He
was free, to be sure, but not free to return to Cyprus. He could go
anywhere else where he was admitted. He decided to go to Greece.

The Cyprus affair continued to be headline news, and
bloodshed on the island was resumed. Now the prime minister of
England, Harold Macmillan, took matters in hand, and he evolved
a new formula. A Tripartite Condominium was to be set up on
the island. Cypriots could opt for any one of three citizenships:
British, Turkish, or Greek. There were to be two legislative assemblies on Cyprus: Greek and Turkish. This was to be a temporary arrangement to last for seven years. After the expiration of
that period, consideration was to be given to a permanent plan.

Archbishop Makarios was now in Athens and his opinion
was sought on the plan. His answer was concise: "It is the old imperialist game—divide and rule."

For two years Archbishop Makarios continued to be the
"itinerant salesman" of the right of self-determination for Cyprus.
He attended the General Assembly of the United Nations where
the Cyprus question was discussed again. By that time, the British
had realized that the Cypriot majority was not willing to lay down
its arms. The pressure of the Western alliance on Britain, Turkey,
and Greece continued to ease the fratricidal animosity of these
three members.

The solution of the Cypriot problem did not come from
the United Nations, as the Archbishop expected. It came from
within NATO, and the peacemaker was a Belgian statesman of world
renown, Secretary-General of the North Atlantic Treaty Organization Paul Henri Spaak. He faced a seemingly hopeless situation

which had defied the ingenuity of other first-class diplomats. The
Greeks of Cyprus wanted union with Greece. The Turks of
Cyprus were violently opposed to it. The British wanted to retain
some rights on the island, an area of great strategic importance.
Could these contradictory interests be reconciled?

The man of iron, Sir John Harding, had failed to solve the
Cyprus enigma and had been replaced by a far more flexible
British civil servant, Sir Hugh Foot, an imaginative and liberal-
minded governor of the island. He was determined to help Spaak
in his work.

The negotiations were arduous and protracted. It was now
1959, four years after the outbreak of the fighting in Cyprus. The
representatives of the two Cypriot communities were absent from
these negotiations. Delegates of the British, Greek, and Turkish
governments were laboring far into the small hours under the
whip of the indefatigable Mr. Spaak.

THEN THE "MIRACLE"

Some of the most successful diplomatic parleys have taken place
in the serene atmosphere of Switzerland. This one did, in Zurich.
On February 11, 1959, the formula was completed which the
representatives of the two Cypriot communities were to sign. Some
observers called the agreement the "Miracle of Zurich." What did
the agreement contain? Before that, however, let us look at the
cost of the Cypriot affair.

Many human lives were destroyed and still more lives were
thwarted. The number of the killed was 506, and about 1,200
were wounded. The largest number of casualties was sustained by
Cypriot Greek civilians: 203. These were the people whom the
British called "loyalists" and whom the EOKA denounced as
"traitors." More than a hundred British servicemen were killed.
It would be difficult to assay the extent of the material damage
and the loss of revenue due to the chaotic conditions.

Now, at long last, peace was to return to the island. And
what were the terms of the agreement?

Cyprus was to become a republic and was not to join any
other country. Thus, *enosis*, union with Greece, was out. The
president was to be elected from the ethnic Greek community;
and the vice-president by the Turkish community. A 70:30 per
cent proportion of the Greek and Turkish communities was to be

represented in the House of Representatives. The Constitution, to be drawn up, provided that the Turkish minority—some 18 per cent of the population—was to receive 30 per cent of the civil service jobs, and 40 per cent of the places in the army and the police. The three signatory powers undertook to protect the island in the event of attack. Britain retained the bases of Akrotiri, Dhekelia—in the Larnaka area—and Episkopi.

The Constitution provided that both the president and the vice-president had the right of veto over legislation and certain ministerial acts. The government was to consist of seven members of the ethnic Greek majority and three members of the local Turkish community. Separate municipalities were to be set up for the Greeks and the Turks.

The spirit of the compromise was graphically expressed by the banner of the republic, two green olive branches on a gold map of the island on a white field.

The olive branch symbolized the reconciliation of the two communities and their establishment of the republic. Because the Turkish prime minister, Adnan Menderes, was lying in a London hospital, after an airplane accident, the final instrument of agreement was signed by Archbishop Makarios in London.

The diplomatic world heaved a deep sigh of relief and congratulations were in order all around. The comment of an English publication expressed the view of many observers: "The Cyprus problem defied all solutions. Now that it is solved it should become evident that there are no unsolvable problems."

The noted Turkish editor, A. E. Yalman, wrote in *Tou Vima,* an Athens daily: "Greece and Turkey have a common destiny. They are destined either to be good neighbors, close friends, and faithful allies, or to commit suicide."

Speaking for the Turkish community, Dr. Kutchuk expressed profound satisfaction with the instrument of agreement and foresaw fruitful cooperation between the two communities. Ethnarch Makarios expressed himself in an unctuous way: "It is the spirit in the hearts of man that counts." Prime Minister Macmillan spoke for the British government: "The claim of *enosis* has been abandoned—perhaps a big sacrifice; the claim of partition has been abandoned—and that is a big sacrifice. We have abandoned our sovereignty, except over the bases necessary for our military needs. . . . Therefore, if you call it sacrifice, it is sacrifice all around."

Archbishop Makarios flew back to Cyprus on March 1, 1959, after an absence of three years. To the ecstatic people who met him on the airfield there was the sign of charisma on his forehead. He was their idol. There were posters all over, hailing him and EOKA. But there were no posters hailing *enosis*.

BUILDING A NATION

As soon as the agreement was signed about Cyprus, the political agitation began. Who was to be the president of the country? Makarios, and he alone, was the national hero. But gratitude for services rendered is one thing, and election to the highest political office is another. The ethnic Greeks of the island demonstrated their attachment to tradition by forming a large number of political groups. They shaped up into the traditional right and left.

The rightists formed the "United Democratic Reform Front," *Enieon Dimokratikon Metopon Anagenniseos,* EDMA, which replaced EOKA; they supported Makarios. Other political factions supporting him were the Cyprus National Party, KEK; the Pan-agrarian Union of Cyprus, PEK; the Union of Orthodox Christian Youth, OKHEN.

The left-wing formed the "Reform Party of the Working People," *Anorthotikon Komma Ergazomenou Laou,* AKEL, which was the nucleus of the Union of Cyprus Farmers, EAK; the Youth Organization, AON; The Pan-Cyprian Peace Committee, PEE; and the Pan-Cyprian Organization of Democratic Women, PODY. AKEL was the successor of the Communist party, and it formed the Cypress Democratic Union for election purposes. It nominated John Clerides as its candidate. The polling took place on December 13, 1959, and Archbishop Makarios was elected. He received the votes mainly of the countryside, while his opponent was successful in the larger towns. The result was 144,501 for the Archbishop, and 71,753 for Clerides.

The policies of the President-Archbishop-Ethnarch of Cyprus were "middle-of-the-road." In foreign affairs he made an earnest attempt to keep Cyprus free of political alignment, describing his country's role as that of a "bridge of understanding" between Europe, Asia, and Africa. Repeatedly he called attention to the special role of the newly independent countries. Speaking to the General Assembly of the United Nations on May 7, 1962, he made his point forcefully: "Unfettered by the complications of power they [the newly independent countries] can with great objectivity examine the moral issues that lie at the root of international problems. Unencumbered by national policies and deep-rooted notions of a past era, they can perhaps more easily gear their policies to new concepts and wider dedications and thus more readily meet the needs of these atomic times."

Moral power as an instrument of diplomacy has been a keynote of many statements of the President-Archbishop, as, for instance, at the conference of the heads of state of non-aligned countries in September 1961.

"My country is small in size and population," he said on that occasion. "It is the smallest country participating in this conference. But this has not been a reason for overlooking it. Because this conference is not being convened for the purpose of approaching world problems in terms of material force, but in order to bring a moral power in the service of peace and the progress of mankind; and moral power does not depend on size or numbers."

And then again, in the same address: "Above all, good will is imperative. Distrust must be removed. It is beyond any doubt that disarmament and international confidence are closely linked."

Then the challenge: "Indeed humanity now as never before is faced with a great dilemma from which there can be no retreat and no escape. The means of total destruction now placed in the hands of man are as deadly as they are global. Humanity will have to abolish war or perish."

Still another keynote voiced in a television interview for an American station. "Each individual country is in duty bound to see itself in a world context. What sense would it make if that one nation were to survive while all the rest of our globe were to go under? Temporary 'victory' would be followed by the most gruesome end. Individuals live in society or else they perish. What is true of them is also true of the nations. They, too, have to live in society, and interdependence is inevitable. If one country suffers, the others suffer, too."

In the same interview: "We are Western oriented. Our traditions are rooted in the West. Also, we are aligned with certain principles. But we are non-aligned in diplomacy."

And what about the *ultima ratio* of independence, the "better life," higher living standards? The British had a ten-year development plan, 1946–55, for an electricity grid, improved highways and communication facilities, better drinking water in the villages, improved health facilities, and a malaria eradication campaign. The total amount to be spent on the plan was £6 million, but little was accomplished, for the program did not attack problems resulting from land overfragmentation, nor did it attempt to alter the direction of investment from housing and transport machinery into agriculture and mining. It did not encourage search for mineral resources. A badly needed deep-water port was not built.

During the 1950's a large share of investment went into luxury housing in the main towns, primarily for upper-income Cypriots and foreigners, and little was spent for building or improving rural homes. Subsequently, the government started financing municipal slum clearance and rehousing projects in Limassol and Famagusta.

"The shortage of water is our biggest problem," President Makarios said in an interview. "We are drawing up a program to build water-dams. We are satisfied with the progress we have been making with our Five-Year Plan."

The Cypriot Five-Year Plan was designed to run from 1962 to 1966, and it received an appropriation of £60 million. The largest amount was appropriated to the building of ports: £11 million. Ten million pounds each were appropriated for water-dams and electrification; five million for roads; six million for water exploration; three million for tourism.

President Makarios welcomed technical assistance from the United States, the United Nations, and other countries. American technical experts were at work to help raise the low standards of production of food grains and meat. The Stanford Research Institute was enlisted to aid in the training of Cypriots in diverse fields of economic development. A UN technological assistance team was invited to take charge of a hydrological survey.

The island has unexploited potentialities for tourism. In certain seasons of the year a tourist can ski in the morning and bathe in the afternoon in the Mediterranean. Nothing much had been done by the British administration to help tourists to enjoy the exotic beauty of the "country of Aphrodite."

During the three-year period up to 1960 living standards had declined. After independence the country started to make some progress. Trade was expanding, money that had fled Cyprus was being repatriated, emigration was dropping, foreign aid was increasing, and tourism was on the rise. But it takes time to find water, and even more time to build dams. The greatest increase in national income was expected from industrialization. Cyprus had a large number of small industries, but the far more profitable large plants required capital and technical competence which was difficult to accumulate on short notice. Still, the prospects were promising. And then the thunderbolt struck.

A NEW CIVIL STRIFE

It happened on December 21, 1963. A Greek Cypriot policeman stopped a Turkish Cypriot in a Nicosia street. Quickly a crowd gathered. There were varying accounts of what had happened, but someone started shooting and two Turkish Cypriots lay dead. Before long, open warfare between the Turks and the Greeks spread over the island.

"The Archbishop," wrote the correspondent of the New York *Times*, "trembled at the sight of the jet fighters swooping menacingly over Nicosia." Dr. Fazil Kutchuk, the vice-president and head of the Turkish community, sat behind sandbags in his official residence with mortar shells bursting outside and bullets flying from two sides.

Trouble broke out in other parts of the island, too, as, for instance, at Dizdarkoy, a village ten miles from Nicosia, on the road to Limassol in the south; in Omorphita, the northern suburb, where fires had been set; at Trakhonas, a suburb west of Omorphita, where the Turkish Cypriots had taken thirteen Greek Cypriots as hostages; and especially in such outlying areas as Xeros and Lefka, in the northwest.

Greek Cypriots reported the appearance of Turkish warships off the coast of the island. The Cyprus government appealed to the Security Council of the United Nations because of alleged Turkish military movements. Both communities of the island had representation at the world body. The official representative was an ethnic Greek, Zenon G. Rossides. The ethnic Turks had their own delegate, Adnan Kural.

President Makarios said that he would seek the abrogation of the Zurich and London treaties because the system they had set up did not work. He was particularly critical of the treaty provisions that gave the Turkish minority the veto power over the legislative and executive actions of the government. He said that the régime set up by the agreements under which the main towns were under dual administration—ethnic Greek and Turkish—was completely unrealistic. Finally, he maintained that positions in the government services, the army, the police, and the gendarmerie should be distributed in proportion to the population figures. When the trouble started, the Turkish contingents of the army and the police took up positions against the Greek contingents. According to the agreements, the Turks had a 40 per cent representation on these forces—more than twice their numerical strength in the total population. Under the treaty system the ethnic Turks were greatly overrepresented.

Most of the able-bodied men of Cyprus were bearing arms either on the open battlefield, at roadblocks, on terrorist raids, or standing guard over their families and homes. Archbishop Makarios now appealed to his former adversaries, the British, to give a helping hand. And British forces came. One of their first tasks was to set up a cordon right across the center of Nicosia, separating the Turks, living mainly in the northern portions, from the Greeks in the south.

And now feverish diplomatic activity on all fronts began. Foreign Minister Spyros Kyprianou, of Cyprus, called for an end of treaty links with Greece and Turkey and the establishment of a government by the island's Greek Cypriot majority to preserve peace. "Under the present circumstances," he said, "the treaty links must be confined only to Britain."

Vice-President Kutchuk of Cyprus, a Turk, declared that separating the two hostile communities was the only way to "save humanity and the world from continuous trouble." He demanded the partition of the island between the Greeks and Turks.

The Greek government said that, as a signatory to the Zurich and London agreements, it had no objection to their abrogation "in principle." But Greece did not want to clash with Turkey over it.

Turkey invited Turkish Cypriot leaders to consultations. One of them was Raouf Denktash, said to be the power behind the throne, and the other one was Osman Orek, an ethnic Turk in the Makarios government. They reported that Greek Cypriots were fortifying the northern part of the island to prevent a Turkish landing. Also they reported that Greek Cypriots were destroying Turkish title deeds to property on the island, which would reduce Turkish claims on the land if the island should be partitioned.

The United Nations was set to name a personal representative of U Thant, the secretary-general, to keep an eye on the island.

It was in the first days of January, 1964, that a cease-fire agreement was reached between the hostile parties through the intermediary of the British government. Britain had flown 2,500 soldiers into Cyprus since the fighting began. A conference on the Cyprus issue was set to begin on January 15 in London. The prime minister of the United Kingdom, Sir Alec Douglas-Hume, said that by intervening quickly in the Cyprus dispute Britain averted war between Greece and Turkey. Had England not acted with speed and decision the island of Cyprus "would have been rent from end to end with civil war." This, in turn, he said, "would inevitably have spread to fighting between the forces of Greece and Turkey."

President Makarios blamed the Turkish minority on the island and the Ankara government for these troubles. In an interview he said:

"What worries me is the Turkish minority following the instructions of Ankara. The Turkish government says that the Constitution must not be changed. And this in spite of the fact that it has been demonstrated over and over again that some of its provisions are unworkable. At the time I signed the agreements we wanted to end the emergency by all means. Also, it was impossible to foresee that the Turkish minority was bent on sabotaging the orderly conduct of the governmental business. I have direct evidence of the interference of the authorities of Turkey.

"Early in 1963 I had a meeting with the representatives of the ethnic Turkish minority of the island. They seem to have realized that it was impossible to have two different sets of administrations—Greek and Turkish—within the same municipalities. They were agreeable to the setting up of unified municipalities under certain conditions. We, on the other hand, agreed that a certain percentage of the funds in the municipal budgets may be spent by the Turkish members of the councils. These stipulations were accepted all around. Within twenty-four hours they informed me that they changed their minds and they insisted again on the separate municipalities. In our opinion, they consulted Ankara and were told to stand pat."

Why did the Turkish government take such a die-hard stand? According to Makarios, it was beset by domestic difficulties and needed therefore a chance to assume a heroic posture. Cyprus presented such a chance. Its unbending policy on the Cyprus issue was calculated to disarm the opposition, which accused Ankara of being ineffective in its domestic and foreign policies.

"Yet, our suggestion of setting up a workable system and cooperating with each other closely would be of benefit to all of us. There are many ethnic Turks on the island—especially in the villages—who had enough of turmoil. They would like to live in peace, and to live with the ethnic Greeks in amity."

The lull was deceptive, and violence erupted again. The Turks barricaded themselves in self-contained enclaves, seeking to secure protected access to the northern coast and, possibly, to Turkish ships—which they were expecting everyday. The Greeks set about destroying the communication lines of the Turkish Cypriots, attacking the strongholds of the neighbors and foes.

The United Nations considered the Cypriot problem of sufficient importance to hold emergency sessions. In the spring of 1964 the world organization dispatched an armed force mission to the island to keep peace between the Greeks and Turks of the island. Again the chancelleries of many powers were "seized" with the Cypriot problem. The situation was no more hopeful now than it had before the Zurich agreement. President Makarios announced the termination of the Cyprus Treaty of Alliance which bound Greece, Turkey, and Cyprus together for their common defense. It provided for a 950-man Greek contingent and a 650-man Turkish contingent on the island. Speaking for Turkey, Prime Minister Ismet Inönü rejected the Makarios move.

The United States was deeply interested in the recurrence of the communal strife and mobilized its diplomatic forces. Also it alerted other members of the North Atlantic Treaty of Alliance, of which both Turkey and Greece were members. President Lyndon B. Johnson asked the chairman of the Foreign Relations Committee of the Senate, J. W. Fulbright, to deliver messages both to the Turkish and the Greek governments, advising moderation, and recommending positive steps to restore peace.

The Soviet Union entered the fray, too. Speaking through the official Tass news agency, it charged that the Cyprus turmoil was caused by outside forces bent on imposing a new foreign "colonial yoke" on the island. Said the Chairman of the Council of Ministers of the Soviet Union, Nikita Sergeyevich Khrushchev:

"The North Atlantic Treaty Powers are seeking to convert Cyprus into an unsinkable aircraft carrier."

THE POLITICIAN AND THE PRIEST

Archbishop Makarios is the most difficult to evaluate of the biographies in this book. This is due not so much to the ambiguity of his personal traits, as to the dichotomy of his callings. He is a prince of the Church and the president of a republic. In the context of Cypriot traditions, he became the head of the state because he was the head of the clergy. People assume that a "man of God" is a godly man. They also assume that a man in politics is a politician, in the American—and therefore derogatory—sense of the word. One refrains from being too critical of men of the cloth while one is almost in duty bound to be critical of politicians—in democracies, at least. It was because of the historic traditions of his island republic that the Archbishop became the chief executive of his country—a heritage rooted in the Turkish system of fusing the temporal with the religious power, as was the case with the Ottoman heads of state, both sultans and Caliphs.

The work of Makarios was predominantly political, and he could not possibly devote much time to his priestly duties. His priestly calling, in fact, served the purposes of the ethnarchy, the secular leadership of the Greek Orthodox majority of Cyprus. It was as a politician that the world came to know him, first as the "traveling salesman" of *enosis,* and later as the chief executive of the republic. It is a matter of record today that he was the *spiritus rector* of the Greek Cypriots' uprising, a role which was not conceded at the time. At first that struggle was directed against the British. Then it degenerated into a civil war with the local Turks. And all the world knows by now that nothing can be more bitter than a civil war. And it was a very bloody war.

Archbishop Makarios did not condemn the shedding of blood. How could he do it, since he was the *spiritus rector?* He acted according to the desires of his constituents, the Greek majority of the island. He would have been denied as the religious head of the Greek-speaking islanders had he acted in the spirit of the Prince of Peace. He was caught up in the ideology of the day, which commanded him to subordinate his priestly calling to the requirements of the nationalistic nostalgia of his flock. In the inner struggle between nationalism and religion the former had to win the day.

As Prince of the Church, Makarios was accountable only to God, prompting him through his conscience. But the god of today is a nationalist, blessing the flags of the contestants and handing out laurels to the victors. In His eyes, might is not only equated with right but is also its corollary and its reward. The political work of Makarios was also sanctified by the approbation of his people, whose welfare—as they saw it—was entrusted to him by Divine Providence.

The supremacy of politics in the career of Makarios was demonstrated over and over again. Let us take a couple of illustrations. He signed the documents that freed Cyprus from British rule and accorded a disproportionately large role to the island's Turkish group. Subsequently, he claimed that these agreements were not merely iniquitous but also absurd. They were iniquitous because they failed to invest the local Greeks with the prerogatives to which they were entitled on account of their numerical superiority. The balance of power between the two ethnic groups was completely awry.

The agreements were absurd, too, as the Archbishop-President saw it, because they set up a governmental machinery that could not work. How were two ethnic municipal governments to operate within the confines of a small town in which the two populations did not occupy ethnically homogeneous territories? Makarios declared his intention to abrogate the treaties. He justified his proposed action on the ground that he had not been consulted at the time the agreements were prepared.

That was true, of course. No less true was the fact that he accepted the accomplished fact and signed the documents. He could have refused to sign them on the ground that they were both iniquitous and absurd. He did not do so. He signed them, possibly, because he realized that no better arrangement could be achieved. Or because he was aware of the fact that the population of the island was weary of the civil war. Or, perhaps, because of strong diplomatic pressures. Or a combination of all of these factors. Or he realized that if he did not sign the agreements another representative man of the Greek community would, and Makarios would remain an archbishop and not become president of the new country.

Let us further assume that he could not foresee the iniquitous and absurd nature of the agreements. He became convinced that the country could not operate on such a basis. In that case two ways would have been open to him. He could have set the diplomatic machinery into motion, and have another "Zurich Conference" called, at which he would have presented his arguments to the delegates. Or he could have made the ultimate decision and resigned from his exalted post. He did not take either of these two courses. He acted as a politician motivated by purely political considerations: determined to weather the storm he had created, he retained his post at the helm.

In his position as the head of state, Makarios was motivated by political considerations in another respect, too. Being a man of the cloth he might have taken a stronger stand against the Communists at home and abroad. He did not do that, although he was opposed to the cause of the Communists. But they were a factor on the island, and the Soviet Union was a tremendous factor in international relations. The Communists might become an even more frightening factor in the course of time, for the Kremlin was operating very skillfully in international relations, especially in the adjacent Middle East.

In one respect only did Makarios appear as a prince of the Church—in his emphasis on the predominance of moral forces in the relations among nations. But how far could one go in the practice of Christian virtues? It is a Christian precept to turn the other cheek if one is struck. As a churchman Makarios should have done that. Had he done it he would have been overwhelmed by the reproaches of his own constituents, some of them as good Christians as himself. By turning the other cheek he may have earned the praise of God. But God has no voting rights at the Cyprus elections, and that was the consideration that determined the actions of Archbishop-President Makarios.

BEFORE AND AFTER

What was the effect of thirteen months of isolation on Archbishop Makarios? Did the tropical sun weaken his ardor, or did he overcome its influence, making the best of his enforced leisure to keep himself in trim? Was he preparing himself for what he hoped might be his destiny?

Compared with the other political prisoners we have encountered, Makarios found himself in a unique position. On his island he was completely quarantined, with extremely limited resources to attend to the usual self-assigned homework. Social contacts were kept at a minimum: Makarios never mastered the curious local patois of the Seychelles, and besides, what could one discuss with people who lived in complete isolation from the events of the world?

We have seen repeatedly that it is the excessive dynamism of the freedom fighters that causes their detention. Were they people of common clay they would sink into apathy in exile and the jail. In that case their captors would have achieved their aim. But the prisoners we have observed did not fall into apathy. Nor did Makarios—and this in spite of the fact that the temptation for him was the greatest. He was detained in the land of the lotus-eaters in a dwelling place the very name of which seemed to reveal his captors' aim—Sans Souci. In spite of that, too, the Archbishop-Ethnarch employed his free time to best advantage—pursuing his post-graduate studies, meditating, drawing up plans for the post-liberation future, discarding them and drawing up new ones, and polishing up his techniques. He also had the leisure to study the weaknesses and the strengths of his opponents.

Makarios is not an intellectual, we have seen. His readings on the island of Mahé related to his practical work, mainly political, and only partly ecclesiastical. Because of the location of the Seychelles and the unusual impediments, the books he could obtain were greatly limited in number. He did read political books which he believed might be of practical use to him in his campaign for Cypriot self-determination. Books about Britain and about America. Books on how the British wrested their freedom from the hands of reluctant masters and how the Americans wrenched their freedom from the British. But detention in the Seychelles presented him with an even more important opportunity.

The British—and this, too, we have seen—exiled him to the islands so as to give his presumably more moderate opponents at home a chance to strengthen themselves at his expense. London was hoping to be able to strike a better bargain with those Cypriots. But the Archbishop's political opponents took no advantage of his absence. Public opinion on the island continued to place its trust in him.

Also the British hoped that the ardor of Makarios would

cool under the influence of Sans Souci—the carefree Seychelles life—and that he would return home a more subdued and "wiser" man. Because of the isolation of his place of exile he might even lose his close contact with his native land. British hopes were dashed in this respect, too, as Seychelles provided the Archbishop with telling arguments for an even more dynamic policy.

He had been exiled from one British colony, in the fulcrum of the world, to another one, on the peripheries of the earth. The civilization of Cyprus was as old as the history of Western man, while that of Seychelles was as primitive as that of man before the discovery of print. The British treated the two colonies with the same even-handed injustice, in spite of the enormous difference between the cultures of the two. The heirs of the mother of Western civilization, Greece, were accorded the same humiliating treatment as the lotus-eating primitives at the very end of the world.

This injustice, in turn, called attention to a related anomaly. The British acted as the master race, a superior breed, which ruled over an inferior strain, the Greeks. And from whom had the English learned their own political ways at home? What was the origin of the word "democracy," that system which the British claimed to practice? Was it not a Greek word and was the institution itself not practiced by the Greeks? The Archbishop's people were already at the pinnacle of Western culture when the British were still wearing animal skins.

The Archbishop compared the cultural level of the Greeks and that of the natives of the Seychelles. What a tremendous span. Then he compared the treatment the British accorded to Cyprus to that accorded to the Seychelles. Both of them were wards of the British—colonies.

He made good use of this comparison in the diplomatic dialogue he carried on after his liberation. The Archbishop-Ethnarch learned a useful lesson in his exile, a lesson he transmitted to his people. And his people felt strengthened by that lesson.

They were strengthened also in their conviction that their miniature world, Cyprus, was a world without end because it shared the paternity of civilization. Withal it was a world of countless problems because of the inveterate habit of people to turn an earthly Paradiso into an Inferno.

7

Janos Kadar: Prisoner on the Danube

Andrássy Ut, the Champs-Elysées of Budapest, extends from the center of the Hungarian capital to the outskirts of City Park. Cutting across the busiest quarters of the city, it is a stately avenue, flanked by the massive homes of the patricians of another age. No. 60 is near Körút, the point where Andrássy Ut and Ring Avenue intersect.

On an April day in 1951 a police wagon arrived in the courtyard of No. 60 Andrássy Ut. The arrival of police wagons here was not an uncommon sight, for here was the headquarters of AVO, State Security Department, the political police. Unusual was, however, the passenger in this particular car.

Andrássy Ut is attractive and quite long, a "Hungarian rhapsody," this beautiful avenue in an enchanting capital. The avenue is to the left of the Danube River, in the section known as Pest. Buda is on the other bank, fading into the distance in a ripple of hills. The affluence of the past of the capital is attested to by the substantial edifices.

Budapest was at its best on this April day. The fragrance of the lilacs that abound on the precipitous hills on the Buda side of the Danube drifted into the heart of the city on the western breezes, blending with the scent of the acacias, "Hungarian trees," that blossomed in City Park. The April day seemed to be particularly radiant. Even people bent on their daily tasks inhaled deeply of the exhilarating air. On the avenues the young women of Budapest also appeared to be in full bloom, as if they were responding to the loveliness of the day. All seemed to be glad to be alive. Yes, life was good, even in this age of terror in the beautiful Danubian city. Yet, when they caught a quick glimpse of the funereal police-wagon turning into the courtyard of 60 Andrássy Ut, it was not about life that they reflected but about death. For this structure in the heart of the great city was, indeed, a house of pain and torture, a house of death.

Up on Rose Hill, on the right bank of the Danube, from the slopes where the lilacs grew, were a number of the top government people. The Old World mansions on this hill were occupied by Hungary's Communist rulers. Most important of these men who followed the dictates of the Kremlin was Mátyás Rákosi, a pudgy little man who walked with a waddle—a gifted little man, too, who had started out in life with a firm determination to help people make a better life and had become the instrument of death. His word spelled damnation for the man who had just been driven into the courtyard of the secret police. The prisoner, János Kádár, was manacled. Not long before it had been he who had caused people to be fettered. Not long before, too, it had been he who, as minister of the interior in the Hungarian Communist government, had been the head of the political police.

"COMRADE HUNGARY"

Hungary was then a Soviet satellite, as she is now, and Rákosi was the mouthpiece of Moscow. In the Kremlin sat "Comrade Soviet Union," Joseph Stalin, the fountainhead of all authority in the Bolshevik world, "Comrade Communism." It was as Stalin's henchman that Rákosi had Kádár delivered to the house of death.

There had been a time when Rákosi himself had been in the house of death. That had been long ago in the interwar period when Hungary had been under an autocratic regime headed by Regent Governor Nicholas Horthy, an admiral who presided over the fate of a kingdom, although Hungary had neither a king nor access to the sea, truly an Alice in Wonderland situation. In that "wonderland" of Horthy the Communists got short shrift. Rákosi had been apprehended while carrying on Communist propaganda, an act for which the punishment was death. He was given a trial— a superfluous performance, for all the world knew that he was destined to swing by the neck.

Solemnly, the judges pronounced their sentence—death on the gallows. Over this sentence there was much uproar throughout the world, so much that Horthy commuted it to imprisonment for life, and Rákosi had remained a prisoner until the outbreak of World War II. Now this victim of one death sentence was to pronounce a death sentence not over a Horthy but over a fellow Communist, János Kádár.

AT AVO HEADQUARTERS

János Kádár was only thirty-nine. He had a pleasant face, with a dimple; it almost was a handsome face. His skin had a coarse texture, for it was a skin that had been exposed to sun and rain. János Kádár had a habit of keeping one of his eyelids half-shut, as if he were about to drop off to sleep. He never looked his interlocutor in the eye, as if he were afraid of him, or perhaps, of himself. Once his eye was caught, however, one could see that it had the blueness of steel. His voice was throaty, "rusty" people used to say, the voice of a man who raised it often, a platform voice.

Although he may have looked drowsy, Kádár, on the contrary, was an alert man. As minister of the interior, he had occupied a key post in the Communist regime. To him any deviation from the party dogma was anathema. He believed in the universal Communist "Church" and believed, too, that heresy must be punished. The only truth for him was the Communist dogma, and the only future the victory of the Communist ideal. It was the radiant image of the classless New Jerusalem that beckoned to him in the distance. The road to it dipped down into dark valleys and then climbed up steep slopes. He had no doubt that, in the end, the City of Communism would be reached.

That being his faith and his dream, why was János Kádár in the house of death on this April day? Because his crime was unspeakable—heresy. He had dared to entertain thoughts that differed from those promulgated by the head of the Universal Communist Church in the Moscow Kremlin, the Supreme Pontiff of the only true faith, Joseph Stalin.

The loadstar that Stalin followed was simply this: there was only one land of the true believers, the Soviet Union, the Promised Land. Its crusading Communists had passed through the hellfires of purification, moving onward and upward. At the beginning they had not been sure that they would ever reach their elusive goal. In the end, the meandering road across the Chasms of Uncertainty led into the wide Valley of Hope.

The Soviets had extended their sway over a broad belt of nations contiguous to their borders—the satellite countries. Some of them were on a higher cultural level than the Soviet people. Taken together, they formed the glacis the Soviets needed for their operations, political if they had their way, and military if their adversaries should have theirs. The ways of life of the satellites had to be meshed and coordinated into those of the Soviets. Culturally, these nations may have occupied the heights, but, in the Kremlin's view, they were wandering in the darkness, unaware of the light which the Soviets had perceived. They were to see it if they followed the Soviets.

Then the thunderbolt. It struck in the Balkans, in the land of the South Slavs, Yugoslavia. The man who hurled the bolt had been one of the most faithful of the faithful, the stout-hearted man who had wrested his country from the grasp of Fascist gangs, none other than Josip Brozovich, alias Josip Broz, alias Marshal Tito. He was the Prometheus who had usurped the prerogatives of Zeus in the Kremlin. Therefore he was to be punished by being abandoned and exposed to cosmic retribution.

To be punished also were the potential Titos whose secret thoughts, ferreted out by heaven knows what methods, revealed even the slightest trace of Titoist heresy.

That heresy was the belief that Communism did not have to be of the Russian variety; that it could be adjusted to the national ways of each individual country, and that, indeed, it must be so adjusted. Predicating this belief was the assumption that the internationalism of the Kremlin was really no more than a Russian imperialism under which the little brethren were to follow Big Brother, asking no questions, firm in their conviction that He must know what was good for all of them. Implicit in this heresy was also the conviction that the *Zeitgeist* of this age called for a national framework and not a supranational ideal that may have looked good on paper but which could not stand up to the pressures inherent in nationalism. The elemental force of nationalism could be blended with communism, in these heretics' view, but not with a "communism" that was a disguise for a great power's imperialism.

This "nationalistic deviation" was the heinous sin which Rákosi, first secretary of the Communist party and deputy prime minister of Hungary, suspected in Kádár. The more the Soviets under Stalin became aggressively imperialist, the more Kádár's nationalist bias became evident to the Muscovites.. He remained a Hungarian peasant. Kádár had never been trained in the Soviet

Union, as were most other top Communists, nor did he speak Russian, as others did.

On the surface he had to remain a faithful follower of the Moscow line. Yet, the "Muscovites" of Hungary knew that Kádár, a product of the Hungarian soil, was different from themselves, and they felt uneasy about him. And when Rákosi began to fret about a co-worker, he could be counted upon to act.

Rákosi was the real head of the Hungarian satrapy; his prime ministers were no more than figureheads. He himself remained at his post at the pleasure of the Zeus of the Communist Olympus, i.e. Stalin in his Kremlin. This was the Soviet Zeus whose brains had been addled, probably by age, but certainly by his stunning victory in the world war. Stalin expressed simple lines of thought, one of which was that Russia must lead the fraternal countries. Should any of them falter or drop away it was bound to defect to the camp of the Western "imperialists" and, once there, to become a mortal danger to the Soviets and their satellites as well. Tito had placed himself beyond Communist dogma. He therefore had to be destroyed. Crushed also must be any and every attempt to follow his example. The weeding out process was to be thorough and merciless. Severe punishment would be meted out for any lack of zeal in following the Kremlin line, and suspicion of a sin was equated with guilt of the crime. The satellite countries must see that Titoism was the most heinous of all sins. And for such reasons Rákosi sent Kádár to Andrássy Ut.

There János Kádár was not at all the Grand Inquisitor he had been before. Now he was caught in the toils of the system he himself had devised. He was to face his accusers—and he knew what to expect from them. Before that, however, in the dark basement of the Andrássy Ut stately mansion, he was to be made pliant.

Kádár was taken into a subterranean cell. From the outside few passersby could guess what a cubicle in the basement of that impressive building could be like. The subsoil in the Hungarian capital is honeycombed with gushing springs, and the floor of the basement was covered with slime. No attempt was made to clean it; that was part of the jailer's design. Kádár was left to languish in the watery cell. Later, he was taken to the office of one of his former subordinates, the chief of the secret police, "General" Gábor Péter.

When Kádár had been the minister of interior the "General" had addressed him in his most mellifluous tone, standing at attention. Péter was a character out of that Dostoevski novel, *The House of Death,* in which is described the author's own experiences in Siberia as a political prisoner. Péter had begun his career as a sleuth, way down the social ladder. When he had been a tailor's apprentice it had been his custom to stand at attention. Now it was he who made his former boss, Kádár, stand motionless in his presence.

Kádár was to be made to "confess" that he was in the service of "imperialist" powers, and whatever the real facts, such a confession was to be extorted. So he was led into the presence of his ex-subordinate, who now played not only a different role but behaved like a different man. His voice, which used to be mellifluous, now had a cutting edge. He did not utter his words but spat them out. Not only did he fail to recognize his former boss, but he treated him as if he had learned his name only a while ago from the prisoner's dossier. Péter ordered Kádár to turn around and face the wall. So the interrogation began, the classical approach: incriminating questions, each of which contained a modicum of truth that prejudiced the answer, searing repetitions with their hypnotizing insistence on guilt, guilt, guilt.

Then came the nocturnal interrogations, again in the classical approach, undertaken night after night, with the light shining into the eyes of the accused, compelling him to blurt out feverish answers. Hours and hours of this and nothing would matter, only the craving to get out of this hell, to slump down on the cot in the watery cell, and perhaps sleep out of fatigue. A miracle might happen and he would never awaken again. There was only one flaw to this dream. What a pity that he could not relish his own death!

Kádár stood his ground. What could happen to him? The torturers did not know enough psychology about his kind of people. They overreached themselves and helped to benumb his senses.

They had other means, too, of extorting confessions: physical torture. The torturer arrived with his kit of tools—the pliers, squeezers, hammers—and for the maximum effect, laid them out carefully before the prisoner. The nails first, then the fingers to be crushed. The male organ next? Did they actually injure the prisoner that cruelly? The fingers were "treated." There were rumors about the male organ, too, but that was one of the subjects about which the surviving victim did not speak. But the tools were used, one after another, in the stately mansion, in the most beautiful city, in one of the most enchanting capitals of the world. It was in the beautiful month of April when the lilacs and the acacias were in bloom. Kádár did not confess.

IN MARKO UTCA AND OTHER JAILS

In those days it was not known but now it is: Stalin was no longer in possession of all his senses. His mind was filled with thoughts of murder. There is a gruesome anecdote about his state of mind.

He was addressing a group one day, this man of iron, this Stalin. People were expected to listen to him with rapt attention; they did, to save their lives. Then the deadly silence was rent. Someone had sneezed. The audience was gripped by fear as Stalin broke off his speech.

"Who sneezed?" He asked in his flat voice. Nobody dared to reply.

The master of the Kremlin gave a signal. A platoon of soldiers marched into the hall. Another signal, and the platoon formed a single line, machine guns at the ready. The third signal, and the guns spat death into the first line of the audience.

As the soldiers marched out, Stalin repeated his question: "Who sneezed?" Still gripped by fear, no one dared to speak. Again the soldiers marched in, and now they mowed down the second line.

At that point the squeaky voice of an old muzhik was heard:

"Comrade Stalin, it was me."

The strong man's face lit up with a benign smile:

"God bless you, Ivan Ivanovich!" he said warmly and continued with his speech.

Such was the climate of terror in those days. One never knew when or how or upon whom the tyrant's wrath would fall. Rákosi, eager to show his loyalty, had to produce a Titoist to prove that in Hungary, too, heresy was being rooted out, and Kádár was the man.

The methods of the torture chamber had failed to produce results, and so the Hungarian Muscovites decided to try another tack. Kádár was transferred to a common jail in Markó Utca, on another attractive mid-town avenue. That was not a place of horror. There was no slime, and Kádár's cell was clean. It was not in the basement but on one of the upper floors. There he could inhale the fragrance of the acacias and the lilacs. He got plenty of food and of good quality. His health was to be restored so that there would be no outward evidence of the tortures he had suffered. He was to be given a very good suit and then prepared for exhibition—at a public trial. He may have been told that the trial was to be a spectacle and that even if he were convicted his life would be spared. Later, unbeknown to the world, he would be freed. All he need do was confess publicly that he had been engaged in a plot with the Western imperialists and with Tito of Yugoslavia. But Kádár was softened not even by the humane treatment in Markó Utca, and he would not sign a confession. What could one do with a man like that?

A show trial was needed to incriminate Tito and to prove that Hungary had got rid of nationalist heresy. Kádár would not cooperate; his stubbornness may have saved his life. Another Communist who could be accused of heresy had to be found. Another was found, and was coerced into a confession. It has been said that the same Kádár who stood his ground in the face of all the tortures incriminated the other scapegoat, László Rajk. Whether that is true is not known, but it was Rajk whom the Communist judges sentenced to be hanged.

Now Kádár was transferred to the Central Prison of Budapest, a massive stone structure, its cell-flanked corridors fanning out from a central dome like the pattern of a star. The common criminals were held in one of the wings to the right, the politicals in the left. Life for Kádár was no longer an endless nightmare, and he was not treated badly.

Then, in March, 1953, a milestone in Soviet and satellite history, Stalin died. It took some time before the consequences of this traumatic event were felt. The death of the Great One turned out to be a blessed event in Soviet and satellite history.

One of the minor results was the transfer of Kádár to the "Little Hotel," the "maximum comfort" section of the Central Prison. The Ice Age in the Communist world seemed to be over, and then a "thaw" began—between individuals, between the government and the people, and also between the Kremlin and the outside world.

In Hungary the Stalinist Rákosi continued to maintain his position in the driver's seat. But he, too, changed his tone. No longer would show trials of Communist stalwarts shake the world behind the Iron Curtain. On the contrary, the tormentors of the "heretics" were now placed on trial, except for Rákosi himself. Kádár was released from jail in November, 1953.

He had been in prison for thirty-one months—really thirty-one years for a man of action. He had been incarcerated at Andrássy Ut for a couple of weeks, in the Markó Utca prison for a couple of months, and the rest of the time in the Central Prison. (These are assumptions because neither he nor any authority in Hungary ever uttered a word to confirm or deny any details.)

What about "General" Gábor Péter, his erstwhile tormentor? He became the sacrificial animal of Rákosi, who was seeking to denigrate the former Ecumenical Master of the Kremlin Universe, Stalin. Péter was placed on trial in the same year that Kádár was released. The trial was held in secret and the charges were never made public. Gábor Péter was sentenced to imprisonment for life. Subsequently, his term was reduced to eight years. He was released in February, 1959. Before becoming a police "General" he had been a tailor, and now, according to information that reached the outside world, he joined a tailors' collective.

Kádár now began the second and, withal, more important phase of his life. Before looking at it, let us cast a glance at his origins.

JANCSI, THE PROLI

The Iron Curtain covers not only the countries but also the private lives of the Communist leaders; Kádár, particularly, keeps mum about his background. "The Short Biography," preceding his selected speeches and articles, 1957–61, under the title of *Socialist Construction in Hungary,* an official publication, contains a single sentence about the first seventeen years of his life.

He was born in 1912, and apart from that nothing is quite sure about his birth. He was an illegitimate child, it seems, and his father, János Csermák, declined paternal responsibility for him. Kádár is his mother's name. He was born in County Somogy, near the river Drava, which was then deep in Hungary but since the end of World War I has formed the boundary with Yugoslavia.

It has been rumored abroad that Kádár is of German origin and speaks Hungarian with a German accent. That is not so. He is of Hungarian peasant stock. "Jancsi," diminutive for János, grew up as a farm *proli,* proletarian. At the time of his birth Hungary was a characteristically peasant country, and Kádár's roots reach down into the poor farmer's soil. János Kádár appears to have conceived an atavistic dislike of the country's traditional ruling system even while he still lived in his maternal home.

Few countries of Europe are as blessed with so much good soil as Hungary. Yet, most of the Hungarians were poor, many of them very, very poor: farm-working pariahs, knocked about by fate and by the landlords. There was nothing lower in the Hungarian universe than the agricultural working class, laboring *vakulástól vakulásig*—from dawn to dusk (literally, "from blindness to blindness"). An uncommonly large portion of the land belonged to the *ezer holdasok,* "thousand-acre landlords." Large estates were entailed to leading families and thus could not be alienated, and peasants could not under any circumstances acquire land from such estates. Most of the peasants owned no land or only tiny slices. Many of them eked out a beggarly life as peons. This semi-feudal spirit persisted into the current century. It was in this environment that Jancsi, the *proli,* grew up.

The peasants may have been a conservative lot, but not so much as to be completely paralyzed by the landholding system. Hundreds of thousands of them turned their backs on their native land and sought a better life in America. Others moved to "America in Hungary," the larger towns where industries offered higher rewards. The Kádárs belonged to this category.

Jancsi was only four when an era ended. After a reign of sixty-eight years, Emperor-King Franz Joseph I died. His Monarchy was at war, fighting the Great Struggle at Germany's side. Two more years passed, an age of agony. To the very end, the Central-European bloc, headed by Germany, appeared to be winning the war, and then, its weaknesses revealed, it collapsed. Most of the people of the Austro-Hungarian Monarchy belonged to various national minorities, an exceptionally large number being Slavs. The war over, they bolted out of the Habsburg realm, joining their own kith and kin. Thus it was that "millennial" Hungary became a rump, a shadow of her former self.

It was just then that Jancsi came of school-going age. His native village, near the river Drava, became a border town. Jancsi chanted the Hungarian creed: *Nem, nem, soha,* "No, No, Never" —never will Hungarians resign themselves to their loss. Jancsi must have joined other children in the defiant patriotic song: *Ha a föld Isten kalapja,* . . . "If the earth is God's hat, then Hungary is a bouquet of flowers on it."

How many years of education Jancsi got cannot be ascertained—that Iron Curtain again. Probably it was not more than the compulsory six years, including evening vocational-school attendance. He was still a very young boy when Hungary went Communist for a few months in 1919. It was an amateurish and grotesque affair. The regime was headed by ex-journalist Béla Kun who thought that well-turned phrases, of which he was not capable, could sway the fates of nations. His absurd regime collapsed in an avalanche of verbiage. Reaction followed in the form of the first Fascist regime in Europe, which was headed by Admiral Horthy.

"Jancsi" became "János" in due time as he moved slowly up the ladder of underprivileged youngsters. He was more intelligent than the average youth of his age—of that there could be no doubt. But of what use was his intelligence? At best he would be able to make a very modest living. As an apprentice he received more blows than food. Then he became a journeyman toolmaker, locksmith, and mechanic—a skilled worker.

Did he ever think of going to America, the dream of so many intelligent Hungarian youngsters? The answer is locked in his own bosom. But he did go to the "New York of Hungary," to Budapest, which no regime, Communist or Fascist, could entirely destroy. The Hungarian capital was always far more astir than the countryside. There János could hope for a job in an industrial plant. One day if he had the tenacity and the good fortune, he might become a foreman.

Would he be able to participate in the life of Budapest that was well known to foreign tourists, in the glamorous ways of a capital with its cafés, filled with chatter? Would he be able to enjoy the music of gypsy bands on the Danube Embankment, while looking at the parade of attractive women? This "Hungarian rhapsody" was not to be János Kádár's treat. His Budapest was Angyalföld—Angels' Field.

Why was that part of the capital called the field of angels? To most people it looked more like the devil's own land. Situated in the northern quarters, near the Danube, adjacent to the industrial suburbs, Angyalföld was anything but glamorous. Its tenements were swarming with poor souls of János Kádár's ilk, working very hard, but to what end? To get wages on which to rent beds for use during the night, but not having enough money to rent a flat. János Kádár became an *ágyrajáró,* "bed-goer," entitled to occupy a bed during the night. He was working during the day. He had to vacate his bed early in the morning to a bed-goer who was working on a night shift. The bed stood in a tenement with one single water pump for all the tenants, and it had one toilet for the population of an entire floor. These were the ways of *Angyalföld* in those days.

UNDERGROUND IN THE AGE OF HORTHY

Kádár prepared himself for his future vocation during the Age of Horthy, which spanned the ends of the two world wars of our century. For fully a quarter of a century Nicholas Horthy de Nagybánya was regent governor, the Hungarian head of state. A former admiral of the Austro-Hungarian navy and an adjutant of the late Emperor-King Franz Joseph, he became the embodiment of the interregnum age. As the first Fascist regime in Europe, Horthy's government was anti-Semitic, anti-liberal, and also violently anti-Communist. It started on its political orbit at the extreme right. In the course of time, however, it moved closer to the center and finally came to rest not far from a middle position, but still somewhat to the right. Horthy made his peace with the Socialists, the Jews, and the liberals, but never with the Communists. The death sentence itself could be imposed in the Age of Horthy for Communist agitation. Yet, a nucleus of the Communist party survived the draconic laws and Kádár began to play increasingly important roles in it.*

There were many unemployed workers in the Hungary of 1930, as there were in Germany, Austria, and in the United States.

---

* The Communist party changed its name many times in Hungary. First it was called the Communist Party of Hungary, its Hungarian abbreviation being KMP (November, 1918 to September, 1944). Communists in those days were international-minded—the party was not "Hungarian," but "of Hungary." Next its name was the Hungarian Communist Party, MKP (October, 1944 to June, 1948). The Communists were now also nationalists. To conceal the Communist dictatorship, the name was a third time changed to the Hungarian Working People's Party, MDP (July, 1948 to November, 1956). Then it was changed to the Hungarian Socialist Workers' Party, MSZMP (From November, 1956). The magic word was now Socialism.

The National Unity Committee of the Unemployed Workers organized a demonstration on September 1, 1930, and János Kádár had a hand in it. The committee was a Communist front. The police used firearms and there were casualties.

Kádár, who was an organizer in the Young Communist Workers' League of Hungary, KIMSZ, an underground organization, became a member of its Central Committee while he was still a teen-ager. The general public did not know in those days but the Communist regime of Hungary today maintains that there was a full-fledged Communist underground even then. Bolshevik literature was smuggled into Hungary from nearby Czechoslovakia: *Dolgozók Lapja,* "Workers' Journal." Even Hungarian papers, wrapping their illicit contents in Aesopian fables, were able to follow the Kremlin line: *Társadalmi Szemle* ("Social Review"), and *Gondolat* ("Thought").

The police of the Horthy regime kept Kádár under surveillance beginning in 1931, according to *The New Hungarian Encyclopaedia,* a Communist government-publication. The same source asserts that he was taken into police custody from time to time, as the shadow of suspicion touched him. He was caught in the dragnet in 1935, as a suspected Communist, tried and sentenced to two years in jail. That was a light sentence for such offenses in those days. The police must have thought him either small fry or just a naïve Red.

Very little is reported about his life during most of that era. He continued to be a mechanic and a toolmaker, and for a time was a streetcar conductor in Budapest. How could a man suspected of being a Communist get a job from a public body, the municipality of the capital? The police black lists may not have been complete and, besides, János Kádár is not an uncommon name in Hungary.

THEN THE BLITZ

Hungary was swept up into the maelstrom of the Second World War. There was a Bolshevik underground in Hungary during that war, Hungarian Communist government-publications proclaim today. The same publications state that Kádár played important roles in the underground. These allegations cannot be verified. During the war the police and gendarmerie were particularly vigilant. Toward the end of it the German Nazi organizations controlled the security services, and in Hungary as in many other countries, the authorities kept a record of the movements of every individual. Although it was difficult to submerge into complete anonymity, it was not entirely impossible; there was, indeed, a Communist underground. How large it was nobody knows, but it could not have been very large. The Communists who became the rulers of Hungary, until the emergence of János Kádár, were residents of the Soviet Union—Mátyás Rákosi, the pudgy little "strong man" of Hungary, and Erno Gero and Imre Nagy, his successors.

The leader of the vestigial Communist underground was Lászlo Rajk, who went under the name of "Khirgiz," a former combatant in the Soviet-sponsored International Brigade in Spain at the time of the Civil War. Other leading Communists were Ferenc Fejto and K. Olt. The name of Kádár as one of the Communist leaders does not appear even in the most detailed accounts of Hungarian developments during the war.

It does appear, however, in the official accounts of the war that have been issued by the Hungarian government under Kádár. According to this narrative, Kádár became a member of the Central Committee of the illegal Communist party when he was thirty. He stepped up one more rung of the ladder in the following year, when he became secretary of the party. He was also organizer of the Communist front Anti-Fascist Movement.

During the spring of 1942 the Hungarian police carried out a series of anti-Communist razzias in the course of which it arrested some six hundred Communists and sympathizers. This was said (not by the Communists, though) to be about 80 per cent of the active trained cadres of the party. Two of the three members of the central secretariat, Zoltán Schoenherz and Ferenc Rózsa, were also caught; they were hanged. Kádár, as the only surviving party secretary, took on an enhanced leadership role.

At first the Germans had appeared to be the supermen of the war, incomparably superior to their foes. However, the British kept the spirit of the resistance awake. Horthy's Hungary had been forced to join the hosts of the Germans, Japanese, and Italians— the Axis—but the hearts of the government and of the majority of the people were not in the war. Kádár and the few remaining Communists sought to capitalize on the unpopularity of the war, and they organized a Peace Front. Again, we are told, Kádár was its moving spirit.

The magic of the Axis powers vanished as their foes, the

Allies, warmed to the battle. The Russians were pushing the Germans back in the east; the Western Allies were doing the same in the south. By the time the Western Allies invaded the heartland of Europe the Axis powers were in retreat. Now, the official Communist version of events asserts that Kádár headed a coalition resistance movement which embraced not only Communists but also democratic anti-Fascist forces and which was known as the Fatherland Front. (After the war the name was revived in another context, to serve as a foil of the Communist seizure of power.)

Even though the Germans were forced into retreat on all fronts, there was enough life in them to wage a war of extermination against their domestic foes. The Soviets were advancing from the east, crossing the protective walls of the Carpathian mountain range, descending into the plains. Kádár now found many others, including democratic-minded persons, who wished to join the underground in physical combat against the Germans. Total war struck the countryside and chaotic conditions ensued. Kádár made an attempt to establish contact with the advancing Russians. He was caught in the attempt by the Germans, who were determined to hold out to the bitter end, and was lodged in the prison of the city of Vác on the Danube. But in the existing turmoil he escaped from jail. And now there are two contradictory versions of what happened.

The official Communist version is that Kádár quickly turned toward the east from where the Russians were advancing. It was on the banks of the river Tisza that he met the first Soviet troops pushing westward. He eluded them, crossed the stream, and got in touch with the Hungarian Muscovites returning to their native land. They were organizing Hungary's first post-war government. It would be named the National Committee and would embrace several political parties. János Kádár was drafted into the Political Bureau of the Central Committee of the Hungarian Communist Party. Also he became a member of the Provisional National Assembly, a handpicked body. Still more important, he was invited to organize the country's "democratic police," anti-Horthy and pro-Communist. Horthy himself was out of the country, having been taken into custody by the Germans. He was freed by the Allies.

There was a shortage of Communists and especially of the "grass-roots" Hungarian type. Kádár, the "peasant," was a rarity among the Communist intellectuals.

According to another version of Kádár's liberation from Vác, as the Russians were sweeping westward they were rounding up able-bodied young men, deporting them to Russia. Everybody became a "Communist" in order to escape that fate, and Kádár, too, who did not speak a word of Russian, may have been on the verge of deportation to Siberia. To avoid that fate he got hold of a huge wooden beam and carried it to Budapest; the very picture of the exploited proletarian. It was in Budapest that he established contact with his Muscovite comrades.

In May, 1945, he advanced one step in the party ranks, becoming secretary of the Budapest committee. The following year he advanced to the post of the first secretary of the Hungarian Communist Party. Then came the crucial year, 1948, important on two counts. Under the leadership of the shrewd Mátyás Rákosi, No. 1 Communist in Hungary, all other political parties were liquidated and the Bolshevik dictatorship was established. A constitution copied from that of the Soviet Union was imposed; industry, banking and mining were nationalized; the influence of the Church on education was eliminated; the old landowners were forced out and the *kolkhoz* system was introduced in their place. Hungarian Working People's Party became the new name of the Communist organization. Kádár became the minister of the interior, a key position, with the police and the gendarmerie under his authority. Now he occupied top positions in both the government and the party. But not for long. Because of the other historic event of the year, the heresy in the Communist Universal Church.

Then came Kádár's entombment in Andrássy Ut and in his other jails.

THEN ANOTHER HURRICANE

After Stalin's death in 1953, for about two years the outside world did not suspect the internal turmoil within the Soviet Union. There was the "thaw," as the reign of terror abated. Then—we know today—there was a struggle for power behind the scenes. The followers of the hard line ranked Stalin with Marx and Lenin. Other Communists seemed to feel that times were different now, even in Russia. A new generation had grown up which was repulsed by the notion of Russia as a House of Death.

The first secretary of the Communist party of the Soviet

Union made a "secret" speech to the Twentieth Party Congress on February 14, 1955. It was a speech that shook the world, when its contents seeped out. Stalin had established a cruel and despotic one-man rule, said the first secretary, Nikita S. Khrushchev, and had introduced a regime which was alien to Marxist-Leninist principles and which subverted the values of the Communist movement. Khrushchev further charged that Stalin had developed a nefarious "cult of personality." Communism, in its present stage, must be the dictatorship of the proletariat, and not the terroristic dictatorship of a tyrant.

A new era dawned in the Soviets and among the satellites. The dead tyrant's lackeys were discredited. Stalin's regime had held probably millions in prison-like labor camps. They were released now. The Russians and their satellites began to breathe more freely. In Hungary, one of the "moderates," Imre Nagy, became the chairman of the Council of Ministers. Although he spent the war years in Moscow, he did not have the reputation of being a Kremlin stooge, and like Kádár, he was of peasant stock. He followed now a non-Stalinist, liberal policy. Kádár, we have seen, was released from jail during his regime. But Rákosi, Kádár's jailer, held on to power in the Hungarian Working People's Party. He was a less savage, a far more chastened man.

Now that Kádár was free again, what was to be his lot? What was the effect of the tortures he had endured, of the long months he had spent in jails? Was he a broken man? Having been tortured by Communists, had he turned against the "God that failed," becoming a Titoist perhaps, or even an anti-Communist?

Kádár's faith was made of a different stuff. Communists may have been unworthy of the cause for which they stood, but communism was beyond cavil. Communism continued to be his creed. Having been hurled from the heights would he be able to start his career anew? Would he be given another chance?

He had to start near the bottom again, but start he did. It was in District XIII—Angyalföld—that he became the first secretary of the local party committee. He did not get stuck there, for, not long afterwards, he became the secretary of the party committee of County of Pest. In July, 1956, he became a member and one of the secretaries of the Hungarian Working People's Party. The top-policy-making body of the party, the Political Bureau, too, elected him to membership.

In June, 1956, another major event had shaken the Communist world. It originated in a city about which the outside world had heard little: Poznan, a large industrial center in western Poland. Severe rioting broke out. The workers demanded more food, better wages, and improved working conditions. Now that there was a "thaw," they wanted to see its results. Their ire also turned against the Russian soldiers stationed in Poland. This was an incredible occurrence, presumed lambs roaring like lions. What if the rioting spread to other parts of Poland, and to the satellite world, including Hungary? Troops and tanks entered into action and scores of people were killed. Eventually the storm in Poznan quieted down, and a more liberal regime took over in Poland. The new government, headed by Wladyslaw Gomulka, was not Kremlinist, but it was not Titoist, either. Although it had a nationalistic tinge, it was still ready to work along with the Soviets, who maintained units of their armed forces in the country. The Hungarians took their cue from the Poles.

A month after the Poznan crisis, Kádár opened a campaign against Rákosi, who had demanded that some four hundred writers and intellectuals should be arrested in order to head off a revolutionary wave. In an open meeting of the Communist Central Committee in Budapest, Kádár told Rákosi that the country had had more than enough of him. Kádár was sustained by other Central Committee members, and Rákosi resigned. It was believed in some circles that Kádár had mounted the offensive against him at the behest of the Kremlin, which was determined to get rid of the "last Stalinist." The No. 1 man of the Hungarian Communists was now Erno Gero, another Muscovite. Gero, an engineer, had been in charge of the reconstruction of Budapest, which had been badly mauled during the war. "Bridge-builder," the Communist propaganda called him, because he rebuilt the Danube bridges that had been blown up by the retreating Germans.

Bridge-builder, yes; statesman, no. Too deeply immersed in Muscovite phraseology, Gero was detached from the actual course of constructive politics. His working tools were slogans representing party dogmas. He was not able to foresee that as a result of the Poznan revolt Hungary would be subject to a rising tide of discontent.

THE EXPLOSION

The events that followed in the autumn of 1956 became known in history as the Hungarian Revolution. While history books tell us that it took place in 1956, a more correct reading of the meaning of history informs us that it began a thousand years before that date. That revolution had been launched in the Verecke Pass, across the Carpathians, far up in the north. The ancestors of the Hungarians were moving across that pass into what was to become Hungary. The Hungarians were surrounded by Slavs. The strongest of these Slavs were eventually to be known as Russians, whom Hungarians came to fear and detest. The Russians ousted the Germans at the end of World War II, to be sure, but that did not change the attitude of the Hungarians toward them. In the autumn of 1956 it was the accumulated weight of a thousand years of Hungarian tradition that thrust against the Russians.

The Western world called the events of those days a revolution, although the Soviets called them a counter-revolution. In the Western world the word "Hungarian" became synonymous with the willingness of brave people to face death rather than accept thralldom. No higher compliment could be paid than to speak of "Hungarian bravery."

It all began with the work of a group of Hungarian writers, who demanded that the nation be given its freedom. The writers demanded that the Soviet troops stationed in Hungary should be withdrawn from the country and that democratic elections should be held. The Communist government in Budapest remained deaf to this demand. On the evening of October 23, a demonstration which consisted mainly of young people was held in front of the Radio Building in Budapest. The demonstrators were faced by a unit of the AVO, the secret police, rushed from the Andrássy Ut headquarters where János Kádár had been tortured. The AVO men opened fire on the crowd, killing a number of people and wounding others. "Insofar as any moment can be selected as the turning point which changed a peaceable demonstration into a violent uprising, it would be this moment," a United Nations report said later.

Thus a demonstration became a revolution. Spearheading it were university students and industrial workers. When the fighting broke out, the government of Erno Gero, being unable to maintain order, resigned. It was replaced by that of Imre Nagy. He was a Communist, but he was also a Hungarian, and he knew that the uprising was a nationalist revolution. More Russian troops rushed into Hungary.

If the revolutionaries won, there was the possibility that

Hungary would break free of the Soviet fortress and join the enemy camp in the West. That, in turn, might have been the signal for the other satellites to break for freedom. That, again, would be the end of the Soviet realm of satellites. Stripped of this shield, the Russians feared they would be on the verge of losing the cold war with the Western alliance.

After a short period of hesitation, Russia moved tank units into Budapest to support her troops. The rifles of the revolutionaries now faced the armor of the Soviets. The embattled Hungarians pleaded with the United Nations for help. The UN, in an emergency session, called for the invaders to halt. Then the revolutionaries addressed their pleas to the United States as the leader of the free people of the West. Washington was deeply concerned.

It was estimated that by November 3 some 2,500 Soviet tanks and about 1,000 supporting vehicles were in Hungary. All strategic centers, airfields, railways, and highways had been brought under control by Russian troops. The government of Nagy included János Kádár, too, at first. Premier Nagy now went over to the side of the revolutionaries. Thereupon Kádár and three colleagues left Nagy's cabinet and formed a counter-cabinet, the Hungarian Revolutionary Worker-Peasant Government. The head of this new government was Kádár himself, and he turned completely against Nagy, announcing over the radio:

"We were prompted to take this responsible step by the realization that within the Nagy government, which became impotent under reactionary pressure, we could do nothing against the counter-revolutionary danger menacing our People's Republic of workers and peasants.

"Respected champions of the working class have been murdered . . . and many highly esteemed sons of the peasantry have been exterminated. . . . We have decided to fight against the threatening danger of fascism and its dangerous gangs."

There were now two rival governments in Hungary. The one headed by Imre Nagy was a coalition cabinet, the "national Communists" predominating, and it broke with the Soviets by declaring Hungary's neutrality in the cold war.

János Kádár, who had slipped out of the Nagy government and had left Budapest, was lost to sight for a time. Where he was and the details of what he did are not matters of reliable record. According to information culled from refugees, Kádár rushed to the town of Uzhorod, on the Hungarian-Soviet boundary, and there he got on the Russian band wagon. Sure it was though, that there was soon formed a rival government, headed by János Kádár. A short while later there was only one government, with Kádár at the helm, the Soviets' choice.

The Soviets' No. 2 man, Anastas Mikoyan, appears to have had a hand in the arrangements with Kádár. He showed up in Hungary in those tragic days. Khrushchev visited Budapest only two years later—celebrating the anniversary of the "victory" of the Communist regime.

It was the radio station of the revolution, operating in Dunapentele (formerly Sztalinváros), which had announced that the battle was on and that it would continue until victory was won. The battle raged in Pécs, in Székesfehérvár, in Dunaföldvar, in Veszprém, and in Budapest.

The main battles were fought in Budapest, and hard fighting took place on the arterial roads leading to the capital. In order to slow down the advance of the Russian tanks, barricades were thrown up. Fighting side by side, units of the Hungarian army and of the freedom fighters, equipped principally with light arms, resisted the advancing tanks. The freedom fighters were transmitting their desperate appeals to the outside world. The writers, who felt a special responsibility for the success of the revolution, made their broadcasts: "Civilized people of the world, listen and come to our aid, not with declarations but with force—soldiers and arms. Do not forget that there is no other way to halt the wild onslaught of Bolshevism. Your turn will come when we perish. . . . Save our souls! Save our souls!"

Addressing the UN the radio station pleaded: "We beseech the United Nations to send immediate aid. We ask for parachute troops to be dropped in Hungary." An hour later an unidentified radio station sent out the following plea: "Peoples of Europe whom we helped for centuries to withstand Asia's barbarous attacks, listen to the tolling of the Hungarian bells which warn of disaster. . . . Civilized people of the world, we implore you to help us in the name of justice, freedom and morality. . . . Our ship is sinking, the light is failing, and the shadows are growing darker every hour over the Hungarian soil. Listen to our cry, civilized peoples of the world, and extend your fraternal hand."

Meanwhile, the Soviet armored units broke through the defenses and acquired control of the Danube bridges, of the central telephone exchange, which covered the entire country, and of other vital services. By that time, the János Kádár government was at the helm. "The events of the day," the new government announced, "have led to the complete dispersal of the reactionary foes."

The following day Kádár's Home Service of Radio Budapest proclaimed: "We are dealing the last blows to the counter-revolutionary forces." But some of the insurgent groups were still on their feet, and the Free Radio Rákóczi—so named after a freedom fighter of another century—stated: "We are not Fascists and we can prove this to the world." A few minutes later this appeal was broadcasted: "Can the world let a small country lose its liberty—the freedom of a country which had maintained it with great loss of blood through a thousand years? Why are only the interests of the great powers important? Why can't you hear our call?"

Late on November 6 the government-controlled Radio Miskolc reported that "Fascist bandits" were still destroying railway stock. A weak voice was heard over Radio Rákóczi on the seventh: "Please forward this appeal to President Eisenhower. . . . We are asking for immediate armed help." Even Kádár's Radio Budapest, which had minimized the importance of the battles, conceded that resistance in the capital itself continued. The stations of Moscow and of the satellite countries denounced the "Fascist counter-revolutionaries and hooligans." Sporadic fighting flared in the heavily industrialized areas of Csepel Island and Dunapentele. There were guerrilla encounters around the coal basins and in the rugged Bakony hills of Trans-Danubia. Former Premier Nagy found sanctuary in the Yugoslav Embassy, and there he stayed for a few days. He left it in the belief that he had the government's pledge of safe-conduct to go to his home. However, as he left the Embassy, he was apprehended by Soviet agents. Eventually, the world learned that he had been killed.

Resistance to the Kádár regime continued as industrial workers refused to return to their plants. Refugee newspapers reported that the Hungarian government sought to starve the resisters into submission by holding up food shipments at the Austrian frontier. The Kádár government claimed that foreign relief was merely a cloak for the shipment of arms. As a result of the workers' resistance to the Kádár government, production continued at a low level. Daily coal output, for instance, was down from 80,000 to 3,500 tons, less than one-twentieth of normal production.

The foreign press reported mass arrests by Soviet and Budapest authorities. Refugees from Hungary claimed that trainloads of Hungarians were headed toward the Soviet Union. Even a year after the revolution, reports appeared about large groups of Hungarian deportees in the Soviets' Central Asian republics, and some of these people were allegedly working on the newly opened Soviet "virgin lands." The UN special report on the problem of Hungary stated: "No accurate figures exist regarding the number of Hungarian citizens deported, but these certainly run into thousands." And the most important loss—the loss of human lives? Neutral observers estimated mortalities at 25,000 people, while the Kádár government itself admitted 2,700 deaths.

THE APPRAISAL OF THE REVOLUTION

The Hungarian revolution of 1956 was unique. A small nation rose against a superpower. The Hungarians could do little more than battle with rifles in their hands. Seldom has Western public opinion been aroused to such a pitch of excitement as during the Hungarian uprising, and no contemporary event has received comparable attention. More copy was filed about Hungary, more pictures shown, more radio and television programs produced, more books printed—sometimes in a remarkably short time—than about any other current event.

Superlatives of the most purple hue were evoked. The Hungarian revolution was described as "the greatest," and "the most awe-inspiring," event of the century. The refugees were received as immortal fighters for human freedom. The gates of countries long bolted to Hungarians were thrown open with amazing speed. The free world could not do enough for the freedom fighters.

The world had known Hungary only superficially, as a small nation somewhere in Eastern Europe, in the vicinity of the fairy-tale countries of "Ruritania" and "Carpathia," a nation with an attractive capital, spiced food, fiery music, and very beautiful women—in other words, as a Hungarian rhaposdy.

Suddenly the world learned that there was far more than that to the Hungarians—that they were an exceptionally courageous people, who had the pluck to do what no other nation had dared to undertake.

DISARMING THE OPPOSITION

János Kádár's stand toward the revolutionaries was ambivalent. He claimed, on the one hand, that "the armed insurrection that occurred in Hungary between October 23 and November 4, 1956, was designed to overthrow by violence the constitutional and social order of the Hungarian republic and to restore the old Horthyite Fascist regime, a regime that was directed against the Hungarian people's social progress." On the other hand, Kádár blamed the "Rákosi-Gero clique," too, for having ignored Hungary's special conditions and having "slavishly" applied Soviet methods.

The regime of Kádár faced a disastrous economic situation. The Communist governments of Hungary had forced the growth of heavy industry at the cost of farming and the production of consumer goods. As a consequence, prices had risen sharply. Hungarian living standards in 1956 had been lower than in 1937. Whereas in the latter year it took the work of ten hours to buy the food requirements of an entire family for one week, the corresponding figure for 1956 was seventeen hours.

The conditions of Hungary after the revolution was such that only the quickest financial aid could help. Hungary's neighbor, Poland, was in negotiation with the United States about such aid, but this was out of the question in the case of Kádár. There was only the Soviet Union to which he could turn. Negotiations were opened in the latter part of March, 1957, on a high level, indicating the urgency of the problem. An arrangement was finally reached. The Soviets undertook to ship to Hungary a billion rubles' worth of goods (about $100 million in purchasing power then), including vital industrial raw materials and food. The Soviet government also granted Hungary long-term loans and canceled a part of the country's previous debt.

The most important innovation in the economic management of the country was the change in the ratio of consumer articles to industrial equipment. Clothes, shoes, and other consumer items were now given priority in the production schedule. The new Three-Year Plan, beginning in 1958, projected a better balance between investments for capital goods and for the manufacture of consumer items. Housing, too, received high priority on the list.

Kádárország, "Kadarland," cost the Russians a pretty penny. How much it was nobody knew, partly because of the Kremlin's secrecy and partly because of the Soviet's monetary conversion. The West estimated that Hungary received about $400 million from the Soviets in the first six post-revolutionary years.

The toilers' life was eased. There were fewer brainwashing operations and more fringe benefits. These included not only the usual and long-established free medical services—traditional among the working people of the European continent—but also government-financed vacations and workers' sanatoria. Lovely Lake Balaton became a summer resort center for the kind of *prolis* Kádár himself had been in his youth.

Kádár had now his office on Castle Hill, but he apparently did not forget his years in Angels' Field. Six years after the revolution the tenements of that Devils' Field were gone, replaced by gaily painted apartment houses with conveniences which the *prolis* had never seen. No longer did the tenants have to use a single toilet for the swarming population of an entire floor. Every flat had a bathroom, and many of these apartment houses were surrounded by garden plots. The larger complexes had shopping centers and even "cultural centers" which were stocked with books and periodicals. There were also some cafés with open-air terraces for the warmer months.

It was not only in Angels' Field that the former "tenement barracks" vanished. It was the same in the other slum areas which used to form a ring around the capital, at Kelenföld, Lágymányos, and in the eastern sections, out on Üllei Ut.

In the course of time the entire countryside was transformed. Tourists to Hungary in the past were familiar with the beauty of Budapest. Some of the smaller towns of the country were charming, too, and there was much romanticism in the villages. But there was also the sign of much poverty. Many of the houses had thatched roofs and their walls were baked mud. It was not uncommon to see such a mud hut completely collapse under the onslaught of persistent winds and rains.

Now the houses were roofed with gay red tiles and the walls were stone. In all villages electricity replaced the old petroleum lamps. Of course, the "cultural centers" were more the centers of propaganda than of culture, but they provided a clean meeting place. Gone were the disreputable taverns with their acrid smoke. The highways over the country were paved: no longer would they become rivers of mud in the rain and winding ribbons of dust under the summer sun.

New industries were in the making, including Hungary's own "Pittsburgh" in Dunaujváros, "Danubian New Town," on the banks of that river. Other parts of the country received a boon

in the form of manufacturing plants that would enable farm workers to get additional employment during the inclement seasons.

A rapid process of urbanization set in, not only in the
growth of the cities but also in the mental attitude of youth. "Peasant girls" no longer looked different from their urbanite sisters;
both could appear in the evening with a stylish hair-do. A fad
originated in Paris or New York would in a short time sweep over
the Hungarian countryside. Gone were the days when the *csárdás*
was the national dance of Hungary. It was now the twist and rock
'n roll.

These were improvements, no doubt, but Kádár alone was
not entitled to credit for them. The foundations had been laid in
the austerity period of previous years. Also the very existence of a
freer regime may have encouraged progress. Material growth was
a hallmark of the age on both sides of the Iron Curtain. Most of
the credit, however, is due to the freedom fighters of 1956. Referring to the apparent improvement in living conditions, Western
newspaper correspondents reported: "It looks as if the revolutionaries had won against the Russians." This was a triumph of
Westernization.

Still, Hungarians kept on complaining about the Kádár
regime, more often and more loudly than before. *Magyarorszag
menyország* used to be a patriotic exclamation—"Hungary is
paradise." Now many Hungarians added: *Kádárország fenyor-
szág,* "Kádárland is a penal colony." This they said not only
among themselves but also to strangers. That was a good sign,
too, of changing times. People in that part of the world are grumblers. History—that is, the heavy hands of Tartars, Austrians,
Turks, and Russians—has made them such. Grumbling, which in
the Rákosi period led to the secret service mansion on Andrássy
Ut, now became almost a social obligation; one was expected to
complain about the regime. The secret police were ever present,
but apparently had little interest in complainers.

AND THE PEASANTS

Although of peasant stock, Kádár could not deal effectively with
Hungary's farm population. First, there was the peasant paradox.
The peasants had not joined the freedom fighters in the Hungarian revolution. As we have seen, the industrial workers and the
students did most of the fighting.

The explanation of this phenomenon is provided partly by technical considerations. The revolution was spontaneous. With no national headquarters or central leadership, it acquired organization as it forged ahead. Rural areas do not lend themselves to a process of that nature, for the villages and farmhouses are widely scattered.

Hungarian history had seen peasant revolts, but there were no signs of a jacquerie in the revolution of 1956. There was also an even more basic reason for the restraint. Up to the end of World War II the peasants on some of the best land of the mid-Danubian area led a wretched life. Much of the land was in few hands, and too little was available for the many. For the first time in the history of the country, the end of World War II brought about a distribution of the estates. The land reform was effected by a coalition government in which the Smallholders, not the Communists, dominated. There were no magnates now in Hungary, not even too many *zsiros parasztok*, "fat peasants"—*kulaks*. Many peasants helped the fighters with free food, but on the whole they decided to sit out the fight.

Kádár, the ex-peasant, was faced with the eternal paradox, the peasant problem in a collectivistic economy. The post-war system of small landholdings did not, and could not, work at all. Small farmers were unable to accumulate the large investments required by the agricultural operations of modern times: the machines and other tools, improved seeds, and fertilizers. In a small country with millions of peasants, the units of farming had to be small. There was only one solution to this problem, and Kádár knew it. It was farm cooperatives. Yes, but the peasant is the most rugged of all individualists, especially if he is accursed with a historic memory. He had never had any land of his own, nor had his ancestors. The soil to him meant not only livelihood and security, but also prestige. His god was the black soil. He could not work it efficiently, but gods are not always merciful. A thousand times better was the inefficiency of his own holding than the perfection of a mechanized cooperative farm.

Rákosi's regime had followed the Soviet line. The farms were to be collectivized. As in Russia, members of the *kolkhozi* were granted the privilege of keeping a slice of land as their own private property. Then came the revolution of 1956. Even though the peasants left the fighting to the towns, they wanted to have their own solution of the farm problem. The peasants left the collectives, which then sunk into limbo, as if they had never existed. Would the Kádár regime accept the accomplished fact? The existence of private property was neither in line with Communist dogma nor with the presumed interests of the state.

Kádár turned the clock back—collectives had to win the day. But his government did not employ the detested term. It spoke about cooperatives. Was there any difference between the two? There was indeed. In the collectives basic ownership rights were extinguished while in the cooperatives they were retained. In the former the members were paid according to their work, while in the latter their previous landholdings were taken into account in the determination of their earnings.

What did the peasants do? They devoted most of their efforts to their own private allotments, on which they produced more farm specialties than on the larger collective properties. The younger generation of the farmers was now thronging at the factory gates, looking for industrial jobs. The labor supply of the villages was being depleted.

THE EX-PRISONER AND HIS WAY OF LIFE

What is János Kádár like in real life, at home, among his friends, before the public? What are his relations with the Russians? What appears to be his future?

At home? One can seldom ask that question about Communist leaders. There is that iron curtain protecting their private lives. Khrushchev became an exception. In his eagerness for coexistence with the West he was embroiled in a process that may be called his "Americanization": revealing his family to the outside world. Only he could afford that.

The proverbial seven seals protected the private life of János Kádár. Yes, he was married. His wife remained so much in the background one got the impression she was a captive in a harem. And nothing else was known about his family.

People asked hopefully: a mistress, a little wine and song? The questioners were disappointed again. Kádár was an ascetic man, who looked sad, too, and "play" was not in his vocabulary. The smile he forced upon his lips for the photographers was unnatural.

He lived in a simple flat, with no more space than he and his wife needed. There were no swimming pools for him as there had been for his predecessors, no mansions in the hills of Buda, no sumptuous summer homes of the kind that the Russians call *dachas,* no large retinues, no underground palazzos for maximum security. He was an ascetic man, indeed.

Kádár was called "rough, primitive, mysterious," by a prominent fighter for Hungary's freedom in 1956, General Béla Király, who spoke out from his American sanctuary. That, maintained other former freedom fighters who had studied Kádár more closely, was an oversimplified description: Kádár was a true believer of the Communist creed.

Was it an abstract creed, for the lips, or was it also for the brains and the hands? Was it floating on the hot air of generalities or was it anchored to realities? Above all, did Kádár have a sense of his own mission?

As a young Communist he was in revolt against the treatment of the Hungarian *prolis,* and being one of them he was struggling *de profundis* on behalf of his own caste. Why, he seemed to ask, were there so many wretchedly poor people in an uncommonly rich land? He could see that the problems of Hungary were the fault of a ruling élite that kept on proclaiming its burning idealism without ever practicing it. After World War II he witnessed what must have appeared to him a miraculous change—the underdogs became the masters. He noticed how many members of the new élite lost themselves in ideological hairsplitting. He himself learned from his own experience as a *proli,* perhaps also as an inmate of several jails, that ideas and ideals fulfilled a useful function only if they were the guidelines of actual improvements that affected the lives of the masses. He became an "ideopraxist," to employ a Carlylean term. He learned to scrutinize his ideas in the light of their practical application.

He considered himself an orthodox believer and protested against the designation of his policy as "demi-nationalistic Communism." He was a true Communist, he maintained, because his creed sustained the conviction that eventually some form of socialism was bound to encompass the globe. The apotheosis of his secular religion was the ultimate integration of Marx with the corollaries of Lenin's teachings. Marx spoke about the *prolis* emancipating themselves, while Lenin's corollary posited the need of establishing a professional cadre of full-time political reformers.

Thus Jansci the *proli* became János *a proletár,* displaying an obvious empathy for people of his own ilk. As a former bed-goer he identified himself with the lowest strata of life. It was precisely the standards on that level that he was eager to raise in a hurry. That is why the flats on Angyalföld today have not only bathrooms but also lifts.

Kádár never became an intellectual, although obviously he would have liked to become one. He interlarded his speeches with references to the "Marxist-Leninist science," about which he spoke with reverence. He kept on quoting Lenin profusely, mostly commonplace, over-generalized passages of practical import. His speeches and articles contained barely any references to Marx, who seemed to be beyond his ken.

However, after his years in Communist jails he attempted to employ Marxist phraseology. In the jails he had easy access to Marxist literature, and probably little else. Also, he had "leisure" to immerse himself in the study of the concept he had been professing. He learned a little more about dialectics and the importance of the materialist interpretation of processes of history. His public addresses proclaimed his belief in the "unified field theory of the natural and social sciences." More than that: He reached the conclusion that the social sciences, as interpreted by Marx, formed part of the natural sciences. It was thus possible to gaze into the future through the correct application of dialectics. ("Correct" is a word which Kádár always liked to use in this context.) This knowledge enabled key people to follow what must have appeared to the uninitiated as history's mysterious laws.

Though not an intellectual, Kádár struck one as a man of intelligence. He learned through bitter experience that most Hungarians would never become Communists. He wanted no more than that they should not be anti-Communists. He learned that his regime would not be accepted unless he proved with deeds what it said in an avalanche of words—namely, that the planned economy was raising living standards faster than the unplanned, capitalistic economy. He burned with the desire to demonstrate the superority of his creed. He spared neither himself nor his collaborators to achieve that aim.

Kádár never acquired any friends outside of the political sphere. He had no time to waste on social contacts. Closest to him were the people with whom he could work best. The No. 2 man in the Communist party was Gyula Kállai, in whom Kádár saw some of the qualities he would have liked to possess. In his youth Kállai had studied philosophy and had qualified as a secondary-school teacher. He had played a well-documented role in the Hungarian underground during World War II. The son of a shoemaker, he, too, came from the grass-roots. Another member of the brain-trust was Lajos Fehér, intellectual farm expert, editor, and deputy prime minister. Béla Biszku, another member of the inner circle, filled the post of minister of interior, having charge over arms of the state authority, such as the police.

In his public appearances Kádár never cut an impressive figure. His speeches struck most listeners as lacking in fire to the degree of being monotonous. True to the Communist practice, his addresses appeared to be long, sometimes interminable. Still, he seemed to hold the attention of his audience, partly because of his prestige and partly because of an inner intensity. He appeared to believe in what he said, and so it was the intense words that counted and not the monotonous speaker.

Kádár seemed to have fallen under the influence of Khrushchev in his speech-making. He spoke not as the boss but as the man of the people, interweaving peasant proverbs and the homespun philosophy of the common people into his policy declarations.

What was Kádár's relation to the Soviets? Although the cult of personality was scorned in Russia, when Nikita Khrushchev spoke, it was the Kremlin talking: the chairman of the council of ministers of the Soviets was still the boss. What was, then, the relation of the two men? Where did Kádár rank among the Soviet satellites? The outside world believed that closest to Khrushchev among the bloc statesmen was Poland's quiet dictator, Gomulka, a Slav himself, who spoke Russian.

Yet, Gormulka was not closest to Khrushchev. The place of honor was occupied by Kádár and this in spite of many handicaps. He spoke no Russian, was not a Slav, and represented a country in which the dislike of Russia was deeply seated. Also, the span in the ages of the two men was considerable.

But, both of them came from the lower strata of society and in fighting their way to the top had faced great odds and bitter opposition. Both of them were known as intelligent men speaking the language of the common people, but lacking in intellectual pretensions. Both of them had what the Germans call *Fingersplitzengefuehl*—feeling in the tip of their fingers—intuition to show them the way.

The Soviet leader was familiar with the story of the Hungarian leader. He knew that Kádár had staked his very life as a member of the Communist underground during the Horthy regime. In those days it was all but impossible to foresee that one day the "scum of the earth" was going to become the leader of the "governing élite."

The Soviet leader, knew, too, that Kádár had not broken down when facing the Gábor Péter bloodhounds. Here, then, was a man who had passed through the most bloodcurdling ordeals at the hands of fellow Communists and had emerged with his trust in his creed unbent.

Kádár went along with the Kremlin on most policies, but he was not a "yes man," and this quality may have impressed Khrushchev, too. The Hungarian disagreed with the Russian on a major issue, for instance. It was the Comecon, closer economic cooperation among the Communist countries, a vestigial common market which was in the blueprint stage. Kádár insisted on maintaining a measure of freedom of movement for Hungary in the economic field. He was apprehensive that countries with older established industries as, for example, Czechoslovakia, would score advantages over Hungary which, in turn, might be dragged down by poorly industrialized nations, such as Bulgaria. Also the Comecon would call for a more vigilant supervision on the part of the Soviets. Finally, what would be the effect of a more highly integrated agrarian policy? Would Hungary be forced into specializations for which her peasants were not prepared?

And now, what about Kádár's future? Of course, it is all but impossible to detect signs of change in the monolithic structure of authoritarian regimes until the inner logic of events overwhelms the participants. Challenges to Kádár's leadership might emerge on three fronts: in the Kremlin; within the Hungarian Communist party; and from a domestic opposition outside of the party.

As long as Khrushchev or someone close to his ideology is at the helm in the Kremlin, such a challenge is not likely to materialize. Kádár was successful in taming the Hungarians' insurrection. Nor could the observer detect signs of incipient rebellion within the ranks of the Hungarian Communists.

The greatest danger to Kádár might have come from the domestic front outside the Communist party, but that power factor had already tried its luck with Kádár's predecessors. The Hungarians had attempted to overthrow the Communists. At that time they had viewed the West and especially the United States as their allies. They called to them for help but received no response. The revolutionaries wanted only a limited engagement of the West; most Hungarians recoiled from the thought of war. They were romantic, as Hungarians are in such matters. They opened their eyes only to one aspect of reality, keeping them closed to other aspects. They did not realize that help from the West might have entailed the risk of nuclear war. When the aid was not forthcoming they became not only disappointed but also bitter and spoke of being "sold down the river." This happened in 1956.

After it was over, the Kádár regime sized up the situation and applied quick remedies. It raised living standards at a rapid rate. Non-Communist Hungarians learned their lesson from this sequence of events. They learned not to be so quick in imperiling the obvious improvements in their material conditions for the sake of an abstract ideal, an ideological victory. Besides, democracy is not an experience with which Hungarians became overly familiar under the Horthy regime or, for that matter, under the House of Habsburg. It was their historic fate to resign themselves to the best in a chronically bad situation, and they have seen far worse days than the Age of Kádár.

The age turned out to be an inescapable compromise between the Hungarians' congenital reluctance to play the role of a satellite and their perception of the monumental reality extending from the boundaries of their own country to the "end of the world." The Hungarian paradox, an anomaly, is not likely to disappear unless there is a shrinking of that monumental Soviet reality. In that case people of the faith of János Kádár would quickly vanish from the revolving stage of history.

8

Poland's Subdued Dictator: Wladyslaw Gomulka

What had been the crime of the man with the sallow face and wistful eyes? He was a patriot and a Pole. Also he was a Communist and a nationalist—a great crime in the eyes of the orthodox believers in the creed of the Kremlin.

Neither in his appearance nor in his conduct did Wladyslaw Gomulka seem to be qualified to lead a dangerous life. When he reached the peak of fame his balding head was rimmed with a fringe of white. Some people try to crush others with piercing looks, with their massive stature, or with the cutting edge of their voice. There was no steel in Gomulka's eyes, his short stature was unimpressive, and his voice faltered from time to time. It was perhaps partly because of his stature and his voice that he could take physical hardships in his stride. He tired less quickly than some of the Polish stalwarts, and a stentorian voice in the entombed underground life of the Polish guerrillas would have been of no use. But he had steel in his will power and a large measure of resilience, especially under conditions that appeared to be hopeless. Appearing to be meek, he had a fanatic streak. Conveying the impression of being a worrywart, he was unafraid. Seldom did he allow his strong emotions to gain the upper hand. Once, however, he let that happen, and he stepped into a mortal danger. More about that further on.

Now he was buried, buried alive in a gloomy house he was not allowed to leave. He was under house arrest. Few people outside Poland ever heard of the location of that tomblike house in Miedzeszyn, a suburb of Warsaw, the Polish capital. His name no longer appeared in newspapers. Dead people could not possibly perform newsworthy deeds. Once he had been No. 1 man of Poland. Now he was the No. 27,564,198 man, the least of the last. He was now an un-Pole, an un-man. The year was 1951, or was it

298

1952? Who knew and who cared? Dead people have no need of calendars. What was the crime of this un-man?

In 1948 the Communist world had been shaken by the Titoist heresy—the view that Communist countries could follow the lights of their own ways and not necessarily those of the Moscow Kremlin. Gomulka was then secretary of the Polish Workers' Party, and a member of its policy-making Central Committee. Polish Workers' Party was a pseudonym of the Polish Communist party, a name that did not sound well to Polish ears. Also, it was a designation that enabled non-Communists to take part in a Popular Front.

Gomulka was a dedicated Communist, but his roots were in Poland, not in Russia. There was no Poland at the time of his birth, only an aspiration and a dream. Poland underwent three dismemberments: the first in 1772, the second one in 1793, and the third and final one in 1795. The deed had been perpetrated by voracious neighbors: imperial Russia, imperial Austria, and the Kingdom of Prussia which, about a century later, was to become the nucleus of imperial Germany. Even though there was no Poland on the map of Europe, beautiful was the Poland of the patriot's fancy, a luminous city of God in the midst of the dark world of sinister barbarians. "Poland is not lost yet. . . ."

This tragic background conditioned even Communists to feel as Poles, and not as denationalized and denatured creatures who owed loyalty to Moscow. Because he was a Pole, Gomulka was not only a Bolshevik but also a nationalist. At the time Yugoslavia's Tito asserted the right of Communist countries to follow their own historic rights, Gomulka made no such declaration. Topography and geography accounted for the difference in the stands of the two men. Yugoslavia is not adjacent to the Soviet Union, as Poland is, and her rugged terrain serves as a shield. Poland is not only next door to the Soviet Union but she straddles the transcontinental highway into Europe's heart. Poland's plains form a geographic extension into the Russian steppes.

That is why Gomulka was in no position to make a declaration of his Polish faith. The lord of life and death in the Communist universe was Stalin, all-knowing, omnipresent, but not all-merciful. He was a revengeful god, and a jealous one. To him and him alone was due the burning of incense and myrrh. In one person he was Caesar and God, head of the Ecumenical Communist creed, and teacher of all faithful Bolsheviks. He kept his eyes on his flock, and should he have failed to do so there were many other eyes to observe heretic acts, as there were many lips to make hushed reports. Those lips were in the habit of reporting suspicions as accomplished facts, for the lips were motivated by jealousy.

The time was past when Gomulka could have craved an audience in the Kremlin. But even if it had not been he would have been kept waiting in the antechamber of the master of the Communist world. The Pole would have been expected then to prostrate himself in the Radiant Presence. Then the word would have been pronounced—perdition or absolution. Gomulka was spared the Kremlin Canossa. And thus he remained an un-man about whom people did not dare to speak. His name was heresy.

In the tomb of the living, certain privileges were extended to him, though. He had many books, in Polish, Russian, and German. They were books of history, especially of Poland and of the workers' movement.

His wife could visit him, a professional statistician. She was a short woman, much younger than her husband. She, too, had been working in the Central Committee of the party. His son could visit him, also his granddaughter, whom he adored. During this living entombment, Gomulka could not indulge in his favorite sport, swimming, which, while free, he credited for his ability to work long hours far into the night.

Gomulka had been arrested at his favorite health resort, Krynica-Zdroj, on the northern slope of the Carpathian Mountains, where he liked to spend his summer vacation with his wife. Ironically, it was almost within sight of the highest peak of the Carpathians, the 8,700-foot Stalin Peak, that he was detained. No less ironically, the name of that peak in adjacent Czechoslovakia was later changed to Gerlachovka, its original name.

Political visitors were forbidden to cross the threshold of the house of detention at Miedzeszyn. Besides, what politician of the Stalin era would have dared to pay such a call?

Knowing his role to be that of a living corpse, Gomulka kept quiet and played dead. He lost his political life in 1949. Year followed year with immutable monotony. Then, one day, he heard that the master of the Kremlin was dead. That was four years after his arrest. Gomulka began to wonder what his fate was going to be. An heir sponsored by Stalin followed in the tyrant's footsteps, but there was a measure of relaxation, the beginning of a "thaw." Still it was not spring, and a tussle for first place in the Kremlin ensued. There were many aspirants, and no clear line of succession. Then emerged Nikita Khrushchev with that historic "off the record" speech at the Twentieth Congress of the Communist Party of the u.s.s.r. in March, 1956. And a new era in history began in the Soviets and, soon, in Poland, too.

Gomulka heard about the speech by way of the grapevine. Now he had visitors, and some of them were politically involved. One could never know; he might yet be resurrected. The Polish political stage was crowded with potential leaders who thought that they could solve Poland's problems. Who could have measured up to the self-confidence of a Jakub Berman, boss of the Polish police and virtual dictator of Poland during the Stalin era, now ready to change his line? Or of Hilary Minc, economic czar of the Stalin regime, ex-vice-premier, and member of the Politburo. The No. 1 Polish leader of the Stalin age, Boleslaw Bierut died while attending the Twentieth Congress in Moscow. In his suburban prison Gomulka appeared to be forgotten. But not altogether, as events were to show.

Khrushchev's remarks about Stalin tolled the end of an era and announced the beginning of another one. The cult of personality was to end, and the Soviets were no longer told that only the *Vozhd,* the "Leader," the Great Stalin in a new guise, could solve their problems. Nor was the Kremlin to tell the "fraternal" countries how they were to behave in every little detail. The broad Communist principles were, however, to be dictated from the Mount Sinai of the creed, from the Kremlin.

Gomulka had never made his political philosophy explicit. Yet the Poles knew that he was one of them, and not a Russian in Polish disguise. They also knew him as a man of moderation, who could reconcile his own creed with the national interests of the Poles.

Then the workers' riot broke out in Poznan, a highly industrialized Polish city. The time was June 28, 1956, the beginning of a new era in Poland's history. The troops suppressed the riot, in the wake of which there were forty-four people dead and a thousand imprisoned.

And Poland remembered the man in the House of the Dead, Wladyslaw Gomulka. He was exhumed from his grave, and lo! there was a living man, ready to work as if he had not been entombed for seven years. The world liked to think of the Poles as romantic people, and yet Gomulka, short of stature and soft-spoken, did not cut a romantic figure. He spoke quietly, but the Poles paid close attention. To him went the confidence of the entire nation: Communists, non-Communists, perhaps even anti-Communists, atheists, and Catholic believers. He was now the first secretary of the Central Committee of the Polish United Workers' Party—the party of the Communists. And this is what he said at the Eighth Plenary meeting of that committee on October 20, 1956:

"The working class recently gave a painful lesson to the party leadership and the government. Seizing the strike weapon and going out to demonstrate in the streets on that black Thursday of last June, the Poznan workers proclaimed in a powerful voice: Enough! This cannot go on any longer! Turn back from the false road! . . . The Poznan workers did not protest against People's Poland, against socialism, when they went out into the streets of the city. They protested the bad which was widespread in our social system and which was painfully felt also by them, against the distortions of the fundamental principles of their idea of socialism."

Before following Gomulka's career thereafter, let us look at the soil out of which he sprang.

A LIVELY BOY AND A TIRED MONARCH

Wladyslaw Gomulka was born into an age and a region that determined his life. He was born on February 6, 1905, in the town of Krosno, province of Lemberg, in the Austro-Hungarian Monarchy. Today Lemberg is known as Lwow, and there is no longer a Monarchy. Krosno was in the southern borderland of Poland. At Wladyslaw's birth, and for thirteen years afterward, the region was known as Galicia, a Habsburg Crown Land. Other parts of historic Poland, we have seen, belonged to Germany and Russia. Austria treated her Poles best. She was by then a tired country, with a goodly measure of *schlamperei,* "slovenly indolence," combined with a dash of *gemuetlichkeit,* "joviality." Galicia had a measure of self-government and, indeed, she was said to have had more of that than the other Crown Lands. German-speaking Austrians were in the habit of complaining, with much exaggeration one might say, that the Habsburg Monarchy was run by Poles.

Young Wladyslaw was born into a farming and oil-producing region, the only petroleum area in the Habsburg realm. In Gomulka's youth most of the oil wells in the nearby areas of Boryslaw, Drohobycz, Stryj, and Jaslo belonged to foreigners, including Standard Oil. Wladyslaw's father, Jan, had been a poor farmer. He had emigrated to the United States but returned to Poland after a few years. Both he and his son obtained work in the oil fields of Boryslaw.

Wages were low in that distant part of the Habsburg Empire, and the oil-field workers were a discontented lot. Many of the monarchy's industrial workers had joined the Social-Democratic party in the course of time, and the influence of the trade-union movement on their lives was strong. The Socialist press of Galicia was patterned on the model of the *Arbeiter Zeitung,* "Workers' Journal," of Vienna, which minced no words about the exploiter and the exploited. "Capitalist-exploiter" appeared to be one single word in the vocabulary of that press, which contained not merely news but also large doses of indoctrination. Such concepts as "surplus value" and "economic interpretation of history"— highlights of Marxist theory—were household words of that journal. Young Wladyslaw, too, became thoroughly familiar with them. He also became saturated with Polish romantic nostalgia. Strong swelled the hope in the Galician oil fields that the triumph of both socialism and Polish nationalism would usher in happier days. Thus the seeds were sown that were to bear their bitter fruits in Gomulka's later life.

A bright young man, Wladyslaw Gomulka became prematurely acquainted with the problems of his native land. He did not live in Poland—because there was no such country then—but he was a Pole. The Habsburgs ruled in Vienna while Galicia was ruled by semi-feudal Polish families. Great wealth was strongly concentrated in the hands of the Polish *szlachta,* the "gentry," many members of which lived in the imperial capital, Vienna, and in Lemberg. Besides the Poles, Galicia had a large number of other nationalities, especially Ukrainians. While the Poles were Catholics, as were the Gomulkas, most of the Ukrainians were Greek Catholics, in which case their churches were in communion with the Pope in Rome and were therefore called Uniates; or they were "Greek Orthodox," under their own religious authorities and not in communion with the Pope.

Wladyslaw also became acquainted with the "Jewish problem" of Galicia. There were hundreds of thousands of Jews in that province. While the Poles and Ukrainians disliked one another, both groups agreed on disliking the Jews. Catholic, Greek Catholic, or Greek Orthodox, they were all Christians; the Jews, naturally, were not. There were also occupational cleavages among the various groups. Most enterprising were the Jews, many of whom left Galicia, crossing the Carpathians into Hungary, the "America of the Danube Valley" in those days, or migrating directly to the United States.

Jews, Catholics, Uniates, no matter—Gomulka was familiar with the plight of the underdog: a very hard life with little to look forward to. Of food there was enough and of fuel, too, after the natural gas resources of the region had been tapped, but the housing was miserable and the clothing often in tatters. Children walked to school in their bare feet. In those days young Gomulka would not have been acquainted with the cause of these harsh facts if he had not heard his father and his working companions discuss the lot of the "exploited" people at the hand of the "capitalists."

Young Gomulka, too, went to school in his bare feet. He was in the third grade of the elementary school when the "Great War" broke out. In another generation, when the experience of the twentieth century was more widely disseminated, people came to speak about it as the First World War.

There was no worse place in all of Europe during that war than Galicia. Northern France was also visited by the scourge, but France had a higher level of material prosperity. Galicia was poor when the war broke out, and it was continuously swept by the hosts of the warring forces. Austria-Hungary joined forces with Germany against imperial Russia. The Galician plains were the extension of the western Russian plains. In those days the world spoke with dread about the "Russian steam roller," the huge armies which the Czar had at his beck and call. That steam roller crashed through Krosno and the rest of the Galician plains, including the petroleum fields.

The Russian steam roller was not as effective as it was noisy, and having crossed the Carpathian crest, it sputtered to a halt. The Austrians were helped by their German allies to push the Russians back into Galicia.

Every young man with two arms and two legs was considered *tauglich*, fit for service in the army of Austria-Hungary. Workers in the oil fields, in shops, and in plants were in short supply. Replacements had to come from the ranks of bright young boys with manual skills. In 1915 Wladyslaw completed his elementary education. Two more years of full attendance would have freed him of his scholastic duties for good. But many teachers were able-bodied, too. Also many schools in Galicia were in shambles; their gaslights gone and their iron stoves, too. Education entered the rank of luxuries.

Vocational schools for apprentices kept going for a while. They held their classes in the evening, sometimes in total darkness and often in subzero temperature. Classes were more often dismissed than they were held. Young Gomulka was matriculated for the next three years in such a vocational school.

There were no I.Q. tests in those days and especially not in Galicia. Still, interested people learned one way or another about youngsters with special skills. So they learned about the young chap in his knickers whose name was Wlaydslaw Gomulka. He got jobs first in the shop of a mechanic, then as the apprentice of a plumber, and then of a blacksmith. Apprentices received no wages, only blows, and those were supposed to be important ingredients for their training to manhood. They got their daily rations, which were small, and a bunk in which to sleep.

Because he was such a smart fellow, Wladyslaw got other assignments, too, the most important of which was known as *hamstern*. It was simple in theory but hard in practice. The *hamsterer* went into the nearby village to induce the peasants to accept his food in exchange for such urban products as matches or an article of clothing. Being a bright fellow, from the grass-roots himself, Wladyslaw got on well with the peasants. Had any of his acquaintances been endowed with prophetic intuition he could have foreseen that the boy was destined for an important role. But who would have paid that much attention to him? Besides, one could not be destined for important roles without the Maturity Certificate of a gymnasium, the classical secondary school. Nothing ranked lower on the educational scale than the vocational school which Wladyslaw attended until he was fourteen.

Meanwhile conditions in Galicia were getting worse—food and fuel scarcer. The war had been dragging on from the beginning of time, or so it seemed to many people. Was it ever to end, or was it to last till Judgment Day? Or was it a prolonged Judgment Day itself? Much of the brunt of the fighting was borne by Galicia in a series of engagements during 1914 and 1915, which history knows as the Battles of Lemberg. The battles were between Russia and Austria-Hungary. The first series constituted the opening campaign when the Russian steam roller crunched over Austrian resistance. Lemberg had to be evacuated. The Austrians were forced to retire in the direction of Sambor, towards the fortress of Przemysl, which was forced to stand a siege. The Russians moved on along the Dniester River, in the direction of the Carpathians, which they breached. The Austrians were defeated and the Russians occupied the whole of Eastern Galicia.

In the general plan of the Central Powers, the main components of which were Germany and Austria-Hungary, the role of the armies of the latter was to engage the principal Russian forces until the German army had overwhelmed France and was free to transfer its weight to the eastern theatre.

The second series was fought some ten months later during the great Russian retreat. It started along the Dunajec and San rivers, in young Gomulka's homeland. The Russians were pushed out of Lemberg. German guns battered the Russian positions and effected a breakthrough along the Rawa-Ruska-Lemberg line. Eventually the Russians were forced to abandon their Dniester River defenses and were pushed up to Gnila Lipa and Zlota Lipa. In spite of this victory, Austria turned out to be a papier-mâché empire. The outcome of World War I was decided when the allies of Russia and of the Austro-Hungarian Monarchy swung into action. The might of Imperial Germany was of solid steel. It rolled back the front of the Russian giant. It scored resounding victories on the western front, too. Because of the new weapons, this turned out to be a war of troglodytes where countless millions lived in subterranean trenches. In the west the Germans dug themselves in on the soil of France. The French and their British allies also dug themselves into the clay and muck. Flexing their muscles the two sides became immobilized. Occasionally, one or the other of the contenders broke loose from its realm of trenches, trying to take the other side by surprise. A few hundred thousand dead young men marked the futility of the endeavor after a major engagement. The front in the west in France was not quite as fluid as in the east, in Russia. The two contenders there lay in a deadly clinch and nothing could budge them. That is why despair counseled the melancholy thought that this was the war that could not be ended at all.

But it did end. Forces from overseas—from the United

States—transfused blood into the tired veins of the West. In the east the war revealed the fatal sickness of two empires—Russia and Austria-Hungary. Behind the times by many generations, the semi-feudal anachronism called Russia could not survive its exposure to the twentieth century. The Austro-Hungarian Monarchy was no less an anachronism, a dynastic structure superimposed on the waxing national aspirations of its many minorities. Its days, too, were numbered.

Thus the paradoxical event came about—the war was lost by both contending parties, Russia and the Habsburg Monarchy. The Germans, meanwhile, had penetrated deep into the land of their Russian foes. They did not know, though, that wars were won or lost not in fights with receding phantoms, as on the Russian plains, but in campaigns against the major foes. The coalition of Britain, France, and the United States wrought the fall of the presumably invincible German empire.

THE AGE OF DISILLUSIONMENT AND OF MIRACLES

Wladyslaw Gomulka was thirteen years old when the Great War ended—not an age when one is politically conscious unless one is a Pole. The political consciousness of the boy, however, was on a higher level than that of other boys of his age. *Jeszcse Polska nie Zginela,* "Poland is not lost yet," Poles of three countries used to hum when informers were out of earshot. For well over a century there had been no Poland as a country. But there had been a Polish nation. The Polish country had been dismembered and annexed by three greedy empires—Russian, German, and Austrian. But Poland was not lost yet, and the tyrants were to learn about that when the Poles rose.

In the autumn of 1918 the three empires collapsed. One of the emperors was killed, the two others were exiled. Could there have been a more perfect set-up for the resurrection of that most gallant of all nations, Poland?

At the peace conference which was to reorganize the affairs of the world Poland was recreated. Every attempt was made to undo the injustice of the past. For generations the Poles had been subject to the wills of alien masters. Now they were the masters of millions of other nationalities, Ukrainians, Byelorussians, Lithuanians, and Germans. To make their lives easier, they were given access to the Baltic Sea. This could be done only by cutting defeated Germany into two parts, which was done. The name of the access to the sea became known as the Polish Corridor, and a corridor to tragedy it was to be.

But not at first, not when Wladyslaw Gomulka was thirteen years old, not even when he was fourteen years old. Resurrected Poland vowed to transform the fervent resolves of the starless nights into blazing realities. Not only a new country but also a new reality was to be created. The "spirit of negation," the bane of oppressed and frustrated nations, had to be made into the "spirit of creation." The policy of oppression to which the people of Gomulka had been subjected under the three emperors was to be replaced by a policy of friendly cooperation among all the citizens of a free republic. Here was a gifted nation, bursting with the energy of creation, to take the leadership in Eastern Europe and to justify the faith of those who had never despaired of its resurrection. The Messianic faith of Poland in her missionary power, of which her great poet, Adam Mickiewicz, sang, was to be the keynote of a new policy. The world was to see the emergence of a country dedicated to progress and justice, engaged in the task of making this a better globe. On the banks of the Vistula, where the old capital, Warsaw, of the new country stood, the Poles were to create a New Jerusalem.

The world-famous Polish pianist, Ignace Jan Paderewski, became the prime minister of Poland. A beloved artist at the head of a resurrected country: what could be more promising, more romantic, or more Polish? The piano virtuoso remained at the head only for months, and then romanticism reached its end. The life story of Wladyslaw Gomulka illustrated the Polish story. He was precocious, bright, and now that the war was over some means should have been found for him to continue his education. But no such means were found. He belonged to the lower classes and his father had been known as a Socialist. So Wladyslaw, a teen-ager now, continued to work as an apprentice to mechanics and plumbers in the New Jerusalem.

ON REVIENT TOUJOURS

New Poland was confronted with a set of inescapable realities. One of them was her neighbor to the east, the Soviet Union. It claimed to be Socialist, working toward the ultimate ideal of communism, the elimination of class distinction, and the good life for all in a reformed society. No sooner was the Great War over than Poland launched a Little War of her own against the Soviets. It was led by Jozef Klemens Pilsudski, a fighter for freedom in those darkest nights of the Poles before the stars came out. First it was the Russians who lost, and then it was the Poles. The West interfered and the frontiers between the two antagonists were drawn.

Young Gomulka was now old enough to follow these events in the popular press. He also learned about Poland's new role in the international constellation. The Soviets proclaimed that their ideology was to be the ultimate victor. It was based—they claimed—on social cooperation and not on individual rapacity, which, they charged, was the motivating force of "free enterprise" and capitalism.

This was a challenge to the Western world—more than that, it was an abomination of abominations. The Soviet plague had to be contained. The Russians now occupied a near-global abode, extending from Europe to the farthest reaches of Asia. Global or not, it had to be isolated, placed beyond the pale, in an ecumenical quarantine. To keep contagion away from the West, a "sanitary cordon," *cordon sanitaire,* was established. It was pivoted on Poland, the resurrected country, the New Jerusalem, out of which was to radiate the true faith of anti-Communism and free enterprise. This was the new role of new Poland in the new dispensation of the world.

And how was Poland to fare in domestic affairs? Old Poland, before her dismemberment, was the "freest" of all countries. There every member of the *szlachta,* "higher gentry," had the right to exercise the *liberum veto* in the assembly. That paralyzed the legislature, paralyzed Poland, too, and paved the way for the aggressors. In New Jerusalem there must be established a more sensible system, a party regime enabling the development of constructive political ideas without immobilizing the machinery of the state.

The legislative system of New Jerusalem was, alas, not unlike that of Old Poland. Parties were mushrooming and it looked, indeed, as if every Pole were the leader of a different political group. The French have a system like ours, too, Poles told strangers hopefully. The world was to know later that it was not a good system in France, either. In the Polish legislature, *seym,* there were thirteen major and countless minor parties. Most of them served the interests of the *szlachta* and other members of the New

Establishment. New Jerusalem began to look very much like the Old House of Iniquity.

The treatment of the minorities did not recall the pledges of the past either. About one-third of the people of the country belonged to the minorities—and that was the Polish estimate. Freedom of religion was written into the Constitution, but in real life the millions of Jews of Poland were pariahs. Yet, many Polish Jews had fought in the front lines of the contenders for freedom. The Jews of Poland were no less passionately Polish than the others. Nor should it have been forgotten that it was on top of a Judean Hill that the promise of Jerusalem had become a reality. The Polish situation after liberation was summarized by an American observer who reported that a "small group of between 50,000 and 100,000 people ruled the country, while all the others, peasants and workers, simply toiled for them, paying tribute for the right to live."

Gomulka's own countrymen—people from Galicia—came to play important roles in new Poland's history. They had a better political education in pre-war Austria than the Poles of Russia. One of these Galicians was Wincenty Witos, leader of the parliamentary Peasant Party.

Whether or not the leaders were politically educated, the country was poorly run, with its fragmented political parties, puny political Napoleons, and lack of purpose and clear-cut orientation.

On May 12, 1926, Jozef Pilsudski, Poland's hero of the Great War, entered Warsaw at the head of his troops. He swept out the old government and set up a cabinet of puppets, headed by Professor Ignacy Moscicki. A few months later Pilsudski swept out many of his own puppets and assumed the premiership. For nine years, until 1935, he was the dictator of Poland. Pilsudski introduced the "law and order" of dictatorships but accomplished little else. It was during this period and under such circumstances that Gomulka became a full-fledged Communist.

A YOUNG MAN GOES UNDERGROUND

He was then one of those whom people called the "faceless ones," human ciphers, and not individuals. The daily wage of unskilled workers was then a *zloty,* worth twenty cents, and a full working day may have lasted eighteen hours. Highly skilled workers were considered Croesuses if their daily take amounted to the equivalent of one dollar. Gomulka observed the working conditions in the New Jerusalem and found that they were no better than in the Galicia of his youth.

In the early thirties, ripples of the tidal wave that had struck the United States began to reach Poland. It was the great depression. Poland had many sizable industries: textiles in Lodz, Bialystok, and Bielsko; oil refineries around Drohobycz; important chemical and metal plants in Silesia—the "Pittsburgh region" of the country—as well as glass, ceramic, earthenware, paper, and footwear industries in various locations. The depression hit Germany, Poland's best customer, with devastating force. Exports fell behind imports. But the trade balances did not begin to reflect the condition of the people. Poland was a rich country of poor people, the richness was in her natural resources, in the quality of her people, and in the capital of the privileged few, the Establishment. The masses were poor, and it was not easy to improve one's condition. The class system being strong, fatalism was inculcated in the workers—it was divine dispensation that the poor should be always with us. How else could the rich practice the noblest of all Christian virtues—charity?

Meanwhile the Soviet Union started on its massive innovation, the *Piatiletka,* "Five-Year Plan," to transform a feudal peasant country into a Socialist industrial community. Privilege was to be dethroned, the common man enthroned. So it looked to Gomulka and many other young idealists. Their New Jerusalem was in Moscow, not in Warsaw. Gomulka was told by his country's leaders that freedom was one of the first casualties of the Five-Year Plan and that it was a Moloch demanding countless lives. He did not believe these warning words because he distrusted Poland's new leaders. He did not see Soviet Russia as a country of physical qualities but as an ideal, as the embodiment of an aspiration. He could no longer believe in the saints of the Catholic Church, but he believed in the Soviet idols—Lenin and Stalin—and he believed in the Holy Script—*Das Kapital* of Marx. He believed himself opposed to religions and yet he became a sectarian of a dogmatic creed. His rules of conduct, the party line, were laid down in the Kremlin. He, the iconoclast in other matters, never questioned them. It was good to believe in a transcendental reality.

THE POLISH COMMUNISTS

Why a Communist, and why not a Socialist, as his father? Because Pilsudski had been a Socialist and because that party was constantly on the defensive, engaged in sectarian disputations, turning its shafts against the New Jerusalem on the Moskva, instead of the feudalism of the Polish *szlachta*. Nor did Gomulka believe that the Socialists' slow-moving "inevitability of gradualness" was adapted to the needs of a swiftly moving age.

The Communist party was outlawed in Poland by the decree of one of the puppet presidents of Marshal Jozef Pilsudski, the real power behind the throne. Membership in the party was a criminal offense, punishable with years in jail. Yet, its underground membership continued to rise, from four thousand at the outset to sixteen thousand in fifteen years. Also, thousands of party members were in jail, and their number in the mid-thirties was estimated at ten thousand. Almost anybody was considered a Communist by the authorities who was overheard to express unorthodox political views. "Politicals" were detained in a number of prisons, placed strategically for maximum deterrent effect. Best known of them and most dreaded was the large camp at Bereza Kartuska, which was on the Brest-Litovsk-Baranowicze railway line, on the Jasiolda River, in Polesie Province, and in the Pripet Marshes region (today the Byelorussian part of the Soviet Union). There were many other places of detention as, for instance, in Bialystok, Kobryn, and Kowel.

The regime of the jails and camps was extremely harsh. Politicals, in many instances, were treated more harshly than common criminals. As a rule, the political convicts were forbidden to engage in conversations. When they were summoned for interrogation by the prison authorities they were ordered to face the wall. This was intended to weaken their resistance by indicating that they were not decent human beings worthy of being looked at. Particularly sophisticated methods of torture were employed in these jails and camps. The object was to turn strong men into craven slaves. The following was one of the "classical" methods.

The inmates were forbidden to go to the toilets and they were unmercifully beaten if they soiled themselves. The convicts contained themselves as long as possible. Suddenly, the warder would call them. With an apparent show of sympathy he told them: "I think it is inhuman that you should be made to hold yourselves any longer. You may now go to the toilet."

In a mad rush the detainees elbowed each other out of the way. When they were halfway to the toilet, the whistle sounded, and the official made the men stop in their tracks. "A mistake," he grinned, "you must come back."

At twenty-one Gomulka became a functionary of the secret Polish Communist party. Submerged in the underground, he lived under aliases, moving from town to town, accepting temporary jobs, installing Communist cells. Particularly deplorable were conditions in the textile city of Lodz. Gomulka's underground work established tunnels into the trade unions. Contemporary records make no mention of his name. Nor are his many aliases known. As far as the government authorities were concerned he was a "faceless" and extremely elusive organizer. Withal he was a dedicated worker, fired by an ambition which seldom failed to make its mark.

Not the world, but certain circles in Poland, gradually began to hear the name Wladyslaw Gomulka. The president of Poland was Ignacy Moscicki, who held office for thirteen years, beginning in 1926. He had been a teacher in a technical high school at Lwow, near Gomulka's native town. All Poland knew the name of President Moscicki, but only the police blotters and Communist underground leaders were familiar with the name of Gomulka. It was under the presidency of Moscicki that Gomulka was first arrested and sentenced to a long term in jail.

The year was 1931, close to the age of the Apocalyptic Monster. Adolf Hitler had scored a great electoral victory in the previous year. It was not long before he was deposited in the chancellor's office in Germany—the highest in the Reich—on the tidal wave of what appeared to be an irresistible popular movement—National Socialism. It combined two extremely potent forces—nationalism, which was the deification of the modern state, and socialism, the unification of social forces for the common weal. The world knew little of the real nature of the movement then. Nor did it know that its programmatic name, socialism, camouflaged a negative idea, opposition to constructive social forces.

Gomulka saw "national socialism"—an extreme form of fascism—not as the "wave of the future" but as the "undertow of history," an attempt to halt social progress. He emerged from the underground at a meeting of the textile workers' union in Lodz, speaking on the danger of fascism and criticizing the Moscicki government. The police officer who had been assigned to watch the proceedings ordered Gomulka to stop. He refused to do so and an altercation ensued. In the melée the officer fired a shot which hit Gomulka in the leg. Manacled, he was dragged into the house of detention. A show trial was staged and he drew a heavy sentence, four years.

So we have seen, Moscicki was the president, but the real

power was Pilsudski, whose hand was heavy on those who had their own vision of a New Jerusalem. Luckily for the prisoners, the authoritarian regime was inefficient and the accelerated program of building prisons did not move fast enough. The jails were bursting with "politicals," and many of them had to be released. Long before the expiration of his sentence Gomulka was set free.

Poles were not supposed to endanger the health of the uncontaminated world by sneaking across the "sanitary cordon," but Gomulka did precisely that. The year was 1934, and he wanted to see the grass that looked so beautifully green across the Soviet border. He reached Russia in devious ways. His view of things there was conditioned by his own sectarian Communist beliefs; all seemed beautiful to him. He would have seen in the Soviets the world's best hope even if it had been a charnel house. Certainly, it was not that for him. The *Piatiletka*—the Five-Year Plan regime—had lasted now for years, and the countryside echoed the blast of the riveters' gun. The Soviets' age of tribulation seemed to be over.

Gomulka remained in the Soviet Union for nearly two years—1934–35. What was he doing there? We will recall that the war, the circumstances of his family, and the uncertainties of the post-war era had cut short his education. He had acquired a primary and vocational school training, and had then entered the hardest of all schools: the Communist underground. His mind was keen, and he had a lot of common sense. But he was a Communist, and thus he believed that there was inspired knowledge in the "Holy Books" of Lenin and Marx. He wanted to apply himself to a methodic study of the Socialist-Communist classics. He matriculated in the International Lenin School in Moscow. This was the information revealed many years later by the *Great Soviet Encyclopaedia*.

A MARKED MAN

Gomulka decided now to return to his native land. Was he discontented with what he had seen in the New Jerusalem on the Moskva? We have no reason to make that assumption. Probably he felt that it was his duty to apply in his homeland the knowledge he had acquired on his pilgrimage. The decision to leave Russia was fortunate, for a short time after his return to Poland, the great purge of the Old Bolsheviks began in Moscow. It was undertaken by Stalin, who was thus to secure his position as the only authentic prophet of the one true Communist creed. Many were his victims among the Russians and also among transient foreign Communists.

Despite Stalin's heavy hand, the Communist movement in Poland, still underground, picked up additional strength. The great danger to the democratic world appeared to be the Fascist powers—Germany and Italy—with their mystic belief in their superiority and their violent advocacy of the dangerous and violent life. They glorified the nation as an immortal, everlasting, and absolutely sovereign entity. It seemed to many democratic countries that their exaltation of the belligerent nation was driving the world to the brink of war. To counteract their influence, some of the democratic European countries established Popular Front governments, in which all political parties, with the exception of the extreme right, participated. There could be no Popular Front in Poland, to be sure. But there was a certain measure of apprehension about the intentions of Hitler's so-called Third Reich. In the democratic world, Communists played a role in the Popular Front governments. In Poland some democratically inclined persons became more reconciled to the Communist views.

Gomulka derived advantage from this change of climate. He now had the self-confidence which his knowledge of Marx and Lenin imparted to him. He was still romantically dedicated to the cause in which he saw only what he wanted to see. He looked anything but romantic with his receding hairline and with a habitual slouch that made it seem as if he wanted to offer a very small target. He got married, too, shortly after his return to Poland. He married a fellow worker in the Communist party, a Jewess, Zofya. She was a professional statistician, we have seen, who was to work in that capacity after the war. The political police, anti-Semitic, as was the entire regime, took notice of this fact, and Gomulka was watched with greater care than before. His police dossier was waxing fatter all the time. Communists were considered more dangerous than common criminals.

Gomulka was seized now by the psychological impulse that seems to be common among people dedicated to quasi-religious causes. He wanted to become a martyr, a "witness" to the truth of his cause. Why, otherwise, did he take a prominent part in the preparation of a May Day parade in Lodz, where he was particularly well known to the police? He helped to organize the parade and he was picked up again as a dangerous Communist organizer. The year was 1936.

Pilsudski had died the previous year, but the dictatorship was not over. His mantle fell on Edward Smigly-Rydz, inspector general of the Polish army, marshal of Poland, and the most powerful man of the country until the outbreak of World War II.

This time Gomulka was sentenced to seven years. His prison was in the small textile town of Sieradz, in the province of Lodz. What was he to do in his jail university? He had to read the books that were available to him. However, nobody could forbid him to read the anti-communist propaganda books in reverse. Many of the volumes were about history, the struggle of a highly gifted nation against alien despots and then the happy end—the national resurrection at the end of World War I. Gomulka detested the heroes of Poland's contemporary history but admired the villains, the rebels. He learned that never in their history did the Poles have rulers who took a constructive interest in the masses. It was indirectly that the people were occasional recipients of some of the good things of life which percolated to them by way of the main beneficiaries, the ruling classes. Was it at all possible to have a common-man-centered regime in Poland?

Polish Communists, observing the preparations of the Fascist powers, expected war to erupt in Europe. While the Communists of Poland had only a few thousand active members, they estimated the number of sympathizers at two million.

Wars did break out, but not in Europe at first. War broke out first in the African empire of Ethiopia, where the Italian Fascists were seeking to find their place in the scorching sun. However, the Great Rehearsal for the massive attack against the "degenerate democracies" took place in Spain, where Nazis and Fascists were leagued against a left-wing government. There it was that the European right-wingers apparently wished to test the patience of the democracies. Spain was also to become the proving ground of their strategies and arms. The meek stand taken by the democracies confirmed the belief of Mussolini and Hitler that the traditional Western countries were not only degenerate but also very weak.

Polish diplomacy was handled by a "colonels' clique" headed by Jozef Beck, whom the Communists denounced as a Fascist and who, they expected, would make common cause with Hitler against the Soviet Union. As the communists interpreted the nationalist view, the Poles of the past had taken part in the West's defensive crusades against the assaults of the abominable Eastern men of Asia. It was they who had deflected the Turkish arms from the walls of Vienna in the late seventeenth century. Now the Poles were expected to march against the Soviets under the sign of the German Hitlerites' Double Cross. The Polish Communists pledged that they would rally to the aid of the universal Communist cause, even if that entailed their turning against the ruling regime of their own nation.

The prediction of Gomulka's comrades failed to hit the mark. The Nazis and the Soviets concluded a non-aggression pact late in August, 1939—a diplomatic event that stunned the world. The German Nazis turned against Poland in league with the Soviets. Their ostensible aim was to recapture the "Corridor" which had belonged to Germany before World War I and which had been assigned to the Poles after the war so as to give Poland access to the Baltic Sea.

On September 1, 1939, Hitler invaded Poland, and the war broke out. The Polish government needed the help and good will of all political views. The gates of the jails detaining the "politicals" were opened. First, Gomulka fled to Lwow. Some of the freed Communists scurried behind the shield of the Soviet lines, which now moved into Poland as had been agreed with the Nazis. What happened to them in the storm-tossed years? And what did Gomulka do?

The resistance of Poland was broken in a matter of days. The Germans occupied Warsaw and established their Government General there. Gomulka went to the Nazi-occupied Polish capital. Promptly he started to organize a Communist underground. Had he been caught this time his penalty would not have been the jail but the hangman's noose.

Meanwhile, the Russian armies had lumbered into eastern Poland, in accordance with a secret agreement between Berlin and Moscow. Hitler had made his pact with Stalin so as to neutralize and immobilize the Soviets for a time. But he was committed to destroy the Bolshevik regime. In his disturbed mind the Communist government appeared to be a Jewish plot, and it was his mission to save Western civilization from the Jews. His Third Reich absorbed the bulk of Poland. Again Poland was dismembered, as at the end of the eighteenth century.

On June 22, 1941, Hitler tore up the agreement he had

signed with the Soviets only two years before. Not since the days of Napoleon had the world seen an army as superior to its adversaries as that of the German *Wehrmacht* of Hitler. It swept across countries as if they had not been on the map. It forced the armies of *La Grande Nation,* France, into submission within a few days. Not only were the Nazi hosts incredibly swift but also they appeared to be invincible. Now they swept into Russia.

LIFE IN THE UNDERGROUND

Had Hitler heard the name of Gomulka it would have carried no meaning to him. He would have had one of his hysterical tantrums if he had been told that the balding little man would have a hand in the destruction of his presumably indestructible hosts. After his long stays in jail, meeker looking than ever, Gomulka turned against the Nazi forces almost as soon as they had crossed the Soviet frontiers. He was a past master in underground movements by now.

There was a Popular Front in the underground—Communists, Socialists, peasants, and fighters from bourgeois groups, too. Some Poles made common cause with the Germans. The underground formed partisan units behind the enemy lines. Guerrilla tactics were employed, and they worked well as long as the population was friendly. A friendly population enabled the partisans to live on the resources of the land. It also enabled them to fade into the countryside by day, continuing the work of harassing the Germans and their allies—Rumanians, Hungarians, and others—by night.

Work in the underground would thus appear not to have been too risky. But it was. The Germans had a large force to ferret out its units, and then there were the traitors among the Poles. Once a partisan member was caught, he was exposed to public view before being put through a fearful ordeal. Torture was preliminary to death. Slowly the partisan was prepared for his end on the gallows or sometimes at the burning stake.

Gomulka was now in the front ranks of the Polish fighters for freedom. He had no doubt as to what would happen to him in case he was caught. In 1942 he became the secretary of the Warsaw group of the Polish Workers' Party. The first secretary of the national group was Marceli Nowotko, the chief party organizer. The Germans did not get him. But he was killed in an engagement between them and a partisan unit. Second in command was Pawel Finder, and the leadership in the national group devolved upon him. He was captured by the Nazis. An official comunique revealed that he had been meted out an "exemplary punishment." We can image what it was. The third person in line was Wladyslaw Gomulka. There was no question that even after these antecedents he would accept the leadership of the party. In 1943 he became the secretary of the Central Committee of the Polish Workers' Party. He was now the No. 1 candidate for death at Nazi hands. But they did not kill him. He retained his party post until 1949.

He was in grave peril, though, many times. Once he was in especially great danger because fellow Poles working for the Nazis found that his unit sheltered a Jew. Renegade Poles were given rewards by the Germans for finding "escaped" Jews. In the insane scale of values of those days there was no greater service than helping the Nazis capture Jews who were working in the underground. Then one day Polish "Jew catchers" pounced upon Gomulka's unit. This could have been the end of the entire unit, but luckily the Jew catchers were as venal as they were cruel; a ransom of two hundred *zlotys* saved many human lives.

The Nazis called the Poles *oestliche Untermenschen,* "Eastern subhumans." This in spite of the fact that many Poles had blond hair and blue eyes. Light coloring is more prevalent among the Poles, who are northern Slavs, than among the Germans. In line with their distorted values the Germans exacted the lives of many Poles for the loss of one German. On one occasion they executed fifty Poles for the death of one of their own kind. Gomulka had learned in his jails and in the underground to act with deliberation. Shortly after the execution of the fifty Poles he came across a casino of German officers. He could not restrain himself on that occasion. His unit was short of arms, especially of hand grenades, and their use had to be rationed. This time he decided to sacrifice one of the precious grenades.

For a long time it seemed that nothing could halt the Nazi juggernaut. But Hitler committed the great mistake of arrogance. He was so convinced that the Slavs, especially the Soviets, were inferior that he overlooked the signals warning him of danger. He overextended himself. Racing eastward, his forces reached Russia's River of Sorrow, the Volga. It was there that his war machine was forced to halt at the end of 1942 in the Battle of

Stalingrad. Not only was Hitler's armor halted, it was forced to retreat. Unaccustomed to see the "invincible" Germans retreat, it took some time before the Soviets began to gain self-confidence and to hit their stride. Although the Germans contested every inch of the way, they could no longer hold their own. The strength did not go out of their steel, but the magic of invincibility was gone. Elsewhere on the global battle front, too, the Axis armies were forced into retreat.

THE BATTLE OF THE TWO POLANDS

The Poland which Gomulka represented was actually only one of the two countries by that name. The armed forces of his underground comprised some 20,000 fighters. There was another Poland, with about 200,000 men under arms. That was Poland in exile, the armed force of which operated in the open. The Polish army corps, under General Wladyslaw Anders, distinguished itself in the Italian campaigns, at Ancona and at Monte Cassino. In the Battle of Britain, every seventh German plane was destroyed by a Polish airman. Polish land, sea, and air forces fought in the campaigns of France and Norway, in the Netherlands, in Belgium, in the Normandy invasion, in Italy, and in North Africa.

The Western Allies recognized a Polish government in-exile, the president of which was the former head of the Senate, Wladyslaw Rackiewicz and the premier of which was Wladyslaw Sikorski. "The old gang," Gomulka commented.

Meanwhile the incredible was taking place: the German superarmies continued to be pushed out of the Soviet Union. The retreating Nazi divisions reached Poland, and the world expected that there they would make a halt. They tried to do so, tried very hard, but the intention and the implementation were far apart. As the Soviets were approaching Warsaw, an anti-German uprising broke out inside that city on August 1, 1944. Gomulka established contact with the Russians on his way to eastern Poland. Then, one day, he turned up behind the Soviet lines. The Russians did not give any help to the Warsaw freedom fighters. What was the reason of their inaction? Was it because the insurrection had occurred at the behest of the Polish government that was recognized by the Western Allies?

The Polish government-in-exile was situated in London.

In December, 1944, another government was formed in the Polish city of Lublin, and in this one the Communists played the leading part. The ring around the beleaguered Germans was to close; the war was approaching its end. Gomulka was appointed deputy premier in the Lublin government. The premier was a Socialist, Edward Osobka-Morawski. The real powers in the government were two Moscow-trained Communists, Boleslaw Bierut, president of the National Council, and Jakub Berman, undersecretary of state. The Soviets recognized the Polish Government of National Liberation on January 5, 1945. The Poles had two governments now, one in England and the other one in Poland. Eventually, the Western powers withdrew recognition from the Western cabinet and extended it to the one in Poland, which now moved to Warsaw. In 1945 Gomulka became the minister for the recovered territories and also secretary-general of the Polish United Workers' Party. He held his jobs until 1949.

THE WESTERN AREAS

What were these Western areas of which Gomulka became the minister?

They included the territory which the Poles had obtained from the Germans after World War I. Far beyond that the Soviets helped the Poles to acquire German territory up to the Oder and Neisse rivers, territories which had belonged to German States and the Reich for many centuries. The Poles say that originally these had been lands occupied by their kin, the Slavs. These western territories contained millions of Germans, most of whom had turned toward the West, seeking sanctuary in defeated Germany.

The Soviets gave these German lands to the Poles in compensation for the territories they took from them. They took the eastern peripheral regions, inhabited mainly by Ukrainians and Byelorussians, which they then attached to their own two component republics known by those names. The Western Allies stipulated that the final decision about the Western areas of Poland should be made at the peace conference.

A high degree of organizational talent was needed to fill the gap left by the German emigrants. Gomulka had to install an entirely new administrative system. In addition to his works as minister for recovered territories, he retained his post as secretary of the Central Committee of the Polish Workers' Party, a top post in the Communist hierarchy. Not only that, Gomulka became the principal organizer of the Communist Information Bureau, which the world was to know as the Cominform. Three such posts for one man indicated not only the recognition of his almost inexhaustible energy but also that there was a shortage of talent in the highest echelons of the Communists.

PROLETARIANS OF ALL COUNTRIES,
EXCHANGE EXPERIENCES!

The Soviets set up satellite regimes as they were pushing into Europe. It seems that there was a master plan for this operation. Between the two world wars the people of the region of the Eastern Belt—"sanitary cordon"—were infused with a strong feeling against communism. The Communists were described to them as an inferior and dangerous breed. Dangerous they may have been, but they were certainly not inferior in beating the German "supermen." As the Soviets swept into Eastern Europe the people of that area stood aghast.

The Soviets were supposed to assist the people of this region to establish democratic forms of government through free elections. They did nothing of the kind. They wanted to turn the area into a field of their operations—a shield, perhaps, against attack from the West, or perhaps a proving ground of communism. At any rate it was to be a "glacis." They wanted these countries to be run by Communists, but they had to reckon with the bias of the population. Communism was an evil system in the people's eyes.

That is why communist regimes were established under various front names, such as the "Polish Workers' Party." On paper, these governments represented coalitions of Communists and non-Communists, though never of anti-Communists. The Communists, being more unscrupulous, better organized, and highly dedicated were eventually to run the show. This happened in the Eastern Belt, all the way from Poland to Bulgaria in the east and Albania in the south. The Soviets controlled this area through "fraternal advice" and also through interlocking directorates in a number of economic ventures. They controlled it also through their armed forces. But they wanted an additional link with the satellites, and the forging of the new link was the task of Gomulka as the head of Cominform.

The proclaimed aim of this organization was to "organize and exchange experience and, in case of necessity, to coordinate the activities of the Communist parties on the basis of mutual agreements."

In the interbellum period there had been a Communist International, Comintern, known also as the Moscow, or the Third, International, a representative body of the Communists of all countries. It attempted to formulate a single policy for the dissemination of Communist ideology and, presumably, for other unavowed purposes. That International had policy-making authority. Stalin dissolved it in the middle of the war so as to create a better working atmosphere with the Western Allies.

It was Gomulka who called a meeting in Warsaw in September, 1947, to launch the new organization. Besides the representatives of the satellites, he also invited those of the two largest Communist parties of the non-Communist world, Italy and France. The Cominform was to meet periodically to discuss matters and to exchange information. It had no policy-making authority. "At first largely directed against the Marshall Plan [for the economic aid of European countries, launched by the United States] the Cominform was established . . . not only to advance the international Communist movement through a close coordination of international policy and tactics but also to insure more complete control by the Soviet Union over the international affairs of other Communist countries."

At the time, Stalin was at the crest of his fame, the great leader of the Communist world, the "father of victory." The idea of the Cominform must have been conceived in the Kremlin and the invitation to Gomulka to set the machinery into motion must have originated there, too. Therefore he must have been *persona gratissima* to the Kremlin at the time.

THE DEAD DO NOT STIR

The Cominform was pronounced dead a year later. What brought about its premature demise? The reasons were given in 3,000 searing words which the Kremlin issued. Communism had been alive as long as it was monolithic, a creed with its dogmas, rituals, and holy books. Now however it was rent apart by a force the existence of which the world had not suspected.

The 3,000 words from the Kremlin dealt with Yugoslavia's Marshal Tito and the Communist party of that country. Tolling like a death knell each sentence of the document was expected to strike the true believer with awe. And these were some of the words:

The Titoist regime "followed a hateful policy toward the Soviet Union." It tended to identify the Kremlin line with that of the "imperialistic powers." It treated Russia "in the same manner the bourgeois states were treated." The leaders in Belgrade had "departed from the Marxist theory of class struggle, particularly in relation to the peasants." Therefore, the Yugoslav party had placed itself outside the Communist faith.

This was excommunication and that meant death. If the heretic no longer believed in the Kremlin creed, what was the purpose of his life? Dedication to his cause had been his purpose, and now he found himself in the midst of a vast vacuum, cut off from the hopes and consolations of his faith. Communism was an international movement under the fraternal shield of the Kremlin, maintained Stalin, the official interpreter of the creed. Titoism, on the other hand, was neither international nor fraternal. It was a national heresy which could not be tolerated in the bosom of the Holy Kremlin Church. Its name was anathema, even a decent burial to be denied to it, its wicked bones to lie in an ideological potter's field.

Stunned by this unprecedented development, the world looked around. Was this the beginning of a movement of Reformation within the Third Rome—Moscow? Was Tito the Luther of the movement? There had been only one Christian Church before Luther, but many national Churches after him. This seemed to be the way of all religious movements of the Western world— monolithic at first, and then polymorphic. This could have been the end of the worldwide Communist movement, whose leader closed his eyes to the world of realities. The world of realities consisted of nations and not of nebulous concepts of internationalism. The Soviet Union itself was not merely a nation but a supernation concerned about its national interest. Its fraternal solicitude for the other Communist countries was no more than the manifestation of imperialism. Titoism was thus to clear the air and show the new way to communism. Was the Kremlin going to be able to halt the trend to nationalism—if it turned out to be a trend—or was national heresy to prevail?

Communism was Gomulka's line of thought. But he be-believed that the Communist thought could be most effectively conveyed to the Poles in their own idoms. The history, traditions, folklore, and folkways of each country determined its political ideology. The coexistence which the Kremlin had begun to preach —capitalism and communism living together—should be applied also to the relation of Communists among themselves. The Soviets had accumulated a vast stockpile of experience as to how to construct the framework of socialism, but it was their own experience. The "fraternal countries" derived great benefit from learning about the Soviets' ways. But they would have to devise their own method of molding conditions into forms which could accommodate the party ideology. This is how Gomulka was consigned to his political grave.

Gomulka, even though a dedicated Communist, was too much of a Pole to ignore his people's history. He was well-read in it even before his long entombment. While under detention he had had ample time to become acquainted with all the details of Polish history. As the top man of the Polish Workers' Party he gave much attention to the twists and turns of mob psychology. Some of the statements he made in his philosophical meditations brought to mind the works of Gustave Le Bon, the French sociologist, and especially his book *La Psychologie des Foules.* That book explained how fruitless it was to ignore the ebbs and tides of popular opinion even in dictatorships. The best leader of the people was the man who knew how to be guided by the deep-seated intuitive forces of the masses. Gomulka knew that communism in Poland was one thing and that Russianism was another. No other country had fought the Russians as bitterly as the Poles. Communism itself would be jeopardized if the Soviets' "fraternal care" were to engulf the Poles.

These nationalistic heresies were often implied by Gomulka, though not articulated at any time. Stalin had the primitive's intuition; he also had direct information, so he knew where Gomulka stood. "Gomulka is building a wall of mistrust between Poland and the Soviet Union," wrote the *Nowe Drogi,* "New Ways," of Warsaw. This accustation was repeated in many ways. Had Gomulka been directly under Stalin's thumb he would certainly have been the accused in a show trial. In the satellite countries, too, the witchhunt was on, and many leading Communists were accused and convicted of "Titoism." Gomulka, however, was not tried; he was merely entombed and embalmed.

Some of Gomulka's close associates were detained and tried,

and among these was the former deputy minister of the recovered areas, Jozef Dubiel, who had "confessed" to having been a Gestapo agent. The former deputy minister of national defense, Marian Spychalski, and the former chairman of the parliamentary group of the Communist party, Z. Kliszko, were also taken into custody. Dark days fell upon Poland.

"We live like miserable wretches," said a letter of a Lodz textile worker smuggled in those days to a French Socialist newspaper, *Le Populaire*, "driven by the Communist party to produce ever greater norms for lower pay and worse treatment. . . . Our trade unions fail to protect us. On the contrary they are against us, the workers. Strikes are considered acts of sabotage and are forbidden. . . . People advocating strikes are subject to penalties meted out to common criminals. . . . We are ringed around by informers picking up rash words uttered in fits of bitterness. One word and the poor wretch goes to a forced labor camp."

AUSCHWITZ AND AFTER

About forty miles southwest of Poland's old coronation town, Cracow, there is a unique museum. It is the museum of a small town that saw the extermination of more people than any other place, not only in modern times, but at any time. The massacres of Attila and Genghis Khan were puny in comparison with the record of this town. The town is called Oswiecim (it was Auschwitz under German rule), and the unique museum was erected in the shadow of the five chimneys that witnessed the extermination of millions of Jews. These acts were perpetrated during World War II. There are exhibited countless broken shoes of men, women, and children in this museum, also shoes of babies. These belonged to the victims. The visitor sees mountains of decaying toothbrushes and of eyeglass frames. The Nazis had removed the good shoes and toothbrushes, and extracted the glasses from the frames.

No less macabre is the museum's filing room. It contains the documents the Nazis drew up about their victims with the dependable thoroughness for which Prussian bureaucracy was known. With that incredible cynicism which was their hallmark they coined a bizarre word for their genocide: *Entwesungskammer,* "Desubstantiation chamber." They never said "gas chamber."

The war over, only a few thousand of the millions of Jews returned to Poland. The Poles themselves were made to suffer so

much during the war that they could have been expected to understand the tragedy of the Jews. Yet, during the years of Gomulka's
detention, anti-Semitism again stalked in Poland, not in the darkness of the night, but in broad daylight. These were the years of
the Stalinist paroxysm.

Toward the end of his regime Stalin indulged in anti-
Semitism. The causes—if any—of this strange anomaly have never
been investigated. The Nazis had denounced communism as a Jewish monstrosity. Jews had played important roles in the early years
of communism. Under the Czarist regime theirs was a sad life.
They were the scapegoats, besides being the outsiders in a national
community which was closely linked to the Greek Orthodox faith.
Some of Stalin's early collaborators were Jews.

He had turned against his early collaborators before World
War II. The field was to be his and nobody else's. During the war
he noted that the virus of anti-Semitism found a fertile soil in
Russia—an atavistic trait. After the war he seemed to be ready to
increase his own popularity by riding the hobby horse of anti-
Semitism. If Stalinist dogma contained a dash of anti-Jewish sentiment, the Polish Stalinists did not want to fall behind. And it was
the paradox of paradoxes that some of them were of Jewish birth,
although not professing any religion. Anti-Semitism in Poland
assumed virulent forms; street attacks on the Jews, loss of jobs,
pressures to move out of certain neighborhoods, bullying children
in the schools. Periodically, anti-Semitism erupted into flash po-
groms in which people were insulted and beaten. The small band
of Jews in Poland saw itself endangered.

Three waves of anti-Semitism struck the country while
Gomulka was under house arrest. The first of these was launched
in 1951–52, when people of Jewish origin were ousted from the
higher party apparatus. The second wave struck during the period
of 1954–55, when many people of Jewish origin were ejected from
the armed forces. The third wave removed many Jews from the
Polish United Workers' Party (*Polska Zjednoczona Partia Robot-
nicza*—the Communist party reformed in 1948 as a result of the
merger of the Polish Workers' Party and Polish Socialist Party).
The party workers known as "activists" undertook the actual work
of purification. They were instructed to probe into the family
background of their comrades. The Jews who fell under the axe
were denounced as "cosmopolitans," people who saw the world,
evidently, not from the parochial Communist point of view. This

period coincided with the outbreak of virulent anti-Semitism not only in the Soviet Union, but also in Czechoslovakia, another Polish neighbor.

The entire Jewish community felt the heavy hand of the purifiers. The Central Committee of Polish Jews was liquidated and its successor, the Cultural and Social Union of Polish Jews, was placed directly under Communist party control. The bulk of its activities was devoted to participation in so-called peace programs and to combating "Zionist fascism" in Israel. "Non-productive elements" in the Jewish community were the special peeve of H. Smoliar, chairman of this allegedly Jewish body.

Only the Communist *Folksztyme*, a Yiddish newspaper, was tolerated. Under the auspices of the Cultural and Social Union, the *Yiddische Szriften*, a "literary and art" monthly magazine was published. The All-Polish Union of Writers inherited the functions of the Jewish Historical Institute of Warsaw. Jewish schools of traditional learning were wiped out, while religious education was denounced as the hotbed of Zionist heresy. Parents were made to send their children to national schools where not only full-fledged communism but also anti-Semitism was their fare. Some Jews had been enabled to leave the country for Israel. Finally, in the spring of 1951, migration of the Polish Jews to Israel was all but stopped. Indeed, people who entertained the idea of going to that country fell under a dark shadow.

At the same time the attacks of the "extreme right of the extreme left" upon the Jews assumed larger proportions. The trouble this time appeared to be that the Jew was too efficient. It was also bad that many Jewish cooperatives were better organized than others, that many Jews were working harder, and that a few were even more prosperous.

Anti-Semitic violence again erupted into the streets. The government attempted to hush up the incidents and therefore the record is sketchy. There was an ugly outbreak of violence in the town of Kielce already in the early days of the Communist regime. The details of this were made available much later to Polish emigre newspapers in France.

An even more dangerous outbreak occurred in Lower Silesia, where the largest number of Jews had settled. Previously, this area had belonged to Germany. The trouble erupted in the town formerly called Waldenburg, renamed Walbrzych, of about 73,000 inhabitants. A Jewish butcher in Waldenburg, according to sketchy reports, engaged in an altercation with a gentile miner. The latter alerted the people of the town, and soon a mob congregated in front of the butcher's house. It was bent on lynching. The butcher barricaded himself. The town police, who had heard the commotion, observed the scene with relish. Thwarted in "getting" the butcher, the mob moved on in search of other Jews. The alarmed would-be victims summoned the police of the neighboring towns, but they joined their local colleagues as interested viewers. Finally, the police of the capital of the *powait,* "county," of Breslau—now Wroclaw—had to be summoned to put an end to the violence.

A FELLOW PRISONER, CARDINAL WYSZINSKI

Not only Communists suspected of the "nationalist heresy" and Jews were affected by the Polish wing of the Stalinist reign of terror. About three-fourths of the population is Roman Catholic. Many of Poland's prominent Catholics were among the victims. The Warsaw government, in Gomulka's absence, concentrated its most venomous attacks on Cardinal Stefan Wyszynski, archbishop of Gniezno and of Warsaw, Primate of Poland, and head of the Polish Catholic hierarchy. The Cardinal protested against the "tendentious, malicious, and untruthful accusations" against his clergy. The "dialogue" between the party and the clergy continued, but it was more a monologue. Edward Ochab, a ranking Communist, accused the Cardinal of "double-dealing." Said Ochab: "This double-dealing is especially obvious in a domain of such importance for our nation and world peace as that of our recovered territories and the Oder-Neisse line." After this exchange of words the Cardinal was arrested and detained in a monastery.

The Polish government declared war on the Church on many fronts. Warsaw forbade church nominees to assume their posts. For alleged wartime collaboration with the Nazis the Bishop of Kielce was sentenced to twelve years in jail. A priest was condemned to death and others to long prison terms for acting "as agents of the American intelligence service." Witnesses were produced to charge that Popes Pius XI and XII had been pro-German and that the former primate of Poland, Cardinal Hlond, had been a man "without a nationality." To top off all these accusations, the government charged the Vatican with refusing to recognize Poland's western frontier, thus promoting "expansionist" West German claims.

The *modus vivendi* observed by Church and State during the Gomulka regime was no longer observed. Religious instruction was dropped in schools. The Committee of Patriotic Priests was formed to stand by the Communist regime in its fight on the Church. Another Communist front was the Committee of Catholic Intellectuals. What the Warsaw government wanted was to foster a Catholic schism.

THE RIOTS AND ITS SEQUEL

Then came Khrushchev's famous "secret" speech which was heard around the world. No longer was Stalin the universal genius, the father of his country, the father image of all "right-thinking people," and the *Vozhd*—"Leader." The dead man turned out to be a senile and bloody tyrant. This historic denunciation ended the Age of Stalin and introduced the Age of Recanting. Was this the signal for a new phase in the Communist world—the Age of Humanism? Khrushchev's speech received that interpretation among many Poles. And thus Gomulka's name was restored to the list of living people.

We saw in a previous chapter how the rebellion erupted in Poznan—Posen under Germany's rule—an industrial city with an articulate industrial-worker population. Clamoring for bread and freedom, some 50,000 people assembled. Such an event could not have taken place in the shadow of Stalin's terror. Had Khrushchev made a fatal mistake in conceding the crimes of the past and opening the floodgates of discontent? History has not yet rendered the verdict on that event.

The Russian armed forces, maintained for the "security of Poland," should be withdrawn, the workers demanded. Polish armed forces had been placed under the command of the Soviets' Marshal Konstantin K. Rokossovski, a wartime hero, born on Polish territory of what had been imperial pre-World War I Russian soil. He was marshal of the Polish armed forces and minister of defense in the Warsaw cabinet. The workers demanded his removal.

For a long time the demonstrators and the security forces glared at one another. Then the street battle erupted. Shots were fired; fifty people were killed and hundreds injured. The Poznan battle appeared to have been the signal for a nationwide revolt.

What was the Soviet Union to do now? The revolt of the Poles might have started a series of revolutions in the Communist satellite world. Should the masses prevail against their Soviet masters what would be the consequence of these events in the Soviet Union itself? Were the omens favorable for a global rebellion against the Kremlin? The decision the Soviets made would be of historic import.

Soviet troops stationed in Poland began to move on Warsaw, set to proceed from there to Poznan and other danger spots. A blood bath between the Poles and Russians seemed inevitable. It was the turn of the Poles to act. They would listen to one man and one man only, and his name was Gomulka. But that man was dead and buried in a Warsaw suburb. No Polish newspaper had dared to mention his name. He could be resurrected, though, by popular will, because physically he was alive. Wladyslaw Gomulka had become more charismatic in his detention; he had acquired that professorial owlish look on his bland face and that quizzical look that appeared to probe motives.

But he could not be resurrected because the very term, "Gomulkism," carried the connotation of the most unspeakable of all heresies, the nationalist deviation. That was precisely the deviation the Poles craved. They wanted to regain their own personality, the national personality of the Poles. Gomulka was their man.

There were other reasons why he was their man and had to become the man of the Communist leadership, too. He was known as a man of extraordinary managerial ability, with a well-organized mind, and a fabulous knowledge of pertinent facts. He had an eye for effective co-workers, too. Gomulka was a martyr who had offered his freedom for the cause in which he believed. But above all, he was the product of the Polish soil, a Pole of the Poles.

The Central Committee of the Polish United Workers' Party remained in session for a long time. It was to decide if the heresy of yesterday was to become the party line of today. There was much heart-searching, because the top Communists realized the import of their decision. They foresaw the possible consequence of the appearance of Russian tanks on Warsaw streets. They dreaded the consequence of a Polish uprising for themselves, for their cause, and for the entire world. There were seventy-five members in the Central Committee. Some of them were Stalinists, while others were against the dead despot's tyrannical policies.

Edward Ochab spoke up, a member of the top echelon, and he urged his comrades to reinstate Gomulka. That was also the line of Jozef Cyrankiewicz, former secretary-general of the PPS, Polish Socialist Party, and prime minister since 1947; of Wladyslaw Bienkowski, a noted writer who was to become minister of education; of Stefan Jedrychowski, member of the Politburo, who was to become minister for national economy; and of others.

Among those who voted there were foes of Gomulka, as, for instance Franciszek Jozwiak, leader of the pro-Moscow group. It was called the Natolin Group because of a meeting the Stalinists had held on October, 1956, in the mansion of the historic Branski family in Natolin, near Warsaw. Among several other members of the Natolin Group were Jakub Berman, boss of the police, and Hilary Minc, the economic czar at that time. On this vital occasion, however, they had to set aside their partisan views and to think in terms of all the Poles. With the exception of one vote— which may have been that of Berman or Minc—all of the participants voted for the reinstatement of Wladyslaw Gomulka.

GOMULKA'S RETURN

He did not cover the short distance from the Warsaw suburb as a conquering hero, nor as a "thief in the night." Wladyslaw Gomulka became the first secretary-general of the Central Committee of the Polish United Workers' Party.

The following year, in January, 1957, national elections took place. Gomulka spoke earnestly to his people: "If you cross the names of Communist candidates off the election lists, you may be crossing Poland off the map of Europe." The majority of his people understood him, and the Polish United Workers' Party got 51 per cent of the votes. The ZSI, United Peasants' Party, received about a quarter of the votes. The Catholic Parliamentary Club elected seven deputies. Voters could cross off any name on the official lists. The elected deputies formed the National Unity Front which, in turn, was controlled by the Polish United Workers' Party. This arrangement took Poland as close to democracy as any satellite country could get.

Gomulka was no less a Communist now than he had been before his detention. Now, however, when he spoke to the Soviets they listened to him. It was he who laid down the conditions that were posed by the Poles through their government. Soviet troops were to be withdrawn from the capital forthwith, and their numbers, locations, and movements in Poland were to be circumscribed. Also it was Moscow and not Warsaw that was to bear the cost of maintaining these troops. The Polish government was free to accept economic aid from the West. The United States became a large contributor. Subject to certain reservations, the Poles were free to arrange their internal affairs.

Gomulka's position was not easy even after his rehabilitation. The Natolin Group had hoped that there would be a Stalin II in the Kremlin. It held that the only language the "imperialists" understood was that of the mailed fist and that Khrushchev's "soft line" was a betrayal of party policy. Several Stalinist members retained their posts in the policy-making committees. Gomulka's own policy spelled out compromise.

A PERIOD OF CHANGE

Educated Poles are *moqueurs,* and many others are grumblers. So they began to mock their government and to grumble. This showed that they were reasonably satisfied with it. Mocking and grumbling are functions of Poland's location in the most dangerous spot of the world, between the Russians and Germans, who, in turn, are the most dangerous people of our globe. The jokes the Poles cracked about their own government were without number.

In the "inter-Gomulka" period grumbling was considered a criminal offense. In those days paeans had to be intoned in honor of the Kremlin's Superman. The official line was simplicity itself: there could be no better place than the hunger-ridden area of the Polish plains. Now, however, under the Gomulka era, criticism reached into the innermost sanctuaries of the Communist party as, for instance, in the columns of the super-audacious *Po Prostu,* "Off the Cuff," which was not only that but off-with-the-gloves. Gomulka did not mind it at first, because he knew his own countrymen and they knew him. He acted only when the criticism became too violent.

Under the Gomulka regime the Soviets' Marshal Rokossovski was relieved of his command, which was entrusted to Marian Spychalski, one of Gomulka's closest associates, who also had been

imprisoned by the UB (*Urzad Bezpieczentswa*), the political police of the Stalinist era, spending six years in jails. Now Spychalski
became Poland's minister of defense.

Poland continued to be a member of the "Warsaw Pact," a
mutual assistance agreement among the Soviets and its satellites.
It was designed to be a counterpart of the North Atlantic Treaty
Organization of the Western world, with this significant difference:
While NATO was a voluntary association, the Warsaw Pact was not.
It provided the Soviets with the legal handle to employ its armed
forces for the crushing of national uprisings, as it did shortly after
Poznan in Hungary.

Anti-Semitism either went underground or faded away under the Gomulka regime. He could not stand for such nonsense,
especially in view of the fact that he had a Jewish wife.

Gomulka also made his peace with the Catholic Church.
The primate of the Church was still the same Cardinal Wyszynski
who had been arrested by the Polish Stalinists in 1953, and had
remained under arrest for three years. He was released about the
same time Gomulka regained his freedom. The Cardinal and the
Communist represented two diametrically opposed ideologies. Yet,
they understood the need of reaching a *modus vivendi*.

The agreement between the Catholic Church and the Polish
government was reached in December, 1956. By the terms of the
agreement, religious instruction could again be given in the schools
on a voluntary basis. The State was not to interfere with the religious lives of the people. An agreement was reached also about
the installation of bishops who had been kept from their sees by
the Stalinist regime.

Gomulka turned to the United States for food and financial
aid for his people. This was the beginning of a detente between
the hostile blocs of East and West and, at the same time, the admission of the economic failure of the previous regime. Would
Gomulka's Poland become a buffer state or a bridge between the
two worlds of clashing ideologies? Poland suggested a bold plan
to encourage a relaxed attitude.

Poland's minister of foreign affairs, Adam Rapacki, came
forth with the plan on February 14, 1958. Under it a nuclear-free
zone was to be established in the most inflammable region of Europe. The area was to include Poland, Czechoslovakia, and the two
Germanies—the Federal Republic and the so-called "German

Democratic Republic" of the Communists. This plan, however, was not acceptable to the Western bloc, which was apprehensive that this was a way by which the Communists would penetrate into Germany and the democratic West.

THE PROBLEMS OF LAND AND INDUSTRY

In the past Poland was a peasant country. It is no longer basically that; her land produces only one-quarter of the total national income. Although the Polish peasant may have observed that the big farm-machines were more efficient than the plow, he wanted to have nothing to do with the Soviet-type collective, the *kolkhoz*. The Stalinists had been pushing collectivization, though, while Gomulka was "dead." When he regained power he undertook one of the most revolutionary reform movements in the satellite world. He let the peasants repossess their individual holdings. Never had the Polish world seen such a stampede. Within a short time the collectives covered only 1 per cent of the farm area. Twelve per cent was devoted to State farms.

Communism equals planned economy, which is presumed to perform better than the fragmented efforts of individuals. Post-World War II Poland had large industries, many of them taken over from the Germans. Poland's Silesia has long been considered Eastern Europe's "Pittsburgh," a concentrated industrial region. In this respect, too, the Age of Gomulka inaugurated innovations. The government continued to control industrial production, about 90 per cent of the total. Investments continued to be concentrated in the heavy industries, which grew by about 31 per cent in the first three years of the 1961–65 plan, compared with 17 per cent for consumer goods. Like most of Eastern Europe's Communist-ruled countries, Poland was spending a staggering 20 to 30 per cent of her national income every year in a headlong rush to industrialization.

But Gomulka's Poland had about a quarter of a million artisans and industrial workers, either self-employed or hired by small entrepreneurs. Gomulka also gave a start to some eighteen thousand retail establishments. Not only that, but this "capitalist sector" of a Communist country received financial aid from the government. It was reported that small-scale fortunes were in the making in Poland. On the other hand, Gomulka tried to keep the capitalist sector under restraint by imposing higher taxes. Some people suggested that Polish private enterprise was fattened for the public slaughterhouse.

THE CHAINED AND THE UNCHAINED

What did Gomulka look like after his long detention? How did he live? How did he appear to his people?

Unlike many ex-prisoners who had risen to power, Gomulka continued to live very modestly. He occupied neither a mansion nor a former presidential palace. While he was under detention, his wife lived in a four-room flat in the Warsaw suburb of Praga, on the right bank of the river Vistula. The house is a unit of a workers' colony built in 1946. Gomulka moved into that apartment after his release.

His days were well organized. Early in the morning he went to the swimming pool in Warsaw's Palace of Culture. He was a passionate swimmer. At the stroke of nine he was at his desk in the massive building of the Central Committee of the Polish United Workers' Party. At twelve he returned to his flat for lunch. Back to work again in the afternoon.

In the evening he read reports and engaged in his studies concerning Poland's problems. He also read Polish and Soviet newspapers. Often he wrote directives, to be given to other party and government officials. His wife did much of the research, and Gomulka wrote his own speeches.

Gomulka and his wife were often seen in a nearby park. They were accompanied by a St. Bernard dog, their only body-guard. They liked to spend their vacations in the Carpathian mountain health resort, Krynica. They lead the lives of the small bourgeoisie.

Even before his detention Gomulka was soft-spoken, and after it he seemed to be even mellower. He learned to brake his habit of occasional temper tantrums, keeping himself under tighter control. It was not his way to act the part of the masses' darling, of the spellbinder. He appeared to be a teacher instructing a class of mature people—a graduate class. And it was not for him to talk down to his audiences. If some people failed to understand him, he believed that they should make an effort to do so.

There was probably no other Communist leader employing the public address technique of Gomulka. Many of them speak in generalities, quoting "party lines," the "correct approach," the application of "Marxist-Leninist science." Gomulka presented facts, lining them up in endless arrays. Here is a specimen, from a speech at a meeting of miners in Katowice, held on December 3, 1960:

"The prospects for the development of the whole national economy depend to a great extent on a speedy growth of coal production and increased investments in mining. According to the provisions of the Five-Year Plan, by 1956 the mining industry is to extract 113,000,000 tons of hard coal and 27,000,000 tons of lignite. Thus, in relation to this year, we have planned to mine 9,500,000 tons more of hard coal and 18,000,000 tons more lignite than in 1965. The average daily output of hard coal should reach. . . ." .and so on, facts, figures, more facts and figures.

In his speech to the Eighth Plenary Session of the Central Committee, shortly after his liberation, Gomulka spoke for nearly three hours, covering such subjects as the "management of industry and material incentives," the "varied forms of cooperation to the road of socialism in the countryside," and also on political questions and international relations. It was interesting to observe the people listening to him.

One would think that his audiences were bored listening to the enumeration of so many facts and figures. But they did not convey that impression. Gomulka himself seemed to be so absorbed in the enumeration of the facts and to attach so much importance to them that his audiences appeared to be carried away by his own absorption in what otherwise would strike the outsider as a scholarly dissertation fit to be reproduced in some esoteric publication meant for specialists. The deep impression of sincerity Gomulka conveyed helped to create the mood of his audience.

In his many addresses Gomulka never made any reference to his detention. He continued to be a dedicated Communist— more dedicated than before, if that were possible. Just because fellow Communists had treated him so viciously he did not turn against the creed that belonged to all of them. Many of his former enemies were readmitted into the higher echelons of the party and to top government positions. Nor was Gomulka ready to concede in any of his public utterances that it was his own comrades who had imposed indignity upon him. He could not concede that it was in the nature of Communists.

In the beginning there was Soviet communism, the Norm and the Guide. Then there was Yugoslavia's Titoism, the "Heresy," decried as such by the Kremlin. Later, the Kremlin was forced to accept it, thereby paving the way to the establishment of new sects. Maoism emerged next in China, in the guise of the Counter-Reformation, some Russians said, *plus Pape comme le Pape*. Tiny Albania's Hoxaism was attached to the Chinese dragon's tail. Then there was the Gomulkism of Poland. Unlike Tito who enunciated a new faith, Gomulka could not afford either to make a reference to his own sect or to stress its significance. He acted upon the belief, however, that both history and traditions were character-forming factors in the lives of nations. Poland's tragic history and traditions called for recognition in the implementation of the solutions of national problems. Geography, too, was a historic fact, Poland's location between the East and West. According to Gomulka, the Poles had been the tools of aggressive Western policies in the interbellum world. Now, however, the Soviets had enough strength to build Poland into the structure of the Eastern bulwark against the West.

Poland's post-1956 policy, with Gomulka at the head, was a new approach in the Communist bloc of Eastern Europe. Was it the product of Gomulka's thinking or of the Polish soil—or of both? In his appearance Gomulka looked anything but a charismatic leader. But the appearance of the man did not coincide with his public image. The way the Poles closed ranks behind Gomulka indicated how highly they thought of him. Few nations are more articulate politically than the educated Poles. They had turned politics into a national passion during the generations they had been an un-nation.

Why did they have to go into the House of the Dead to search for Gomulka? Could they not find a living man? They looked for Gomulka—we have seen—because they recognized a grass-roots Pole in him, moderate even in his dogmatism. Yes, he appeared to be comparatively undogmatic in a dogmatic world. They saw a man who could speak the language of the Kremlin, too, and thus could carry on the dialogue between Warsaw and Moscow. And they realized that the dialogue had to be carried on, for without it there would be no Warsaw.

The Poles made a search for Gomulka in the House of the Dead mainly because they recognized the sign of the charisma on his forehead. And it was a special type of charisma. Not the *baraka* of Ben Bella or the charisma of Sukarno, or of any of the others. It was a Polish charisma. The Poles had selected the world's worst location. Between the Germans and the Russians, they were in a part of the world where they stood in the way of powerful neighbors. Their country had no natural frontiers and was wide open to East and West. They suffered much—suffered more than it was fair for people to suffer. They carried their crosses when Poland was only a dream, and continued to be Poles, and continued to dream. They were, perhaps, proud of their sufferings. And from time to time they got tired of being kicked around. Then they revolted. After each of these revolts they suffered even more. The Poles developed the habit of being attracted to fellow sufferers. Gomulka suffered more than most of them, and so they were even more attracted to him. The Poles are a romantic people.

Gomulka's long detentions seem to have seasoned him to assimilate moods and policies that would be rejected by people less dedicated to their ideologies. While he was isolated from his people, Gomulka entered into a more intimate communion with them. His work at the helm after his liberation bears out this view. His emergence from the House of the Dead was a historic event for Poland. It required all of Gomulka's charisma to fit the Poles' temperamental individualism into a collectivistic system. The product, Gomulkism, a term of eulogy and not of shame any more, may become the beginning of another Protestant movement against the High Church of the Kremlin. And thus it may become an immensely significant historic event for the entire satellite world. It may show other nations how to detach themselves from the dead weight of an ideology that took no account of national ideals.

It is too early yet to say the last word about the Gomulka experiment. Many are the traps into which he may fall, because all of Poland is surrounded by snares, the curse of her location. One thing is sure, though. The ultimate success or failure of Gomulkism may turn out to be the most important indication of portentous events to come.

EPILOGUE

And when the heavy gate shuts behind the released prisoner, what then? Does the un-man become a man? In the case of each of the biographies in this work he reaches the pinnacle of power, and thus represents in himself the awesome might of the modern sovereign state, the nearest human embodiment of our concept of the Almighty.

He stands in front of the gate a free man. Behind him he has left degradation, before him looms near-deification. Punished, corrected, disciplined, castigated, chastised—he stands alone between two eternities: the eternity of infamy and the eternity of immortality. Purged out of him, presumably, is the "evil" for which he had become an un-man. And the evil came only from his attempt to follow his own light—a light that was to lead him to recognition. Now he is presumed to be chastened, purged so to speak, of the desire to see the light.

Then there is that other view of the influence of the jail, sadly conceded by penologists, and expressed here by a famous victim of incarceration:

> The vile deeds like poison-weeds
> Bloom well in prison air,
> It is only what is good in man
> That wastes and withers there;
> Pale anguish keeps the heavy gate
> And the warder is despair.
> . . . .
> .All that we know who lie in jail
> Is that the wait is strong;
> And that each day is like a year,
> A year whose days are long.

And not merely in Reading Gaol and not only for Oscar Wilde.

"Prison life with its endless privations and restrictions makes one rebellious. The most terrible thing about it is not that

340

it breaks one's heart—hearts are made to be broken—but that it turns one's heart to stone."

Perhaps the heart of the common man. It was the prison which inspired these words of Wilde in his *De Profundis* and in his *Ballad of Reading Gaol.* Imprisonment also encouraged some of Socrates's wisest observations; and Cervantes' in *Don Quixote de la Mancha,* and Dostoevski's in *Memories from the House of the Dead.* Prison enabled Lajos Kossuth, champion of Hungarian independence in the mid-nineteenth century, to become one of the great English-speaking orators by studying the King James version of the Bible and Shakespeare, two books available for the prisoners' use. There were many others, too.

Political prisoners are our concern here—their rise from shame to glory. What did jails do to them? What was the plus or the minus, stimulation or destimulation, acceleration or deceleration?

In quest of the answer one faces the danger of falling into the error of *post hoc, ergo propter hoc,* "after this, therefore because of it": that is, taking as a cause something that merely occurs earlier in time. But then that is a risk one cannot avoid.

Let us not look only at the samples which have appeared so far in this work. There are many cases of great leaders who have spanned the chasm between the House of Glory and the House of Shame. For comparison we may turn to the previous century and also to the examples of two contemporary leaders who were born in the nineteenth century.

There was, for example, that young rebel Silvio Pellico, who wrote one of the classics in the literature of political prisoners. His crime was great. He wanted a free Italy, a united nation, and not a conglomerate of alien satrapies. So he made common cause with the *carbonari,* members of a society organized to establish a republic. Silvio Pellico the *carbonaro,* was a dramatist and a poet of note. While he thought that Italy should become a nation, that great statesman, Prince Metternich, knew that Italy was merely a geographic expression—and who would have known about such things better than the man who not only studied history but who also helped to make it on a grand scale? And so Venice was annexed by Austria, over which the Prince ruled through his imperial puppets. And then Milan was taken, too. Silvio Pellico looked at Venice, at Milan and all of Lombardy, and at the rest of that "geographic expression" which is Italy, and found it was a perfectly natural unit ringed by seas and mountains and—more important—that it was united by a strong national will. In his eyes, this Italy should be a nation.

"Blasphemy!" thundered Metternich, and Europe echoed the thunder a thousandfold. The infamous Silvio Pellico wanted to subvert the God-given right of the Austrian Emperor to rule in Venetia, Lombardy, and elsewhere. A halt had to be put to such heresy.

And so this godless *carbonaro* was marched to the gallows. A deep silence descended upon the thousands who had come to see him die. The sentence was just. An investigation had been made of his activities and words. He had voiced the *carbonaro* motto: "Revenge must be exacted for the lamb mangled by the wolf." The lamb was Italy—a geographic expression—and the wolf was good Emperor Franz, who ruled by the grace of God. And the accused did subscribe to the heretic's view: "Every *carbonaro* has the natural and inalienable right to worship the Almighty according to the dictates of his conscience." Blasphemy of blasphemies, the judgment said. How could weak man—weak as a reed—worship the Almighty according to his own conscience? How could he even know his own conscience? He needed the intercession of the Holy Roman Church and the orders of the Emperor, who, by virtue of being the earthly representative of the heavenly Prince of Princes, was the Defender of the Faith. Worse than that, the criminal mind of the accused subscribed to the absurd idea that all men were created equal, thus teaching the perverse creed known as democracy. All the world knew that Divine Providence prescribed the fates of all its creatures, and that there were those who had to rule and those who had to serve. Silvio Pellico deserved the ultimate punishment.

For his unspeakable crimes Silvio Pellico must suffer death on the gallows. The sun shone brightly on the Venetian public square where judgment was pronounced. A sigh fluttered through the spectators' ranks—as much of expectation as of sympathy. They were to see the hanging of a man. Then there was a short pause. The reading of the judgment was not yet at an end. His Majesty in His Infinite Wisdom commuted the death sentence to fifteen years in jail.

That is how Silvio Pellico in his cells came to write the classic: *Le Mie Prigioni*, "My Prisons." "Each day is like a year," he wrote, and he purged his sins during 3560 years. One of his prisons was in one of the most beautiful palaces of Europe, the Palace of the Doges, in Venice, one of the most entrancing cities of the world. Was that such an awful punishment? From his cell he saw a corner of St. Mark's Square, and he looked down upon the roof of its church. Yet, Pellico's prison was in the midst of Inferno. "Piombi" it is called to this very day because of its leaden roof, the heat from which seared not only the skins but also souls of the prisoners.

Then he was transferred out of the hideous Piombi to the town of Bruenn in the lovely Moravian province of the Austrian Monarchy, far in the cooler north. Up the hill his guards took him, depositing him in a jail that had been a fortress. The hill was known as Spielberg, "Play Mountain." Play, however, was not for people like Pellico. His legs in chains, he was left to rot in a dank cell. It was in the Piombi and on the Spielberg that he wrote his famous book.

In his prison Pellico heard no word from his kin, knew nothing of their lives. Not only were they dead to him, he was dead to them. Entombed, and scarcely expecting to survive the torment, his thoughts were turned from earthly life. Then another miracle. Because of the infinite kindness of the Emperor of Austria he was released after ten years in jail.

However, by consigning him to the Piombi and to Spielberg, Pellico's judges had achieved their aim. Pellico's *Le Mie Prigioni* is a testimony to his change of heart, for in prison he turned away from politics—hardly a word on which appears in his work. Turning his back on the false gods of prejudice and pride, Pellico became a better Christian, accepting his fate as a visitation of providence. Alone, forsaken by man, he could not have sustained his spirit. But he was not forsaken, neither in the Piombi nor on the Spielberg, not by any means. The dazzling light he saw in jail was different from the light he had seen as a *carbonaro*. In his cell he was constantly in the company of God, and in that company he triumphed over his weakness. This political prisoner was "reformed" in jail.

Fyodor Mikhailovich Dostoevski was an even more famous political prisoner who ran afoul of the established order. In his day, about a quarter of a century after Pellico, at the pinnacle of the hierarchy of the Russian world order, stood the "Flogging Czar," Nicholas I, who so loved his subjects that he had them whipped. They were all his children. Some he ordered hanged and others sent to Siberia. To discuss a different mode of government was, in his eyes, a criminal act, the penalty for which was death.

Dostoevski, a member of the Petrashevski Circle, was an example of what Germans used to call *Schoengeister,* "beautiful souls," harmless intellectuals who dream about utopias, neither able nor willing to break new paths. The Russian authorities were not concerned with what the members of the Petrashevski Circle did not want, only with what they were talking about. The very act of discussing philosophies beyond the bounds of the dominant social ethics was an affront to the Father Czar, and that was high treason. Members of the Circle were tried, but the trial was a mere formality. The sentence was routine. Dostoevski and his associates were to be executed by the firing squad.

Under a brooding dismal sky of December 1, 1849, the condemned men were lined up and the execution squad marched forward. The death sentence was read. Only a few minutes were left for the condemned men to meditate before the rifles fired. In the very last minute a commutation of the sentence was read. So the dead were restored to the living—more correctly, to the living dead: banishment to Siberia.

Dostoevski was banished to Siberia for ten years. Four of these years he spent in the House of the Dead—among people who had no legal existence, many of them closer to animals than to men. Some of them were as hard as steel, others as soft as wax. Hardened criminals and saintly martyrs mingle in these situations; all are prisoners. The rest of his sentence Dostoevski served in semi-detention as a military man on the Mongolian border.

What was the impact of such an inhuman ordeal on a sensitive artist, later to become one of the great novelists? Did the horrors of the House of the Dead and the cruelties of the regime turn his thoughts even more against the Czar? Far from that. Like Silvio Pellico, he, too, turned to Christ. But his was a different kind of conversion, for his was to a national Russian Christianity. He saw the Russians as the chosen people, a consecrated community, tried in the crucible of suffering, invested with the mark of the elect, *sobornost,* the "hallowed congregation." He turned away from political non-conformism, and toward the Cross. Thus in his case, too, political self-assertion was transmuted into religious zeal.

The third figure, Oscar Wilde, had not been sentenced to jail because of political views. A darling of the gods, he had been endowed with all the gifts men dream of—dazzling talent, boundless self-confidence, and great success. But he was also cursed with an abnormality which Britain deemed a crime against society. His homosexuality was revealed in a public scandal, and that is how he came to stand trial and to be sentenced to jail. His shining presence became anathema. Could he survive the searing indictment now that he was forsaken by the world? He was not entirely forsaken because the plaudits of the world were replaced by an even more universal presence, the radiance of which filled his cell. It was to the Immanent Presence and not to a human companion that the convict turned his face. "He who can look at the loveliness of the world and share its sorrow, and realize something of the wonder of both, is in immediate contact with divine things, and has got as near to God as anyone can get."

Here, then, we encounter three unusual creative men. Endowed with uncommon gifts, and recognized as men of genius by the world, they were confined to the House of Shame; and though severed from the normal ministrations of their fellow men, they managed to survive their ordeals. They did so by turning beyond and outside the everyday world, into the realm of man's fondest dreams, where justice prevails. Not only were they no longer cut off from the mainstream of life; they, the sufferers, became the elect and the beneficiaries of God's bliss.

This, then, is one kind of reaction to life in prison; the convict seeking solace in the tangible intangible, the unexplainable reality, the invisible presence. The solace they found came from an intuitive recognition that man does not have to stand alone in the world, that he can turn the symbol of his shame into a halo and move closer to the Throne of Glory. Soren Kierkegaard called this the "existential period," the time of the most acute personal crisis, when the deeply hurt human creature, realizing his helplessness in the company of men, is brought face to face with despair. Only when man abandons all pretense of self-reliance, according to Kierkegaard, the high priest of religious existentialism, can he accept the supreme figure of Christ, in whom the greatest paradoxes, those of time and eternity, of God and man, are reconciled.

THE MAN FROM YUGOSLAVIA

Now we must turn to others who have found solace and solutions in other ways. The eight subjects of this work were imprisoned by their governments for political reasons. They were born in the twentieth century, with the exception of Kenyatta, whose date of birth is in doubt. We will turn our attention now to two political prisoners who were born in the nineteenth century. Their careers need not be summarized here, for that has been done many times before. Only the highlights of their lives need concern us here. From these points we can arrive at the common denominators that support men who ascend from jail to power.*

It was Josip Broz Tito who launched the Reformation within the Oecumenical Communist Church, and whose very name has become immortalized in "Titoism."

What was the effect of a long prison term on the man whom the world was to know as Marshal Tito, President of the Federal People's Republic of Yugoslavia.

Under the inter-bellum Yugoslav royal regime it was a criminal offense to be the member of a Communist party, and Josip Broz was that. Under the Law of the Defense of the Kingdom he was therefore subject to heavy penalties. Josip Broz had disseminated Communist propaganda, the prosecutor of the Crown charged; not only that, he had purchased and concealed arms, ammunition, and hand grenades. On November 14, 1927, in the city of Zagreb, the sentence was pronounced: five years in jail. Upon hearing the sentence, young Broz unvanquished, shouted: "Long live the Revolution!"

That was Day 1 of his incarceration as a convict. Would he have the strength to stand up and shout pridefully after five years in jail? He served most of his term in the prison of Lepoglava, a town near his birthplace, Kumrovec, in the Croatian province of Yugoslavia.

Several times we have observed that jail cells serve as classrooms for self-generated "great books" courses. But Josip Broz was not a bookish person, nor an intellectual. His father was a peasant, the head of a lower-class family of fifteen children. As a boy, Josip liked to read *The Adventures of Sherlock Holmes.* With little schooling he became apprentice to a locksmith, and went on to become an electrician, and a mechanic. He seemed to be more skillful with hand work than with brain work.

---

* The Heretic. The Life And Times of Josip Broz-Tito, by Fitzroy Maclean (Harper and Brothers, 1957), written from a politically neutral point of view, is particularly revealing.

Jawaharlal Nehru. A Biography, by Frank Moraes (The Macmillian Company, 1956), is detailed and incisive.

The Lepoglava jail—a former Pauline monastery—evinced signs of old age: it needed a mechanic, and so Josip Broz was assured of activity with his hands. It was while doing electrical repair tasks in the jail that he ran into his future and, probably, his career. The man he ran into was Moshe Pijade, a little Sephardic Jew with an abnormally large head, who was there for a jail term of fifteen years. He had been convicted for illegally editing and printing a Communist paper. Pijade was literally an encyclopedia of Marxism and Leninism, a man who knew all about dialectical materialism. He was the prison's substitute for a well-stocked library. Although Pijade was awkward with his hands, Broz appointed him his assistant. Moshe, the brilliant, was greatly impressed to learn how easily a blown fuse could be replaced. Josip Broz learned about other matters.

The two men set up a party cell in the jail and established contacts with Communists still at large. Here Broz acquired both the theoretical and pragmatic knowledge of how to run a unit of the Communist underground. Through the course conducted by his assistant, Broz was in training to assume greater responsibilities. Now, with all that work on their hands, the prison term did not seem long enough. As soon as Broz was free, he put himself to the work which led him eventually to the pinnacle of power.

By 1935 he was Yugoslavia's No. 1 Communist, important enough to be summoned to a conference with Stalin in Moscow.

Josip Broz became Marshal Tito during World War II. His role in the war became an epic of history, for the success of the underground resistance against the Axis powers that occupied Yugoslavia astounded the world. The years he had spent in jail now came in good stead. He had acquired knowledge of the Communist party literature, and jail had strengthened his dedication to the cause.

Once installed in the seat of power, he turned against a new foe, fellow Communists who—in his opinion—had deviated from the path of Marxism and Leninism. As we have learned in previous chapters, his Communism was to succeed within the framework of his own nation and not within that of Russian imperialism.

THE BRAHMAN FROM KASHMIR

Jawaharlal Nehru became "Mr. India," the leader of a nation beset by as many problems as the human family could endure.

The jail terms of Jawaharlal Nehru began in 1921 when he received a six-month term for distributing notices about a *hartal,* the suspension of business and civic activities as a protest against the condition of India. Freed, he was back in jail six weeks later because he had advocated the boycott of foreign cloth.

Unlike Tito, Nehru was not a man of the people. He was an aristocrat of the Kashmir Braham castle, and also an aristocrat of the intellect. In the Lucknow jail this Brahman found himself in the same cell with fifty other convicts, most of whom were common criminals. Nehru disliked the pickpockets, the sneaky, shifty-eyed petty crooks. Those he disliked least, it seemed, were the murderers. Apparently he could sympathize with these poor creatures who were often the victims of their own hot tempers.

The authorities jailed him often; he was imprisoned not only by the British but also by the judge of a native state. He had arrived in the Indian princely state of Nabha one day with the harmless intention of merely observing a *hartal.* That was enough for the local authorities. He was not only arrested but also chained and carried away from the street as if he were a dumb brute. The native judge who tried him could not write English—or perhaps could not write at all, so at least Nehru thought. He was placed in so low a cell that he and his companions could touch the roof. As they slept, rats scurried over their faces.

For three speeches which he delivered to peasants Nehru was thrown into the Gorakhpur jail. The speeches had been excellent, but the penalty for delivering them was heavy—four years. A year after this last sentencing Nehru was released—the tragedy at Pearl Harbor had taken place, and Britain needed the good will of leaders. "Freedom will enable India to resist aggression," the Indian National Congress, in which Nehru was a powerful force, declared, "with the people's united will and strength." The British view of will and strength differed from Nehru's, and soon he was back in jail, this time in Ahmadnagar, for three years, until the summer of 1945. He had good company —twelve members of his party. They could accomplish much, indeed, in jail.

In some of his jails, Nehru confessed, he enjoyed himself. In the town of Almora, on a Himalayan spur from which he could view the snow-clad giant, the Nanda Devi peak, he occupied an immense prison dwelling, a huge hall of fifty by seventeen feet, where he was waited upon by two score sparrows who nestled in the eaves. In another prison he had an opportunity to tend a garden.

Incarcerations were not merely opportunities for Nehru to engage in the study books. During some of his incarcerations he himself wrote notable books. "This book was written entirely in prison," Nehru said in the Preface of his autobiography, *Towards Freedom.* "The primary object in writing these pages was to occupy myself with a definite task, so necessary in the long solitudes in jail life, as well as to review past events in India."

The Discovery of India was the title of the volume he wrote while he was in Ahmadnagar jail in order to convey to his daughter, Indira, the knowledge he could not transmit in person. He began to write on April 13, 1944, and finished his manuscript five months later. In freedom he would not have had the time to work that rapidly; it was a substantial work indeed, a chronicle and an analysis of events and of his reactions to them.

His prison sentences aided Nehru to gain stature in his people's eyes. He suffered for their sake and so merited the honor conferred upon him when India became free and he was made the prime minister of an independent nation. He had gained stature in his own eyes, too, because he had come to know himself better, and India had become more familiar to him. He crystallized many details of his *Weltanschauung,* his philosophy of life, in prison. As in the case of so many other political prisoners he moved leftward: "Socialism is for me not merely an economic doctrine which I favor," he wrote, "it is a vital creed which I hold with all my head and heart."

No lesss significant, as he told Field Marshal Montgomery, he had changed in prison from a political agitator to a responsible prime minister.

LEADERS IN PRISON CELLS

The men we have observed became the leaders of their nations. Leadership is the "capacity and the will to rally men and women to a common purpose and the character which will inspire confidence."

A different kind of leader of men, Field Marshal Montgomery, provided this definition. Contrary to the popular view that leaders are born, not trained, he supported the thesis that leaders

are made rather than born. Many men who are not natural leaders may have a small spark within them, he maintained, but this
spark must be fanned into a flame.

Potential leaders must have a tremendous vitality and an
infectious optimism, Montgomery said further, and surely this was
true of our ex-prisoners.

Prisons are the breeding places of melancholia—and those
who succumb to it are lost. Our political prisoners became noted
for a large measure of optimism. They were able to overlook the
dismal present and concentrate on the radiant future. Jails enabled
them, too, to become engrossed in their studies to prepare their
plans for the morrow. They became classrooms of post-graduate
studies, places of reflection and meditation—"think tanks."

It was their enthusiam that made them turn—in many instances—to philosophies that envisaged the basic improvement of
the society within which they expected to work. They learned
about Nietzsche at one extreme, and about Marx at the other. Or
perhaps these two philosophers did not represent extremes. For
how can a superior society flourish without the aid of the superior
man? Or how shall the superior man reveal his best qualities except within the superior society?

The prison setting accentuated the hypomania of these
"politicals." In their "existentialist" environment, not sustained
by the social institutions available to free men, they were in a better position to fan that spark to which Lord Montgomery referred.
Social conventions, at the same time, did not force them to con-
form to the accepted norms.

It was within the prison that they were enabled to develop
their charismatic traits. The Golgotha exposed them to the admiring glances of people in search of a savior. The Christ of modern
times is not the Universal God-Man but a nationalist hero.

Charismatic authority was needed when the prisoners became the leaders of developing nations. Charismatic leadership is
one of the three ways in which authority may gain legitimacy, according to Max Weber, the German sociologist. Such authority
rests upon faith in a leader who is believed to be endowed with
great personal worth. A second avenue to legitimacy is through
tradition. The third way is via the rational-legal authority that
exists when those in power are obeyed because of the popular acceptance of the system of rules under which they have won and are
holding office. Legitimacy is a basic problem faced by all nations.
David Apter has shown, in *The Gold Coast in Transition,* how the

government of Ghana gained legitimacy from the charisma of Nkrumah. The same could be proved of many of the other leaders of the new countries.

THE JAILED BECOME JAILERS

Charismatic leadership, because it is so personalized, is, however, extremely unstable. "The source of authority," writes Seymour Martin Lipset in *The First New Nation*, "is not something distinct from the various actions and agencies of authority, so that particular dissatisfaction can easily become generalized dissatisfaction. The charismatic leader must therefore either make open criticism impermissible or he must transcend partisan conflict by playing the roles of the constitutional monarch. Even where opposition to specific policies of an individual—or informal factional—basis may be tolerated, there cannot be an opposition to him that is organized into a formal party with its own leader. But the difference between these options can have fateful consequences for the entire nation."

The prisoners who have become national leaders have, in many cases, become the jailers of their opposition. Have they not learned from their own experience that the prison may glorify the political convict? Are they not, in other potentially charismatic leaders, fanning the spark into the flames that might consume their own regimes?

However, the ex-prisoner-leaders of the new nations see this problem in a different light. They become charismatic only after a hard struggle against non-charismatic, oppressive, and alien regimes. The opposition, on the other hand, rises—as the new leaders see it—against a charisma that has provided the legitimacy, the very foundation upon which the new society rests. In their jailed existence the Elect fought the non-Elect. The new leaders feel that the opposition is composed of anti-Saviors who have undertaken to grapple with the Saviors.

There may be, of course, another reason, put into poetic words by Shelley:

> *Power like a desolating pestilence*
> *Pollutes whate'er it touches.*

The prisoners reached their goal—power. Will they be able to employ this power for the purposes of statesmanship? The answer to this question may be more meaningful in the future than the reader may think. And linked to this question is an even more comprehensive one? Has the fragmentation of the world into a large number of new countries—a result of the "nationalism explosion"—led to a happier and more productive world or are the new nations likely to stultify the potentialities for which so many "witnesses" to the cause of freedom have suffered the ultimate in disgrace?

Furthermore—and this thought might well give pause to every new leader who, in his turn, has acted as harshly to his political opponents as the earlier regime did to him—since prisons never truly stifle freedom and, indeed, as we have shown, often serve only as schools for freedom fighters, may it not be that in prison cells everywhere this very day, there may be languishing in physical torment and mental anguish but yet undefeated in spirit, the men who on some tomorrow—destiny being so capricious—may achieve freedom, reach power for themselves, and take the seats of the mighty?

Mechanical as our age has become, it still has not succeeded in mechanizing the human being blessed with the seeds of greatness. FROM PRISON TO POWER will undoubtedly have many sequels as long as history is written. The arduous road from the depths to the heights tests the climber's strength. No less trying is the struggle to hold his own on the peak in the face of adversities.

Biographical Index

Biographical Index

Introduction

Chapter 1

A JAILBIRD NEAR NOWHERE: KWAME NKRUMAH

Chapter 2

Chapter 3

Chapter 4

THE MAN FROM TUNISIA: HABIB BOURGUIBA

Chapter 5

THE ISLAND COSMOS OF INDONESIA'S SUKARNO

Chapter 6

Chapter 7

JANOS KADAR: PRISONER ON THE DANUBE

Chapter 8

POLAND'S SUBDUED DICTATOR: WLADYSLAW GOMULKA

Epilogue

About the Author

EMIL LENGYEL was born in Budapest in 1895, but he has
since the Thirties been associated with the American
university scene. He is today Professor Emeritus in
History at New York University and Chairman of the Social
Science Department at Fairleigh Dickinson University.
For thirty years he has traveled and lectured on
international topics and has achieved a worldwide
reputation as an authority on the statesmen of our
generation. He is the author of the best-seller *The Danube,*
and has written other works of international fame, among
them biographies of Hitler, Atatürk of Turkey, Krishna
Menon of India, and studies of Hungary, Central Europe, the
Middle East and Siberia. At present, when he is not teaching
or lecturing, he is a resident of New York City.